CODENAME:
RENEGADE

British born Richard Wolffe was most recently *Newsweek*'s senior White House correspondent. He covered the length of Barack Obama's presidential campaign, travelling with the candidate from his announcement through to Election Day, 21 months later and was granted Obama's first print interview inside the Oval Office. Prior to writing for *Newsweek*, Wolffe was a senior journalist at the *Financial Times*, working as its deputy bureau chief and US diplomatic correspondent in Washington, D.C. He is a political analyst for NBC, appears frequently on MSNBC, as well as on international media including the BBC and CBC. He lives in Washington.

Also by Richard Wolffe

The Victim's Fortune (with John Authers)

CODENAME:
RENEGADE

THE INSIDE ACCOUNT OF
HOW OBAMA WON THE
BIGGEST PRIZE IN POLITICS

RICHARD WOLFFE

Published by Virgin Books 2010

4 6 8 10 9 7 5 3

Design by Maria Elias

First published in Great Britain in 2009 by
Virgin Books
Random House, 20 Vauxhall Bridge Road,
London SW1V 2SA

www.virginbooks.com
www.randomhouse.co.uk

Addresses for companies within The Random House Group Limited can be found at:
www.randomhouse.co.uk/offices.htm

The Random House Group Limited Reg. No. 954009

A CIP catalogue record for this book is available from the British Library

ISBN 9780753519790

Penguin Random House is committed to a sustainable future for
our business, our readers and our planet. This book is made from
Forest Stewardship Council® certified paper.

Printed and bound in Great Britain by Clays Ltd, St Ives plc

For Paula, Ilana, Ben, and Max

CONTENTS

CODENAME:
RENEGADE

ONE

CHANGE

Election day starts, in the small hours, where the candidate has spent most of his last 626 days: on a plane. Stuck to the gray plastic walls of the pressurized cabin are snapshots of his odyssey across cities and fields, mountains and deserts, continents and oceans. A snowstorm in Iowa, a press conference in Downing Street. Camera crews dozing onboard, Secret Service agents sharing a joke. The candidate signing books, reporters holding audio recorders close to his face. Now, between the empty candy wrappers and the drained beer bottles, he walks back one last time from his spacious first-class section, through his staffers' business-class seats, to the coach class of the press. "You know, whatever happens, it's extraordinary you guys have shared this process with us, and I just want to say thank you and I appreciate you," he says, shaking everyone's hand. One reporter asks how he's feeling, but he insists that he won't answer questions. Even obvious ones. He thanks the young TV producers who have trailed his every move from the start, admires the photos on the overhead bins, then pokes fun at a magazine reporter who was parodied on *Saturday Night Live*. He gives a birthday kiss to a young photographer, shakes hands with every member of the aircrew, and finishes with a simple farewell: "OK, guys, let's go home."

The last twenty-four hours felt like the longest day of the long campaign. It began with the news that the last living person to raise Barack Obama through childhood, his grandmother Toot, had lost her struggle against cancer. At his penultimate stop in Charlotte, North Carolina, it rains so hard, and for so long, that it's hard to see the streaks running down both his cheeks. They don't come obviously or immediately. Hardened by two years of campaigning and many more years of self-control, his voice never breaks as he announces the news. "Some of you heard that my grandmother who helped raise me passed away early this morning," he says calmly. "Look, she has gone home. And she died peacefully in her sleep, with my sister at her side. So there's great joy as well as tears. I'm not going to talk about it too long, because it's hard a little to talk about." His face remains composed as he talks about the "bittersweet" sensation of losing his grandmother while his campaign draws to a close. He betrays little emotion as he describes her as "a quiet hero" and sketches out her life story. But when he starts to read his stump speech from his teleprompter, when he talks about the broken politics in Washington, he surreptitiously strokes one cheek with his thumb. He condemns eight years of failed Bush policies, and casually strokes the other cheek. Two minutes later, as the crowd chants "Yes We Can," he finally takes a handkerchief out of his pocket and wipes his face down. It is one of the rarest moments of the entire election: a display of raw emotion from a candidate whose mask almost never slips before the dozens of cameras that trail him every day. Even then, at his most vulnerable point, he defers the moment and dissipates its impact.

The cracks in his self-control spread to those closest to him. Standing at the back of a leaking tent in a parched yellow field is the candidate's friend and strategist David Axelrod. "He's at peace with what happened. It wasn't unexpected. He just wishes he had some time to deal with it in his own way," Axelrod says. "But I'm finding this hard right now. The enormity of it all is almost overwhelming. I love him; he's my friend. This election is ridiculously long and there are many stupid things about it. But you really have to earn the presidency. And he's been tested. You can't hide it or fake it."

Yet the candidate has partly passed the test by hiding himself away. By the time he reaches the final campaign rally in Manassas, Virginia, he has regained full control. Close to the site of two Confederate victories in the Civil War, the nation's first major African American nominee—a Democrat, no less—speaks to some 100,000 people at Prince William Fairgrounds. As a community organizer two decades earlier, Obama often feared that no one would show up to his meetings. Now there are so many people the traffic is snarled for hours and miles around. These crowds, he says, have enriched him, moved him, and lifted him up when he was down. Now he's so inspired he tells his signature story from Greenwood, South Carolina. The tale of a little woman who lifted his spirits, on a dismal day early in the campaign, with a simple chant: "Fired Up! Ready to Go!"

"It shows you what one voice can do," he concludes. "One voice can change a room. And if a voice can change a room, it can change a city! And if it can change a city, it can change a state! And if it can change a state, it can change a nation! And if it can change a nation, it can change the world!"

Yet at the start of this historic election day, in the early hours of the morning, the candidate seems weighed down. Determined and spirited perhaps, but also crushed with exhaustion and emotion. The gray wisps on his head are now visible from a distance, like the lines scored close to his eyes and across his cheeks. He sounds fired up, but looks ready to drop.

It is one in the morning when he lands at Chicago's Midway airport. The polls have already closed in the small New Hampshire town of Dixville Notch, which has not voted for a Democratic president since 1968, but favors Obama by fifteen votes to six. The candidate walks down the stairs from his plane and steps into his armored SUV to a flash of cameras. Behind him is a new addition to his motorcade: another SUV filled with a black-clad, heavily armed Counter Assault Team.

Obama liked to describe his journey from freshman senator to presidential front-runner as an improbable one. It was also preposterous and quixotic, at least in the judgment of the greatest political minds in the nation's capital. In February 2007, as Obama was readying the formal launch of his campaign, President Bush cast his expert eye across the contenders who wanted to succeed him. Sitting in the yellow oval room of the White House, on the second-floor residence of the executive mansion, the president conceded he had no idea who would win the GOP nomination. But he was clear about the other side. "I think Hillary Clinton will be the Democratic nominee," he said with his feet propped on a glass coffee table. "I'll tell you why. I think she will because I think she has staying power, star power, and money power. She brings a big organization that is well funded right off the bat, and one of the lessons I learned is you have to be able to play the long ball." As for Obama, who was on the verge of announcing his candidacy, Bush was deeply doubtful. "Certainly a phenom and very attractive. The guy is very smart," he said before realizing he sounded like Joe Biden, who had just stepped into the racial minefield for calling Obama "articulate and bright and clean." Bush was so taken aback with the public criticism of Biden that he called in his African American secretary of state Condoleezza Rice. "I don't get it," he said. "Condi, what's going on?" Rice told him what everyone else had said: that white people don't call each other articulate.

No matter. Only the tough and battle-scarred could survive, and Obama wasn't one of them. "This primary election process is rough," Bush said, popping an endless stream of peanuts into his mouth. "It's really tough and rightly so. It exacerbates your flaws and tests your character. And I don't think he's been around long enough to stand it. I may be wrong. The process may forge a steel that I didn't anticipate."

In some ways the forty-third president was correct: Obama was untested, unforged. Not even his closest aides and friends knew whether he could really survive the trial by fire of a presidential election. There was only one way to find out. Winston Churchill once said, "No part of the education of a politician is more indispensable than the fighting of elections." Well, the education of Barack Obama was protracted and often painful. He was a political upstart, the candidate named Renegade by the Secret Service, and he repeatedly broke the rules. He did not wait his turn to run, and had no resources in the bank when he set out. He sunk his money into lowly fieldwork, and rejected public finance. He took his campaign overseas, and staged his acceptance speech in a football stadium. He kept his tone mostly positive, and spent millions on a prime-time TV show. His middle name was Hussein, and he wasn't even conventionally African American. No, he didn't look like the presidents on the dollar bills, as he once quipped. For that matter, he didn't look or sound like other candidates for president. But he was highly disciplined and driven, supremely self-confident, and he possessed the rare ability to act both as a team player and a star athlete. Although he was a renegade, he was also a cautious and pragmatic one, who played by the rules when he needed them to win. On the surface, his performance was as steady as his resting heart rate of just sixty beats a minute. But his private moods were far more variable: he could be cocky and grumpy, impatient and withdrawn. He was often an inscrutable character. Yet he struck a rare emotional connection with those around him, no matter the size of the crowd or the ego of the person he was wooing.

There was a nagging question that cropped up at the beginning and the end of the election. It was posed at the start of his presidency and will likely be posed as his term finishes as America's commander in chief: who is Barack Obama? The mystery of Obama may seem simplistic but is nonetheless hard to unwrap. Simple questions about a president can still be stubborn and enduring ones: there remains plenty of debate about President Bush's intellect. But while there is a long Bush record to study for clues, there is relatively little that is public about the private Obama. In fact, the best evidence lies in the extraordinary presidential campaign of 2008, in which the candidate exposed himself to intense examination. He wrote one memoir and one highly personal political treatise, both of which were minutely dissected through the course of the election. He debated two dozen times and delivered hundreds of speeches. Yet something remained hidden about his character, suppressed about his moods, deep-rooted about his thoughts. And something remained unsettling for many pundits and voters who couldn't quite pin him down, as a black leader or pop celebrity, as a fiery preacher or closet radical.

In one way at least, his critics were surely correct: Obama lacked Washington experience. But the voters seemed to find reassurance in the way he campaigned, the way he built from scratch the most formidable election machine in history, the way he endured twenty-one months of public examination and private stress. They may not have all the answers about Obama, but the ones they heard and watched seemed satisfying. The 2008 election was by far the biggest undertaking of Obama's life, the only real executive experience on his résumé, and the biggest clue to his future performance as president. It changed America's view of itself, the world's view of America, his friends' view of Obama, and Obama's view of himself. It was a drama of political biography performed on the biggest stage in the world: an outlandish, extraordinary spectacle that veered from inspiration to exasperation, from the mundane to the faintly insane.

This is the making of a president, witnessed from a front-row seat, as it unfolded from its first day to its last. With the help of more than a dozen one-on-one interviews with the candidate and then president—as well as scores of sessions with his trusted aides, friends, and family—this account is an attempt to translate the enigma of Barack Obama, to answer the questions of who he is and what lay behind his rise from freshman senator to forty-fourth president of the United States of America.

Six hours after Obama lands at Midway, the polls are open across the East Coast and Midwest, as they are in the Fourth Ward, Twenty-third Precinct, in Chicago—otherwise known as Beulah Shoesmith Elementary School—where voters are already lining up outside. A few blocks from the candidate's home in Kenwood, the school is a humble, brown brick building that is showing its age. Inside the cinder-block gym, the amber wooden floor feels warm but the old backboards have no markings on them. In three corners, there are flimsy voting booths that collapse into the form of a small plastic briefcase; when opened for voting, the handles stick over the top. Affixed to the walls are bilingual voting instructions that are entirely ignored. Election officials have squeezed reporters, photographers, and TV crews onto a three-foot-high stage, draped with burnt orange curtains. Their intention is to stop the media from interfering with the voting process, but the stage only serves to elevate and exaggerate their presence. Unlike every other school gym the campaign has visited for the last twenty-one months, this one has no musical sound track, no adoring crowds stuffed onto bleachers, no speeches amplified through towers of loudspeakers.

The crowd is two-thirds African American, one-third white, and entirely informal—with two exceptions. The only people in jackets are the Secret Service agents gathered at the door and a handful of Obama's anxious aides: his senior adviser, Robert Gibbs, wearing his trademark blue blazer, white shirt, and khaki chinos; and his body guy, Reggie Love, in a blue jacket, campaign T-shirt, and blue jeans. A single Chicago police officer stalks the gym sternly, her braided hair tumbling down from an old-fashioned peaked hat over the back of her bulletproof vest. The voters are a cross section of the mixed neighborhood close to the University of Chicago: students in sweatshirts, South Siders, and the professional class that lives in the large homes close to the candidate. "I voted for Barack Obama," says Addison Braendel, a forty-three-year-old lawyer who lives four houses down from the Obamas. "He's sort of a hometown favorite."

Across the gym, glancing repeatedly toward the cameras, is a balding, overweight, late-middle-aged man with an earring in one ear, and a

New York Times under his arm. He wears a black short-sleeved shirt un-buttoned to reveal a long-sleeved red T-shirt hanging loosely over faded blue jeans. When he starts posing for photos with voters, his face be-comes clear: Bill Ayers, the former 1960s radical and proxy for Republi-can attacks on Obama's supposedly soft touch on terrorists. Only here, he looks like a schlub, more threatening to a cinnamon roll than to the Pentagon. The candidate once dismissed him as "a guy who lives in my neighborhood," but now Obama's staffers are alarmed at his showing up in the neighborhood. Back at campaign headquarters, Obama's tightly wound campaign manager, David Plouffe, pops off an e-mail in disbelief: "What is this? The bar in *Star Wars*?"

At the back of the stage, Reggie Love perches on the edge of a table to text-message on his cherished iPhone. Nobody knows the candidate better than Love, who plays the role of little brother and personal assis-tant rolled into one. He accompanies him to the gym in the morning, hands him water and snacks through the day, adjusts the height of his teleprompter before every event, watches ESPN with him in their down-time, and entertains him with stories of his after-hours partying. So how bad was the last day of the campaign for the candidate? "It was a tough day for him," he says. "All the feelings about the end of the campaign and everything with his grandmother. But it would have been a lot worse if he hadn't gone out to Hawaii a week before. That was a good thing to do." Drained by sleep deprivation, Love felt revived by last night's encore about being fired up and ready to go. "That got us through Iowa," he said with a tired smile. "It got us *all* the way through." And now that he's gone all the way through, was it worth it—all the early mornings, all the rallies, all those days on the plane? "Are you kidding me? Hell, yeah," he says as he relishes the prospect of change. "This is the start of the next phase. All those people who say they're going to get their lives back—it doesn't happen that way. It's like Barack says: All these people go to Washington to serve other people but they forget why they should be there. They just hang on to what they've got."

At 7:30 central time, the candidate walks into the gym looking like a changed man, in a dark suit with a gray striped tie and flag pin fixed to his lapel. He long abandoned his distaste for tacking the Stars and Stripes to his chest, after many months of resisting the token patriotic gesture. Beside him are Michelle, dressed simply in a black knit top and black pants, with her hair tied back, and their daughters, Malia and Sasha. As they walk over to a voting booth in the corner of the gym, his young staffers finally drop their guard and show some excitement. "It's election day!" whispers Katie Lillie, a long-suffering press handler, as she hugs Arun Chaudhary, who handles video production on the road. Standing behind the voting station, the candidate holds up the long paper ballot to show his wife an important section at the bottom. He completes the complex ballot easily while his wife crouches over hers as if reading a high school exam paper. He leans down to hug Malia, who is standing close to her mother, and kisses her gently on the forehead.

Within minutes, all other voting activity has ceased. A handful of voters stops to take photos with their cell phones; soon there is a cluster of gawkers at the halfway line. The scene is a mix of groupie worship and high-minded civics, which seems to accompany the candidate wherever he travels. A young white guy wearing an Oprah sweatshirt stands next to a young African American woman wearing a Mikva Challenge T-shirt, commemorating a program (named after one of Obama's mentors, Abner Mikva) to help Chicago's inner-city youth enter politics and public service. Next to her is a young white woman who is so excited at the sight of the candidate that she is fanning herself. Only a couple of people are still voting in the gym, and the Secret Service has closed the school to new voters. Election officials try to move some of the cell phone paparazzi away, or at least quiet them down, but it is hopeless. Even the stern police officer, now smiling broadly, is snapping photos with her phone. Obama's aides join in the circus: Gibbs takes a photo of Love with the Obamas voting behind him.

The candidate finishes voting and talks to his older daughter, who cracks a private joke. Michelle remains hunched over her ballot, while her husband glances at his watch and the press cameras machine-gun the moment. The wristwatch is one of his most treasured mementos of the campaign: a gift from one of his first Secret Service details in the early days of the primary contests. He was unusually friendly with his agents, playing basketball with them on primary days and sharing food with them when they waited outside his home. He seemed genuinely touched by their gift and would show it off with pride. But he does not need it to be punctual; even on long campaign days across several states, he ran on schedule, while his rival candidates were notoriously late. Today is no exception. Michelle finally completes her ballot, and stands up to her full height. "OK!" says a relieved Barack, pointing to the ballot box machine.

He feeds the long ballot into the reader, with his daughters on either side of the box, blocking the photographers' shot. The gym bursts into cheers and applause. An election official hands him a small ballot receipt officially called Form 10. "November 4, 2008 General Election," it reads. "Thank you for VOTING!" Barack looks up at the cameras, perched on the stage, barely twenty feet from where he stands. "I voted!" he says with a grin. He turns to the gawkers, shakes hands with them all (including the police officer), and walks out to more cheers shortly before 8:00.

Outside, it is an unseasonably, irrationally warm day for late fall in Chicago. The air is clear, the morning clouds have burned off, and the sun dapples through what is left of the yellow autumn leaves. Across the street, local fans and press are jammed behind barriers trying to steal a glimpse of the candidate as he steps into his black SUV. The motorcade leaves to cheers as it speeds through Kenwood, passing the voters who just cast their ballots in the school gym. The candidate drives by the home of his friend Marty Nesbitt and his nonfriend Louis Farrakhan, past the Kenwood/Forty-seventh Street Metra rail station, and onto Lake Shore Drive toward the downtown Loop. He speeds beside the deep blue waters of Lake Michigan, reflecting a sky that is almost perfectly clear, then turns onto a parkway named after the last Democratic nominee from Illinois: the erudite, and doomed, Adlai Stevenson. Along the railway tracks, through an industrial neighborhood that is home to A1 Fasteners and K3 Welding, past a Payless ShoeSource, the junked cars of some body shops, and through the rear gate of Midway airport. Slowing down, the motorcade follows the edge of the tarmac by the hangars, then turns left along the perimeter to the parked planes and a white Boeing 757 with a deep blue tail sporting a giant O. It could be a flying billboard. Above the windows at the front of the plane, where the senior staff sit, are the words CHANGE WE CAN BELIEVE IN; below is the campaign's Web address.

The candidate grabs his overstuffed black leather bag from the back of the SUV and glances toward the cameras gathered under the wing of his plane. "How's it going?" asks one TV producer. "I feel great," he says. "It was fun. I had a chance to vote with my daughters. I feel really good." Another TV producer asks if he's feeling sentimental. "You know, I'm sure I will tonight. That's when polls close. The journey ends. But voting with my daughters, that was a big deal. I noticed that Michelle took a long time, though. I had to check to see who she was voting for." With that glimpse of humor, he flashes his widest smile and walks up the metal stairs.

There is an unbearable lightness of being. Onboard, the candidate kicks back in his spacious front section, where the chairs could comfortably seat Captain Kirk on the bridge of the *Enterprise*. There is so much space between them that you can barely hear the next person speak over the noise of the engines. He is joined by some of his closest friends: Marty Nesbitt, Eric Whitaker, Valerie Jarrett, and her daughter, Laura, who has taken the day off from Harvard to witness history. Valerie woke at 4:00 a.m. to make sure she could vote before traveling today. The first in line at her polling place, she was surprised to find her hands trembling as she marked the paper ballot for her friend's name.

The flight to Indianapolis is short and the plane is emptier than normal, with many reporters staying behind in Chicago to work on election-day stories. The candidate spends his time joking with Marty and Eric as they select basketball teams for his traditional election-day game. What started out as a superstition during the primaries, played at run-down YMCAs across the country, has grown into a full-blown ritual with friends jockeying for slots. Obama categorizes the players by ability levels to divide the teams fairly, while Marty makes the final picks. The team selection drags on, and Laura Jarrett (hoping for more history on her only day of travel with the candidate) observes that psychologists say men feel comfortable with their emotions about sports. "This is a way for you to be in touch with your feminine side," she says to their bemusement. "You can pat each other on the behind, give each other a hug, you can cry. Anything is OK in sports." The candidate breaks off to autograph a pile of reporters' credentials, as the press turns its thoughts to campaign souvenirs. By 10:30, he is on the ground, bouncing down the steps with new energy. On the tarmac, Reggie throws a football to another young aide and catches the return with one hand while carrying the day's briefing binder in the other.

The motorcade speeds to a drab United Auto Workers hall where two dozen volunteers are phone banking around long plastic tables. There are flags on the wall and streamers in patriotic colors tied to the white metal roof supports. None of the decorations can hide the white cinder blocks and blue plastic floor tiles. Obama posters, in the propaganda style of artist Shepard Fairey, are taped to the walls. The press rapidly starts tearing them down as more souvenirs. At the side of the room, at the back of a small stage, is a giant plastic sign saying Indiana for Obama, Vote November 4th. Obama himself walks in with a spritely "Hi guys!" His shirtsleeves are rolled up to the elbow, and he looks like he means business. Turning the corner past the front desk, he sees the phone bankers. "Here's where the work is being done back here," he says to nobody in particular. "That's what I'm talking about." When the applause subsides, he greets every volunteer and walks around the tables like a sports coach pepping up his team. "Are we going to win Indiana?" he asks. Yes! "You got anybody on the line? If you've got any live wires over there, bring them on," he says.

Three hours ago he was the suit-wearing candidate voting with his family in a tableau of semidignified democracy. Now he is the community organizer firing up his small band of volunteers and trying to stir up voters along the way. "Hi, Michael, it's Barack," he says on the phone to one voter. "How are *you*? Well, listen. I wanted to find out if you've made up your mind. Don't be discouraged by the lines out there. Take your iPod or whatever it is you use to pass the time." He walks over to another phone to take another call. "Hello, Lindy? This is Barack Obama. How are *you*? I'm in Indianapolis. We're trying to make sure everybody is going out to vote and taking their friends or their neighbors . . . I'm so grateful to you for waiting in line. . . . Grab some of those folks who haven't voted yet."

He points across the room to another phone. "All right, what have you got?" The volunteer says it's his wife. "I don't want to talk to your wife," Obama says. "Unless she needs some persuasion." She didn't. So he picks up another phone, thanks them profusely for voting, then strides to the other corner of the room. "How are *you*? Thanks so much for the prayers and thanks for the vote," he says. "Make sure you call your friends and neighbors. Stay on it. God bless you." By now the volunteers are in the swing of it. "OK, I'll be over there in a second," he shouts to the other side of the room. He pretends to jog over to a waiting call, saying, "This is how I get my exercise." Bouncing from one side of the room to the other, the candidate is thrilled to be active, as if it relieves the stress and boredom of the endless waiting of election day. "This is Barack Obama. How are *you*?"

Another group photo and a quick drive back to the airport. Before his last flight of the entire campaign, the candidate stops at the bottom of the stairs to pose for a photo with the press corps. Inside, the cabin is morphing back to a normal charter plane: the photos have come off the walls, leaving small squares of sticky photo mount. The aircrew hands out bottles of red wine to say thank you. The candidate returns to his basketball strategy, playfully arguing with Marty over the team selection, which he claims is skewed. His mood is markedly better than twenty-four hours earlier, when his grandmother passed away. "Yesterday was tough for him, especially at the moment he spoke about it," says his friend Eric Whitaker. "But he's very good at compartmentalizing."

On the ground at Midway, a small group of fans at an airline mainte-nance building cheer his arrival. Marty walks off with a bottle of red wine in his left hand and a basketball spinning on his right index finger. The air is warm, and the sky is clear, blue and sweet, as the candidate drives downtown to the Hyatt Regency hotel: his base for the afternoon and evening.

At Manny's old-style Jewish deli, ten minutes southwest of the Hyatt, Obama's political brains have gathered to fill their stomachs to bursting point. Sitting around the cheap plastic veneer tables, their plates piled high with corned beef or roast turkey breast, is a large group gathered by David Axelrod. More than anyone else, except Obama, this campaign is Axelrod's creation: shaped by his vision of political contests, executed by the operatives he most respects, guided by his love of the candidate. Ax-elrod helped lift Obama from a long-shot primary candidate into a United States senator, and from a freshman senator into a presidential nominee. He is more than just a consigliere to the candidate; he is his number one fan and his close friend.

The deli is Axelrod's favorite lunch spot, especially on election day, and the staff and regulars love him almost as much as he loves one of Manny's grotesquely large turkey legs. He eats the leg with a medieval flourish, tossing the bare bone onto the table with a flick of his wrist. At some point in midflight, or possibly before takeoff, oil and gravy splatter his shirt. Around the table with him today are pollster Joel Benenson, ad maker Jim Margolis, and Axelrod's business partner John Del Cecato, who is sporting an untrimmed beard—a superstitious growth until the election is over.

Together, these are some of the most nervous of Obama's advisers, a fretful bunch who search for trouble in focus groups and polling data. Today they are exceptionally relaxed. There are no more ads to cut, no more press to massage. "It's what I call the what-do-you-know day," says Axelrod, who has spent the day calling everyone he knows to ask them what they know. He tried to sleep in that morning but failed. Over the course of the last two years, he has trained himself to wake by 6:00 a.m. to read the news clips. Yet there is little news today. Earlier, he called over to campaign headquarters, only to hear a bland response of so far, so good. He kicked around his old consulting firm's office, which he hasn't visited for weeks on end. But with little to do, he just ambled over to Manny's.

The candidate calls him with his own what-do-you-know queries. "Everything looks fine," Axelrod says. "What about Pennsylvania?" asks Obama. Pennsylvania seemed to be tightening on the last night of internal polling, from eight down to four points. They knew about the McCain campaign's bluster about its internal numbers in Pennsylvania. But they also knew there were so many more Democrats registered to vote there this year that they could expect double the margin of Kerry's victory in 2004. In their own polls across the battleground states, Obama is up by eight points and well ahead of public expectations in Florida. All the signs are positive, so far. Axelrod has just spoken to Chuck Schumer, the New York senator running the Democratic push to reach a sixty-seat, filibuster-proof majority. Schumer's latest prediction is fifty-eight senators, an enormous leap in terms of Senate strategy, and what an Obama White House might achieve. The only point of contention is about North Carolina: Benenson thinks it remains out of reach, while Axelrod feels confident. "The early vote was just so big, I think we'll win," he says. Benenson's final prediction, before he walks off to pick up his daughter from the airport, is a 5.7-point margin of victory across the country.

Axelrod drives back to campaign headquarters and almost swerves into another car as he passes Grant Park, where the victory celebration will be staged. There are lines of people along several city blocks waiting to enter the site many hours before the polls close. Although a native New Yorker, Axelrod loves Chicago almost as much as he loves Obama. He sees the city's history in each landmark, savors its skyline, its sports, its politics. When he looks at Grant Park, he sees in part the violent clashes between police and antiwar demonstrators at the Democratic convention of forty years ago. "Wow, a lot of people are lining up!" he says innocently, as if the tens of thousands of supporters at campaign rallies were unusual. "It's kind of cool that forty years later, everybody gets together in Grant Park to celebrate." Axelrod is normally lugubrious, his droopy mood matching his unruly mustache. But today he is surprised by his own contentedness. Two days earlier, he breezed through two Sunday talk show interviews after drinking past midnight at the hotel bar. And the light mood hasn't left him. "Even my mother is happy with the campaign," he says. "And that's unprecedented."

Axelrod parks his car at his home and walks over to headquarters on the eleventh floor of a corporate office block. The numbers from Florida and Virginia are already good, and Axelrod knows what that means if they hold true: a surefire victory in the electoral college. He stops by the office of Jon Favreau, Obama's young speechwriter, to make a few minor tweaks to Obama's victory speech. But the serious work is going on eight floors above, in a largely empty office on the nineteenth floor, where the number crunchers in the boiler room have been tracking turnout since 4:30 a.m. Run by Jon Carson, the campaign's national field director, and Jen O'Malley, director of the battleground states, this is the nerve center where they will follow the evening's returns and watch the news unfold on television. In the big bull pen, each battleground state has a team composed of a strategic staffer to monitor turnout and a lawyer to investigate any voting irregularities. The goal is to measure turnout against the campaign's targets, as defined by an enormous database compiled from millions of phone calls and door knocks. When a group of volunteers fails to show up in Cleveland, the Ohio team focuses on turnout in that area. If the ground staff needs extra help, they can target that area by calling local radio shows to boost turnout. Walking around the boiler room Axelrod takes a call from ABC's George Stephanopoulos, who shares the exit poll numbers. Wary of exit polls from 2004, when they were wildly wrong, Axelrod is still cheered by the prospect of sweeping the battleground states from Florida, through North Carolina and Virginia, to Ohio. But the strategists in the boiler room want to hear none of it, fearing that the exit numbers might distort their thinking or weaken their drive.

Axelrod goes back to his condo, with a sweeping view of Lake Michigan. He showers and talks to the normally stressed David Plouffe. Plouffe likes what he's seeing from the turnout patterns, but can't shake the last four days of tension in his sinews. Last night Plouffe was so torqued up that Axelrod told him he had a lot of pent-up energy. "I know," said Plouffe. "I feel like I should go out and rob a bank or something."

The candidate releases his pent-up energy with his superstitious game of election-day basketball. According to the official story, he played basketball on the day of the Iowa caucuses and won; he skipped playing on the day of the New Hampshire primary and lost. But basketball is much more than a good-luck charm for him. In his drifting teenage years, he dreamed of joining the NBA, and the game was the first point of focus of what would become his formidable self-discipline. Basketball was also a source of friendship and identity, not least for a fatherless African American boy growing up in a white family in Hawaii.

But on days like this, it is even more raw and teenage: a channel for his competitive spirit. Shooting hoops is like returning to his roots. Three high-school buddies from Hawaii have traveled to Chicago, staying with Marty Nesbitt, to join him on this big day. The election is not entirely out of mind, however. His old friend and hoops rival Alexi Giannoulias, the youthful Illinois state treasurer, has printed up shirts for the occasion. One team is called That One, the other is called This One—a parody of the way McCain disparaged their friend in the second TV debate. The only outsider is someone who became a close friend through the longest, most painful primary: Pennsylvania senator Bob Casey. Nesbitt's team wins, and the competitive candidate feels justified in his earlier suspicion of team skewing.

"See, Nesbitt? I told you," he jokes. "You rigged it."

By nightfall, the concentric inner circles of Obama's campaign are gathering at the Hyatt Regency hotel on Wacker Drive, next to the river. The polls have closed in nearby Indiana and Axelrod calls in to the boiler room from the sidewalk outside the hotel. "I really like what we're seeing from Indiana," says Carson. "We're exceeding our vote goal." Axelrod allows himself to believe in the exit polls after all. Inside the hotel, the lobby is bubbling with excited friends, financial backers, and political allies. Thirty-five floors above them is the suite where the Obamas and Bidens will watch the results. But for now, the Obamas are eating a quiet steak dinner at their Kenwood home alone, and the insiders are eating in the hotel bars and restaurants. At Daddy O's bar, some of the biggest names in Obama's finance team meet up, including Mark Gorenberg and John Roos from California. The mood is so upbeat that talk quickly shifts to the long-shot Senate races that might just succeed tonight. Inside the lobby, Eric Holder, who ran Obama's vice presidential search with Caroline Kennedy, is trying to eat dinner with his family while pacing up and down to glance at the TV screens. At the next table Rodney Slater, the former Clinton transportation secretary, is eating at a high round table with Wes Clark, the former NATO commander.

Across the street, in the hotel's west lobby, Axelrod has just finished a long evening of satellite TV interviews. With each new phone call, he has grown ever more confident but has played a cat-and-mouse game with TV anchors to avoid saying anything too cocky. Just before his final interview on CBS, Plouffe e-mails him to end all interviews: "Let's shut it down now and let's stand down until Obama speaks."

Now at street level, his phone rings: it's the candidate. "What's going on?" he asks.

"Look, I'm not going to say congratulations yet, but boy, it looks awfully good," says Axelrod. Axelrod wants to avoid the premature congratulations offered by his 2004 counterpart Bob Shrum, who saw the exit polls four years ago and offered to be the first to call John Kerry "Mr. President."

"It sounds like we're going to win," replies a low-key Obama.

"Yes, it sure does," says Axelrod. They thank each other and hang up.

A few moments later, Axelrod's phone rings again: they just called Ohio. He grabs his wife, Susan, and tells her the news. She starts crying, so he starts crying, and they embrace, silently and tightly. All around them, the lobby is filling and emptying with Obama's special guests: elected officials, donors, staff, friends, and family, heading toward Grant Park on a series of trolley buses, bouncing along on hard wooden benches.

Axelrod tries to call the candidate but can't get through; he e-mails him instead, but later realizes he used the wrong address. He walks half a block to campaign headquarters and meets his team of consultants leaving the building on their way down to Grant Park. He hugs his direct-mail ace, Larry Grisolano, telling him that he loves him. Then he takes the elevator to the boiler room, where the mood is frothy. He walks into the bull pen to talk to his deputy Karen Dunn, who is manning the Virginia desk among dozens of other staffers, when the boiler room bursts into applause. Plouffe walks out of his office to see what the commotion is all about, and an embarrassed Axelrod turns the spotlight on him. "Plouffe will go down in history as the greatest presidential campaign manager of our time," Axelrod declares. "He took a campaign that started at zero and built the greatest campaign organization anybody has ever seen." Plouffe deflects the praise to the staff, the organization, and their achievement. As they walk back into their strategy office, Axelrod apologizes for creating a stir. "Ax, you create a stir wherever you go," Plouffe says, as they sit down to watch the reports on TV.

Still nervous about the final results, Axelrod takes a plate and piles it with ravioli, eats it clean, and piles it high again. Then the messages start pinging in from news organizations: the Associated Press and the networks are ready to call the whole election at 10:00 p.m., as soon as voting ends on the West Coast.

Back at the Hyatt at 9:30, just before the polls close in California, the candidate walks into a tan hotel suite, where he intends to watch the results with his family on a giant flat-screen TV. First, he shares a quiet moment that has nothing to do with his own election. He sits and talks with Lane Evans, a former Illinois congressman who is suffering from Parkinson's. He leans forward, holds his hands, and listens to the progressive politician who supported him early in his quest to become a United States senator. Then he moves to a red, orange, and green sofa with Michelle and her mother, Marian Robinson, as the results come through rapidly.

Down at Grant Park, in a giant white tent set up for the world's media, his young staffers are punching the air and bursting into tears as the networks call Virginia for Obama. Within minutes, the TV screens declare Barack Obama the forty-fourth president of the United States. Inside another tent, his family and friends erupt into hoots, hugs, and applause. A crush builds from the tents to the stage. Reporters rush to the risers; campaign insiders run toward the stage. Stars like Oprah Winfrey and will.i.am bustle alongside political players like Bill Daley and Howard Dean. Inside the boiler room, Obama's senior strategists have given up their raw numbers and are transfixed by the news of their state-by-state success on ABC. Axelrod is overwhelmed, struggling to understand the words about his friend becoming the next president. Hugs and high fives bounce around the room, and Axelrod and Plouffe walk out to meet the president-elect in his hotel suite.

There is no crush or high-fiving on the thirty-sixth floor of the Hyatt. With his feet propped up on a coffee table, the president-elect tilts his head back on the sofa and finally looks relaxed. Michelle and her mother allow themselves a smile at the corners of their lips. Malia walks over to her father, flashes a cheeky smile, and offers him a fist bump. The Bidens enter and embrace the entire Obama family. Then come Axelrod and Plouffe. Axelrod walks over and shakes hands with the president-elect, who says wryly, "Well? Can you congratulate me now?" Obama talks to Plouffe and the hard-edged campaign manager tears up as he hugs the next president. He still looks bleary as they pose for a group photo with Robert Gibbs.

Obama returns to the sofa to watch McCain concede the presidential election. He leans forward and listens intently to a generous, high-minded speech from his often bitter rival. Sitting beside him, his mother-in-law, Marian, reaches over and gently touches his shoulder. He relaxes and holds her hand. While his wife and daughters watch McCain on TV, his senior aides are thumbing their BlackBerrys. "That was very gracious," Obama observes.

A few moments later, President Bush calls to congratulate his successor, twenty-one months after predicting that he would never survive the ordeal of a presidential election. "I know we have our differences," says Obama, "but you've always been very gracious to me and I appreciate it." He asks the president to thank the First Lady for defending his wife for her miscued comments about being proud of her country for the first time.

The conversation over, Malia walks over to her father with a simple question. "So, Daddy, can you tell me the first thing you're going to do as president?" she asks sweetly. Obama looks at the room. "Malia is working for the school newspaper now," he deadpans. "I'm going to buy a dog." The answer doesn't satisfy her. "No, I mean the first *political* thing you're going to do." The laughter fades as Marvin Nicholson, the campaign's levelheaded trip director, walks in to say it's time to head down to Grant Park.

They pass along Lake Shore Drive, watching people scream in the streets along the route of some fifteen city blocks. To Axelrod, it feels like the city he loves is shining. When the motorcade arrives, the Obamas hold hands with their daughters as they walk through a tented runway to the stage. Beyond the white plastic sheeting, there are more than 200,000 people in the park. Above is Chicago's illuminated skyline and one building whose lights now spell USA. Opposite the stage is the world's largest and tallest concentration of live TV cameras; to the left there is an anthill of stills photographers. Overhead six shafts of light stretch above the stage like the stripes of the flag, while twenty-eight Stars and Stripes line the back of the stage—just in case the flag pin is lost on camera. Four thick plates of bulletproof glass shield the left and right of the podium, dwarfing anyone in between. Across the nation, city streets are crime free and Obama crazy. Reports come in of crowds celebrating in Washington, D.C., at the historically black U Street corridor and on Pennsylvania Avenue in front of the White House.

The event starts with the music that normally greets the end of an Obama stump speech: Stevie Wonder's endlessly upbeat "Signed, Sealed, Delivered," then Brooks and Dunn's eternally hokey "Only in America." Backstage, Obama calls over Axelrod with his first executive decision. "I just want you to know I killed the fireworks," he says. "I don't think it's appropriate." Obama catches sight of Valerie Jarrett and walks over. He smiles, tilts his head, and shrugs. She smiles, tilts her head, and shrugs back.

The family walks onstage, with no music, and Obama closes his eyes to savor the moment. He kisses his daughters, his wife, and then is alone. The giant image of his face projects on the JumboTron, a few feet to the side of the real thing: a thin man with big ears, boxed in by walls of bulletproof glass.

A whole campaign is condensed into a few minutes of his greatest hits, as he threads his campaign stories into the familiar weave of American history. He reaches back to the 2004 convention in Boston to celebrate neither the red states nor the blue states, but the United States of America. He pays homage to the voters who put their hands on the arc of history, like Martin Luther King Jr., as he urged them to do at the start of his journey. He thanks his family, his senior aides, his supporters, and the three early states that gave birth to his campaign: Iowa, New Hampshire, and South Carolina. He quotes from Lincoln's first inaugural address to reach out to Republicans. And he speaks of an African American woman from Atlanta whose life spanned an American century to reach this point. He ends with a determined, defiant message to all those who said his campaign could never succeed: a message that started as a rallying cry in the defeat of New Hampshire, then grew into a viral music video. Yes We Can.

The stirring music that follows is not a classical masterpiece or an American anthem. It's the theme from the movie *Remember the Titans,* the story of a football team that helps integrate a suburban high school in Virginia, where Obama has just won the decisive victory of the election. His family reemerges, along with the Bidens, before disappearing into the tents below to celebrate.

Beside the stage, Axelrod is in tears, catching sight of several African American children in the crowd. They, too, are crying as they wave American flags. He recalls the earliest days of their quest for the White

House, when Michelle asked Barack what he thought he could accomplish as president. "I know this," he told her almost two years earlier, in Axelrod's conference room. "The day I take the oath of office, the world will look at us differently. And millions of kids across this country will look at themselves differently. That alone is something."

For Barack, Michelle, and their best friends, there was no such moment of catharsis, no tears of joy or flood of emotion. Were they cold to the moment of history, or exhausted by the long campaign? "It's like the golfer who hits a hole-in-one and all his friends run up to congratulate him, saying how improbable it was, and asking him if he's surprised," says Marty Nesbitt. "'No,' says the golfer, 'it's exactly where I was aiming.'" Barack and Michelle come to shake hands in the tent full of their family and friends, and spot Marty on the other side of the rope line. "I don't want to have a conversation with you divided by a rope line," says Marty. "Well, what are you doing on that side of the rope line?" asks Barack. "Come over here and let's walk. Come with me through all these other tents." Soon Marty realizes that his friend will be shaking hands for hours, and he gathers his family to drive home.

Almost two hours later, Barack and Michelle are delivering their final thank-you to the people who brought the campaign to life: his financial backers. The news is still hard to believe for those inside the walls of the big white tent. "Hello, Mrs. Future First Lady," says Wendy Wanderman, a Los Angeles fund-raiser. Michelle looks shocked and laughs. "Are you talking to me?"

This is one of the most trusted groups inside the campaign, but the candidate never saw them solely as a way to raise record sums of cash. He tried to organize them, just as he organized his young field directors and volunteers, and before them, his adopted community on the South Side of Chicago. He steps onto a low stage and picks up a small microphone to apologize that he can't speak to them all individually. "I think all of you know that had it not been for you, there's no way we could have accomplished this," he says. "But what made it special is not just that you guys raised the money. It's that you put your heart and soul into this thing. You organized, you went out, you knocked on doors, you made phone calls. You were committed to the mission, as opposed to simply being engaged in a transaction. And that made all the difference. It meant that when times were tough, when things didn't look like they were going where they needed to, you knew the facts."

He steps through a flimsy glass door into the night, leaving the white tent cheering behind him. "All right, do we have anything else?" he asks an aide behind him. A handful of supporters tries to snatch his attention by calling out "President Obama!" But the title still sounds unfamiliar, unfeasible, unreal, when matched with a Kenyan name so often confused with something far worse.

Even the self-made, self-possessed president-elect seems bemused. Has the result really sunk in?

"No, you know, it's all pomp and circumstance," he tells me, his hand on my shoulder. "It sinks in when you're quiet."

Has he had a quiet moment?

"No, not yet. I'll get one. Don't worry."

He may not savor the history of the night, but he already senses the change of the morning.

"You know, unfortunately now I've got to really . . . ." He trails off as he contemplates his new schedule. "Everything has to be a lot more screened. Now I've got these bigger obligations."

Michelle follows him, hugging friends and supporters, her campaign frown transformed into a victory smile. Together they walk into the darkness of Grant Park, shadowed by men in black suits, beyond the last clutch of giddy fans, into another armored SUV, toward a family home they will soon leave far behind.

TWO

THE DECIDER

He decided to make up his mind on the beach. The same stretches of Pacific waters and sand where he had walked and talked with his mother about the troubled state of the world, where he had conjured up teenage images of an absent father, and where he now tried to relax with his wife and young daughters. Hawaii was Barack's escape, for sure. A place to kick back, feel connected to his family and his memories, and retreat a little farther into his own mind. But it wasn't clear what he was escaping from. For the decision he faced would take him further away from his family and friends, from the privacy and simplicity of his home in Chicago and his holidays in Hawaii. Flowing through that easy Christmas break in December 2006, there was a looping conversation—often with his friends but mostly in his head—about his restless ambition, the cost to his family, the tugging gravity of history, the fleeting moment of opportunity. After several weeks of talks with his most trusted aides and friends about a presidential run, Obama had promised to clear his head and decide his future—and perhaps the course of a nation. So between the beach and the barbecues, the golf and the basketball, the pool and the movies, he looked at his easy life and pondered the prospect of leaving it all behind. As he watched his daughters play in the sand and chatted with his wife and friends, he wondered whether he could say good-bye. "Hawaii reminded me of what I might be giving up," he later told me. "At that point I was known, but could still go out and live a quasi-normal life and have a quasi-normal time with my kids. Was I prepared to give that up, certainly for the short term, if not for the long term?"

The huge Hyatt Regency hotel on Waikiki Beach was not a perfect refuge. People were beginning to recognize him in restaurants, on the beach, wherever he stopped. The outside world—his fame and the stratospheric expectations—were already encroaching on his private life. One morning, after working out, he took the elevator back to his room and a white couple in their early sixties walked in. The couple said nothing as they climbed several floors, but stared at Obama as they tried to figure out who he was. They reached their floor and walked out, but just as the doors were closing, the tall, burly man stuck his hand in the doors and wheeled around. "You gotta run," he told Obama. "You gotta save us. We're from California, and you *have* to run." He pulled his hand back, and the doors squeezed shut. Obama smiled and shrugged, but the attention was beginning to concern him. He phoned one of his political advisers to report on what he was seeing. "It's different now," he told David Plouffe. "I really can't go down the street. This feels different." Plouffe was deeply skeptical that Obama would really decide to give up his happy life while in Hawaii. He figured that Obama would back out at the last minute, like so many other politicians he had advised over the years. "Well, you know this is not a done deal, that's for sure," Plouffe told him. "You really have to think about this because it's only going to get worse. You already are a recognizable figure. Whether you win or lose, your life is going to change forever. You'll lose all privacy."

As long as he kept moving, Barack could avoid the intrusion and attention. Early mornings were best, when the beachfront was almost deserted and the children were still sleeping. He and his old basketball friend Marty Nesbitt would exercise along the beach and stop at a nearby Starbucks to stare out at the ocean and contemplate a possible presidential campaign. "You know, if you *didn't* do it," Marty observed, "we could retire in ten years, buy a place here in Hawaii, go golfing." Barack was conflicted, torn between the life he loved and the life he wanted. He knew that this kind of attention was nothing compared with what he had seen on his recent book tour, and what lay ahead on the campaign trail. He realized that his family time would disappear, that every word and every vote would be scrubbed, parsed, distorted, and exploited. But he also knew this moment might never come again. "What makes a great president?" Marty asked him one day. "Well, I think that probably everybody who has been elected president was a great person in some aspect or another," Barack began. "But what makes a great president, as opposed to a great person, is the juxtaposition of that president's personal characteristics and strengths with the needs of the American people and the country. And when you are a president who happens to come into office at that juxtaposition, there's an environment for you to be a great president." Some presidents were great individuals with extraordinary talents, but their timing was wrong. The great ones were needed by their nation at that point in history. For all that he opposed the policies of the era, Barack was thinking about Ronald Reagan. "Reagan would probably go down as a great president," he said. "It was just his time."

Was it Obama's time? You'd never really know until you started. Besides, the questions were just as important as the answers. He was testing himself and those around him, probing to see if they were all ready for the endurance test of a campaign, and for the changes that lay ahead.

Hawaii was home to his closest family beyond his wife and daughters: his younger half sister Maya Soetoro-Ng and their grandmother, Madelyn Dunham, known as Toot. Obama talked to them just as he had consulted them before proposing to Michelle fifteen years earlier. He wanted them to feel part of the process, that their questions were answered, that they were onboard. Maya was well aware of the Draft Obama movements across the country, and she knew that he felt their pressure. Maybe they knew her brother was ready to be president before he did. Still, she was fearful of losing him to the rest of the world, of him placing their demands above the family's needs. She thought of her own daughter, of his daughters, of the students she taught in Hawaii, and how his presidency would shift their horizons. Maybe those possibilities were worth the challenges and the sacrifice. Maybe there was nobody else who could affect people in the same way.

Time and again, in talking to his friend Marty, Barack returned to the meaning of an Obama presidency. "I wonder what impact it would have on African American boys if I were to be elected president," Barack said as they walked back to the hotel together one morning.

"Wow, that might be the single most influential event since the Emancipation Proclamation," Marty replied, fueled by his fresh cup of coffee.

"Yeah, it might be. Yeah, that could be very powerful," said Barack, sipping his bottle of water.

"Even if you didn't do anything beyond that," Marty continued. By now, the almost-candidate was imagining what he could do for a generation of children.

"But just think if I went to an inner-city school once a month," he said. "I wonder what impact that would have?"

"What would it really say about the country?" Marty wondered. "And what would it say about incumbent politicians? What would be the message to them if the American people elected *you*?"

Obama savored the thought. "Well, they'd be quaking in their boots."

To his entourage in Hawaii, Barack's fortune seemed unreal. It was only two years since he overcame enormous odds to become a United States senator. And it was only six years since his disastrous run for Congress, a campaign that had left him broke and disillusioned, and strained his marriage to breaking point. Now he was seriously considering a campaign for president, upending all the rules of conventional politics by running for the White House so soon after leaving Illinois. The field was hardly open: he would be taking on the Clintons, the biggest brand in Democratic politics, with little name recognition and no money of his own. "Either you made a deal with God or a pact with the devil," his old Harvard friend Eric Whitaker told him in Hawaii.

Or maybe Obama had just made some kind of deal with himself. Maybe he could detach his emotions to study his own situation just as his anthropologist mother had studied foreign countries and cultures. Obama took several steps away from his own life, mixing a cold assessment of his chances with all the self-confidence of a self-made man. "I came to the conclusion," he later told me, "that the times might be such that I would have to give it a shot."

If Obama was a renegade, he was a cautious and calculating rebel. There were no sudden moves, no rash judgments as he plotted to overturn the natural order of the Democratic Party. And if that seemed like a personal paradox, Obama had plenty of family role models for his peculiar combination of risk and self-discipline, of high-minded dreams and practical details, of restlessness and roots. Both his parents were rule breakers who were raised with discipline but rebelled against it. Both often chose their careers over spending time with their son. Obama inherited his father's burning ambition for himself and his mother's burning sense of injustice about the poor and the powerless. "My fierce ambitions might have been fueled by my father—by my knowledge of his achievements and failures, by my unspoken desire to somehow earn his love, and by my resentments and anger toward him," he wrote. "But it was my mother's fundamental faith—in the goodness of people and in the ultimate value of this brief life we've each been given—that channeled those ambitions."

However, Obama possessed something even more powerful than his parents: his own abilities to weave the two together, to create his own order out of disorder, to write his own story. "Someone once said that every man is trying to either live up to his father's expectations or make up for his father's mistakes," he wrote, "and I suppose that may explain my particular malady as well as anything else." Yet Obama is rarely casual enough to suppose anything about his own identity, or his relationship with a father who abandoned him when he was just two years old. His entire memoir revolves around his search for a father and an identity that was absent. What fills the hole is not his father; it is his own quest, his self-reflection, and his storytelling.

Those powers of self-creation ran in the family. Obama's Kenyan grandfather was a tough, independent spirit: a self-made man with an unyielding mind. As a boy he was so restless that people said he had "ants up his anus." Yet he was also ambitious enough to learn to read and write, and work as a domestic servant to the colonial British. He converted to Christianity, changing his name to Johnson, but found the ideas of mercy and redemption to be effeminate. So he converted once again to Islam, which was more attuned to his austere sense of discipline, and he took the name Hussein.

His son grew up herding his goats in a village near the shores of Lake Victoria. Barack Obama, the candidate's absent father, escaped from goatherding through study: he was a gifted student who won a scholarship to Nairobi, another to the University of Hawaii, and yet another to Harvard. He was also a perennial rebel, whose antics got him expelled from his elite school and earned him a severe beating from Hussein. He married a young Kenyan woman, had two children, then left for Hawaii and met Barack's mother.

Obama senior was a commanding presence on campus in the early 1960s: tall, loud, and opinionated, he was part of a fresh generation of Africans who thought their destiny was to lead the new nations emerging from colonial rule. In late-night conversations, fueled by beer and pizza, he would hold forth on the world's freedom movements stretching from anticolonialism in Kenya to civil rights in the United States. "When he came into a room, you knew it right away," recalls his friend Neil Abercrombie, now a Hawaii congressman. "He had a big heart and a brilliant, brilliant mind. He was a very engaging conversationalist, who always had an opinion, but was always respectfully listened to because he was so well-read." Obama was charming enough to marry an eighteen-year old girl from Kansas and win over her doubtful parents; persuasive enough to convince a racist drunk in a Waikiki bar about the folly of his bigotry and take $100 as compensation for being called "a nigger." He was also selfish enough to turn down a scholarship at the New School in New York, where he could have lived with his young wife and son, in favor of living alone at Harvard. "He came out of the 1950s in Africa and was affected by the patriarchal culture, as well as his own sense of destiny to participate in this movement," says Abercrombie. "In the end, he went to Harvard because it was the top of the heap." There he met another woman who followed him back to Kenya and became his third wife. He worked for Shell Oil and then the Kenyan government, before tribalism—and his outspoken nature—led his career to collapse. He turned to drink, suffered a serious car crash, and lived a penniless existence before returning to government. He died in another car crash, when his son was just twenty-one and living a solitary existence as a student at Columbia University in New York.

The woman he married in Hawaii was just as unconventional and almost as ambitious. She was a wanderer and romantic, a citizen of the world and unreconstructed liberal, but with the drive to wake up her young son at four each morning in Indonesia to teach him an American correspondence course.

In many ways she was the sum of her parents' contrasting characters. Her father was a bighearted but sometimes frustrated and violent man who lacked the discipline to make a success of his life and family. His attempts to discipline his grandson largely failed: Stanley Dunham set petty rules for the teenage Obama in Hawaii, when Obama's mother was still living overseas, and the teenager rebelled by cutting him down in argument. His relationship with his grandson was an echo of his own childhood. Dunham was himself raised by his own devoutly Baptist grandparents after his philandering father abandoned the family and his mother committed suicide. At fifteen, he was expelled from high school for punching the principal, spending the next three years hopping on railcars across the country. He was known as the charming dreamer of the family, another restless soul, whose failing career as a salesman took his family from Kansas to Texas to Seattle and then Hawaii.

His wife, Madelyn, led a far more respectable life, with a stable home where temperate, Bible-reading Methodism was the order of the day. Her parents disliked Stanley so they eloped. It was Madelyn, a flinty and rational woman of few words, who would turn into the breadwinner as she climbed the ranks of the Bank of Hawaii.

Their daughter, Stanley Ann, combined Stanley's romantic wanderings with Madelyn's drive and discipline. She was bookish and studious enough to gain early admission to the University of Chicago (which her father opposed). Instead she took her undergraduate degree at the University of Hawaii, where she met the charismatic Barack Obama in Russian class. She married at the age of eighteen, in a quiet civil ceremony, six months before her son was born. The contrast between Stanley Ann and her new husband was striking. Neither in personality nor in culture was the couple a good fit. "When he brought her to our gatherings, we were pontificating all the time," recalls their friend Neil Abercrombie. "It was clear she had a very adventurous spirit, but she was very calm while he was very voluble. She was an observer and a quiet participant. I think she concluded after little Barry was born that when Barack had an opportunity to go to the mainland, that his ambitions and her ambitions weren't going to work out."

Two years later, she divorced and later remarried another student, this time an Indonesian man named Lolo Soetoro, who abruptly left Hawaii when he was conscripted in the army. Ann moved with her six-year-old son to Jakarta, oblivious to the dangers they faced in the aftermath of a bloody military coup that left thousands dead. There she lived in a strangely half-immersed world: separate from the American expats who thought themselves superior to Indonesians, yet critical of the local culture for its lack of straight talk. "My mother always distinguished between certain aspects of Americans abroad that she was embarrassed by," Obama told me. "The expats who would never eat in a local restaurant or never socialize with Indonesians or had a patronizing attitude. She was always concerned about me never thinking I was superior to Indonesians in that way. But certain values that were very important to her were clearly midwestern, traditional American values that she was very proud of and cared a lot about. Being truthful with people in a way that Indonesian culture, which put a premium on conflict avoidance, or at least Javanese culture, wouldn't allow. So she believed in saying what you mean and meaning what you say, even if it made a situation uncomfortable. To her, that was part of her American tradition that she was proud of, and she wanted to make sure was part of me."

Ann had a second child, Barack's half sister Maya, but was worried about her son's safety and education, so she sent him back to Hawaii to live with his grandparents. She later left Lolo and returned to Hawaii herself to get her master's in anthropology, raising two children on her student grants. Three years later, she left her teenage son in Hawaii once again, this time to work on her Ph.D. in Indonesia. For the next two decades, she returned to Indonesia working for international agencies, especially on women's issues and microfinance.

For all her wonkish interest in development policy, Barack's mother was deeply idealistic and, at times, naive. She drilled a sense of empathy into her son and left him with a deep commitment to social justice. She idealized the civil rights movement, its leaders, and its stars: Martin Luther King Jr., Sidney Poitier, and Harry Belafonte. She liked to inspire her children with poetry or music. Sometimes she would wake her son up in the middle of the night to stare at a magical moon. As an anthropologist, she viewed the great religions as one, sharing their rituals with her children and touring temples and churches on their travels. One of her favorite TV shows was *Joseph Campbell and the Power of Myth,* a set of six PBS interviews with Bill Moyers, tracing the common themes of religions and mythologies across the world.

Obama adored and idealized his mother. Her struggle with cancer, and her early death in 1995, was a sudden, lonely snatching away of her life, and he tried repeatedly to find some greater meaning in her loss. "In my daughters I see her every day, her joy, her capacity for wonder," he wrote almost a decade later. "I won't try to describe how deeply I mourn her passing still. I know that she was the kindest, most generous spirit I have ever known, and that what is best in me I owe to her."

He also owed to her—and perhaps to his father—a certain rebellious, restless spirit, a spirit that pushed him away from his mother's life and her worldview. Where his mother lived a rootless life, he yearned for stability. Where she romanticized the civil rights movement of the sixties, he saw a grittier side of race in America in the seventies. Where she was absent from his life, he grew self-reliant. At times, he actively rejected his mother's example. He was happy to travel but wanted to return to a home. "The idea of being a citizen of the world somehow didn't feel right for me," he told me. "I wanted to be rooted in an American city and an American context and then venture forth. There was a weightlessness to that life, in the sense of at some level always being an outsider. But also at some point, it wasn't where I wanted to be. Even though there's a part of me that still has that. There's a wanderlust. It's much stronger in Maya than it is in me. Or at least she hung on to it longer."

Obama found himself, and his roots, in his own version of the three Rs—reading, self-reflection, and writing. The process started in his early teens, when his mother returned to Indonesia to begin her Ph.D. fieldwork. Obama was self-assured and independent enough to reject her offer to stay together as a family, wanting to remain in Hawaii rather than start a new life once again. He found his mentors in books—Baldwin, Ellison, Hughes, Wright, DuBois—and locked himself away as he tried "to reconcile the world as I'd found it with the terms of my birth."

Alone, without his parents and with only distant grandparents, Obama forged his own identity. What he was looking for was certainty, stability, and he disliked the self-doubt of the classic African American writers. Except for one: Malcolm X, in the autobiography cowritten with Alex Haley. Like Obama's own memoir, which includes composite characters, Malcolm X's autobiography includes fictional elements and techniques (it is "told to" his biographer), as does Haley's best-known book, *Roots: The Saga of an American Family*. Of all the characteristics that Obama picks out from the cowriting of Malcolm X and Alex Haley, the ones he values are not the unsettling and challenging aspects that spring to mind in the mainstream culture. (He rejects Malcolm X's "religious baggage" and especially his hatred of his "white blood.") But they are the qualities that would be critical to Obama's writing, life, and career—reinvention, discipline, and willpower. "His repeated acts of self-creation spoke to me," he wrote. "The blunt poetry of his words, his unadorned insistence on respect, promised a new and uncompromising order, martial in its discipline, forged through sheer force of will."

It was in New York City, while studying at Columbia University, that he developed his capacity for self-control, self-creation, and self-confidence. Obama was attracted to the bigger stage of New York, the dense, urban, polyglot city—not for fun, but as a test. "That's when I stopped drinking. I stopped partying," he told me. "This was my ascetic phase. Everything was stripped down." He lived like a recluse, talking to nobody but himself. "I literally went to class, came home, read books, took long walks, wrote," he explained. "I really think that during those two years I had to look inward and gather myself. That is when I started writing the journals which gave me then the information to write the book, and in fact where I probably learned to write. Writing journals during those two years gave me not only the raw material for the book but also taught me to shape a narrative in ways that would work." Shaping a narrative was invaluable for more than just a book author: it would prove to be one of his most powerful tools as a politician and orator.

It was a time of emotional turmoil and enormous self-discipline for Obama. He learned of his father's death while he was in New York. And he devoted himself to his studies in international relations, as well as his extracurricular reading of religion, literature, and philosophy. As in his own teenage years, and like Malcolm X, he taught himself through books. He read Saint Augustine, Graham Greene, and Friedrich Nietzsche. He played basketball in Harlem and sat in the pews of Abyssinian Baptist Church. He walked the city, and sometimes fasted (in the style, but not the excess, of Gandhi). And when he had visitors, including his family, he was poor company, lecturing them on politics, personal discipline, and world affairs. He was even cold and distant to his mother as he searched inward, and in books, for his own black identity. "I remember wanting to make sure that she understood that me embracing an African American identity in no way meant that I wasn't affirming or embracing her," he told me. "But I think that there were tensions there that weren't always articulated but that I sensed and felt in retrospect I could understand."

This was the period when Obama grew up, creating himself anew through force of character. Around this time, he split with a white girlfriend whom he dated for a year, unable to bridge a cultural gap that separated them. He felt alienated by her privileged background on a weekend trip to her family's country house, while she couldn't understand African American culture—especially the mixture of humor and anger that coursed through a newly written play they watched together. And he changed his name from Barry—the name his family had always called him—to his birth name, Barack. "Here's what it wasn't," Obama said. "It was not some assertion of my African roots. That was not a racial assertion. It was much more of an assertion that I was coming of age. An assertion of being comfortable with the fact that I was different and that I didn't need to try to fit in, in a certain way." By the end of his studies, he had decided to make a career out of community organizing, inspired by the cause of Change.

Later, the writing process that led to *Dreams from My Father*—a memoir written in his early thirties—helped Obama reconcile himself to his past and his identity. It also helped create a political narrative and identity: the book was about his experiences as a teenager and young man, but it was written by the adult Barack Obama, just as he was about to embark on his political career by running for the Illinois legislature. The book spoke of compromise and unity, of community organizing and social justice, of seeking and finding common ground with people thousands of miles from America's comforts and calm. When he finished the manuscript, he shared it with his half sister Maya and they discussed how important it was to him personally. "We talked about this journey and how it was a challenge. It was very important for him as part of the process of excavating his father," she said. "For him I think this was a very cathartic process. Then he's able to move on in a very healthy way and feel quite peaceful, which is interesting for us." His narrative, his collection of people and their tales, seemed to take the place of the stable family he never enjoyed. "All my life," he told a photographer around the time his book was published, "I have been stitching together a family, through stories or memories or friends or ideas."

In his family life and youth, Obama shared little with the woman he would marry. Instead of his disrupted childhood with multiple father figures, Michelle LaVaughn Robinson grew up in a stable family with her older brother and both her parents. Instead of Hawaii and Indonesia, her home was a one-bedroom apartment in a brick bungalow on Chicago's South Side, where her mother, Marian, lived until after the presidential election. Marian stayed at home until Michelle went to high school, cooking lunch for her daughter and a half dozen school friends every other day. "We would just talk—about the morning and all the ridiculous things that happened, and the unfairness and the injustice of education and something bad that our teacher had done," Michelle told me. "Oh, that's terrible," Marian would reply, as she readied them for an afternoon of school. "OK, let's go and get back in there."

Marian, who helped raise her granddaughters through the presidential campaign, is no dreamy romantic. A competitive spirit, she took up running in middle age and ran in athletic races until the moment she fell and knocked herself out. When she came to, her first question was "Did I win?" After her fall, she found that she couldn't run as fast in races, so she quit. "If I couldn't win," she said, "I didn't want to do it."

Yet for all her competitiveness, the power inside the Robinson home was Michelle's quiet but forceful father, Fraser. An athlete in his youth, Fraser was struck with multiple sclerosis in his thirties. His determination to overcome his disability left a deep impression on Michelle and her brother, Craig. Their father struggled to work at the municipal water department every day with no complaint or self-pity. "My father was sort of the emotional presence," Michelle told me. "There was something about my father that just touched us. You never wanted to disappoint him, even though he rarely raised his voice, he never gave out spankings. It was always just the 'I'm *disappointed.*' And then, huh, you bawled. We would be bawling. I think it was something about his consistency and his disability. He was always the model of the kind of people we wanted to be." Fraser compensated for his disability by phoning relatives and taking pride in his children. "He basically lived his life through us," Michelle said. "He couldn't run or jump. So he was deeply invested in my brother's basketball career, went to every game, even went to many games when Craig was at Princeton. He would have to drive around the country." Fraser remains the voice in Michelle's head, pushing her to achieve more, assessing her performance. "What defines me, and what I think about every day, is what my father would think of what I am doing," Michelle said. "How would he feel? Would he be proud? Would he be encouraging the choices that I was making in terms of my career?"

The desire to overcome the odds, just like her father, became Michelle's driving force, masking her own insecurities and self-doubts. Michelle was a bright student in the public schools she attended, skipping second grade, but she was not at the top of her class. She relied on hard work much more than her gifted brother and seemed intimidated by his easy success. "She was disappointed in herself," Marian told me, echoing her husband's most devastating line. "She used to have a little bit of trouble with tests, so she did whatever she had to, to make up for that. I'm sure it was psychological because she was hardworking and she had a brother who could pass a test just by carrying a book under his arm. When you are around someone like that, even if you are OK, you want to be as good or better." Craig was swooped up by Princeton, but

Michelle was overlooked by college counselors who advised her not to apply to the Ivy League. That was when her own competitive drive kicked in. "When it was time to apply to college," she told me, "it was the test scores that essentially said 'these are the schools that you should apply to.' Even though I was looking at my brother who was at Princeton, and thought, 'Well, I'm as smart as he is. So why wouldn't I reach for that?' So there's always a sort of nagging insecurity because of the way society measures preparation—test scores, what school you go to, what neighborhood you grew up in. There are all these indirect indicators that said 'You should be doing it differently.'" Determined to succeed, and drawing on her self-belief, she applied to Princeton anyway and secured a place, partly through her own talent and partly through her brother's.

What she found at Princeton, and later Harvard, was that her drive and determination had taken her to a place that was deeply unsatisfying. It turned out that overcoming her self-doubts and disadvantages did not lead directly to happiness. At Princeton, she became close friends with her roommates, Angela Acree and Suzanne Alele. The three would often talk about the racial divide on campus, how white students would pass them by, pretending not to see them. They hung out at the Third World Center on campus and stayed apart from the white party scene. That sense of separation found its clearest expression in Michelle's senior thesis, entitled "Princeton-Educated Blacks and the Black Community." Princeton had made her feel more black than ever before, yet it also left its black students feeling uprooted when they returned home. "Regardless of the circumstances under which I interact with Whites at Princeton," she wrote, "it often seems as if, to them, I will always be Black first and a student second." Yet she didn't tell her parents of her problems, preferring to work even harder to get departmental honors and proceed to Harvard Law. She returned to Chicago as a successful and ambitious corporate lawyer at the white-shoe firm of Sidley Austin.

It didn't take long—three years, in fact—for Michelle's carefully executed career plan to fall apart. First her father passed away, from complications after a kidney operation. A few months later, Suzanne Alele was also gone. Alele offered Michelle the hope of something beyond her father's focus on work and career. Born in Nigeria and raised in Jamaica, Alele was freewheeling, easygoing, and something of a rebel. "She was always a carefree spirit and didn't take life too seriously," Michelle told me. "Her parents were doctors and she didn't want to be a doctor. She wanted to travel. She never took things seriously—unlike me. I was like, 'I've *got* to get into Harvard.' And then once you get in, you've got to focus and now I'm practicing." Alele's death came quickly: in December 1989 she was diagnosed with lymphoma, and six months later, at the age of twenty-five, it was over. Michelle was with her in her final moments. Alele had recently taken the time out to travel through Asia with her mother, and Michelle suddenly realized she had focused on the wrong things in her own life. "I just thought, 'If I died in four months, is this how I would have wanted to spend this time?'" she recalled.

Between those two devastating losses, Michelle had lost her life's compass. "All my life I had felt I was on sort of this automatic path," she said. "You do well in high school, you apply, you get into a good college. I got into Princeton. You go, you do well. I never thought about getting off the track. I went straight into Harvard Law, didn't take any time off, although there were people deferring. I thought, 'Why would you defer?' Then at Harvard, I did the Harvard Legal Aid Bureau, but the plan was you go into a corporate firm. So that's what I did. And there I was. All of a sudden, I was on this path. I was sitting as a second-year associate at Sidley Austin and I hadn't really thought about how I got there. It was just sort of what you did."

Barack Obama showed up in Michelle's life just before her crisis would unfold, six months before her father died. He, too, was reexamining his life's plan, fearing that he had sold out by giving up community politics for Harvard Law. Still, he needed the cash he could earn from a summer at Sidley, and his assigned adviser at the firm was one Michelle Robinson. When she first heard about him from other office workers, she was unimpressed with the stories about the Harvard hotshot with the unusual life story. "Yeah, he's probably a black guy who can talk straight," she said to herself. "This is a black guy who's biracial who grew up in Hawaii? He's got to be weird." Over an unhurried first lunch, he noticed something behind the 1980s, career-driven facade. "A glimmer that danced across her round, dark eyes whenever I looked at her, the slightest hint of uncertainty, as if, deep inside, she knew how fragile things really were, and that if she ever let go, even for a moment, all her plans might quickly unravel," he later wrote. "That touched me somehow, that trace of vulnerability. I wanted to know that part of her." He wore her down, and their first kiss came when they shared some Baskin-Robbins ice cream after an office picnic. Their first date was watching Spike Lee's movie *Do the Right Thing*—a classic struggle between Martin

Luther King's nonviolence and Malcolm X's anger. But Michelle only fell in love when she heard his stem-winder speech to one of his community organizing groups. He loved her stability, her rootedness, her *Leave It to Beaver* family; she loved his dreamy idealism and his exotic sense of adventure.

Michelle's family feared he'd never survive her toughness. "The first thing I was worried about was 'Is this poor guy going to make the cut? How long is it going to be until he gets fired?'" wondered Craig Robinson. "My mom and dad used to joke that if we ever got to meet any of her potential suitors, we had to really make hay while the sun shined because it was going to be fleeting." But Michelle's hard shell was beginning to crack. The process began even before the twin losses of her father and best friend. Michelle was already looking around her corporate law offices and wondering what the point was. "People were very nice. I had dozens of mentors. People were very supportive. I knew I would make partner. There were people behind me. I was being assigned to the right things," she told me. "But I also didn't see a whole lot of people who were just thrilled to be there. I met people who thought this was a good life. But were people waking up, just bounding out of bed to get to work? No. And with the older associates, the longer you stayed, the harder it was to get out. The golden handcuffs." Obama shared something with Alele, a free spirit who also seemed driven. "This completely unconventional character, who was very smart, very capable, but who took more of a winding path to his life," she said of her future husband. "It wasn't as direct. Yet he seemed to have just as much clarity about who he was and what he wanted to be. And all of that led me to start thinking, 'What do I want?'" By now, Michelle was beginning to think that her education had taught her little about life. "I thought, 'This isn't education.' You can make money and have a nice degree. But what are you learning about giving back to the world, and finding your passion and letting that guide you, as opposed to the school you got into?" She wrote letters to charities and city agencies, and one landed on the desk of Valerie Jarrett, deputy chief of staff to Mayor Richard Daley. After a ninety-minute interview, which turned into a heart-to-heart about the meaning of life and the purpose of a career, Jarrett offered her a job. Michelle had one moment of doubt, asking Obama to meet with Jarrett before accepting the offer, which paid half of her Sidley salary. But she was already set on a new and renegade life.

After months of dismissing marriage as unnecessary, Barack finally proposed to Michelle over dessert at the end of a dinner at a Chicago restaurant. They married in 1992; she was twenty-eight years old, he was thirty-one. They were almost reflected images of each other. He was a restless dreamer who discovered the power of self-discipline; she was a competitive striver who discovered the freedom of breaking out of convention. They were both outsiders who had gained entry to the inner sanctum of the establishment, only to find that they preferred to stand somewhere in between. Together they wanted to belong—to family, community—yet they also wanted to shake up the old world. She wasn't just a South Side girl anymore, and he wasn't just an exotic guy from Hawaii and Indonesia. There was no turning back to their old lives, and there was no abandoning their past, either. Both overcame enormous challenges to succeed in a traditional, Ivy League world; yet both were determined to leave that world and set their sights on new challenges.

After editing the *Harvard Law Review* and securing a book contract, Obama returned to Chicago to work on a voter registration drive in the 1992 elections that helped the Clintons to win the White House. He could have joined a big corporate law firm like Sidley; instead he joined a small civil rights law firm and taught constitutional law at the University of Chicago. She could have stayed in the bureaucracy in city government; instead he suggested a job running a new nonprofit group called Public Allies, whose board he sat on. Public Allies aimed to inspire and train the next generation of community leaders: talented young people who were committed to public service rather than corporate work. It paid even less than her city job, but she could finally offer to young people what she only experienced herself in midcareer: the chance to start an unconventional life and give something back—to be a Princeton-educated black who still had a relationship to her community. "It sounded risky and just out there," she told me. "But for some reason, it just spoke to me."

It was politics that spoke to Barack Obama. Four years later, as they started thinking about a family, he ran for the Illinois state senate and won. Over the next eight years, he would split his time between Springfield and Chicago, between campaigning and home. They would have two daughters, Malia and Sasha. Michelle would shift to more stable, more lucrative work at the University of Chicago and its hospital. But his restless political ambitions took their marriage and finances to the brink. Obama gambled and lost an unlikely race for Congress in 2000, then saw his moment three years later in the United States Senate. It was supposed to be his last shot at politics, and it hit the mark. He burst onto the national scene with a single speech, trounced his opposition, and secured a handsome book contract. The outsider had made it to the inside track of American politics.

The United States Congress was supposed to be a big deal, a huge leap for a humble state senator who would likely have quit politics altogether if he had lost. Instead, by the time he arrived, Barack Obama was already too big for Capitol Hill. His Senate victory was one of the few bright spots in a dismal election year, as he seized a Republican seat amid the wreckage of Bush's victory over John Kerry. It was only ironic that Kerry had helped to launch Obama's national career by picking him to deliver the keynote speech at the Democratic convention in Boston. Kerry had briefly campaigned with Obama in Illinois, and Obama was hardly expecting a speaking slot in return. But his Senate race was critical, his message fit with the positive tone of the convention, and he was the biggest symbol of diversity in the party. After his Boston speech, and an endless series of high-profile national interviews, Obama was launched into orbit. He was a ready-made star, at a time when Senate Democrats sorely needed something to believe in. They had just lost their leader, Tom Daschle, and faced a president who proclaimed he owned enough political capital to do whatever he wanted.

Out of those ashes, Obama found some rare opportunities. Daschle's defeat offered the newcomer the chance to hire some of the most experienced and best-connected Democratic staffers in Congress. At the top of that list was a rumpled gray head who was Daschle's friend and chief of staff: Pete Rouse. Rouse was ready to retire after three decades as a congressional staffer, perhaps to join Daschle in the private sector, when Obama suggested a meeting late one evening after an orientation session for new members of Congress at the luxurious Mandarin Oriental hotel. Obama asked for his advice in setting up an office, then wondered if he would consider being his chief of staff. Rouse demurred, saying he was focused on packing up the Daschle archives and finding jobs for his soon-to-be unemployed staffers. Three weeks later, Obama told him he could have the job if he wanted it, but Rouse declined, citing the job search for his Daschle staffers. "Well, look, can you give me an hour a day?" Obama asked. Rouse said that wasn't fair to the freshman senator, but Obama suggested it would tide him over to the end of the year. Rouse felt it was important to help Obama get a good start in the Senate, and was intrigued by his pitch.

"I know what I know and I know what I don't know," Obama told him. "I know what I'm good at, and I know what I'm not good at. I can give a good speech."

Rouse liked his attempt at modesty. "Yes, Senator, you can," he replied.

"I know policy and retail politics," Obama continued. "But I don't know how to build a large staff and negotiate the potential pitfalls of being a relatively high-profile newcomer to the Senate. I have no intention of running for president in 2008 and just want to get established in the Senate. I'm looking for someone to partner with me to make sure I get off on the right foot."

Rouse sensed he was getting reeled in, but was under pressure from his old friend Daschle. Besides, he was disarmed by Obama's frank and direct approach. Obama told him that he knew he would never be as close as Daschle, but he wanted to work with him in the same way. Fifteen years older than Obama, Rouse wasn't looking for a friend; he wanted to be a fully trusted adviser, and Obama promised to let him run the office with as much leeway as he wanted. He interviewed a handful of senior staff, but trusted Rouse completely. "I left most of the decisions up to Pete," he told me.

Obama needed to lean on Rouse. In Springfield, his staff comprised one person; in Washington, he had little idea whom to recruit and how to chart a course through the Senate. Rouse wrote a strategic plan for Obama to do just that, spelling out how he would operate over the course of the next two years. There were three main phases. In the first, he would concentrate on Illinois, earn the respect of his voters, and avoid the fate of Carol Moseley-Braun, the former African American senator from Illinois who looked like she had lost interest in her own state. In his first year, Obama refused all out-of-state speaking offers, with a handful of exceptions: an NAACP award ceremony in Los Angeles complete with red carpet and movie stars, another NAACP award dinner in Detroit, and an event marking Martin Luther King's birthday. Instead of appearing on the Sunday shows, he traveled back to Illinois every weekend. In the first nine months, Obama held thirty-eight town hall meetings, of which thirty-one were downstate, far away from his base of progressives and African Americans in Chicago. "I came down here looking for votes before the election," Obama told his aides. "I won big. I don't want people to think I just forgot about them once I got their vote."

Phase two was supposed to begin at the one-year mark, when Obama would be free to turn his focus back to Chicago and its suburbs. Within two years, he would have a solid foundation across Illinois, from rural towns to the big city. In the meantime, he worked on the highway bill to bring federal dollars to his home state, along with ethanol and alternative energy funding to help farmers in rural Illinois. By the fall, his approval rating was over 70 percent.

Later, a third phase would begin: venturing onto the national stage. This was the model built by Hillary Clinton—the only other national media star in the Senate, having entered the world's greatest deliberative body with an even bigger profile. In the first phases, Obama would be a loyal member of the Democratic caucus and avoid the press. The strategy was designed to dull his star power and prove that the unconventional outsider could play a conventional game. "Here comes a guy who is the only African American. He has this notoriety from the convention. People start looking at him and saying, 'Is he going to be a hotdog, grabbing all the big issues, looking for national press?'" said Rouse. Obama and his staff were acutely aware of the caricature. They overheard one long-serving liberal senator trashing Obama at a Washington party in his first month on Capitol Hill, saying, "This guy is too big for his britches, he needs to be taken down a notch." Obama knew he needed to charm an older generation, to befriend those inclined to distrust an ambitious newcomer.

He also wanted to impress his own Democratic leadership, helping to raise money and get more Democrats elected to Congress. His first assignment—and his only national event in the first six months—was a press conference at the National Press Club with James Roosevelt, FDR's grandson. The target was President Bush's plans to privatize part of Social Security, but Obama was deeply reluctant to go, even though most freshman senators would have relished the chance to appear before the TV cameras. "I don't know why I should do this," he chafed at his staff. "I have nothing interesting to do or say on this." The answer was simple: because the leadership wanted him to get some publicity for their message. Obama spoke at the event with minimal staff and returned looking pleased with himself. When asked how it went, he replied with a broad grin, "Excellent. But some people might just say very good." The line became a standing joke between his staffers as they echoed his supreme confidence about the smallest task. Even as he tried to keep his head down, Obama was always stumbling into something higher.

There was no serious planning for a presidential bid in the first year, according to staffers and internal memos. "I'm sure at the time I had no intention of running," Obama told me. Still, he believed he could do far more than play the role of a respectful rookie. He made all the right moves, seeking out the advice of Ted Kennedy and Hillary Clinton. But his mind-set suggested something more: to be both a successful junior senator and someone who punched far above his weight. "My assumption was that I'd be in the position to work across the aisle as well as within my own party to continually nudge issues forward that I deeply cared about, like nuclear proliferation. I thought I'd be able to make some immediate progress on veterans' issues, which I'd taken a deep interest in when I was campaigning," he told me. "I anticipated on the big-ticket items that I cared about, like universal health care, that I would be second chair, or third or fourth chair, to people like Ted Kennedy, who'd been working on it for a very long time. But I thought that I could contribute good ideas and help shape the agenda."

In fact he was far lower than second or third chair in the Senate; he was ninety-ninth in seniority out of one hundred senators. He soon realized the Senate didn't work at the same pace as either his old legislature in Springfield or his ambition. Obama was a very junior member of the minority party, and his fame counted for little beyond the cameras. "I think fairly quickly I realized that it was going to be hard to get things done in the minority. But that wasn't a surprise. That was true when I was in the state legislature," he told me. "People forget that I had been in the legislature for a very long time and knew how legislatures work. And I also understood that the Senate is an institution that still runs on seniority and that it would be some time before I was actually calling the shots on any committee. But I have always believed that if you are willing to work hard, and not take credit, you can get things done." Obama was happy with small-bore issues like veterans' benefits and Illinois infrastructure. His bigger achievements, on ethics reform and nuclear proliferation, were substantive but not controversial. However, he found he could work hard in Washington and still not get things done—at least, not at the gridlocked speed of Congress. "I was surprised by the slow pace of the Senate," he told me. "In the state legislature, we could get a hundred bills passed during the course of a session. In the Senate it was maybe twenty. And that I think made me realize how resistant to change Washington is generally."

Yet he wasn't exactly pushing for dramatic change himself. As an outsider, he owed the establishment little, but chose instead to play by its rules and stuck to his strategic plan with strict self-discipline. He was cautious and compromising, disappointing the progressives who saw him as an antiwar hero because of his 2002 opposition to the invasion of Iraq. Indeed, he chose not to speak out on Iraq until his eleventh month in office. "He got to the Senate and now had access to more information and more points of view. He wanted to digest that," said Rouse. "To get out on national TV and rally the base did not fit our plan of earning your spurs and getting accepted in the Senate as a serious legislator. If he'd known he would be running for president in 2008, he may have made a different calculation at the time."

If Obama was a rebel, he seemed most interested in rebelling against the expectations of his liberal fans. He spoke out against a date certain to pull out of Iraq in 2005, voting against such a proposal the following year. He preferred instead the more cautious "time frame" for a phased withdrawal. He voted to confirm Condoleezza Rice as secretary of state, taking an unexpected amount of heat from liberal Democrats. Despite his liberal rankings, he sided against the trial lawyers by voting for tort reform that pushed class-action lawsuits from state to federal courts. He worked closely with Tom Coburn, the social ultraconservative, on good-government issues. He even considered voting for John Roberts on the Supreme Court, which Rouse argued strenuously against.

"You know, I would hope, if I'm president someday, twenty years down the road, Republicans will judge my nominees on the merits, whether they agree with them philosophically or not," he told his staff.

"This isn't Harvard Law School's moot court," argued Rouse. "This is the political arena. If this guy is technically qualified and a brilliant legal mind, that's fine. But in the real world votes have consequences. If I really thought Republicans would say, twenty years from now, Barack voted for John Roberts so we're going to vote for a Larry Tribe, that might be different—but that's not gonna happen. The reality is you're going to have to live with the consequences of this vote for twenty years and they're not likely to be good." Not content with his political positioning, Obama wrote a post on Daily Kos castigating progressives for their attacks on his fellow Democrats who voted for Roberts, as he had wanted to.

The final phase of the national rollout had a very distant goal. "The original thinking was—and I never heard Barack articulate this specifically—we want to get established in Illinois by delivering for the state, so we're politically unassailable," said Rouse. "We want to have the option in 2010 to run for governor or seek reelection to the Senate. And we want to be in position to consider running for president in 2012 or 2016, depending on what happens in 2008."

Instead Obama's fame and ambition were constantly pushing to the fore, as the political clock began to speed up. In late August 2005, Obama embarked on his most substantive overseas travel, to weapons sites in the former Soviet bloc. As he flew out to Moscow, a tropical storm developed over the Bahamas before heading toward southern Florida. Over the next four days, as Obama toured weapons storage and destruction sites in Russia, the storm burst into the Gulf of Mexico and swelled into a monstrous category five hurricane. Obama was sitting down with political and military leaders in Kiev, Ukraine, when Hurricane Katrina slammed into the Louisiana coastline. He returned, at the end of the week, to a geographical and political landscape that was utterly changed. He had missed most of the indelible TV pictures of rooftop rescues and lootings in New Orleans, of Americans chanting for help outside the Convention Center. But by the time Obama landed on American soil, President Bush looked weak and incompetent less than a year after winning reelection as a strong national security leader. And rapper Kanye West was on national television accusing the president of not caring about black people.

Obama tore up his strategic plan. He stood as a prop with Hillary Clinton, as they both accompanied former presidents Bush and Clinton to Houston for the announcement of their new Katrina fund. He toured the Astrodome where Katrina evacuees were sheltering, saying nothing to the press while others in the arena drew far more attention to themselves: Oprah Winfrey, Jesse Jackson, and Bishop T. D. Jakes. And he returned to Washington knowing that he was uniquely placed to give voice to the evacuees, as the only African American senator in the nation's capital. "What I realized was I might be able to offer a unique perspective on Katrina, in that my voice could amplify the voices of people who had been forgotten during that crisis," he told me.

He could have plucked the heartstrings, but preferred to strike a different note about class. When he finally spoke on the Senate floor, he stuck to his personal strategy of combining conventional politics with an unconventional message. He rejected Kanye West's accusations of Bush's racism, and preferred to quote one woman in the Astrodome who told him, "We had nothing before the hurricane. Now we got less than nothing." Obama used his star power to focus less on race than on an age-old tolerance of poverty and criminality in the inner city. "I hope we realize that the people of New Orleans weren't just abandoned during the hurricane," he said. "They were abandoned long ago—to murder and mayhem in their streets; to substandard schools; to dilapidated housing; to inadequate health care; to a pervasive sense of hopelessness." He took the message to a national audience, breaking his self-imposed exclusion from the national media to appear on ABC's *This Week*. To his staff's surprise, his Illinois voters didn't seem to mind his higher national profile or his message about race and class. "Katrina sort of forced him to go out publicly," said Rouse. "Lo and behold, we realized we weren't taking a hit in Illinois. People weren't upset about that. And we sort of came to the realization that we could be a little more forceful and speak out on these issues a little sooner than we had thought."

Around this time, Obama mentioned to his aides for the first time that maybe they should start to think about something bigger. Not planning, just thinking. "We ought to see how this goes and after the election just talk about whether or not we ought to consider running," he said. "Nothing serious."

As President Bush's political capital collapsed, Obama and his organization were hardly ready for the political opportunities. Restless and ambitious, for sure, but neither committed nor all that competent. With a heavy year of campaigning ahead, along with a trip to Africa and a tour for his second book, his team had set up a fund-raising organization to help the midterm candidates in 2006, called the Hopefund, which suffered from a lack of adult supervision and professionalism. While Obama raised a respectable $4.4 million for candidates, the fund failed to translate that cash into what every national politician needs: a network of contacts and favors. Obama's office eventually brought in a seasoned Democratic consultant, Anita Dunn, to set their political operation on a more organized footing. "A tactical miscalculation was made initially because he had no intention of being a national figure that quickly," said Rouse. "The original course was fine for just getting ready to run again in six years. But there was no priority placed on putting together national lists or building national contacts. In retrospect, we didn't do what we could have done because we didn't know we needed to do it. We were doing the basics of raising money for ourselves and other people. But we weren't taking it to the next level of trying to develop the political infrastructure that a rising star in the Democratic Party ought to have."

Obama himself thought his political fortunes might dim by the time of the midterms. He was often frustrated by the business of Washington—the press conferences and hearings—and sought inspiration from a lonely jog along the Mall toward the Lincoln Memorial, where he would read the Gettysburg Address and imagine the crowd listening to Martin Luther King. "Our working assumption was always that the air would slowly go out of the balloon during the course of 2005 and 2006," he told me. "The interest, the hype, the crowds."

Yet his own crowds kept gathering, and Obama's closest aides sensed distinct turning points through the year. For Pete Rouse, the moment came in May 2006, when Obama traveled to Omaha, Nebraska, at the invitation of Ben Nelson, the Senate's most conservative Democrat and the only Democrat among Nebraska's members of Congress. Obama took some shots at President Bush, pleasing the crowd at the Hilton hotel. "We all remember that George Bush said in the 2000 campaign that he was against nation building," he told the crowd of 850 people. "We just didn't know he was talking about this one." Rouse was struck more deeply by Nelson's observation that Obama was the only national Democrat he would think of inviting to speak at the dinner. "I thought to myself, a progressive African American from Hyde Park who is in his first year in the Senate is the only national Democrat you'd invite to Omaha? Something's happening here." Obama's aides didn't realize how much of a draw their noncandidate would be on the campaign trail. Soon, they were fielding requests not just for Senate races but also House races, too, thanks to Obama's close relationship with Rahm Emanuel, the aggressively competitive Chicago Democrat running the party's congressional election effort.

Obama's popularity at home was only eclipsed by his stardom overseas. On a trip to his father's homeland of Kenya in August 2006, the media crush looked tame compared with the surging crowds of adoring Kenyans. In Kisumu, not far from his ancestors' farm, Obama took an HIV/AIDS test with Michelle outside a local hospital to encourage Kenyans to take their own tests. Outside, the crowd was so intense that

Obama picked up a microphone and pleaded with them to stop pushing. The entire trip left Michelle overwhelmed and embarrassed by the public outpouring. But Obama sensed something else. "We're on a roll here," he told his staff. "Let's see what happens."

Inside the Senate office, the highly disciplined mood gave way to some calculated opportunism. At the start of 2006, the working assumption was that Obama would be in no position to make a decision to run for president in 2007—unless there was what they called a perfect storm of personal and political factors. By midyear, the storm was gathering and Obama's staff started to map out the decision-making process of whether or not to run. By early fall, they were ready to roil the waters. Obama was invited to be the keynote speaker before thousands of Democrats at Senator Tom Harkin's annual steak-fry event in central Iowa. "If we're going to do it," said Rouse, "let's have some fun."

The fun involved some mischief: an invitation to one of the party's best operatives to accompany Obama at the steak fry. Steve Hildebrand was a friend of Rouse's and a former staffer of Tom Daschle, a fellow South Dakotan with a soft western lilt to his accent and a romantic view of the political trenches. He believed in grassroots politics, the kind of door-to-door campaigning that was key to winning Iowa's arcane caucuses. And he had a track record that any candidate would covet, having managed Al Gore's knockout win in Iowa six years earlier against Bill Bradley. Rouse thought there would be an instant chemistry. "He'll be taken with Barack so if we ever end up doing anything, he'll be our guy," he reasoned. Above all, Obama's team wanted to mess with the other campaigns and the media. They leaked Hildebrand's name to the press, sparking a round of intense speculation about Obama's presidential ambitions. "They wanted to fuck with the other campaigns," said Hildebrand. "I was a pawn, and that was very clear."

The political operative quickly turned into a starstruck fan. Hildebrand picked up Obama from Des Moines' airport and drove him to a couple of fund-raisers before the main event. He had never met Obama before and never heard him speak; he had even missed his keynote speech at the Boston convention two years earlier, as he was running Tom Daschle's doomed reelection contest in South Dakota. Instead of staffing Obama in Iowa, or laying the groundwork for a presidential run, Hildebrand spent the day observing the noncandidate closely. He saw him surrounded by admirers at the fund-raisers, where they asked him to sign books and pose for photographs. Then he watched him enter the steak-fry site in the tiny town of Indianola, where the crowd rushed Obama as he left his van. Hildebrand was so concerned by the surge that he asked three of Harkin's male staffers to manage the fans and the press, which included fifteen television cameras and sixteen still photographers. The operative was astonished as he looked on. "I estimate about four hundred people brought his first book and asked him to sign it," Hildebrand recalled. "Each time he would ask people if they had read it and they would say yes and talk about their favorite passage. I saw nineteen-year-old men shake when they got near him. I saw elderly women just ask him for a hug. I saw person after person after person say, 'Thank you for giving us hope.' A lot of people asked personal questions about his life and who he is. At the end of this three-hour steak fry, he literally must have met every single person there." Hildebrand paid close attention to how Obama shook hands with the crowd, curious to see whether he could succeed at the kind of face-to-face politics that Iowa demands. Instead of just slapping hands and moving on, Obama would reach in, three or four people deep, fix them with his eyes, and ask them for their names. "He was *very* good at it," said Hildebrand. "He was very genuine about wanting to meet people and caring about the exchange he would have with them." At the end of the day, as they walked back to the car, Hildebrand asked Obama if this was a common reaction.

"It's like this everywhere I go," Obama said.

"How do people know so much about you?"

"I have no idea," Obama shrugged.

On the four-hour drive back to South Dakota that evening, Hildebrand called everybody he knew in politics to tell them what he had witnessed. "This guy is the real deal," he told anyone who picked up the phone. "This guy has something that others don't have. There's a connection here." Hildebrand knew there were no serious plans for Obama to run in 2008, but he wanted to be there in case they decided to move ahead. He had already met with Senator Clinton to talk about her campaign, and was intending to hold fire until Tom Daschle, his old boss, made a final decision about his own campaign. Instead, the next morning, he walked into his office in Sioux Falls and sat down at his computer to paste together the news clips about Obama at the steak fry. He e-mailed it to 120 people—a mix of political reporters, operatives, donors, elected officials, and former officials, plus staffers to rival candidates. That was the start of a three-month e-mail campaign that extended to four hundred insiders, which Hildebrand pulled together at six each morning. "I became obsessed," he said. "I drank the Kool-Aid. I started my own little movement to convince people that this guy was ready and our party needed him to run." A couple of times, Obama's aides asked him to stop, but Hildebrand refused. Instead he convinced them to return to Iowa just days before the 2006 elections, to stage a get-out-the-vote rally for Chet Culver, who was running for governor. Hildebrand promised they could get a big crowd in a student town like Iowa City, and argued that helping Culver was worth enduring another round of speculation about an Obama campaign. In case anyone was unclear about his own wishes, Hildebrand showed up with five hundred buttons saying Obama for President.

The steak fry served its purpose. Rouse wrote a memo to Obama's inner circle suggesting they meet in Chicago the day after the elections to talk about whether or not it was crazy to consider running for president.

In fact, Obama had already entered a world of irrational exuberance before the midterms began. In mid-October he began touring a dozen cities to sell his latest book, *The Audacity of Hope,* mixing campaign stops alongside his bookstore sessions. The book tour was orchestrated to lift Obama's profile in the midterm elections, allowing him to sit for TV interviews that would sell his book to readers and sell Democratic candidates to voters. The response was overwhelming. Oprah Winfrey invited him on her show and all but urged him to run for president. Fans lined up for hours to see him; thousands crowded into theaters to hear him; the media offered him big interviews; and the author skillfully sidestepped presidential questions while still inflating the bubble. On NBC's *Meet the Press,* Tim Russert confronted Obama with his own firm pledge, on the same show just twenty-one months earlier, that he would serve out his full six-year term as senator for Illinois. "Well, that was how I was thinking at that time," said Obama as he grasped for an artful response. "And you know, I don't want to be coy about this, given the responses that I've been getting over the last several months. I have thought about the possibility. But I have not thought about it with the seriousness and depth that I think is required."

The book tour marked the moment of no return for Obama. "What became clear was that the mood for something different, for change, was strong," he told me. "When we were in Seattle for a book signing and put out free tickets over the Internet, they were gone in two hours.

When people were scalping tickets for a free book signing, you got a sense that people's interest was still high."

Despite all the hype it looked like a longshot: the notion that a freshman senator with an exotic name, just two years out of the Illinois statehouse, could beat the biggest names in the Democratic Party and win the White House in just twenty-four months. But there was something extraordinary about that moment in politics, as Barack Obama sat down with his inner circle to explore whether there was any reality to his far-fetched dream. It was the day after an unexpectedly large victory: the Democrats had reclaimed control of both the House and the Senate. Anything seemed possible at a time when the Republican Party was collapsing and President Bush was so deeply unpopular. All the same, the group of friends and political aides knew they were discussing something outlandish in the simple office in Chicago's River North neighborhood. They had no political machine to set in motion, no Rolodex of contacts and favors to recall. They were on their own, inside the conference room of Obama's political guru David Axelrod.

A razor-sharp mind in a shambling body, Axelrod was sometimes compared to a bumbling history professor (although the comparison elicited complaints from history professors). He was the dominant Democratic operative in Chicago, the man who had helped pluck Obama out of obscurity and thrust him into the national spotlight and ultimately the United States Senate. Yet Axelrod still thought of himself as a former political reporter from the *Chicago Tribune*. He liked to craft the broad narratives of a campaign, but he also maintained the competitive spirit of an old-time newspaperman. He wanted to write the lead story of the election, and he wanted to win.

Axelrod loved to talk about his favorite newspaper stories, of the mass murders and train crashes he covered as a metro reporter, and the zeal that drove him on. One weekend, while visiting family in New York, he heard a local news bulletin about the former vice president Nelson Rockefeller dying suddenly while working on an art book at his home. Axelrod called his news desk to find there was no wire story, so he raced to Rockefeller's home to report and file his story. "The only true words of that story were that he died," Axelrod recalled later. "Everything after that was a lie. He died in the height of passion with a network news correspondent." On the basketball court with Obama, Axelrod had no style but a sharp eye and plenty of hope: he would wildly miss a half dozen three-pointers before effortlessly swishing the next half dozen.

Behind his wilting mustache, there lay a wry sense of humor and languid voice that hinted at darker moods. Axelrod was a worrier. He liked to think of himself as a multitasker, but he often looked like he sweated the small stuff. He had good reason to act like a weight sat on his slumped shoulders. His depressed father committed suicide when Axelrod was just nineteen, and his eldest daughter lives with developmental disabilities brought on by epileptic seizures. Even his political life was marked by loss. His heroes both passed away prematurely: Paul Simon, the United States senator who gave him his first job in politics, and Harold Washington, Chicago's first African American mayor, who died in city hall.

What leavened Axelrod's politics was his passion for the story and his sense of idealism. As a five-year-old in Manhattan he watched Jack Kennedy campaign in his neighborhood. Eight years later, he was volunteering on Bobby Kennedy's short-lived presidential race. He loved politics and he wanted to fall in love with his candidates.

To Axelrod, Obama was far more than just his highest-profile client; he was his friend. He was convinced that Obama had a shot at winning, but had plenty of doubts about Obama's desire to suffer the freak show of presidential politics. Axelrod was conflicted by the prospect, sensing Obama's potential but wanting to test his desire for the job. "Anybody who has been through presidential politics doesn't lightly recommend it to a friend," he told me. "Because it's a ghoulish, nasty gauntlet and you commit yourself to this terribly difficult process. And if you win, then you have the honor of the most difficult job on the planet." Other politicians seemed to be yearning to fill a hole, to fulfill their lives with a presidential campaign. Not Obama. "Many other folks who run for president have a kind of pathological drive or ambition. And I just didn't see that in him. I didn't see that," he said. "I mean, I knew he had ambition. But you've got to wake up every morning and have this burning desire to be president of the United States in order to put yourself through the really inhuman pace and pressures that it entails. And I think the prospect of that has weeded out a lot of people in recent election cycles. Many before they start."

Axelrod had spent the previous cycle with one such driven candidate:

John Edwards. The experience was not pleasant. Axelrod barely knew Edwards before the election and he lost several rounds of infighting. He ultimately lost control of one of the most important levers of power: the candidate's TV ads.

Obama was entirely different—a close friend who deferred to his judgment. Still, Axelrod reluctantly approached the idea of another presidential campaign after the wrenching experience of 2004. He looked forward to resting through 2007, and was talking to some newspapers about writing a column on politics. To the campaigns that asked him for his services, Axelrod had a simple response. "I'm not going to be involved unless Barack runs," he said. "And I'm pretty certain he isn't going to run."

His certainty came from a simple observation: Barack liked his own life. After several years of turmoil, the Obama family felt more rooted and stable. Barack was still splitting his time between politics and Chicago, just as he did while serving in the state senate in Springfield. But the children were older, and his marriage with Michelle was much stronger. His books were selling exceptionally well and the family finances were comfortable for the first time; they had even moved into a large home, their first after several years of living in condos. To unwind, he loved time with his children or flopping on the couch to watch ESPN with friends. "I don't really need to do this," he told Axelrod at the time, "because being Barack Obama turns out is a pretty good gig."

Being Barack Obama was not enough. Even as he savored his family life, he was deeply restless. He had just spent the last several weeks campaigning for other candidates and selling his book—and he loved it. Politics was always taking him away from his family, the place he yearned to be. Maybe there was a different kind of yearning that made him seek out some new contest every few years. Maybe he wasn't running for office so much as running away. Away from the failures and indiscipline of his father and grandfather. Away from the failure of his own congressional election in 2000, a disastrous effort that almost drove him from politics. Away from the aimlessness of his own youth filled with drink and drugs and lazy days in Hawaii.

Barack couldn't have the stability and the restlessness, the rules and the risk taking, the home and the road, without one person: Michelle. It was Michelle who had to agree to a presidential campaign before he could, and the early meetings were aimed, in large part, at answering her questions. More than agree to a campaign, she needed to want to take part. She hated the failed race for Congress in 2000, and their marriage was strained by the time their youngest daughter, Sasha, was born a year later. There was little conversation and even less romance. She was angry at his selfishness and careerism; he thought she was cold and ungrateful. Even as he ran for the United States Senate in 2004, she still harbored very mixed feelings about her husband's love of politics. Politics seemed like a waste of energy to Michelle, at least when compared with the serious work of government and public service. She believed deeply in a sense of duty to the community, to helping others. But campaigns and elections seemed less serious and substantive. So she had played no part in Barack's previous contests and preferred to keep her distance. This one would be different, of course. But how different?

At least she was ready for change. The children were older and more self-sufficient. She had built a network of friends and family in Chicago to help her through the school days and after-school activities. She had taken control of her fitness, working out in punishing predawn sessions and improving her diet. And she had created something out of nothing at work, turning the idea of community relations into a reality for the University of Chicago Medical Center. By the time Barack reached Washington, Michelle had even reconciled herself to the fact that their home life would never be the same as the nuclear family she had known as a child, with a father who was home every night for dinner. Instead, there were phone calls and video conferences with Barack, bike rides and soccer games for him and the girls, and a routine she could manage. Initially he wanted her to move to D.C. so the family could be together. But even he now admitted that she was right to stay in Chicago.

So, Michelle wanted to know from the assembled political brains in Axelrod's office, what exactly would be left of their happy life if Barack entered the presidential contest? "What would his schedule look like?" she began, as she peppered them with questions. How often would he be home? What time would he have available for the girls and her? Would there be any flexibility? Could he take weekends off?

The answer was simple. "No, no, no, no, no," said David Plouffe, one of Axelrod's business partners. "There are no shortcuts." Plouffe's lean frame and soft voice masked a heavyweight operative with sharp political instincts and an eye for detail. He tried to lighten his brusque judgments by frequently flashing a toothy smile. But the Plouffe punch landed hard, just the same, and he thought he knew where this conversation was headed. Axelrod was merely concerned about Obama's desire and drive; Plouffe believed there was no drive and the entire notion was dead on arrival. Like the rest of the political professionals in Axelrod's office that day, he was tired after an exhausting, but successful, set of campaigns in the 2006 elections. He was looking forward to some downtime with his family and had no interest in a brutal presidential campaign that would begin almost immediately. Plouffe thought he could make the same stark argument to Obama himself. "As you make this decision, just think: your 2007 and 2008 could be wonderful if you don't run," he began. "You don't have reelection until 2010, you can take most weekends off, you can spend all the time with your family that you want. You could have a wonderful period of time. The book is selling well. But if you run, you'll never see your family, you'll be under pressure the likes of which you can't imagine, and it will be absolutely miserable from a personal standpoint."

Obama's friends were taken aback but impressed by the frank advice. "I'm so glad I'm not running for president," quipped Marty Nesbitt, to lighten the mood.

"Oh, but you are," Obama replied. "This is going to affect your life, too."

The meeting looped around the pros and cons of running, following the contours of a meticulous memo typed up by Pete Rouse several weeks earlier. Ever the pragmatist, Rouse wanted to lay out the issues and the steps to make a rational decision about a seemingly crazy idea. With no groundwork done, no national network, and no personal experience of a presidential contest, what would it look and feel like?

Barack wanted to know everything, to vacuum up the information. Most of all, he wanted the answers to these questions: "Could we win? Could my family survive? And should I win? Was there something unique I could provide that would justify me running this soon?" He knew that Hillary Clinton was likely to enter the contest as the front-runner— a prospect that shaped the follow-up questions. "How would you organize a campaign against the best brand name in Democratic politics? What would be the unique message that I would be able to bring?" he asked. "We knew it would be change, that it would be a change election. But how would we describe the changes that were needed? What would the schedule look like? How much money would I have to raise? How would I raise it?"

Michelle wasn't exclusively domestic in her concerns, either. A competitive player in everything she touched, from card games to careers, she wanted to know if the campaign would be worth the sacrifice. "OK," she told the aides, "if once we get over the hurdles and I'm sufficiently comfortable that he'll be available to be the father that we want him to be, can we actually chart a course to victory?"

That was harder to answer than the question of weekend leisure time. The political aides knew they would be starting far behind the Clinton juggernaut in money, organization, and name recognition. Sure, Obama had some obvious strengths: he looked and sounded fresh at a time when the country wanted change. But the campaign needed to be perfect to stand any chance of winning, and even with an ideal operation, Obama would still be a very long shot. Maybe they should think about trying to avoid embarrassment rather than winning? With no existing relationships in any of the early states, especially Iowa and New Hampshire, the prospect of total failure was very real.

Just one person inside Axelrod's office argued strongly for Obama to move ahead: Steve Hildebrand, who was desperate for him to run and deeply disillusioned with the rest of the Democratic field. Having watched him in Iowa earlier in the fall, Hildebrand wanted an antiwar candidate who could inspire him to dive into another campaign. "The timing is right," Hildebrand insisted. "If you wait four years, you'll have no idea. You can't predict that the time is going to be right then."

By the end of the meeting, Plouffe thought there was a very low chance of Obama entering the race, and the senator seemed to agree. "Well," Obama said as he wrapped up the conversation, "I think it's very unlikely I'm going to do this. But let's have another meeting in a month."

The Obamas left the meeting with their friends Valerie Jarrett and Marty Nesbitt to eat dinner at Jarrett's favorite Tuscan restaurant, Coco Pazzo. It was time for a gut check after all the professional advice. Michelle and Barack approached the conversation coolly, analyzing their own situation with a high degree of detachment. "I know you'll make an outstanding president," she said, "but have you really thought through whether the timing is right now?" They all agreed that time was key to the contest. Was there enough time to beat the Clintons? Wasn't the country at this time searching for someone like Barack? Was it easier running now when the girls were younger rather than adolescents? And were they ready as a couple for what lay ahead? "We're going to be fine," said Michelle. "We just have to make sure the girls are fine. We're strong enough to take anything on and be OK at the end."

Over the course of the next ten weeks, Barack and Michelle engaged in an endless conversation with each other, their friends, and his political aides. A conversation that would change their lives forever, and maybe the history books, too. The whole prospect seemed as unreal and unlikely as it was audacious and hopeful. The discussions continued back in Washington with a group of more than a dozen friends at a downtown law office. There were former Harvard friends like Michael Froman, Julius Genachowski, and Cassandra Butts, along with newer friends like Broderick Johnson, a former Clinton official. Their concern was more practical than political, about what it would take to win the nomination. In Plouffe's view, it was a pure question of delegates, and he rattled off Obama's prospects in each state as the primary timetable progressed. Still, Obama's friends leaned against running, warning that it was too early in his career and would create too much upheaval for his family. Yet they all pledged to be with him, should he decide to move forward.

Feeling conflicted, Obama sought out the opinions of an even more experienced Washington Democrat: Tom Daschle, the defeated Democratic leader. The soft-spoken Daschle had met Obama in Chicago four years earlier, as the young state lawmaker was thinking about running for the United States Senate. As he sat through an education press conference at a Chicago school, Daschle was impressed with Obama's poise and natural political skills. But he thought his chances of winning the Senate nomination were low, partly because his competition was formidable and partly because Obama had only recently lost his attempt to enter the House of Representatives. This time around, Daschle wasn't so quick to write Obama off. Daschle himself had only just decided against running for president, after exploratory trips to Iowa and New Hampshire. Daunted by the money required to run, and ready to turn the page on his old career, Daschle felt he could not put together a winning campaign in time. And timing, as he told Obama, was everything. The young senator and the former Senate leader chatted for three hours at the kitchen table in the back of Daschle's favorite Italian restaurant, Tosca, in downtown Washington. Obama seemed to be leaning toward running, but said Michelle remained unconvinced. Daschle, in contrast, seemed to be pushing for a yes. He argued that the Democratic field, including Clinton, was lackluster, and that Obama enjoyed at least three strengths: his newness in Washington, his national fame, and his natural gravitas. If he needed any more persuasion, he should just look at what happened to Daschle himself. Four years earlier, Daschle had passed up a presidential campaign for something further down the line. "I didn't know in 2003 how limited the window of opportunity really is for things like this," Daschle said. "I thought I was young enough with a safe enough future to look to the next couple of cycles, and had the option to choose one of them. But that wasn't the case, and the same could be said of you. I don't know what the future holds but don't count on having another window. And even if you had another window, your persona is going to be different than it is right now, I guarantee you, in four years or in eight years. If you don't go for it this time, you may never have that chance again."

Back in Chicago, Obama continued to consult with his closest friends. Over dinner at home, or at his friends' homes, the conversation came into focus. They all agreed that the country was hungry for change, to break the deadlock in Washington and end the disaster of the Bush administration. And they believed that voters were looking for someone new with the kind of unifying, hopeful message that he offered at the Democratic convention in 2004. To his friends, Barack was no empty vessel but someone who could learn and adapt under pressure. Marty Nesbitt liked to point to businesspeople and sports stars they both admired. Barack had the capacity to learn from his mistakes, to synthesize new information, to change his game—just like Michael Jordan could change himself from an individual star to a team player. "That capacity would make someone really capable of being president," he told him.

Rarely did Barack ask his friends the most direct question of all about whether or not to run. At one black-tie dinner for the Chicago Urban League, inside the Hilton hotel ballroom in mid-November 2006, he briefly stopped to talk to Valerie Jarrett between greeting hundreds of supporters and contacts. "So, do you think I should run for president?" he asked her.

"You're asking me this *here*, with thousands of people," she sputtered.

"Nobody's listening," he deadpanned.

"I think it's a go," she said. "I think it's your moment."

Obama continued to fire questions at his political advisers, but he was already authorizing them to sound out potential staff discreetly. One night after ten he woke Hildebrand at home, following several phone conversations earlier in the day. "How will we win in Iowa?" he asked.

"You're going to have to spend a lot of time there, make sure that you know how to connect clearly with people. You're going to have to build relationships. Michelle and the kids are going to spend a lot of time there, too—that's an important part of connecting with voters. And we're going to have to have a very large operation."

By the time of his final meeting, before his traditional family vacation, Obama was ready to break the political rules of presidential campaigning but remained cautious about his final decision. Axelrod leaned the same way, but even more cautiously. "My reading of history is that people rarely suffer for having run too soon," he pointed out, thinking of Dick Gephardt and Mario Cuomo. "They more often suffer for having run too late, for passing up opportunities." Breaking the institutional rules seemed like the only way to avoid becoming institutionalized. "I'm inclined to do it now," he told his advisers, "but I'm going to go to Hawaii to think about it." He was so inclined to run that he had already asked Plouffe to manage his probable campaign. But his reservations seemed so deep that Plouffe still believed there was only a fifty-fifty chance that he would return from Hawaii as a candidate.

His hesitations were unusually protracted for someone who had displayed so few self-doubts about his career until now. As a new graduate, he eagerly turned his back on New York finance for the thankless work of a community organizer in Chicago. After Harvard Law School, he showed little caution when he joined a small civil rights law firm instead of a corporate law giant, and instead of taking a high-powered court clerkship. As a lowly state senator, there were no serious plans behind his run for Congress in 2000, and no second thoughts after his decision to run for the Senate two years later. At those moments in his old life, he had little to lose with a risky decision. Now he was an insider—with money, status, and fame—preparing to gamble it all for the uncomfortable life of an outsider.

Obama returned from vacation with a decision that he reserved the right to rescind. He wanted a cooling-off period from his own chilled-out time on the beach. "I've decided to do it, you can plan that we're going to do it," he told his advisers early in the new year. "But don't do anything yet, because I want to go home to Chicago this weekend and make sure I don't have buyer's remorse."

Obama drove to Axelrod's office and talked, once again, through the pros and cons for two hours. The two had hashed this out for weeks, comparing Obama's qualities with those of President Bush, as well as the rest of the field of presidential contenders. However, this moment seemed less about strategic positioning than spiritual well-being. "You don't have to do it," Axelrod told him. "You need to know you don't have to do this."

It looked and sounded like Plouffe might be right: maybe Obama was going to back out after all. "I'm going to give it a few more days," Obama replied.

A week later, he called his senior advisers with his final, final word: "You can go ahead and start offering jobs to people."

It was almost two weeks into the first quarter of the presidential contest, and they were only just starting from scratch. Obama called his friend Nesbitt to share the news. "OK," he started casually, "I think we're going to do this."

Unlike the political pros, Nesbitt had no doubt where the decision would lead: "I think you're going to win."

Winning or losing was the simplest test of whether his decision was the right one. The greater measure of success or failure was whether he could run for president as a renegade. Could he win an insider's game while keeping hold of his outsider's character? No insurgent candidate had won a major party's nomination in a generation of American politics. But winning the nomination would be meaningless if he lost his soul. Barack Obama's challenge was not making the decision; it was surviving and thriving in what followed.

THREE

RULES FOR RADICALS

He looked and sounded crushed as he slumped into the black leather sofa onboard his campaign bus in early January 2008. It was the night before the Iowa caucuses, the end of a seventeen-hour day, and there were just a handful of staffers at the back of the bus. Barack put his arm around Michelle and pulled her close after a rare event together—another late-night rally in an overcrowded, overheated school gym. Their last stand, in a town called Waterloo. Michelle had been traveling on the bus for the last few days, and her staff covered the walls with pictures of her and hand-painted signs saying We Love Michelle. With his voice hoarse, he started sipping tea from a steel travel mug. So how was he feeling on the eve of the make-or-break event of his eleven-month career as a presidential candidate?

"I feel calm," he croaks.

Really? Not nervous about the results, or plain exhausted after all that time on the road?

"No. Because this is the campaign I always wanted to run. That makes me feel calm. If it doesn't work, it's not because of the organization we built or the respectful tone that we set."

The organization counted for more than anything else. It was the key to his strategy and his identity. Fatigued, the candidate drifted off, his eyes fixed on the TV screen showing ESPN over his left shoulder. But his wife was only just getting warmed up. "We complain that politicians are mean and cynical and angry, but we've been doing the same thing over and over again," she says. "We have been making the same irrational decisions. When faced with the most rational choice, we hesitate—and that is what we have to break out of. We're not in Kenya or Pakistan. Democracy works here."

Barack stirs himself, looks up, and leans forward. "She's scary," he whispers. Michelle isn't amused: she pokes him and forces a weak smile.

There always was a certain earnest romance to their politics, especially grassroots politics. Michelle says she fell in love with Barack while listening to him lead an organizer training session with a group of community leaders. He was a Harvard student; she was his summer mentor at Sidley Austin. As he attempted to woo her into a date, he tried a new gambit: to come see part of his old life from his community organizing days, in a church basement. They drove to Gary, Indiana, with Obama's old boss Jerry Kellman, who gave him his first organizing job in Chicago. Obama needed the money from the training session aimed at a group of around 120 black and white church leaders. There Michelle watched him take off his jacket, roll up his sleeves, and talk about "the world not as it is, but as it should be." Eighteen years later, driving through Iowa, Michelle still credits that moment with sparking her love. "I remember being in that church basement and he was so good," she told me. "There was really something powerful there. And I was like, 'This guy is different. He is really different, in addition to being nice and funny and cute and all that. He's got a seriousness and a commitment that you don't see every day. You just don't see that every day.' And I liked that. I thought, 'Well, you know, I'd like to be married to somebody who feels that deeply about things.'"

Community organizing lay at the heart of their game plan in Iowa, the character of the campaign, his philosophy as a politician, and her image of him. It would shape the candidate and his quest through the presidency for the entire election cycle. But "the world as it is" and "the world as it should be" were not Obama's phrases. They belonged to a twentieth-century Chicago radical who, despite his own rhetorical firebombs, mapped out a rigorous, methodical approach to grassroots activism.

Saul Alinsky was less of an ideologue than an advocate for political action by neighborhood leaders, through the alliances they formed with the help of an organizer. Above all, he was an analyst of power in government and business. He explained how self-interest could be harnessed at the community level, and detailed the tactics needed to work within the system. Unlike the Marxists, antiwar protesters, and self-styled revolutionaries of the 1960s, Alinsky hated dogma and even the idealism of civil rights leaders, preferring instead the cold-eyed action of labor organizers. He disliked Martin Luther King Jr., and admired John L. Lewis, the founder of the Congress of Industrial Organizations. "The basic requirement for the understanding of the politics of change is to recognize the world as it is," he wrote in *Rules for Radicals* in 1972, his practical book of advice to the young activists disillusioned with the failures of the late 1960s. "We must work with it on its terms if we are to change it to the kind of world we would like it to be. We must first see the world as it is and not as we would like it to be. We must see the world as all political realists have, in terms of 'what men do and not what they ought to do,' as Machiavelli and others have put it."

There was no place in Alinsky's model for the kind of idealism that Michelle fell in love with. In fact, Obama's training session totally reversed the Alinsky worldview, even as he taught community leaders some of Alinsky's concepts. A photograph of Obama at the time shows him at a blackboard drawing a diagram titled "Power Analysis," which details "relationships built on self interest" linking corporations, banks, and utilities through money to a city mayor.

To some of his conservative opponents, Obama's work as an Alinsky-style community organizer meant he was clearly a socialist subversive, determined to launch an assault on American liberty and capitalism. (Those same critics had attacked Hillary Clinton for writing her senior-year thesis at Wellesley College on the Alinsky model.) To others, community organizing was an alien idea that underscored Obama's weirdness and inexperience. "He worked as a community organizer," Rudy Giuliani, the former New York mayor, said at the Republican convention in St. Paul. "What? I said, OK, maybe this is the first problem on the résumé." Vice presidential nominee Sarah Palin took the notion one step further a few minutes later, by comparing her own experience with Obama's. "I guess a small-town mayor is sort of like a community organizer," she said to hoots of laughter, "except that you have actual responsibilities."

In fact, as an organizer, Obama was an idealist, not an ideologue, in a thankless job that was always easy to ridicule—until it turned into a powerful model for a presidential campaign. Even as he decided to work as a community organizer in 1983, Obama had a better grasp of his dreams than the drudgery of the work. "When classmates in college asked me just what it was that a community organizer did, I couldn't answer them directly. Instead, I'd pronounce on the need for change. Change in the White House, where Reagan and his minions were carrying on their dirty deeds. Change in the Congress, compliant and corrupt. Change in the mood of the country, manic and self-absorbed. Change won't come from the top, I would say. Change will come from a mobilized grass roots," he wrote a decade before launching his presidential campaign for change. "That's what I'll do, I'll organize black folks. At the grass roots. For change."

He dreamt of the civil rights movement, but he was two decades late. He turned down a job with a traditional civil rights group that wanted him to organize conferences, working instead for a Ralph Nader group in Harlem. Then came the job in Chicago with an offshoot of the Alinsky movement, although Alinsky himself had died more than a decade earlier. The church-led Developing Communities Project was trying to revive the communities of South Chicago after the devastating loss of manufacturing jobs in the early 1980s, at a time when the city had just elected its first black mayor, Harold Washington. It was the perfect place to discover street-level politics and himself. The word *radical* comes from the Latin for "root," and Obama's work began at the roots of his new community.

Discipline lay at the heart of Obama's experience of community organizing. "Issues, action, power, self-interest. I liked these concepts," he wrote. "They bespoke a certain hardheadedness, a worldly lack of sentiment; politics, not religion." Yet he was neither a slavish Alinsky acolyte nor a bleeding-heart do-gooder. With its vague title and abstract jargon, Obama's job was easily caricatured by political opponents as leftist agitation, or misunderstood as an endless set of fruitless meetings. Instead, his training involved a rigorous approach to working with his new community. It was here that he developed the personal and social skills that were critical to his success as a politician, the analytical tools that would help him negotiate his way through political battles, and the writing talent that could inspire large crowds to follow him. As a presidential candidate he talked about bringing people together as one of his political gifts. For a community organizer, the task of bringing people together was the essential, and often thankless, challenge.

Earning $10,000 a year (plus $2,000 in travel allowance), Obama started his training as a community organizer with two challenges: to interview people to find the common thread between them, and to understand how power was exercised in Chicago. It was hard work, especially at the beginning. "The initial month was very crucial," said his boss and tutor Jerry Kellman. "Think about someone who is twenty-five. They burn out very quickly, especially people who have had some success in academia. They begin to get frustrated, there's not much incentive, they're not getting paid much, there's no status and there's no prospects."

The goal was to organize a community to influence the city's power. But for the most part, Obama's work was far more prosaic. He would watch Kellman conduct interviews, then interview his own people and write reports about them. "If you can't do that basic piece and get people to tell you their story and build a relationship around the story, then you're never going to be any good in the long run," said Kellman. "He was very good at it; partly he was fascinated by narrative. He was still entertaining being a fiction writer." Understanding the power of a story—or the combination of stories—would be central to his book writing and speechwriting in his political career.

With no political experience of his own, Obama was taking a crash course in how elected officials are influenced by their family, friends, and business interests: a "Power Analysis." Together with Kellman, he would analyze the reports and talk about how decisions were made in a city that was still dominated by the Democratic political machine. After some time in the real world, he attended more formal training sessions at Alinsky-inspired institutes like the Industrial Areas Foundation and the Gamaliel Foundation. There he learned the tactics of organizing, but he largely rejected the hard edged philosophy that underpinned the theory, preferring the idealism of the civil rights era. "In Chicago, more than anywhere else, I had to grind his nose in the ugly hard reality of how power really works," said Kellman. "But at the same time the people he worked with, and his own instincts, said that people often do more out of ideals than naked self-interest. Although there are things that people working in civil rights learned from Alinsky's organizing, what changed this country was the civil rights movement, it wasn't community organizing. But community organizing changed Barack."

As he integrated himself into a new community, Obama learned personal skills that were just as crucial to his future career. Despite the color of his skin, he was an outsider: a college-educated single man from Hawaii, who had grown up in a white middle-class family. Yet he also wanted to belong somewhere, to put down his roots while he worked at the grass roots. In time, as he gathered up other people's stories, he began to share the stories of his own family and life overseas. Just as he was teaching his community leaders to act politically, they were teaching him how to become part of a community. The stories he was gathering were more than just instances of Alinsky-style self-interest. They were "some central explanation of themselves." Sacred stories, even. When he would tell his own exotic tales, his new friends would share their own. "They'd offer a story to match or confound mine, a knot to bind our experiences together—a lost father, an adolescent brush with crime, a wandering heart, a moment of simple grace," he wrote. "As time passed, I found that these stories, taken together, had helped me bind my world together, that they gave me the sense of place and purpose I'd been looking for."

The work was politically small in scale: removing asbestos from public housing projects and retooling job programs. But it was personally outsized in scale for the community leaders he worked with, and for Obama himself. In community organizing in Chicago, Obama found his racial identity, a political worldview, a sense of faith and a church, and ultimately a wife. By the time he left, after three years of community work, Obama had found himself. "Socially, someone who is bright has confidence because of what they can do externally," said Kellman. "But there's another kind of confidence that comes from a better sense of who you are, what you're about. You can be incredibly facile on the outside and not have any of that on the inside. School didn't do that for him, and Harvard didn't do that, either. The centering piece happened during organizing and, later on, his marriage to Michelle."

For the biggest speech of his career, Barack Obama was remarkably late and loose in preparation. He only finished the first draft at four on Thursday morning, barely two days before the formal launch of his presidential campaign. The delay had driven his closest aides to nervous meltdown. When it arrived, the speech was too long and overflowing. "Cut down what you will, but I like my ending so leave it there," Obama told his speechwriter Jon Favreau. His ending traced a line from Abraham Lincoln to the current day, and it twice quoted from the Great Emancipator. Twelve hours later, the candidate turned up at his office to edit a few lines. He made a halfhearted attempt at a read-through for a couple of aides, then sent the speech to his policy team for vetting. The speechwriting was over.

At eleven the next night, Obama was in the basement of the old State Capitol in Springfield, Illinois. Tired and grumpy after a late-running CBS interview with *60 Minutes,* Obama stumbled his way through his first rehearsal with a teleprompter. "Is he going to be good tomorrow?" David Plouffe asked out loud.

"I *think* so," said Favreau. "I *hope* so."

The candidate himself was unruffled. "Don't worry about it," he told his anxious aides. "Don't worry about my diction. When I get up there, I'm going to be ready to go."

Twelve hours later, he walked onto the long stage outside, wrapped in a dark woolen coat and wearing long johns under his suit. It was frigidly cold, no more than fifteen degrees outside, and the ground was so frozen that anyone standing in the crowd found their body heat seeping through their feet. The winter sun struck the sandstone pillars to cast a golden glow behind him, but it did little to warm the ungloved hands of the new presidential candidate. Only a heater hidden inside the wooden podium could do that job, and it had little impact. His wife and daughters wore hats and scarves as they waved from the stage to the sound of U2's "City of Blinding Lights." The candidate, facing dozens of TV cameras, could draw no such comfort. Opposite the stage, MSNBC's Chris Matthews had decamped from Washington to host a live show, but found himself cursing the cold throughout.

It was February 2007, just one month since the senator made his decision to run for president, and barely six weeks since he was thinking through his prospects on the beach in Hawaii. "Look at all of ya," Obama said, gazing at the fifteen thousand souls who screamed through the numbing temperatures. "Look at all of *you.* Goodness. Thank you so much. Giving praise and honor to God for bringing us here together today." Then he turned to the two teleprompters on either side of his podium for the speech he had only finished writing forty-eight hours earlier.

He started out, as all good organizers do, by telling the story of why they were all gathered there that day—first narrating his audience's story, then narrating his own. Their self-interests were now shared. "We all made this journey for a reason," he said.

It's humbling to see a crowd like this, but in my heart I know you didn't come here just for me. No, you came here because you believe in what this country can be. In the face of war, you believe there can be peace. In the face of despair, you believe there can be hope. In the face of a politics that's shut you out, that's told you to settle, that's divided us for too long, you believe that we can be one people, reaching for what's possible, building that more perfect union. That's the journey we're on today. But let me tell you how I came to be here.

His own story began with community organizing and his move to Chicago, where he said he wanted to play a small part in building a better America—and where he learned how to do so. "My work took me to some of Chicago's poorest neighborhoods," he said.

I joined with pastors and lay-people to deal with communities that had been ravaged by plant closings. I saw that the problems people faced weren't simply local in nature—that the decision to close a steel mill was made by distant executives; that the lack of textbooks and computers in a school could be traced to the skewed priorities of politicians a thousand miles away; that when a child turns to violence, I came to realize that there's a hole in his heart no government alone can fill. It was in these neighborhoods that I received the best education that I ever had, and where I learned the meaning of my Christian faith.

His policy ideas were Democratic boilerplate. He promised better schools, more affordable college, a living wage, and cheaper child care. Universal health care, alternative energy, improved alliances, and an end to the war in Iraq. What was new was his newness, the fresh political style that tied his story and purpose to his audience, and his presumptuous claim to being a historic figure like the man who once worked in the building behind him. "By ourselves, this change will not happen. Divided, we are bound to fail," he said. "But the life of a tall, gangly, self-made Springfield lawyer tells us that a different future is possible." When the tall, gangly, self-made former Springfield politician had stopped speaking, his new aides rushed across the street with the media to the warmth of an empty office that now served as a press filing room. "What did you think of the speech?" asked two excited staffers. "Great speech," one reporter said. "But in terms of policy, John Kerry could have delivered it."

The new candidate and his family rode in their first motorcade, escorted to the airport by Springfield police but no Secret Service, for the campaign's maiden flight on a Boeing 757 that the crew had dubbed *Obama One*. It would be another year before he would fly with his staff and press on such a big plane again.

Ahead lay a sometimes awkward weekend of campaigning in Iowa and a rally on his return home to Chicago. There was a testy press conference in Ames, where he criticized the media for caring less about his policy positions than a photo of him in black swim shorts in Hawaii. There were the hecklers in the Chicago arena who wanted him to cut off funding for the troops in Iraq. At John F. Kennedy High School in Cedar Rapids, his first town hall meeting was cohosted by a local Democratic official whose dull delivery made the event sound like it was staged for CSPAN. The Iowa crowd of more than two thousand people—a huge number in a state where new candidates normally count their supporters in the dozens—did not seem to care. They listened attentively to his long, wonkish responses to questions about North Korea, the military budget, and No Child Left Behind. Many reporters believed Obama's early style was professorial, emotionless, and clinically cold. But it was more accurately the sound of the community organizer at work, coaching his audience to ditch their cynicism and step up to solve their own problems. "I want to win, but I don't just want to win," he told the crowd in Cedar Rapids.

> I want to transform this country and the only way that I'm going to do it is if *you* make this a vehicle for *your* hopes and dreams. The one thing I'm absolutely certain of is no matter how able the individual, no matter how many good speeches he or she gives, that ultimately the country changes when millions of people come together and speak out on behalf of change. So what I hope is going to happen through meetings like this . . . is that we see the kind of reengagement, excitement and energy of ordinary citizens. Because when ordinary citizens are awakened they accomplish extraordinary things. And I want this campaign to be open to that process of people taking it upon themselves to bring these changes about.

Organizing voters. At the grass roots. For change. That was Obama's strategy from the outset as he mounted an audacious challenge to his own party and the political system. Not its policies, where he remained stubbornly conventional, but its way of doing business. Judging from the pictures on the wall of his Senate office, his role models were giants in transforming a nation: Abraham Lincoln, Martin Luther King Jr., and Gandhi sitting in self-sufficient contemplation beside his spinning wheel. Obama saw Gandhi, and his self-styled experiments with truth, as an inspiring example of how ordinary people could come together to change the world. "That is why his portrait hangs in my Senate office," he told an Indian magazine. "To remind me that real results will come not just from Washington—they will come from the people."

But apart from engaging with the grass roots, Obama had only a vague sense of the challenges he faced and how he would overcome them. In late January, just a few weeks before formally launching his campaign in Springfield, Obama met with his inner circle at the D.C. offices of his new campaign lawyer, Bob Bauer. "I'm really excited about getting going with this," he told his new team. "I feel very comfortable putting this campaign together. But remember: none of us are ready to govern today. So this is something we're going to have to work on." One of his trusted aides scribbled a sarcastic note on his own legal pad: "That's inspiring."

To succeed, he needed to play the game better than anyone else. Therein lay a vast contradiction that had crushed every insurgent candidate before him: Could the outsider run an inside game? Could he raise enough money, and build a big enough organization, without a machine or a national name behind him? Could the renegade master the rules? If he did, would he still be worthy of the name? For Alinsky's radical, the question was easily answered. "That perennial question, 'Does the end justify the means?' is meaningless as it stands," he wrote. "The *end* is what you want, and the *means* is how you get it."

Obama's greatest ally in his pragmatic pursuit of power was David Plouffe, the steel-edged operative who tried to convince him not to run in the first place. Plouffe got his start in politics while a political science major at the University of Delaware. Having worked every summer—one year selling knives door-to-door, another year sweeping chimneys—he saw an ad in the campus newspaper calling for field staff in the Democratic primary for the United States Senate. His candidate, Sam Beard, was declared the winner for one day, until election officials discovered a tallying error. Plouffe's man lost by seventy-one votes, leaving a scar for the rest of his career. "It struck me, if any of us had worked harder or

68 **RENEGADE**

smarter we could have gotten another seventy-two votes," he recalled. "I learned that every vote matters. If that race had ended up differently, I don't think I'd have stayed in politics. It was so searing." The next year, as he was teaching tennis for the summer, one of his campaign friends asked him to go to Iowa to work for its Democratic senator, Tom Harkin. He never graduated from Delaware but found an education in politics, working for Harkin's failed presidential run two years later. After working on Senate campaigns across the country, Plouffe ended up as a senior staffer to Dick Gephardt, the House Democratic leader, who planned to run against Vice President Al Gore in 2000. For two years he built an outsider's strategy against a front-runner candidate, but Gephardt ultimately decided against running. In 2004 he worked on Gephardt's short-lived presidential run that ended after Iowa. His experience in Iowa would prove invaluable, as he mapped out what he called a long-shot strategy for Obama. "I knew Iowa very well," he said. "But it was clear to us strategically: the only way we could win the primary was to destabilize Hillary early or she would be off to the races." The goal was to finish ahead of Clinton in Iowa, but probably behind John Edwards. Edwards had built a loyal following there in 2004 and still enjoyed a commanding poll lead three years later. From there, Plouffe believed they needed to win in New Hampshire and the nomination would soon be theirs.

Plouffe hated the thought of a presidential campaign, of what he called "the vortex of hell," of the brutal hours and professional stress. With a young child and a new home, he was deeply reluctant to sign up, even though his business partner, David Axelrod, was so close to Obama. Still, Plouffe was intrigued by the history of his candidacy, and by the freshness and change that he promised. He sorely needed Obama's inspiration: much of his reluctance to join a campaign lay in his deep sense of dismay with politics over the last two decades. "I thought we needed to turn the page on both the Clintons and the Bushes," he said. "I was very motivated by the need to usher in change in our party. I thought we squandered a lot of opportunities. I was in the House of Representatives having to spend a lot of time convincing Democrats not to impeach Bill Clinton. I felt we needed a clean break, and I thought the process was fundamentally broken. In any election cycle you had people who were right on the issues, but there was a careerism to it. There was very little song in politics."

The two men clicked, sharing a quiet intensity and calm management style. Obama's orders to Plouffe were clear: He wanted a small circle of decision makers, no drama and no mercenaries. He wanted staff who would fight their corner but do so in a respectful way. Beyond that tone, they were free to run the campaign they wanted. "We weren't burdened by any prior expectations," said Plouffe. "It was such an improbable candidacy that we felt no great sense of pressure to win." Plouffe knew he could shape something new, unlike the stress-filled, top-heavy Clinton campaign, without worrying about second-guessing from the candidate or senior staff. Knowing the candidate was a long shot, Plouffe crafted a radical plan to find new voters in the sleepy corners of Iowa. "He was willing to embrace a strategy in Iowa that was completely untraditional," said Plouffe. "The great conventional wisdom is that there's a finite universe of old and white caucus goers, give or take twenty-five thousand people. Barack was willing to roll the dice on the strategy of building a new coalition, getting out young people and bringing in every minority community in the state. It was a gutsy move."

That gamble required Plouffe's singular focus, since it meant avoiding the traditional paths in Iowa. The goal was to find new voters, not the same old hacks who showed up to the usual party events. So Plouffe turned down invitations to county dinners and even big party fundraisers. "One of the things from day one I tried to instill around here was just discipline. I think the most important word in politics is *no*, and we said no a lot," he said. "It was clear that the only way we had any chance to win in Iowa was to expand the electorate. If we go to a county party fund-raising dinner, we're just going to see the core group. When we did our own events inviting independents, Republicans, and Democrats who never give money to the party, those were our prime targets. Even though you're in Iowa a lot, you're only in certain counties X number of times. And if you shot your wad on something that didn't produce the kind of numbers you needed, it was a real tragedy."

Plouffe's team in Iowa was led by the people who won the state for Al Gore in 2000. Seven years earlier, Steve Hildebrand and Paul Tewes had helped kill off the last superstar insurgent in the Democratic Party, the former senator and Hall of Fame basketball player Bill Bradley, by building one of the largest field organizations Iowa had ever seen, with eighty full-time organizers. After the multiple defeats of 2004, they set up their own business together specializing in grassroots campaigns. Their first big success: defeating President Bush's plans to privatize part of Social Security by organizing voters to contact politically weak or undecided members of Congress. They were an ideal fit for a presidential campaign built from the grass roots of Iowa.

Hildebrand was a true believer in Obama and the Democratic Party. The youngest of nine children, he and his family relied on social programs after his father died when Hildebrand was just five years old. Growing up in Mitchell, South Dakota, he shared a hometown with George McGovern, and as a ten-year-old boy shook the candidate's hand at a rally in front of the town's corn palace. From that moment, he was acutely aware of campaigns, and he worked on McGovern's final Senate race in 1980. On his big sisters' advice, he went to nursing school but dropped out in favor of political science. After selling cars for a year, Hildebrand got a job working on Tom Daschle's first Senate campaign in 1986 and never left politics again.

If anything, Tewes was an even more dedicated Democrat. His first childhood memory was casting a mock election vote as a first grader for Jimmy Carter over Gerald Ford; four years later he was crying at the news of Carter's defeat in 1980. As a political operative, he was the kind of devoted, obsessive leader who turned the downtrodden foot soldiers of a campaign—the field organizers—into adoring, dedicated fans. He could motivate his poorly paid, overworked staff not only by giving them ever greater responsibilities, but also by goofing around. He would set impossible targets for them, yet also go door-to-door with them and make long lists of phone calls to voters. For Tewes, it was a perfect fit to work for a candidate who was himself a former community organizer and wanted his staff and volunteers to feel empowered. Fieldwork was no longer an obscure, overlooked corner of a presidential campaign but the organizing principle behind it. All it took was a little fibbing to the candidate about the effort required to make it work. At their first sitdown in his Senate office, Obama asked Tewes how many times he needed to travel to Iowa. "I think I lied to him," Tewes told me later, chuckling. "I said, 'Maybe three times every two months.'" Tewes arrived in Iowa and spent the rest of the year pressing Obama to spend every spare hour in the state.

The only problem was, it all cost money. The headquarters, the consultants, the travel, the advance staff, the huge ground operation: it all needed vast sums of cash that no outsider had ever raised until they won a state or two. And by then, the infusion of dollars was typically too late: insurgent candidates always died at the first sign of life, like Dick Gephardt in 1988 and John McCain in 2000. It was no small irony that a campaign inspired in part by community organizing needed so much money to work at the grass roots. How else could you build a network of field staff to recruit all those volunteers? The only way to harness people power was with the kind of financial muscle that belonged to the super-wealthy.

Obama had one friend in mind to build a money machine that could take on the Clintons—the greatest fund-raisers in the history of the party—and bring his grassroots dream to life. Penny Pritzker, the grand-daughter of the founder of the Hyatt hotel group, was a friend and busi-ness partner to one of his closest friends, Marty Nesbitt. A decade earlier, Nesbitt had convinced Pritzker to take her children to a YMCA basket-ball program coached by Craig Robinson, big brother to Michelle Obama. Over the years, Pritzker had invited the Obamas to her weekend home in Michigan and the families became good friends.

Still, as Obama contemplated running for president, Pritzker had no desire to take part. She was trying to scale back her commitments, which included not just her family time and her business (running Hyatt's non-hotel investments) but her civic life in helping to reform Chicago's public schools. As a friend, she met with Barack and lunched with Michelle, of-fering a distinctly corporate view of their new ambitions. What kind of organization was he planning to build, what would his executive team look like, and what kind of culture did he want to create? Pritzker ad-mired the Obamas but believed she could identify the leadership chal-lenges they faced. "You're going to have to create an organization of a size and scope that you've never done before," she told Obama late in 2006. "How are you going to do that? You possess certain great skills and capabilities today and there's others you don't, and people are going to have questions about them. They're going to have questions about your executive leadership skills. They're going to want to know about your national security expertise. They're going to want to know about your expertise on the economy. So how are you going to demonstrate to the American people that you have that capacity?"

Obama came back to Pritzker with some of the answers, but part of the solution lay in Pritzker herself. Nesbitt worked on her reluctance to take a leadership role in the campaign. They talked about her deep sense of dismay with President Bush, her strong belief in Obama's integrity, and his ability to inspire the country to live up to its values. Nesbitt also appealed to Pritzker's entrepreneurial interest in calculated risk taking: the Obama campaign was a substantial but rewarding gamble.

Pritzker had never led a fund-raising campaign at any level—local, state, or national—and by the early weeks of January 2007, she was still a firm no. On her way home from her office in downtown Chicago, she called her husband, Bryan, with an alarming insight. "I think Barack is going to ask me to be his national finance chair," she said on her Bluetooth headset. "There's no way I can do this. This is crazy." Back home, she began preparing a family dinner with her husband in their galley kitchen, when he started knocking on the kitchen door.

"What are you doing?" she asked.

"Penny," he said, "this is destiny knocking at the door of our country. You've got to find a way to help. I'll take care of the kids. I'll take care of the house. I'll support you in any way I can. You have to figure this out." When they talked to their teenage children, the reaction was the same: she had no real choice.

Ten days later, Pritzker flew to D.C. for dinner in a private room at the Park Hyatt with Obama's senior finance staffer, Julianna Smoot. Smoot had raised millions for Tom Daschle's failed reelection effort in 2004, and was well known to the ex-Daschle aides who were now at the center of Obama's inner circle. Together, Pritzker and Smoot worked through the basic questions of how to build a national finance network for a top-tier presidential candidate who entirely lacked one. For most of the next month, Pritzker jetted around the country talking to the people who had built John Kerry's presidential fund-raising operation in 2004. Lou Susman, a Chicago banker who chaired Kerry's finance effort, shared his Rolodex and ideas over frequent sandwich lunches. Susman made introductions to some of the biggest stars in Democratic Party finance, including Mark Gorenberg in San Francisco and Orin Kramer in New York.

On the day of Obama's announcement speech, Pritzker gathered her new network of three dozen fund-raisers at the Hyatt Regency in Chicago to sketch out their plans. Building on the grassroots political model, Pritzker and Smoot envisioned a decentralized network of regional teams with the freedom to control their own fund-raising efforts. But there were far more questions than answers. Most of the donors had strong feelings about previous campaigns. Most of them hated the titles that other campaigns had popularized—the Rangers and Pioneers for Bush, or the Hillraisers for Clinton—as hierarchical and demeaning. "I wasn't looking for ways to put people in boxes so they felt trapped," said Pritzker. "I wanted to tap into people's entrepreneurial spirit so that they would be successful for us. So I was open to what they had to say because I didn't know any better."

The contrast with the opaque, controlling Clinton campaign was striking but still daunting. From a standing start—in fact, starting six weeks late in mid-February—Pritzker's team was budgeted to raise $12 million in the first quarter. Inside Obama's inner circle, they could only foresee how $9 million would come in. "We were pretty nervous about the first quarter," recalled Hildebrand. Before the end of the quarter, Pritzker knew they would exceed those targets, but she had no idea how that would compare with Clinton's numbers. Before announcing their own totals, the Obama campaign wanted to be sure they were accurate and planned to wait two weeks for a final tally. On Sunday, April 1, the day after the end of the first quarter, Pritzker was at Loeb House in Harvard Yard for a governing board meeting of the overseers. Her personal phone rang in the middle of the meeting; it was former treasury secretary Bob Rubin calling to set Obama straight on economic policy. In the middle of Rubin's unprompted call, Pritzker's campaign phone rang. It was Smoot calling to say that the Clinton campaign had leaked what they thought were record-breaking numbers to the press: $19 million for the primary contests. Obama's team had beaten their rivals by more than $5 million.

Pritzker's phone rang again; this time it was Susman, her campaign finance mentor. He had heard rumors of Obama's big totals and wanted confirmation. "That's interesting," Pritzker said. "I'll have to get back to you on that." Discipline was paramount inside the insurgent campaign. They would wait several days after the Clintons' premature celebrations before announcing their own eye-popping totals.

How did they do it? Contrary to their own carefully cultivated image, the money did not grow at the grass roots. "It wasn't the Internet," said Pritzker. "We tapped everybody and did every event we could. He'd do seven events in New York, back-to-back-to-back-to-back." Internet donations totaled less than 15 percent of Obama's fund-raising through 2007. Money only started to cascade through the Web after Iowa in early January 2008, and it would take another several months, as the primaries dragged on, for the grass roots to represent half the campaign's fund-raising.

In the early days, what mattered most were old-style fund-raising events and the donor networks of candidates who dropped out early, like Kerry and the former Virginia governor Mark Warner. By the second quarter, with press expectations raised even higher, Obama was constantly fund-raising alongside his huge rallies across the country, where he was attracting general election–sized crowds in the tens of thousands in cities like Austin, Atlanta, and Oakland. "We were running scared but we were having fun," said Pritzker, "because we felt like we were on a mission." At the same time, some of Clinton's biggest fund-raisers complained privately that they were at a deep disadvantage because they had none of their rivals' energy, and all of the pressures of working for a front-runner. "For them it's all so new and exciting," grumbled one Clinton friend. "They're doing it for the first time. We're not, and we don't like being treated this way." Halfway through the year, the results were even clearer than they were in April: Obama outraised Clinton by $10 million, reaching a second quarter total of $31 million for the primary contests.

From its first days of life, the Obama campaign was a hybrid of corporate management and community organizing, drawing half its drive from an executive boardroom and half from the street politics of its young staff. The countervailing cultures were captured by the campaign symbol affixed to Obama's podium in Springfield: an O shape over a red-and-white field that looked like a cross between a Life Saver and the Bank of America logo. Axelrod's graphic designer had dreamt up the logo, inspired by an old pin that the campaign strategist treasured from Harold Washington's successful campaign to become Chicago's first African American mayor. The pin was a rising sun, representing a new dawn, a new hope. Washington had the Democratic machine in Chicago to help his sun rise; Obama had Pritzker's new money machine.

With money and hope, Obama could buy some credibility, invest in his organizers, and plan ahead for a bruising contest against the Clintons' conventional campaign. "The money was very impactful because for the first time people thought maybe this guy could really give her a run for her money," recalled David Plouffe. Initially, Plouffe figured they would only have enough money for Iowa and New Hampshire. But when the second-quarter numbers came in, he raised all his budgets, built infrastructure across all the early states, and set aside $5 million for the Super Tuesday contests.

"What the fund-raising in the first quarter told me was that this was real," Obama said later. "We were going to be able to raise enough money to compete. The second thing it told us was a grassroots strategy could generate not just money, but volunteers and support in ways that nobody had anticipated." Now Obama could afford to break the rules.

Bill and Hillary Clinton walked into Iowa's state fairgrounds together, two days before July 4, with every advantage in their hands. It was 2007, their first joint campaign event of the election, and if they were troubled by their position in Iowa—or by their upstart challenger who had just beaten them at fund-raising in the second quarter—they didn't show it. Their warm-up acts were two of the biggest names among Iowa Democrats—former governor Tom Vilsack and his wife, Christie—and the sound system had just played The Monkees' "I'm a Believer." Ringing the outdoor stage that night were yellow bales of hay, a few thousand supporters, and a bright blue banner proclaiming the front-runner candidate "READY for change, Ready to LEAD." Judging from the capital letters, the word *change* had fared worse with the focus groups than the business about leading. Resplendent in a mango shirt that crested over his khaki pants, Bill Clinton rested his hands on the shoulders of his wife, who wore a raspberry jacket over a raspberry top. They listened intently to yet another prominent Iowa Democrat endorse them: Ruth Harkin, the politically active wife of the state's long-standing senator.

Then the last Democratic president took the microphone for a sales pitch that swerved from the self-indulgent to the sly put-down. Pointing out an official-looking sign in the crowd that said Husbands for Hillary, he insisted he would be onstage whether they shared a name or not. "I'd be here tonight, if she asked me, if we weren't married," he said, as if anyone could imagine such a scenario. He assured the crowd that he liked the rest of the Democratic candidates: "Senator Biden, Senator Dodd, Governor Richardson have rendered great service to our country." The other two, not so much. "I'm always interested and I like to see what Senator Edwards and Senator Obama have to say," the former president said of the candidates who happened to be running strongly in Iowa. "I have nothing bad to say about anybody," he added. He also had little good to say about a couple of them.

As for his favorite candidate, he praised her international experience and crowned her the second-best candidate ever, after his own reelection bid in 1996. Hillary was, he said, "the best-qualified non-incumbent I have ever had a chance to vote for in my entire life."—a slogan that was only marginally worse than the half-capitalized banner on the front of the stage. He ended with a moist-eyed story about a golf caddy who had been a New York firefighter. The take-home was both moving and overblown: Hillary had saved lives by securing health care for those who got sick after the towers collapsed on 9/11.

The front-runner herself took the microphone with the kind of modesty and low-key delivery that her husband never displayed. "If I was as smart as Bill seems to think I am," she began, "I would say nothing." For the next thirty minutes, Bill clasped his head in his hands as if he preferred her to say nothing. The front-runner told the crowd how much she loved fairgrounds while campaigning in New York State. She rehashed some of their best-known catchphrases about taking a village to raise a child and building the bridge to the twenty-first century. The crickets chirped in the silence of early evening. She talked of universal health care, photovoltaic roof panels, and the rule of law. Her husband glared at her, and clusters of his supporters drifted home. Six weeks earlier, the campaign's deputy manager wrote a memo recommending they skip the Iowa caucuses because the costs were high and the organizational challenges too great. Now they were doubling their marketing. After all, they owned the brand.

The next day around noon, Renegade was standing on the bed of a red and gold pickup truck on a school playground in Keokuk at the southeastern tip of Iowa, close to Illinois and the banks of the Mississippi River. His microphone cut in and out as he told the modest crowd of no more than a couple of hundred about the tens of thousands he had attracted in Austin, Texas, and even Iowa City. "When I'm in front of these big crowds," he said to the small crowd by the basketball hoop, "I love to take the credit myself and say, 'Oh, it's because I'm so terrific.' But I have to say, that isn't the reason folks are coming out. The reason folks are coming out is because America is hungry for change all across the country." After talking about education and the war in Iraq, he made his basic appeal not for votes but for volunteers; not to win but to take part. "Here's the only catch, guys," he said. "I'm ready to lead this country. I know where America needs to go. But I can't go there by myself. Change in America doesn't happen from the top down. It happens from the bottom up."

Two decades earlier, one of Barack Obama's worst moments as a community organizer was when he staged a police meeting about gang violence in Chicago. A local church leader opposed his efforts to hold a meeting, and only thirteen people showed up. "I realized then, standing in an empty McDonald's parking lot in the South Side of Chicago, that I was a heretic," he wrote. Now the heretic was standing on a pickup truck in a playground, challenging his party's leaders, and it was far from certain that the crowds would show up when he needed them, on caucus day.

Instead a camera crew showed up to capture several moments of campaign Americana for future TV ads, under the direction of Obama's image maker, Jim Margolis. Whatever was happening on the ground with his grassroots volunteers, Obama had the money to reach voters the old-fashioned way: through expensive commercials. If he was going to stand alone in a parking lot or a playground, there was going to be a camera to record the heretic moment. It was an idyllic, but not perfect, scene in rural Iowa in the summer of 2007. In Mount Pleasant, a church pastor introduced the candidate in front of an ivy-covered barn. There were baskets of cookies next to a large jug of lemonade on a table welcoming supporters. Obama had just started his stump speech when he broke off to say, "Don't film this!" A bug had flown into his mouth. "It looked really small but it can't be," he said. "I haven't had lunch yet." A few minutes later, a huge freight train rumbled, forcing another interruption to the filming, just as he told the tale of his gritty experiences as a community organizer on the South Side.

The candidate campaigned across a celluloid version of Iowa. The next day, on July 4, he joined his family to stop at the retro-style Smokey Row coffee shop in Oskaloosa, opposite a Mexican restaurant and a bail bonds office. Inside, there were old Pepsi ads and a fake movie theater sign wishing happy birthday to the candidate's daughter Malia. En route to their next stop, the Obama family played the card game Uno around a small table at the back of a modest Sunseeker RV. The candidate won the game, teased his ultracompetitive wife, and hugged his daughter Sasha— all watched by a magazine photographer and his TV ad crew. At their next stop, in Pella, the Obamas stood on the porch of a blue and green clapboard home while their daughters played on a trampoline in the garden. On their own, the Obama family outnumbered the rest of the African American faces in the overwhelmingly white crowd. After Michelle introduced him in glowing terms, the candidate picked up the microphone by lifting back the stage curtain. "You know, she doesn't say all that stuff about me at home," he said. "I've got to come out to hear all that good stuff."

An hour later, in an activity room above Pella's memorial building, the candidate was executing his real strategy backstage. Away from the cameras and the press, eating their lunch in the hall below, he listened patiently to a half-dozen community leaders. Sitting on a bare metal chair, with gym mats piled behind him on the floor, the organizer asked about their concerns and soaked up their views on schools, the rural economy, and the state of the nation.

Were the stories and the scenes less genuine for all the cameras and the self-conscious staging? Maybe so. But there was no way to win as a renegade without mastering a campaign's language and look, its conventions and protocols. They were taking enough risks by running against the Clintons; anything else was beyond their powers of self-control and team discipline. For any other insurgent candidate, there would have been no press, no public, and no money for TV ads. That would have forced him to take more risks and create more opportunities. But even six months before the first votes of the 2008 election, there was no freewheeling phase for Obama. His campaign was a magic lantern show, projecting something once real, and now sometimes hidden, onto a large blank screen.

Change, at the grass roots, began and ended in a single-story building in the East Village of Des Moines, a run-down but half-revived neighborhood close to the State Capitol, known for its trendy lefty crowd in an otherwise dull, conformist town. Five minutes' drive away, in an office park, were the semicorporate, semiscreened, soulless offices of the Clinton campaign. But in the East Village, Obama's headquarters were a cross between a college dorm, community center, and personality cult. On the wall of the reception desk was a motto that sounded more suited to the side of a police cruiser: Respect, Empower, Include. Opposite was a rendering of Grant Wood's *American Gothic*, with the elderly couple holding a sign saying Obama for America instead of a pitchfork. Where the Clinton campaign worked on PCs with flat-screen displays, the Obama campaign worked on laptops squeezed between empty Diet Coke cans and cups from The Village Bean coffee shop across the street.

The slacker vibe belied a meticulous strategy focused on a series of metrics and ultimate victory. Starting early in 2007, even before the campaign was formally launched, Paul Tewes sketched out his plan on butcher paper at the Embassy Suites hotel in downtown Des Moines with caucus director, Mitch Stewart; his deputy state director, Marygrace Galston; and political director, Emily Parcell. Over the next six or seven hours, they mapped out how they would avoid the mistakes of previous campaigns. The key was to send as many staff, and open up as many regional offices, as early as possible, to give their young field organizers a chance to set down roots in the community. By June, they wanted to have their organizers in place across the state, six months before the caucuses. "Traditionally you hire in waves of staff; we hired a lot of our staff early so they could get indoctrinated into these communities," said David Plouffe. "These people didn't know Obama so we needed to work on those relationships a lot longer. And we knew we had to find people unconventionally so it would require more people on the ground."

Voters could be organized geographically, but that did not reflect the lives of many people who might come to caucus. In addition to their regional offices, Obama's team wanted what they called multiple points of entry, and reached out to distinct groups: young voters, African Americans, Latinos. Previous campaigns had just assumed there were no significant numbers of such groups who would ever turn up to caucus in Iowa. But the Obama campaign stuck a number to their hopes: they wanted to recruit more than one hundred congregation captains at churches, and set up two hundred "Barack Star" groups aimed at high school teenagers (who would be eighteen years old by the time of the general election). The congregation captains would work their church communities each week; the Barack Star captains would work the high school cafeterias every day. Meanwhile, the press team focused on small-circulation newspapers and local bloggers, such as the *Woodbine Twiner*, as well as the mighty *Des Moines Register*.

The goal was to expand methodically the universe of caucus-goers far beyond the traditional, older group of steady Democratic voters. They wanted independents and Republicans to join in, too. By the summer, their contacts with traditional voters amounted to a handful a day, with limited success. In contrast, the targeted effort found lots of infrequent voters and plenty of support among young Iowans. For more wonkish Iowans, there were even opportunities to talk directly to Obama's policy advisers—who were dispatched around the state on their own or in groups—and shape what might become the White House agenda.

Was it real or just another version of the doomed Howard Dean campaign? Dean promised a perfect storm of a ground game in 2004, only to sink into third place with an operation that relied on young out-of-state volunteers. Plouffe spent the summer swatting away reporters who obsessed about the national polls, urging them to look instead at his field offices in Iowa and the energy of his young staff and volunteers. And no, he insisted, they weren't anything like the Deaniacs. "We are much more focused on making sure that every one of the people supporting us is firmly with us, committed to attending the caucus. We reconfirm people all the time," he told me in the fall. "Secondly, our organization is much deeper than Dean's. It's ninety-nine counties strong and down to the precinct level. We're not going to have a lot of out-of-state volunteers coming in at the end. Our organization is Iowa based. The discussions with Iowa voters are happening between Iowans." Volunteers were encouraged to tell their personal stories to regular voters—the moment of crisis, revelation, or inspiration that brought them to that voter's front door at that time. Sometimes, they were moved by Obama himself; sometimes, by greater concerns for the nation or the planet. If things were going well, they would ask their targets to share their stories about their hopes, fears, and dreams. It sounded like a giant self-help group where the therapy was politics.

Obama's young field organizers, many of whom idealized their candidate's community organizing days, were central to his Iowa strategy. By the end of the year there would be 159 of them across the state, supported by some 10,000 volunteers. By midsummer, the machine could generate huge numbers. On one day in mid-June, the campaign made 8,279 phone calls. By December, they would be calling three times that number of voters every day. The field staff staged mock caucuses to demystify the process, training 10,000 people in the byzantine process of voting in Iowa. Their target for knocking on doors was 363,000 in a state where only 125,000 Democrats had showed up to caucus four years earlier. In return, the field organizers received special attention from high-level campaign staff, acting as focus groups to brief the pollsters and consultants.

Nothing was more special than the shout-out delivered at the top of each event by the candidate himself. Obama would explain to his crowds that he had started out as a community organizer with no money and no recognition; now he had all these hardworking, poorly paid organizers of his own, and the least he could do was to give them some public accolade. If the organizers were well known and successful, the crowd would cheer wildly. If not, the staff would sense that something was not working. In any case, the voters knew that the organizer had direct contact with the candidate; if they spoke to a lowly staffer, they were only one step removed from Barack Obama. "Paul and Barack meshed so well in philosophy because Paul's whole worldview was empowering the lowest person on the totem pole," said Tommy Vietor, Obama's press secretary in Iowa. "At Barack's events, he'd have the organizers onstage with him. It would make us cry seeing these kids onstage."

The candidate himself felt empowered by what was happening in Iowa. "We had a strategy at the outset," Obama told me. "I had confidence in that strategy. Not only did I have confidence in that strategy, but it was the only strategy available to us. There was no way we could compete with Hillary Clinton nationally given her name recognition, and endorsements and contacts. We knew we had to take advantage of the retail politics, the intimate nature of Iowa and New Hampshire, and use wins there to catapult ourselves into Super Tuesday." That meant keeping a close eye on the numbers in Iowa. "I was paying attention to them," Obama explained. "Because Plouffe and I would talk every day, and I talked to our field organizers every day when I was in Iowa, which was a lot of days. We just monitored, 'Are we hitting our goals?' And if we weren't, what adjustments did we need to make?" In fact, there was a limit to what the candidate wanted to hear. For the first few months when he visited Iowa, Obama would hear the latest numbers and news from Tewes. Then one day he listened patiently, before signaling that he didn't need them to justify their work. "You know, I trust you," the candidate told Tewes. "You guys know what you're doing. Keep doing what you were doing."

For Tewes the effort was far more than a set of numbers or targets to chase. There was a team that he needed to inspire every day. "You aren't here for Barack Obama," he told his young staff and volunteers. "You're here for something inside you that's more powerful." He would often make his senior team pick the name of a distant county out of a hat; that was where they would be spending four hours canvassing voters on Saturday. Over the July 4 weekend, as the Clintons arrived in Des Moines and Obama prepared to tour the state with his family, Tewes challenged his organizers to fill out a ridiculously high number of supporter cards. The deal was simple: if they met their targets statewide, Tewes promised to shave off his eyebrows. At the end of the long weekend, his young staffers reported their numbers on a conference call, only reaching the magic number with the help of the last, distant regional office. When the cheering died down, Tewes debated whether his eyebrows would ever grow back, before staying true to his word. It would take several weeks for his face to return to normal, and for his jogging to be less painful: without his brows, the sweat ran straight into his eyes.

From his first few weeks in Iowa, Tewes identified several key dates to flex his team's muscles. Stuck on one of the walls of the headquarters was what the staff called their Domination Plans. At each event, they would test their own skills and intimidate the daylights out of the opposition. Their initial test was the ABC News debate at Drake University in mid-August, the Democrats' first verbal contest in Iowa. Outside each debate site, supporters of the rival campaigns would take positions to scream at one another, passing motorists, and the gathering press corps. The Obama team planned their positions like a SWAT operation. The debate's organizers allowed the campaigns to set up at five on the morning of the debate, and a handful of Clinton staffers made sure to show up on time. But they were already too late: by that time, one hundred Obama volunteers had been on-site for five hours, plotting diagrams for the best corner positions and rehearsing their chants. On air, the candidate joked that he had been in the bumper cars at the state fair to prepare for the debate. Off air, he went to a sub restaurant nearby to thank the volunteers who had done the real preparation by staying up all night for a coveted street corner in Des Moines.

One month later, it was time to execute the Steak-Fry Domination Plan for the annual party-building event hosted by Senator Tom Harkin in Indianola. The traditional method of getting supporters to a distant event in Iowa is to buy them tickets, hand out free food and drink, and offer a chance to meet a candidate. Obama's unconventional plan was to bus three thousand supporters from distant staging locations to an early pre-rally. He then led them a mile and a half to the steak-fry site, marching behind the Isiserettes drum corps from Des Moines—the best, and perhaps only, African American drum corps in the state. As they marched together, his volunteers and supporters felt they were part of something bigger across the loosely populated state. From the steak fry, rival staffers could only watch Obama's marching army dip down and up again into the main site.

Iowa was an elixir for Obama's senior staff back in Chicago. For David Axelrod, the crowds were more than just a demonstration of strength. "Based on what we'd seen in the previous eight months, the crowds he was drawing and the enthusiasm, I felt like he had the power to change the equation in Iowa in a way that hadn't been done before," he said. "That he could actually attract tens of thousands of new voters, who could make a real difference. It was a quality to his candidacy that was really unique. I believed in the Iowa dream."

Obama's field of dreams was either an Iowa fantasy or something unprecedented in American politics. Either way, it felt unreal, especially by the fall, when the Clintons reasserted their own domination in finance and national polls. In early October, the Clintons announced they had outraised Obama for the first time, beating him by $3 million in cash for the primary contests in the third quarter, at a time when the national polls gave them a lead of thirty points or more.

How could the insurgent campaign continue to motivate its organizers and volunteers? With several intravenous doses of inspiration and mythmaking. On the fifth anniversary of his speech against the war in Iraq, Obama recalled his greatest moment of political courage before deciding to run for president, by delivering a series of speeches to remind voters of his early opposition to the war. "I'm not running for President to conform to Washington's conventional thinking," he said. "I'm running to challenge it. I'm not running to join the kind of Washington groupthink that led us to war in Iraq. I'm running to change our politics and our policy so we can leave the world a better place than our generation has found it." His introducer across Iowa was Ted Sorensen, special counsel and speechwriter to John F. Kennedy. Sorensen, who ghostwrote *Profiles in Courage*, said there were several similarities between Obama and JFK. Their critics cited their youth and inexperience, but there was something even more essential. "People said Kennedy had lost his chance to be president the day he was baptized," Sorensen told a crowd of a few hundred supporters in a gray concrete convention center in downtown Des Moines. "Like they say Obama lost the day he was born black."

Obama's campaign wasn't the only one to summon the ghost of presidents past. A few days later, Terry McAuliffe, the hyperactive chairman of the Clinton campaign, was at his seventh event of the day, in Cedar Rapids. Just two dozen supporters had bothered to show up at a union hall, leaving the room two-thirds empty and the sign-up sheets unfilled. "The campaign is on fire," he beamed. "We're doing great. Of thirty-seven states, right now Hillary is leading in thirty-five of them. You can clap for that." His small audience applauded weakly. Sensing a problem of complacency, or perhaps the energy levels of his rivals, McAuliffe urged Clinton's supporters to go out and work hard. "What happens in your state here is going to be a huge determinant of who the Democratic nominee for president is. Don't believe the polls. Four of the last six polls have put Hillary in the lead here. We are not in first place. We're bunched up in a three-way tie . . . We've got to run like we're twenty points behind."

Were the polls a reason to applaud or a reason to be worried? McAuliffe wasn't the only confused person in the room. Standing in the audience was Wally Horn, an Iowa state senator who spent thirty-five years in the legislature. He had introduced McAuliffe but admitted he was only really there because of Bill Clinton, not Hillary. "He asked me three times in fifteen minutes," Horn said, recalling that Clinton had visited him as a sitting president in 1994. "He said, 'I want you to be for Hillary. I remember coming here and remember doing those things.'" Horn seemed in awe of the former president. "Anytime he's around people, he convinces them. The charisma is there. You know when he walks in the room. You don't have to look around. You just know he's there," he explained. "What's so sad, for me anyway, is he tries to hide it now because of Hillary. He can inspire a room, but he has to act like he's small." Horn had no doubt that Hillary could be president; he just didn't see that Iowans would show up to vote for her. "I was a Dick Gephardt supporter before, but people didn't show up at the precinct caucus," he said, recalling another failed Iowa campaign from 2004. "This is what concerns me with Hillary. You almost know it's a natural for people to get out for Obama for the precinct caucus. But Hillary is going to have to get her people there and it's not a natural. . . . You know, in Iowa people are so nice, they'll say anything to you. They say they'll show up to caucus, but then they don't."

*   *   *

Obama's first lessons on the streets of Chicago taught him to match organization with inspiration. Early in his community work at the Altgeld Gardens housing project, he was struggling to motivate his base of church leaders and their congregations. A much-hyped job bank was failing to deliver on its promise of work and yet another steel plant was ready to close. When his handful of community leaders said they were quitting, Obama begged them for more time and he glanced out of a church window in anger. He saw a group of young boys tearing up a vacant apartment and pointed to them. "You say you're tired, the same way most folks out here are tired," he said to his fading team. "So I'm just trying to figure out what's going to happen to those boys. Who's going to make sure they get a fair shot? The alderman? The social workers? The gangs?" They had no answer but to believe in his commitment to their cause. Obama pulled his group back on track, then set about finding new recruits on the streets. He and a couple of volunteers handed out flyers for meetings on street corners instead of church basements. Soon he had a group of thirty motivated leaders instead of a handful of people who wanted to leave.

His presidential machine ran on the same principles—of personal pep talks and street-level teamwork—backed by the kind of money he could never imagine on the South Side. For behind his field organizers in Iowa, there was a corporate organization in Chicago. On the eleventh floor of a downtown office complex just south of the Chicago River sat the unlikely headquarters of an improbable campaign. Where the Iowa nerve center was a college dorm, Chicago's was a public-interest law firm: a quiet but casual clustering of neutral desks and low partitions, where the students were grown-up but not totally sold-out. An entire floor once occupied by the management consultant firm Accenture had turned into a supersized campaign consulting firm. Taped to the wall of a huge conference room, with views of Lake Michigan, were four maps of the early states: Iowa, New Hampshire, Nevada, and South Carolina. Taped to the wall of the unisex restroom nearby were two signs: one reminding the gentlemen to lift up the toilet seat, the other reminding everyone to use password protection on their BlackBerrys. Protect the Campaign, it declared.

The protector of the campaign was David Plouffe, the wiry, edgy campaign manager who sat in a small, glass-fronted office on the river side of the building. By early November, he was incredulous at the lack of organization in the Clinton campaign. To Plouffe, the timetable and the rules of the game were clear: each candidate needed to rack up delegates in a series of states. Since many of the states ran caucuses, not primaries, that meant even more preparation than usual. Plouffe had just opened an office in Idaho, a small caucus state that voted on Super Tuesday, and the Clinton campaign was nowhere. "We're in Minnesota, Colorado, Kansas, Idaho, Missouri," he said. "But she doesn't have staff in any of these places. And in the caucus states, you can't wait. This is all about organization. These are turnout caucuses. That's how we have approached it." As for Iowa, Plouffe believed they were heading for a record turnout based not just on organization but on inspiration. "We feel comfortable about our people because they feel inspired by this guy," he said with his low-toned but impatient delivery. "If people feel inspired, they will come out." The focus groups in Iowa suggested that even older Democrats, the regular caucus-goers, were sick of Washington and its ways. And if Obama could win in Iowa, there would be no stopping him, in Plouffe's view. "Obama could be the momentum candidate of our generation, if not our lifetime," he said with unusual hyperbole. "If we can get out of the gate strong."

The candidates stepped into the starting gate ten days later at the traditional fund-raising event for Iowa Democrats: the Jefferson-Jackson dinner. It was there that Al Gore had taken the contest to an insurgent Bill Bradley in 1999, whipping up the crowd with his repeated cries of "Stay and fight!" And it was there that John Kerry had started his comeback against the front-runner Howard Dean in 2003 with the rallying cry of "Bring it on!" Now it was Barack Obama, whose campaign more closely resembled those of the outsiders Bradley and Dean, who needed the big moment. His challenge was to show not just his organizational power but his inspirational force.

For at least a month, one young staffer in Chicago had been fretting about this moment. Jon Favreau, Obama's twenty-six-year-old chief speechwriter, had one of the best and worst jobs inside the campaign. His boss could deliver his speeches in ways that could move a crowd and inspire new legions of fans. But Obama could also be an exacting writer himself, and was a hopeless procrastinator, who left his writing to the last minute. Favreau got his start in speechwriting four years earlier when the Kerry campaign imploded almost at birth (before recovering again in

Iowa). At the time, he was just a lowly aide in the press office, straight out of college, putting together the overnight audio clips, a summary of the radio news. "They couldn't afford to hire a speechwriter," he recalled. "And they couldn't find anyone who wanted to come in when we were about to lose to Dean. So I became deputy speechwriter, even though I had no previous experience." When Kerry lost the general election, he joined Obama's Senate office as his speechwriter and developed a mind-meld with the young senator. They would sit together for half an hour, Obama talking and Favreau typing. Then he would write up and expand on those early thoughts, and send the first draft to Obama to edit and rewrite. After some back-and-forth, a full speech would finally emerge. Their relationship was more than senator and staffer: they were cowriters.

Favreau knew Obama well enough to realize what was going on. The Jefferson-Jackson speech was a seminal moment in the Iowa schedule, and it had to be delivered perfectly without notes and without a teleprompter, in the round. At the steak fry, Obama had winged the event from his regular stump speech. That was fine; the event was all about organization. This one was different. "We got to get to him," Favreau told the senior staff. "He has to memorize this."

The only problem was, they were all procrastinators: Favreau, Axelrod, Obama. All the people dealing with the speech. Conference calls about the speech were wasted exercises in group blather. And when he delivered a draft to Axelrod, the chief strategist wanted to see some changes. "I know it's not quite there," Axelrod told him. After a series of all-nighters, Favreau finally reached Obama on the phone for a forty-five-minute conversation. The candidate wanted to stress that this was a defining moment, a time for urgency. He was impatient for change, and wanted an impatient White House. The old tactics would not work; this was no time to let the moment pass with old ideas.

Favreau recalled that a month earlier, speaking at Howard University in D.C., Obama had hit the same impatient note in talking about this generation's duty to build on the civil rights movement. "I am not just running to make history," he told the historically black college. "I'm running because I believe that together, we can change history's course. It's not enough just to look back in wonder of how far we've come—I want us to look ahead with a fierce urgency at how far we have left to go." Martin Luther King Jr. spoke of the fierce urgency of now, forty years earlier, in New York's Riverside Church, a year before he was assassinated. This was King's landmark speech against the war in Vietnam, linked directly to the civil rights movement that he led. "We are now faced with the fact, my friends, that tomorrow is today," King said. "We are confronted with the fierce urgency of now. In this unfolding conundrum of life and history, there is such a thing as being too late. Procrastination is still the thief of time."

Favreau broke the spell of their procrastination with a speech delivered in Spartanburg, South Carolina, a year ahead of the general election. The crowd went wild, and Obama turned to Robert Gibbs, his communications director, as he left the stage to say, "This is the JJ speech. We got it. This is what I was talking to Favs about." That night, Obama was in New York taping a skit for *Saturday Night Live*, when Axelrod called Favreau from NBC's greenroom at Rockefeller Center. "Barack really likes the year-out speech," he told Favreau, who was ready to watch the show on TV with his friends. "But he knows it has to be cut down to a ten-minute speech for the JJ, and he wants to see something by tomorrow noon." Favreau hung up, kicked his friends out of his apartment, and went to bed. He awoke at 3:00 a.m., walked into campaign headquarters, and spent the next seven hours hacking the speech down to its bones. He e-mailed it to the candidate, who made some edits and added some lines. The next day, Obama was in the office running through the speech for the first time on a teleprompter.

"This is it: the JJ," he told his senior aides.

"Well, you got one week," said Favreau. "Good luck memorizing it."

Three days later, the speechwriter flew to Des Moines for the first real run-through in Obama's hotel close to the airport. "Nah," the candidate said. "I don't want to do it tonight." Favreau was as stunned as he was anxious. They were now going to have their first run-through just twenty-four hours before the dinner, at a time when the candidate also had to prep for the biggest of TV interviews with NBC's Tim Russert.

Obama stood up for his first rehearsal in front of Favreau, Axelrod, and Gibbs on Friday morning in his hotel. "Shit, does he have it?" thought Favreau. None of Obama's aides knew that the candidate had been rehearsing in his Des Moines hotel room all week. Gibbs had walked by his room a couple of times, heard a loud television behind the door, and wondered what was going on. Obama had turned the volume up to practice the speech to himself, out of sight and earshot of even his closest staff. On his first run-through, he forgot only a couple of lines. By the evening, he nailed it. The cocky effortlessness was partly a performance. He was enough of a renegade to leave the big speech to the last minute, but self-disciplined enough to rehearse in his own space, in his own way.

Showtime began early the next evening inside the concrete Hy-Vee Hall, close to the dinner. There, three thousand Obama supporters were gathered after traveling by bus from four staging posts across the state. Their reward for showing up early: a free concert by the young song-writer-pianist John Legend. This was a team-building exercise that would test the Iowa machine two months ahead of the caucuses. The plan was to bring in at least one supporter from each of Iowa's ninety-nine counties, accompanied by their respective local field organizers. And part of the bonding experience was the impression of intimacy that Iowa was normally famous for, despite the size of the crowd. "There's this guy. He's kind of cute. He's tall, skinny, and his ears stick out," said Michelle Obama as she began to introduce the candidate. "But I love him very much because he's a wonderful father. He went trick-or-treating this year. He had to wear a mask. It wasn't a Barack Obama mask. And he went trick-or-treating. He's running for president, and he went trick-or-treating. And I love him because he's a wonderful husband. He still sends me flowers for my birthday and anniversary. It's sweet, ladies. He's decent and honest and he tells the truth, even when the truth isn't easy."

When the candidate walked out, his message was all about organization. He asked them if they were fired up and ready to go. He gave a shout-out to a fifteen-year-old volunteer who canvassed on her birthday. And he reminded the crowd there was a statewide canvass the next Saturday. After a brief stump speech about the ills of Washington, he and Michelle reappeared outside, close to two huge signs for John Edwards and Hillary Clinton. Ahead of them were the Isiserettes drum band; behind them were three thousand supporters. Together, Barack and Michelle Obama danced, marched, and half-jogged their way around the block to the dinner site. Along the way, they waved at the groups of rival supporters gathered outside the Veterans Memorial arena before disappearing inside.

Outside the main entrance, Terry McAuliffe was spinning a group of reporters while a small group of Hillary fans beat white plastic buckets nearby. The noise from the makeshift drums almost drowned out the ebullient campaign chairman, but not quite. "The pressure isn't on us," he shouted. "We're up in thirty-four of thirty-six states. We put a lot more staff in here this week. A couple of the campaigns have gotten frisky in the last month or two. We're staying positive. We're not going to go negative." A few moments later, Governor Bill Richardson started to stroll in with a handful of aides. Rather than walk the gauntlet of rival supporters, he summoned his car and disappeared around the back of the building.

Inside the arena, there were dozens of round candlelit dinner tables on the floor for special guests, with banks of campaign supporters in the tiered plastic seats all around. The muted lighting was a feeble attempt to create intimacy among nine thousand Democrats and the nation's media. All the campaigns were rolling out new slogans, and testing their organization. The Clinton team promised to "Turn Up the Heat," which sounded like a warning about climate change, but was actually intended as a promise to beat up the Republicans. Rows of seats remained empty in the Clinton section of the arena.

On opposite sides, Obama's supporters were screaming "Fired Up" and "Ready to Go" at each other. At regular intervals there were lighted tubes carrying the names of Iowa's counties, as if they were seated at the state convention rather than a public relations stunt. Their organization troubled Clinton's senior team. "Mark Penn went into the bleachers to see the average age of Obama's people," said Mandy Grunwald, Hillary's ad maker. "They are high school kids. Ours are sixty-five." Older voters were the traditional caucus-goers, and the Clinton campaign was nothing if not traditional. Obama had John Legend, but sitting next to McAuliffe was Quincy Jones, the legendary trumpeter, producer, and composer. "I was here fifty-five years ago with Lionel Hampton," he recalled.

The evening spread out like a patient on a table. After a series of Iowa speakers, House Speaker Nancy Pelosi introduced each candidate as the next president of the United States. They delivered their speeches in turn over the course of four hours. Edwards attacked the GOP candidates for being George Bush on steroids. Bill Richardson condemned torture and demanded a deadline for withdrawal from Iraq. Joe Biden said the next president would literally, *literally*, shape the direction of the world, insisting that wasn't hyperbole. The speeches paused while Leonard Boswell, the congressman for Des Moines and much of central Iowa, conducted an extended auction for Pelosi's scarf and a stuffed donkey signed by the candidates. "It took nothing short of an act of God to wake that room up," recalled Tommy Vietor, Obama's press secretary in Iowa. Instead they got Chris Dodd, who imagined himself getting sworn in as president on inauguration day in January 2009. Then Tom Harkin, the Iowa senator, who talked at length about his work on the farm bill. The night wore on so long, the speeches missed the newspaper deadlines on the East Coast.

Finally, the crowd awoke from its etherized state with the arrival of Hillary Clinton, three hours after the program began, in a black pantsuit with a canary yellow top. "I know that as the campaign goes on it's going to get a little hotter out there. But that's fine with me," she said in a subdued tone. "Because, you know, as Harry Truman said, if you can't stand the heat, get out of the kitchen. And I'll tell you what: I feel *really* comfortable in the kitchen. So we have to ask ourselves what is this election going to be focused on? Well, I'll tell you what I want to do. I'm not interested in attacking my opponents. I'm interested in attacking the problems of America and I believe we should be turning up the heat on the Republicans! They deserve all the heat we can give them!"

The last speaker stood at the side of the stage while Pelosi introduced him as a new leader for a new century. His arms were folded across his chest, his head tilted up at forty-five degrees, his eyes blinking frequently: a studied pose in collecting himself. There was one final moment of gamesmanship. He walked onstage to the theme music of the Chicago Bulls and an introduction by the Bulls' announcer Ray Clay: "And now, from our neighboring state of Illinois, a six-foot-two-inch force for change, Sen-ator Ba-rack O-bama!" Maybe he couldn't make it to the NBA, but he could make it as a presidential candidate.

Without naming his main rival, he eviscerated Hillary Clinton for her style of campaign at a time when the nation's challenges were so great. "That is why the same old Washington textbook campaigns just won't do in this election," he said. "That's why not answering questions because we are afraid our answers won't be popular just won't do. That's why telling the American people what we *think* they want to hear instead of telling the American people what they *need* to hear just won't do. Triangulating and poll-driven positions because we're worried about what Mitt or Rudy might say about us just won't do. If we are really serious about winning this election, Democrats, we can't live in fear of losing it."

Sitting a few feet away was the woman he had just accused of being a coward. Vietor and Favreau watched her purse her lips and stare at the synchronized Obama crowds. "I wonder if we went too hard on her," Vietor told the speechwriter. "*You* think we went too hard?" replied Favreau, newly nervous.

Before they could reflect on the killer instincts of their own candidate, and the way he escaped public criticism for his attacks, it was time for the crowd to kick in. Through the run-up to the speech, the Iowa organizers wanted to know how to choreograph the crowd. Struggling to write the speech, Favreau had fobbed off the Iowa staff, disdaining the idea of a corny slogan. When they kept returning for a slogan, he threw out a line about standing up. "I will never forget that the only reason that I'm standing here today is because somebody, somewhere stood up for me when it was risky," Obama said as a section of his bleachers rose to its feet. "Stood up when it was hard. Stood up when it wasn't popular," he said, as another two sections stood up. "And because that somebody stood up, a few more stood up. And then a few thousand stood up. And then a few million stood up. And standing up, with courage and clear purpose, they somehow managed to change the world." By the end, the candidate was hoarse, snatching for his breath and for the moment.

As he wrapped up his speech, his three thousand supporters shouted "Fired Up! Ready to Go!" to the beat of Stevie Wonder's "Signed, Sealed, Delivered." Standing on a chair close to the stage was a middle-aged woman wearing a Hillary pin. "Fired Up!" she shouted. "Ready to Go!"

It was only now that the candidate started to believe in his own chances of success. The JJ speech was strong enough that his ad team simply turned it into a sixty-second ad of the candidate talking to the arena. Two weeks after his JJ speech, a *Des Moines Register* poll—the most respected of the statewide surveys—placed Obama ahead of Clinton by three points. "At that point we said, 'All right, there's something real here,'" Obama told me. "You could just feel the campaign lock in. We were doing five or six events a day, and you could just feel that people were responding to the message."

Inside the Clinton camp, the feelings were a little different. Frustrated by Obama's attacks and his positive press coverage, and torn by their own internal tensions over their Iowa strategy, Clinton's staff could barely contain themselves. "The idea that Barack Obama is going to Kumbaya his way by the Republicans is so fucking ridiculous," said one senior Clinton adviser. "These guys are going to kill him. As sure as the sun comes up tomorrow, Barack Obama will lose the general election. He has no idea how to fight. They're going to *kill him*. He hasn't the stomach for fighting. He doesn't like it. He actually believes that he's this transcendent person. They don't."

Instead of fighting the Republicans, Obama's team continued to break the rules of traditional campaigns. After the Dean debacle in 2004, most campaigns believed that young voters would never show up to caucus. Instead, the Obama campaign ignored that nugget of conventional wisdom. They paid close attention to the university schedules and organized Iowa's students ahead of the winter break. And they announced a new policy speech on national service and the Peace Corps, directed toward students.

They also cast out another old idea, that endorsements counted for little in a close election, especially in the later stages of a race. Obama had tucked away a unique endorsement: Oprah Winfrey, the queen of daytime television, whose reach extended far beyond politics and pop culture. There was an art and science to Obama's Iowa campaign, and Oprah combined both. Her star power would dominate the headlines and swamp the other candidates; it would also generate new data about voters the campaign had never reached before. "There's going to be an enormous amount of interest in this," promised David Plouffe a week before Oprah's Iowa tour. "There will be people who go to these events who will go to caucus. This is a great motivational tool for our supporters and organizers. But it's also going to put thousands of people in the room who might not normally attend a political event or go to caucus."

At the same Hy-Vee Hall where John Legend had played, a crowd of more than eighteen thousand filed in from a bitterly cold day that would later deliver an ice storm. In the hallways, volunteers passed out supporter cards to newcomers, and checked the identities of old supporters to see who had flaked out. The flake-out data was just as valuable as the new names, allowing organizers to follow up and figure out whether they needed extra help or persuasion on the day of the caucuses. Along with the crowd at a second event in Cedar Rapids, Oprah would be speaking to more than twenty-five thousand people—around 20 percent of all the Democrats who voted at the caucuses four years earlier.

Onstage, Oprah delivered the first endorsement speech of her life with perfect timing, mocking the media for their breathless anticipation. "You know, so much has been said about what my jumping into this arena does or does not bring to the table of politics," she began. "I really don't know. I'm going to leave that all up to the pundits, who all say, 'Will it all be the same influence as her book club? Will it be like the Favorite Things show?' I don't know about all of that. Despite all of the talk, the speculation, and the hype I understand the difference between a book club, and free refrigerators—that was a nice refrigerator. I understand the difference between that and this critical moment in our nation's history. And so I bathed—yes, I did—and I got dressed to come out here for I suspect the same reason you did. Because I care about this country. And as we were driving in here today, I said, 'You have to care about this country to come out in this kind of weather.' Twelve degrees, freezing rain, and snow: you love America, I can see that you do."

In the days after she swooped in, Oprah's glitter faded. The conventional wisdom in caucus politics was to get hot late in the process; but the TV star arrived a full month before voting began and left the campaign cold. For ten days before she touched down, the Iowa offices were buzzing with volunteers and precinct captains who needed to work additional hours to secure their tickets. Tewes feared that Oprah reinforced the notion that the candidate was all style and no substance. Moreover, he thought the Des Moines event was soulless, and he watched a few thousand people leave early, after Oprah had finished speaking. Then came the deadly quiet. "The day after she left, I felt like this silence," he said. "After that, I sensed this lull. We had expended so much effort going into Oprah, I felt we were flat coming out of Oprah." His feelings were confirmed a few days later, as they staged house parties in every precinct as a dry run for caucus night. The turnout was dismal, leaving the precinct captains and organizers demoralized. "I spent probably a week making phone calls to our precinct captains, who said, 'I made one hundred calls for that event, and only four people showed up,'" recalled Tewes. "I think Oprah hurt us."

Long ago, Obama had learned that fame could hurt his organization. Back in his days as a community organizer in Chicago, he succeeded in getting a new job center opened by the city. Harold Washington, the city's first African American mayor, would come for an opening ceremony and Obama wanted his group to ask him to come to their rally. Instead they swooned over the mayor and posed for pictures with him. Their young organizer was infuriated by their failure. "We're trifling. That's what we are," he told them. "Trifling. Here we are, with a chance to show the mayor that we're real players in the city, a group he needs to take seriously. So what do we do? We act like a bunch of starstruck children, that's what. Standing around, cheesing and grinning, worrying about whether we got a picture taken with him."

★ ★ ★

The last ten days of Iowa would prove whether his new team was a trifling bunch of children or real players who needed to be taken seriously. The final phase began just before Christmas, on December 23, in the West End Diner in West Des Moines, a fifties-style restaurant with chrome and black bar stools. The candidate spent his time in earnest, one-on-one conversations with customers as if his political life depended on it. One middle-aged lady said she worked in life insurance, prompting the candidate to say that his grandfather had worked for John Hancock for a long time. "Did he make a lot of money?" the voter asked.

"Well, no. He made some," the candidate said, his attempt to connect with the voter taking him only halfway there. "But he was one of those guys who'd get in conversations with people and show them pictures of me. Instead of focusing, he liked to talk. He was a storyteller."

As his story dried up, he turned to policy: the importance of saving for retirement, of Social Security and annuities. Clustered six feet away was the small group of reporters and cameras that trailed Obama. "A tutorial on annuities," he declared to the press after a few minutes. Only in sleepy Iowa could a conversation about life insurance be considered a way to win votes, a little more than a week away from the caucus. One reporter asked the candidate why there were still so many undecided voters at his events, and why he wasn't closing the sale. "It's true there are a lot of people who are undecided. But I don't think you can assume I'm not closing the sale," he replied. "A lot of those folks have never seen me before. That's exactly why we're doing these events. And we keep track of those supporter cards that we're coming out of there with, and we're doing very, very well. Typically when I see a show of hands, we're getting a third of the people who haven't decided yet, and we're getting a sizable chunk of them. For some, they may decide but not want to fill out a supporter card because they're shy or don't want to be called. And some may not feel the need to make a commitment until the day of the caucus."

He left the diner to drive to a steamy school gym in Greenfield on a sleek black bus rented from a company called myluxurybus.com. But he was only the most visible feature of his own campaign. Just as important was the message delivered by a high school student before the candidate walked onstage. It was a personal testimony to the candidate and to political activism: community organizing from the mouth of a teenage motivational speaker. "One person really can make a difference," he said, as he recalled his own experience at an Obama event where he felt fired up and ready to go. If he could feel inspired, then so could the rest of the audience. Just look: the source of his inspiration was walking onstage. All they needed to do was listen, fill in a supporter card, and turn up to caucus in ten days.

Four years earlier, Howard Dean liked to say that his audiences—not politicians—were in the driver's seat. "*You* have the power," he would chant. In Iowa in 2008, people power needed processing at a back office; there was a method to the motivation. Back at the campaign's offices across the state, Obama's organizers and volunteers tracked supporter cards and relentlessly contacted voters, making between twenty-five thousand and thirty thousand phone calls a day. That was a daily number equivalent to the giant crowds that lined up to listen to Oprah Winfrey. But the numbers did not always succeed on their own. By December, Paul Tewes figured out that his team had contacted one single voter 103 times, by phone, by mail, or in person. After all that effort, the voter remained undecided.

Two days after Christmas, Obama stood in the basement of the Scottish Rite Masonic temple in downtown Des Moines, one floor below the ritual room, to deliver the kickoff speech of the final phase in Iowa. There was little he could say or do that could change the dynamic as much as his field staff now. All the same, the room was heaving with a sudden influx of reporters practicing the rites of campaign journalism. Many of them crowded around David Axelrod to hear what the political strategist thought about the assassination of Benazir Bhutto, the former prime minister of Pakistan. Would the international news make voters lean toward Clinton? Obama's senior aides shrugged off the question as media mumbo jumbo. "Yes, people think the world is scary," said a weary Robert Gibbs. "I just don't think they are convinced that longevity in Washington is a surefire cure for what ails a scary world. If that was the case, then Dick Cheney and Donald Rumsfeld would not have given their party the worst foreign policy disaster in living memory."

Just in case any voter needed reassurance, Obama was introduced by two former Republicans who could speak to his nonscary credentials: Tony McPeak, a retired air force general who looked and sounded like Clint Eastwood, and Monica Green, a local voter from Ankeny who switched her party affiliation to caucus for Obama. The candidate had his own response to the Clinton question, and it boiled down to her vote on Iraq. "You can't fall in line behind the conventional thinking on issues as profound as war," he said, "and then offer yourself as the leader who's best prepared to chart a new and better course for America."

If the Obama campaign was concerned about anything in the final weeks, it was a possible assault by a North Carolina trial lawyer, not international terrorists. John Edwards threatened a late surge in the polls, at least according to the most recent news reports. And his rhetoric was starting to bite as he belittled Obama for being too nice, too compliant to fight the special interests and change the nation's capital. Five days before the caucuses, Axelrod chatted with reporters over a cheap Mexican dinner in Ottumwa, a town that left a vivid memory with the overpowering stench of its pork slaughterhouse. Four years earlier, Axelrod had worked for the Edwards campaign, only to find himself cast out of the circle of trust amid internal squabbles, which he could barely fathom. Now he was railing against a new pro-Edwards group, run by a former Edwards aide, which was spending hundreds of thousands of dollars on TV ads. "I've seen this before," he warned vaguely as he slopped his chips and salsa across the paper-covered table and the bright green margaritas. Even Obama felt concerned about the rise of John Edwards. "We thought in the last week or two that Edwards was more competition for us than Hillary," Obama told me. "His base was very loyal. He had been there four years earlier and they were passionate about him. We weren't going to move those folks off him, so he had a bloc that wasn't subject to a lot of volatility."

Like the closing performances of a Broadway hit, the last seven days of Iowa drew an eclectic crowd of family, friends, senior staffers, elected officials, high-profile journalists, and celebrity gawkers. Obama's family and close friends swapped their annual vacation in Hawaii for a hotel in downtown Des Moines in winter, their children spending the frigid days on day-camp-style excursions. At one event in rural Iowa, his friend Marty Nesbitt was surprised to find himself standing beside a seventy-year-old farmer who turned out to be an Obama organizer. At the end of the speech, Nesbitt went to Obama and said bluntly, "You're going to win Iowa. If that guy is your organizer, I *know* you're going to win Iowa."

Deval Patrick, the Massachusetts governor, stepped onto the campaign bus, sharing stories about his personal and political connections to the candidate. The next day, in a middle school, Kent Conrad recalled how much ham he had eaten thirty-five years earlier when he campaigned for Edmund Muskie. The North Dakota senator then endorsed Obama—his first endorsement in a primary in two decades in Washington. Later in the day, Tim Russert wandered into the back of another school gym after taping *Meet the Press* with the candidate. Russert caused enough of a stir that the candidate recalled an anecdote he had told on the show about his wife saying they weren't going to run for president again. "She wasn't just talking about the fact that I've been away from her and the kids so much this year, and the strains and stresses it's placed on the family," he explained. "She said, 'You know what, I think one of the reasons you would really make a good president now is because we're not that far away from being normal.'"

Perhaps they were not that far away from normal in terms of their family finances. But their life in Iowa seemed less than normal on the campaign trail. At the end of the day, in a vaulted church hall in Indianola, Obama's introducer was Brandon Routh, the young Iowa actor who played Superman on the silver screen. A newly married couple left their reception to watch the candidate give his stump speech. The bride was still wearing her wedding dress.

The candidate spent the final hours of 2007 in the wood-paneled hall of the Memorial Union at Iowa State University. Silver balloons in the shape of 2008 were fixed to the wall, but Obama's team had something more important to celebrate. The final, most respected poll of the cycle had just landed at the *Des Moines Register;* Obama was ahead of Clinton by seven points. "It's beyond the margin of error," a hoarse candidate announced onstage. "So we might just pull this thing off. We might just pull this thing off, Iowa. Who woulda thunk it?" At the back of the hall, David Axelrod could barely contain his spirits. "From a psychological standpoint, it's huge," he said. "Because so much of this has to do with the groupthink of the political community and the media." Back in the Des Moines campaign office, David Plouffe and Paul Tewes tried to tamp down the celebrations of their young staffers. Many of them were close to tears in any case, exhausted by the long hours and stressed by the weight of expectations to launch Obama into orbit. "Polls don't matter," they told them. Both were concerned that the *Register* poll didn't match the campaign's internal polling, although it did tally with their own numbers coming in from the field. Still, they thought like Axelrod that the poll itself could add a sense of momentum and become something of a self-fulfilling prophecy.

The next morning, Obama started the new year inside yet another gym, this one in Theodore Roosevelt High School in Des Moines. A candidate who began his campaign with Alinsky-style visions was ending his first real test with a statewide, one-day expression of community organizing. After all the dry runs and muscle flexing, the phone calls and door knocks, it was time to see if the machine could deliver real voters. "Happy New Year, everybody," Obama said after his wife introduced him onstage. "I think 2008 is going to be a good year, that's what I think. I think some big things might happen in 2008." He retold the story of his own life as an organizer before expressing his admiration for the small army of organizers now working for him in Iowa. "As I've traveled around the state over the last ten months I have been so inspired by the young people who have been organizing for us in counties all across the state," he said. "They have put their heart and soul into this campaign, they have believed when others did not believe. I am so proud of what they have accomplished so far." He called up a dozen organizers for the Des Moines area, hugging and high-fiving them as they walked onstage. "This is the team that's put this all together," he explained. "That's a good-looking bunch, too, isn't it. They're like a Benetton ad. You remember those?"

Behind the press riser, where the cameras were positioned, the organizers had put together a precinct-by-precinct operation to canvass voters. There were flyers to hang on front doors, saying "Caucus for Barack!" on the front and "Change the World on January 3rd" on the back. There were hand warmers for the canvassers as well as some written advice. "While canvassing for the campaign, you are acting as a representative of Senator Obama," the paper said. "It's absolutely imperative that at all times we remain respectful, polite and overly nice to the people we encounter." On a plane journey across the state later that morning, Obama explained that his role now was to support his organizers. "I'd bet my money on my organization," he said. "I'm just trying to help them carry us over the finishing line. All I can be confident about are the things I can control."

The next day his speechwriters were holed up in the back room of The Village Bean coffee shop, opposite the campaign offices in Des Moines. Jon Favreau had only just heard from Obama about what he wanted to say on caucus night, and it was simple. "Make sure we talk about the organizers and what they did," he said. "Make sure we talk about how hard it's going to be. Make sure we talk about how we've got a lot to do. We have to win this for these kids. They have worked too hard." Favreau took the thank-you idea and turned it into the pivot of the entire speech. Where other candidates might start their election-night speech with a few thank-yous, Obama would spend the key middle section of his address talking about his young staff and volunteers. Community organizing would become not just the model for Iowa but the message of the entire campaign as it broke onto a national stage.

On caucus day itself, Obama entrusted his political destiny to his Iowa organizers. After a game of basketball with his friends and staffers, he got in a car with his closest aides and drove to a caucus site at a school in the Des Moines suburb of Ankeny. The parking lot was so full, there were no spaces for their cars to park. Valerie Jarrett turned to Obama and said, "Something's going on here. There are just too many people."

The idea was for Obama to greet voters before they went into their caucus rooms, but the small group was stunned by what they witnessed: their vision for their Iowa electorate was walking into the school and shaking hands with the candidate. "Senator Obama, I'm a Republican switching my registration," said one voter. "I'm a Democrat and I've never been to caucus," said another. "The truth is that in Iowa, we re-shaped the electorate," said David Plouffe. "It's the holy grail of politics. It rarely happens."

One young African American mother didn't notice the candidate as she struggled to walk her stroller and her young son through the door. "Mommy, there's Barack Obama," the four-year-old said. The mother's mouth fell open as she shuffled by. "Why don't you go over and take a picture?" Jarrett asked the mother. "Everybody else is." The young mother seemed embarrassed and said no. "Oh, but you really should," Jarrett told her. Obama picked the toddler out of the stroller and played with both children for a couple of minutes. It suddenly struck Jarrett how much an Obama victory would mean to regular voters, and how much the photo would mean to those young children as they grew up.

There was the entire cross section of Obama voters. A strange bearded devotee walked into the caucus site holding a wooden staff with a video iPod attached to the top of it, playing Obama's TV commercials. A social studies teacher was there with one of her students to take part in presidential democracy. As he left the school, Obama seemed moved to the point of tears by the sight of the teacher together with her student. "This is why you do this," he told his aides. "When you see that, and you meet that person."

Obama was eating dinner with his family and friends at Fleming's Steakhouse in West Des Moines when Plouffe called him with the early results. He had won by almost eight points ahead of Edwards, pushing Clinton into third place. "That's great," Obama rasped in his scratchy voice, with little obvious emotion. "I'll be over there soon."

Across Des Moines, Tewes had spent the evening alone, overwhelmed with anxiety and unable to look at his BlackBerry. He returned to headquarters, answered phone calls from confused voters looking for their caucus site, then sat in his empty room until the networks declared his candidate the winner. He walked into the main office and watched his young staffers spraying champagne over one another. A few minutes later, he finally caught up with Obama at the Hy-Vee Hall, where Oprah Winfrey and John Legend had drawn such big crowds. He walked into a reception for the campaign's big donors and hugged the candidate for the first time in a year of working together.

"We made history," Tewes said, tearing up.

"Yes, we did."

In the main hall, the caucus-night crowd seemed relatively small, but more than compensated for their numbers with wild cheering. "You know, they said this day would never come," Obama began, before turning to thank the organizers and volunteers who worked for him.

> While I may be standing here tonight, I'll never forget that my journey began on the streets of Chicago doing what so many of you have done for this campaign and all the campaigns here in Iowa—organizing, and working, and fighting to make people's lives just a little bit better. I know how hard it is. It comes with little sleep, little pay, and a lot of sacrifice. There are days of disappointment, but sometimes, just sometimes, there are nights like this—a night that, years from now, when we've made the changes we believe in; when more families can afford to see a doctor; when our children—when Malia and Sasha and your children—inherit a planet that's a little cleaner and safer; when the world sees America differently, and America sees itself as a nation less divided and more united; you'll be able to look back with pride and say that this was the moment when it all began. This was the moment when the improbable beat what Washington always said was inevitable.

★   ★   ★

More than a month later, sitting on his new campaign plane as he flew from Maine to Virginia, Obama sounded far less confident that his gamble would pay off. But he had no doubts about his desire to change the direction of the country. "You know, I actually believe my own bullshit," he told me with a big smile. "I don't just want change for the sake of it. I want it for better schools for the kid on the streets. I want it for health care."

Still, he didn't know if his rules for radical change would really succeed across the country. He had spent almost a year in Iowa, traveling across a small state, pouring in staff and resources to reach just a few hundred thousand voters. Could he replicate Iowa, with all its volunteers and organizers, throughout the United States? Or was it part of a grandiose, Gandhi-style testing of himself, his theories, and the nation? "You see, I don't know if this whole experiment will work," he said as he glanced out of the window at the clouds below. "I *think* it will work. This is what I've been doing since my days as a community organizer. But it's an experiment to take it across the country."

FOUR

FAILURE

They flew to New Hampshire in the early hours as the giddy, insurgent winners of the Iowa caucuses. Ahead on the runway was Clinton's plane, heading for the same destination. But Obama and his team were already somewhere over the horizon, their dreams spinning out of control. Who knew when they would be back in Iowa, they said excitedly across the aisle. Probably the general election! The candidate loosened his blue tie at the collar and walked back to the press seated several rows behind him. Even he cast aside his innate caution to make some heady predictions about what would take place across the United States. "My throat is hoarse but my spirits are good," he said. "What I was so pleased with isn't just the fact that we won, but what it showed about the country. I think it's fair to say that there were some who were skeptical that young people would come in, that independents and Republicans would be voting in a Democratic caucus, that we would see the kind of turnout that we had anticipated. It was really a victory for the people of Iowa, and it's a sign of what is going to happen in the country."

A few hours later, after too little sleep in a small New Hampshire inn, Obama stepped into a clear, frigid dawn. Streaked across the ice blue sky were wisps of clouds that crested in waves. His convoy drove a few minutes to a half-empty aircraft hangar with old Pan Am jets parked inside, next to rows of spare aircraft seats. An elephants' graveyard of airline travel inside a freezing, echoing shed, where some eight hundred supporters had gathered to hear the croaky candidate deliver his stump speech. A few hours earlier, the candidate thought there were just signs of the country changing; now, in the cold light of morning, he believed this small New England state would decide the presidency. "New Hampshire, if you give me the same chance that Iowa gave me last night, I truly believe I *will* be the president of the United States of America," he predicted.

At the back of the crowd, the normally low-key David Plouffe was still grinning the morning after Iowa, marveling at how little time the Clinton campaign had to catch them up. It was Friday; Tuesday would be primary day in New Hampshire. Like the rest of the campaign, Plouffe was a believer in momentum theory—that Obama could bodysurf from Iowa across the rest of the early states into Super Tuesday and claim the nomination. Not everyone around the candidate was so convinced the theory would hold. Marty Nesbitt, Obama's friend, wondered out loud in July what would happen if the early-state scenario failed. As a businessman, as well as the campaign treasurer, he felt obliged to explore all contingencies. "What if we win Iowa, New Hampshire, and South Carolina, and it's still not over?" he asked the senior aides. "Shouldn't we be prepared?" The experts brushed his concerns aside. What a political neophyte.

It took a certain arrogance, a stubborn streak of independence, to run a renegade campaign: to take big gambles, break the conventions, and succeed against all odds. It could also be a lonely experience, especially if you lacked the preparation or foresight to avoid falling to earth. Through the four days before the New Hampshire primary, the intoxicating feelings of triumph and hubris overpowered the workaday sense of caution and humility that had characterized Iowa. In private, the candidate seemed uncomfortable, unsettled with his success; in public, he drank deep from the adoring crowds. Barely twenty hours after his historic victory in Iowa, Obama was sitting alone in a teacher's small office inside Concord High School, bent over his knees as if looking for a comfortable position to rest his head. Nursing a steel travel mug of tea for his scratchy voice, he seemed ill at ease with himself and the public attention, both defensive and confident about his abilities. With one victory behind him, he already felt that he had proved his leadership skills to the nation. "Just look at how we've handled this campaign, where others who supposedly are far more seasoned and ready to lead maybe haven't always handled the pressures or the ups and downs of the campaign as well," he told me. "I've said from the outset that starting from scratch, starting from zero, we've built the best political organization in the field. And I think that yesterday confirms it. I have managed this operation without any drama. My staff is famous for being courteous and treating people with respect. At some point people have to stop asserting that because I haven't been in the league long enough, I can't play. It's sort of like Magic Johnson or LeBron James who keep on scoring thirty and their team wins. But people say they can't lead their team because they're too young."

He could lead a team, all right. But that didn't ensure his success; it just assured him of his own star qualities. His Himalayan-sized mistake was to confuse the two.

In some ways, the sensory overload of New Hampshire was bound to lead to confusion. Obama was overwhelmed with the crowds and tried to stay above the fray. In Nashua North High School on Saturday morning, January 5, the line of supporters stretched out for one long block, then turned the corner and continued down a long driveway. Such crowds were exceptional in a state where two hundred people was considered a blowout. Eight years earlier, when John McCain was barnstorming his way to victory, his crowds of a few hundred supporters were the early signs of success. Obama was far ahead of that measure already. At the front of the line, Obama's supporters had been waiting in the early-morning ice for almost three hours. It took so long to fill both the main gym and a practice gym (for the overflow) that the event started unusually late. "There must be a hockey game going on somewhere," the candidate began, as he repeatedly marveled at the size of his own crowds.

All the candidates seemed to have lost some sense of judgment that evening, at the only debate of the New Hampshire primary. Clinton accused Obama of being inconsistent on universal health care; John Edwards jumped to Obama's defense and savaged Clinton. "What will occur every time he speaks out for change, every time I fight for change, the forces of status quo are going to attack," Edwards declared. "Every single time." Clinton responded aggressively, prompting howls of mock horror inside the press room at Saint Anselm College. "I think it is clear that what we need is somebody who can deliver change," she began. "And we don't need to be raising the false hopes of our country about what can be delivered." The fourth surviving candidate, Bill Richardson, punctured the bubble of self-righteous indignation. "I've been in hostage negotiations that are a lot more civil than this," he quipped. A few minutes later, Clinton had regained her composure, when the local TV moderator asked what she could say to voters who found Obama more likable. "Well, that hurts my feelings," she said, feigning injury. "But I'll try to go on. He's very likable. I agree with that. I don't think I'm that bad." As Clinton looked at her rival, then at the audience, Obama kept his eyes fixed on his notes and glanced up. "You're likable enough, Hillary," he said, smiling wryly to himself.

New Hampshire was masked in false hopes, false anger, and false modesty.

The next day, Obama took the bait of Clinton's attacks on hope and could talk about little else. At the gilded Palace Theater in Manchester, the crowd waited two hours on a Sunday morning for a glimpse of the performer, who arrived late because he was sleeping. At the back of the theater stood two cousins of Obama's speechwriter Jon Favreau, Pete Favreau and Jim Soucy, wearing black leather jackets with the insignia of Manchester's police force on their arms. "They're hard core Republicans but they're going to vote for Barack Obama," Favreau said, "and not because of me." Favreau's cousins said they liked Obama because he sounded different. But his stump speech sounded so different, so abstract, that it amounted to little more than a defense of Hope—not a plan to change the nation. "That is what hope is, imagining and then working for and fighting for what hasn't been done before," he said. "Believing in things unseen."

A belief in the unseen could be visionary, or it could be delusional. The phrase was born in the book of Hebrews as the definition of faith: "The substance of things hoped for, the evidence of things not seen." Obama had borrowed the phrase to explain the uniquely American nature of ambition and idealism, or the audacity of hope, as he put it four years earlier in his breakthrough speech at the Boston convention, echoing the most famous sermon of his pastor, the Reverend Jeremiah Wright. But by that heady weekend in New Hampshire, the once-rich, once-resonant phrase was boiled down to an argument for believing not in American ideals or religious faith but simply in his own campaign.

What were Obama and his aides seeing in New Hampshire? It wasn't clear if they were dreaming or living the dream. Standing at the back of another steamy gym, this one in Exeter, David Axelrod was rubbing his eyes. "You know, this is just a little bizarre for him and for me, frankly," he told me. "Back in 2002, when he was starting his run for the Senate, I had to get his friends into a room to explain why he stood a chance. It was just him and me. We couldn't get people to believe he had a chance.

Now look at this," he said, sweeping his hand toward the crowd. Diane Sawyer of ABC's *Good Morning America* walked in, preparing herself for an interview with the candidate at the end of his rally.

Axelrod's disbelief was only matched by his disdain for the Clinton team. A day earlier, Clinton's chief strategist Mark Penn wrote a memo headlined "What Bounce?" pointing to minimal movement in the New Hampshire polls after the Iowa results. Today the polls suggested Obama was ahead by more than ten points. "He can stick his bounce up his ass," Axelrod deadpanned.

That night the campaign staff and reporters swarmed into a cheap motel around midnight, convincing the sleepy bartender to stay open for just another hour. Almost everyone in the Obama orbit was in New Hampshire and they seemed ready to celebrate. Around the wooden horseshoe bar, Obama's political staff joined his policy advisers Susan Rice and Karen Kornbluh, who were campaigning independently through the small towns of New Hampshire. Drinking beer past midnight, the policy wonks and the political hacks agreed there was no shadow of doubt: Clinton would lose the early states and could only stage one comeback, on Super Tuesday, a full month away.

Overnight the campaign and the media grew ever more convinced of the outcome. Just twenty-four hours before the primary voting began, the candidate attempted to warn a crowd in Claremont not to be complacent, but he seemed only half credible. "Do not take this race for granted," he said. "I know we had a nice boost over the last couple of days. But elections are funny things. You actually have to wait until people have voted and counted the votes before you know what's happened. So it's very important for us all to be clear that we have not won anything yet," he declared. Not *yet*, but surely soon. At the same time, Axelrod was speculating how Clinton's aides would start to resort to their traditional backstabbing. Could they start dumping money into attack ads in the Super Tuesday states where Obama had barely campaigned? Axelrod thought the rival campaign was almost spent. "I think they'll have a problem raising money, actually," he said. Moments later, the candidate was so confused that he mangled one of his signature lines from his Iowa victory speech. "We can actually start bringing together the American people, Democrats, independents, and Republicans, and proclaim that we are one nation, that we are one people," he declared confidently, "and the time has changed for come."

The time had indeed changed: yesterday it was Diane Sawyer, today it was Brian Williams. On the bus ride to the next stop, the NBC anchor interviewed the candidate on the black leather sofa of his latest luxury bus, showing him the new edition of *Newsweek,* with a gauzy cover photo of him smiling on a rope line. Next to his head was the correct quote from that heady night in Des Moines: "Our time for change has come." "How does this feel of all the honors that have come your way, all the publicity?" asked Williams, as Obama took the magazine and stared at the cover.

"Well, I had not seen this," he said. "So, it's quite something." He paused and sighed, and Williams sensed the moment to tug on his heart-strings.

"Who does it make you think of? Is there a—is there a loved one?"

Obama started flicking through the magazine as a football game played on the flat-screen TV above his shoulder. "You know, it makes me think of my mom, and the fact that, you know, she's not around to see it. I think she would have, she would have been, you know, proud and she would have cried and that's how she used to deal with stuff like this. Her chin would tremble and she would get all weepy," he said, sounding a little wobbly himself, before stiffening his chin. "But we have obviously started something. Now we've got to finish it."

Never mind finishing the job; controlling the crowds was a far more pressing challenge. At the next stop, in the small town of Lebanon, the crowd had filled the opera house and another five hundred people had gathered on the steps outside. "You took us a little bit by surprise," the candidate told them. "Even though we can't get everyone inside, we're all still in this together. Outside and inside." Inside, two hand-painted banners were hanging vertically on either side of the stage, proclaiming in large capital letters HOPE. That morning, ABC broadcast his interview with Diane Sawyer, where Obama expressed dismay with Clinton's criticism of his raising voters' hopes. "I find the manner in which they've been running their campaign sort of depressing lately," he noted dryly.

Yet his crowds seemed anything but depressed or downtrodden by Clinton's admonition. A few hours later, when he tried to stop to talk to voters at Jack's restaurant and coffee shop in New London, he could barely move inside for the reporters and cameras. "President Obama," said one excited voter, "can I get a picture of you with my wife?" The candidate smiled, but did not try to shake off the dream. He bought a cup of hot tea with lemon and honey, then some cookies and cupcakes for the press. A reporter asked whether Clinton should drop out of the race if he won New Hampshire, and he tried to tamp down expectations. "I would never presume to say anything like that," he said, not mentioning that he and his staff were thinking something like that. "We have had one caucus. This would be one primary. And right now, I'm just focused on tomorrow. We have got to get our voters out." He turned to leave and walked into a group of teenage girl basketball players, still in their sports gear, who hyperventilated Omigod! Omigod! Omigod! The candidate calmed them down by talking about their favorite game, before walking out to shake more hands on an improvised rope line by his bus. Managing the excitement, not driving turnout, seemed to be his full-time job.

There was something freakish about the scenes surrounding him. Inside another packed opera house, this one in Rochester, police officers frog-marched out two young men whom they discovered hiding inside a closet. "Why were you hiding in a closet?" asked one officer. "Because we wanted to get a better view," said one of Obama's fans. At the edge of the crowd, struggling to get any kind of view, was another network TV anchor, Matt Lauer. A group of abortion activists were next to get frog-marched out of the opera house, chanting, "Abortion is an Obama-Nation." Outside, a group of orthodox Jews were protesting about the nation of Israel, whose existence they opposed. The circus had little to do with the star performer and everything to do with the audience that trailed him with their cameras, as if the freaks could hijack the tent while they staged their own show.

The emotional spectacle was playing out all across the snowy Granite State. Hillary Clinton had shifted gears after her dismal third placing in Iowa, signaling to the press that she would get more aggressive against Obama, and signaling to voters that she would be less regal by taking their questions. While Obama was struggling with overflow crowds, Clinton was patiently enduring town hall queries. At one roundtable with undecided voters in Café Espresso in Portsmouth, the day before the primary, a freelance photographer asked about her hair and appearance, and how she kept "upbeat and so wonderful." "It's not easy. It's not easy," Clinton explained, holding her stick microphone so close to her mouth that you could hear her exhale. "And I couldn't do it if I just didn't passionately believe it was the right thing to do. I have so many opportunities from this country. I just don't want to see us fall backwards. You know? So . . ." Her voice trailed off and her eyes grew moist, as she rested her chin in the palm of her hand. "You know, this is very personal for me, it's not just political, it's not just public. I *see* what's happening," she continued, clenching her fist and then lowering her voice to an almost whisper. "And we have to reverse it. And some people think elections are a game, they think it's like who's up and who's down. It's about our country and it's about our kids' futures. It's really about all of us together."

The talking heads on TV speculated wildly about Clinton's melting down under the pressure of an imminent defeat. In Manchester, NBC's Tim Russert was shaking his head at his latest conversation with Clinton officials. "They don't have any idea what to do," he said before speculating that Mark Penn would get fired within days, and would never get paid the millions of dollars in fees he normally charged. "At least they won't have to pay his accounts receivable." At Clinton headquarters, the first reports suggested that Clinton had been weeping. Her senior aides feared she had just behaved like Pat Schroeder, the Colorado congresswoman who ended her run for president in 1987 with a tearful press conference that became a standing joke on *Saturday Night Live.*

In public, Obama was immensely cautious about reacting to the news. Gone was the sentiment of his morning-show interview when he found the Clinton campaign depressing. "I didn't see what happened," he told reporters. "I don't know the context of it. I know that this process is a grind. So that's not something I'd care to comment on." In private, he was deeply troubled and even sympathetic. Riding on the campaign bus between events, Obama and his senior aides started to take calls and e-mails from friends and staff about Hillary's supposed breakdown. One of Obama's aides pulled up the Web video on a laptop, and several scoffed at Clinton. The testosterone-charged team, with no women among them, suggested that Clinton had just experienced an Ed Muskie moment, dooming her in New Hampshire just like the 1972 candidate who cried in a snowstorm while defending his wife outside the offices of the *Manchester Union-Leader.* Obama declined to join in. "Hey, guys, I've got to tell you something," he began. "This isn't easy. It's hard. I have some sympathy for her. I don't know how people are going to react."

Obama and his senior team were balloons floating over New Hampshire. They had spent almost a year planning for and campaigning on the ground in Iowa; in New Hampshire they dedicated comparatively little time beyond the four-day contest. They simply assumed it would follow the example of 2004, when John Kerry swept through the state after winning in Iowa. That led them to end their internal polling on Sunday night, missing entirely the huge swings of the last twenty-four hours and any response to Clinton's emotional moment. "We were still basking in the afterglow of Iowa and Hillary looked like she was working her ass off. She looked like she really wanted it," said David Axelrod. "It felt like we were up at twenty thousand feet and she was at ground level, grinding out the votes. It looked like she was working harder than we did."

The Clinton team was indeed working harder than Obama's campaign. Obama pushed back against his aides' plans to pack his schedule. When they planned an event for 11:00 p.m., he said, "I don't want to do it. I'm tired." His aides forced him to do it anyway, but the rest of the team was not performing at the top of their game, either. In place of Obama's rapid response in Iowa, his operatives allowed Clinton's attacks to stand with little effort at rebuttal. One attack had started a month earlier in Des Moines, when Ellen Malcolm, president of EMILY's List, held a press conference to decry Obama's "present" votes on antiabortion legislation in the Illinois state legislature. Malcolm conveniently set aside the fact that Obama had a 100 percent pro-choice voting record in the United States Senate. As rebuttal, Obama's Iowa operatives explained how his votes were designed to thwart pro-life Republican tactics, and had the full support of pro-choice groups in Illinois. And they discredited Malcolm by handing reporters a fawning letter penned by her in 2006, when she thanked Obama for supporting the cause and speaking at a lunchtime conference of her leadership team.

In New Hampshire, however, the rebuttals were limp, if they existed at all. Mailings to New Hampshire Democrats painted Obama as weak on choice compared with Clinton. "A woman's right to choose," read one mailshot, "demands a leader who will stand up and protect it." Underneath, next to a picture of Barack Obama, ran the ominous headline: "Unwilling to take a stand on choice." Next to that was a smiling picture of Hillary Clinton with the headline: "Standing up strong on choice." Automated phone calls drove home the attack, with belated robocalls from the Obama campaign in response. "We should have lifted those up and had a public discussion about her tactics," said David Plouffe. "Because anytime we put the Clinton tactics on display we benefited from it. That hasn't gotten much attention, but as I look back on it, that's the thing I most regret."

It was unclear that a debate about tactics could have broken through the overwhelming crowds and their intoxicating effect on the candidate.

On the eve of the primary, at his final rally in Concord High School, the young audience was celebrating. They clapped and chanted and danced while they waited. When the candidate finally walked onstage, friends hugged one another. "Awww, this is something, isn't it?" Obama began. "Something is going on. Something is *going* on. Something is going *on*. What an unbelievable crowd."

Something unbelievable was indeed going on. The polls were already open when Obama drove to Dartmouth College the next morning. En route a church sign proclaimed its own message of doom. "This new year begins with the end in mind," the sign said. Four days earlier, the campaign seemed to be unstoppable. Now the gym was two-thirds empty, and there was a certain fear of the unseen. "The polls are out of control," Axelrod told me before his candidate started to talk. "It's not going to be ten or fifteen points. A win is a win. But I don't buy into this tidal wave idea." All the same, where were all the students—the very demographic that delivered victory in Iowa? "Do you know how difficult it is to wake up five hundred students at nine in the morning?" Axelrod asked. Walking around the press area were three refugees from Los Angeles: the celebrity blogger Arianna Huffington, the comedian and writer Larry David, and the superagent Ari Emanuel. Soon after the candidate started his stump speech, a woman collapsed in front of him. It took nine minutes for the medical team to arrive, a silent eternity that Larry David tried to fill with a bizarre joke. "Sinatra had that effect on people, too," he quipped. Even more strangely, Obama pretended like he understood the reference. "I know!" he snapped back.

That afternoon, the campaign looked for a coffee shop with some voters inside for the candidate to greet, but they struggled to find anywhere that had any customers. They eventually found a Dunkin' Donuts in Manchester, but there were still more reporters than voters. Obama sensed something was going deeply wrong with the day. "The day of the New Hampshire primary, it was all off," he told me later. "We were doing that event at the university and it wasn't very well organized, and there's not a good crowd there and the sound system is bad. And the person collapses, so I'm having to wait as they carry them out. Everything is just off. We try to go to a coffee shop, a Dunkin' Donuts, and there were three people there. And the whole thing just felt *off*."

The bus drive to the hotel in Nashua, where the candidate would watch the results and prepare for his speech, was almost unnaturally beautiful. Bright sunshine warmed the midmorning as if it were already spring, and no winter wind chilled the air. Inside, most of the senior team was exhausted. Michelle rested her head on Barack's shoulder and tried to doze off. David Axelrod felt it was time to step out of the moment and wax wisely about politics. A friend once told him that campaigns were either going up or they were going down, and Axelrod felt they were losing altitude. Maybe not the full ten- or fifteen-point lead, but enough to make the contest uncomfortably close. "We should keep in mind that campaigns have cycles, and there are ups and downs," he said with all the assurance of someone enjoying the ascent. "Of course, we're up today. But you know, before it's all over, we'll have downs." Sure, sure, the rest of the team brushed him off. Who had the energy to look that far ahead?

The decline was steady through the afternoon. The first exit polls gave Obama an eight-point lead, well below the double-digit leads before the primary, but still healthy. The final exit numbers shrunk Obama's lead down to just three points. Inside the boiler room set up inside the hotel, several floors below Obama's room, Axelrod felt his gut instincts were correct: they had closed the race poorly. Matt Rodriguez, the campaign's intense state director in New Hampshire, was distraught as the early precinct returns came in from the Manchester area. "Something is really wrong here," he said. "We're underperforming in all these Manchester precincts. We can't make it like this."

They waited for a little more data to confirm their worst fears, then Axelrod, David Plouffe, and Robert Gibbs took the long walk to the elevator and to Obama's suite. The news was as stunning as it was dismal. The polls were wildly wrong and so was their strategy. There was no tidal wave. Iowa's momentum had rippled and faded. The much-loathed Mark Penn might have been right after all: where was the bounce?

Obama's closest aides walked down the hotel hallway dreading every step, but they wanted to deliver the news themselves. They knocked on the door and the candidate answered. Obama was immediately struck by the morose look on the faces of all three aides as they stood in the hallway. "I think we may not have made it," Axelrod told him. "We're going to be a couple of points short."

They were a couple of points away from steamrolling their way to the presidential nomination. A couple of points was all it took to destroy their yearlong strategy for emerging out of nothing to beat the Clintons and make history. A couple of points had restored the old rules, the natural order of politics, and threatened to make Iowa look like an aberration.

"I wonder what happened," Obama replied, trying to compute some analysis.

Nobody could really explain it. Nobody had seen anything like it: a huge late swing that the polls missed entirely. Every undecided woman voter chose Clinton. It was a tidal wave heading in the other direction. Some Democrats voted in sympathy for Hillary's emotional moment; some independents and Republicans switched their attention to the Republican race. None of them thought it mattered because Obama was sure to win, right? And New Hampshire's famously independent-minded voters sorely wanted to matter. Everything looked too easy for a candidate who had not yet proved himself worthy of victory. Whatever the reason, their public reaction was key. They all had to remain upbeat.

Obama shook his head and leaned back against the wall. "This thing is going to go on for a while, isn't it?" he said with a wry smile. "I guess we've got to win Nevada and South Carolina," he added, before snapping back to the present. "Let's pretty much give the same speech. And I'd better get ready for it."

His aides were looking for clues: signs of his response and guides for their own. They needed to know if he could survive the blow: if he had the stuff of a leader, a nominee, and a future president.

Plouffe was even more stunned walking back than he was walking there. "This guy really has what it takes to be president," he thought to himself. "There's not a lot of people who would react like that." As for his own reaction, Plouffe was reassured that the results seemed so weird, so out of line with the polling. "Something strange just happened here," he comforted himself.

A few minutes later, Barack and Michelle walked out of their room on their way to Nashua South High School where several thousand supporters were waiting in another gym, cheering and booing as the vote totals showed their candidate narrowing Clinton's lead, then falling behind once again. They stopped by the senior staff room where their friend Valerie Jarrett was trying to think of something upbeat to say. Before she could speak, Obama said, "It's going to be the best thing that could have happened. We're going to be fine." Where Barack was comforting, Michelle was much more competitive. "It's a test," she said. "It's just a test to see how steadfast our support is really." The holding room in the high school was full of elected officials, from New Hampshire and beyond, who had risked their reputations and careers to back Obama. Jarrett started to cry as she watched the scene, and the candidate walked over.

"Are *you* OK?" he said, putting his hand on her shoulder.

"I'm OK if you're OK," she replied, taken aback by his concern for her feelings at his moment of defeat.

"I'm fine," he said. "This is a test. Who said it would be easy? It will make us stronger. This is going to be all right, you'll see."

Other insurgent candidates had wilted in such moments. Howard Dean yelped and screamed on the night of his Iowa defeat as he tried to pump up his depressed supporters; his team spent the next week wondering out loud when the obituaries would be written. Obama's self-discipline and temperament took him in another direction. There was no panic, no firings, no frantic spinning of the press. In fact there were no press handlers present at all in the vast practice gym that became the campaign's media room in Nashua.

Even his speech—once a victory cheer, now a pep talk in defeat—was a study in steadiness. His speechwriters tweaked some wording, but it needed no major reworking. The main theme had surfaced in the TV debate that he mostly flunked three days earlier. "The truth is, actually, words do inspire, words do help people get involved, words do help members of Congress get into power so that they can be part of a coalition to deliver health-care reform, to deliver a bold energy policy. Don't discount that power," Obama said as he rebuffed Clinton's suggestion that he was all empty talk. "Because when the American people are determined that something is going to happen, then it happens. And if they are disaffected and cynical and fearful and told that it can't be done, then it doesn't. I'm running for president because I want to tell them, 'Yes, we can.' And that's why I think they're responding in such large numbers."

Watching on TV, Obama's speechwriters Ben Rhodes and Adam Frankel loved the line. "Why don't we use that?" they asked their young boss Jon Favreau.

Favreau brushed them off. "Because I don't want to have everyone chanting 'Yes we can.'"

On the eve of the primary, Rhodes was driving Favreau back to their hotel in Manchester. It was one in the morning and Favreau was typing about the meaning of hope when his phone rang. It was the candidate. "I got thoughts about New Hampshire," he began. "Here's what I want to say. Obviously it looks like we're going to win, but I don't want us to get complacent. I don't want us to think this is going to be easy, and it's going to be over. So I want you guys to write in how hard it's going to be from here. How much work we've got left to do. How change isn't easy, and it never has been all through our history. All these times we've done it, it's because people stood up and said they could." Yes We Can, thought Favreau. When he finished typing, on the morning of primary day, the reaction was instant. "This is better than Iowa," pollster Joel Benenson told Favreau. "This is your best speech."

The candidate minimized his personal reaction to the defeat, but his public comments were anything but small. "We have been told we cannot do this by a chorus of cynics," he said in a voice worn down to its cords by the cold weather and endless speeches. "They will only grow louder and more dissonant in the weeks and months to come. We've been asked to pause for a reality check; we've been warned against offering the people of this nation false hope. But in the unlikely story that is America, there has never been anything false about hope. For when we have faced down impossible odds; when we've been told we're not ready, or that we shouldn't try, or that we can't, generations of Americans have responded with a simple creed that sums up the spirit of a people." He paused for a second, blinked a couple of times, and quickly licked his lips.

"Yes we can." And his crowd rose to cheer.

"Yes we can." And he raised a finger and nodded, while the cheer grew to a roar.

"Yes we can."

The crowd began chanting "Yes we can," just as Favreau had feared. The candidate turned to look over his shoulder, and smiled. "Yes we can."

He raised his hand to quiet the Yes We Cans, as he began to weave together the stories of the founding fathers and the slaves on the underground railroad, the nation's immigrants and its pioneers, JFK and MLK. "It was a creed written into the founding documents that declared the destiny of a nation," he began. "Yes we can.

"It was whispered by slaves and abolitionists as they blazed a trail toward freedom through the darkest of nights. Yes we can.

"It was sung by immigrants as they struck out from distant shores and pioneers who pushed westward against an unforgiving wilderness. Yes we can.

"It was the call of workers who organized; women who reached for the ballot; a president who chose the moon as our new frontier; and a King who took us to the mountaintop and pointed the way to the promised land," he said, pointing his own finger upward, and leaning into his microphone for greater volume. "Yes we can to justice and equality."

The crowd chanted and cheered, and even his raised hand could not calm them. So he folded his hands, smiled, and soaked up their energy. "Yes we can to opportunity and prosperity. Yes we can heal this nation. Yes we can repair this world. Yes we can."

He and his campaign were the defiant idealists, the immodest inheritors of the great American story, as retold by this young political narrator and his even younger speechwriters. Just a few minutes earlier they were despondently watching cable news calling the primary night for Clinton; now they sounded resurgent. Yes We Can.

Back at campaign headquarters in Chicago, the chant lifted their depressed spirits. "We were all feeling terrible until we watched that speech," said Tommy Vietor, who had left Iowa for Illinois. "Then we thought it was going to be OK." Later that evening, around midnight, Plouffe arranged a conference call for the entire campaign staff. He detailed with precision how they would compete in Nevada and South Carolina, then the Super Tuesday contests, and ultimately gain enough delegates to secure the nomination outright. There was a detailed strategic plan and they would execute it. "Now let's go win this fucking thing," he signed off.

This is a test. Did the candidate have what it takes? Did he have the stomach for the fight? This was the moment when his staff and supporters were watching most closely for answers. Obama spent the next twenty-four hours trying to revive his most important supporters in those early days: his fund-raisers. He started that night, when he talked to his dispirited national finance committee straight after his speech. "You guys have been with me for so long," he began. "It didn't work out our way, but this will make us stronger. This was a good thing. It shouldn't be this easy. We need to earn it." They would ultimately prevail, he assured them. The crowd clapped and cheered as if he had won, not lost, New Hampshire by two points.

Early the next morning, after little sleep, he drove to Boston for a breakfast fund-raiser with his friend Deval Patrick, the Massachusetts governor. Obama spent the journey in silence, reflecting on his defeat and the message he had to deliver. There was no text prepared for him to read, just an expression of his own early thoughts. *This is a test.* "You all know that we had a little setback yesterday. This may sound like spin to you, but I've been thinking a lot about it since yesterday," he told his donors in a private club, looking across the Boston skyline on a clear, sun-filled morning. "We were a little like Icarus flying too close to the sun. It all looked too easy. But that isn't the way change happens. Change is a struggle. Change is a fight. The status quo doesn't yield easily, and certainly not to a candidate like me. We just have to redouble our efforts, roll up our sleeves, and fight harder."

Whether it was conscious or not, Obama echoed the author he admired in the depths of his own failure as he told his Icarus story in Boston. For Malcolm X had also thought of Icarus, four decades earlier, when he was invited to speak at Harvard Law School, Obama's alma mater. Glancing through a window toward Boston, Malcolm X realized he was looking toward the apartment that had once served as a hideout for his old burglary gang. "Awareness came surging up in me," said Malcolm X, "how deeply the religion of Islam had reached down into the mud to lift me up, to save me from being what I inevitably would have been: a dead criminal in a grave, or if still alive, a flint-hard, bitter, thirty-seven-year-old convict in some penitentiary, or insane asylum." At that moment, standing inside the elite walls of Harvard, he thought of the story he had encountered in prison, when he was reading Greek mythology. "Soaring around, this way, that way, Icarus' flying pleased him so that he began thinking he was flying on his own merit," Malcolm X recalled. Icarus's death was not just the result of his breaking his father's rules; he failed because he was too arrogant, too self-indulgent.

Obama didn't need religion (especially Islam) to lift him up, and he dismissed much of what he called Malcolm X's "religious baggage." But pride could easily lead to his fall all the same. The same self-confident impulses that lent him the qualities of a risk-taking renegade could—without the checks of self-awareness and self-discipline—lead him to fail. It had happened eight years earlier, when he staged his first bid to escape the Illinois legislature. Nearing the end of his first term as a state senator, he decided to challenge a former Black Panther and four-term congress-man on the South Side of Chicago: Bobby Rush. Rush was popular, widely known, and drew on deep roots in the South Side; Obama was an unknown and rarefied figure, a Harvard grad and part-time lecturer who lived in the white enclave of Hyde Park. Obama saw weakness in Rush where there was little: Rush had challenged Richard Daley as Chicago mayor a year earlier, and failed. But he also saw strength in himself where there was little: the support of his Hyde Park friends and the *Chicago Tribune* made him an outsider among South Siders. "I still burn," he wrote just a year before running for president, "with the thought of my one loss in politics, a drubbing in 2000 at the hands of incumbent Democratic Congressman Bobby Rush."

The contest was the flight of Icarus, a case study in hubris, poor planning, and worse judgment. Rush "had been there for a long time, and he had a long record," he told me, sitting in his Senate office seven years later. "I may have believed that I could do a better job in highlight-ing some issues, but I think that it was a young man's mistake. Just be-cause you think you're smart and you think you can shake things up, that everybody else is automatically going to see that." Obama commis-sioned his first poll two weeks after announcing his candidacy, which turned out to be two weeks too late. "The issue in that race was the fact that I didn't do a poll until after I announced and I discovered I had 11 percent name recognition and he had something like 95. People just didn't know who I was," he said. "As people got to know me, we ended up moving from single-digit support to—I think we ended up with 31 percent. Without any TV advertising, it wasn't bad. The problem with that race was not in execution. It was in conception. There was no way I was going to beat an incumbent congressman with the limited name recognition that I had."

However, there were problems in execution, too. Rush's grown son was shot and killed by some drug dealers outside his home, and when the legislature was called to vote on new gun control laws, Obama was on his family vacation in Hawaii. His daughter Malia was sick with a cold and his wife was unhappy with both his political career and their mar-riage. She disagreed with his decision to run, was dismayed by his failure to help around the house, and was barely on speaking terms with him. The vote failed and Obama faced tough questions from the press about why he had skipped his duties to stay on a beach vacation. Rush said there was no excuse for his rival to miss the vote, and Obama was left pleading that his daughter's health had been hanging in the balance. The primary was effectively over, barely halfway through the contest. He ultimately lost by more than thirty points, and showed up to his own election-night party too late: the race was already called by the time he arrived. Yet that was only the first phase of his defeat. He returned to Springfield in a subdued state of mind, and felt down about the people he had failed along the way. "He wasn't disappointed in his own loss for himself, he was disappointed that he'd let so many people around him down," said his friend Marty Nesbitt, who led the fund-raising for the congressional race. "There's a certain confidence in his own abilities, but also an obligation to help others."

His disappointment soon turned more personal. A few months later, he tried to attend the Democratic National Convention in Los Angeles, but he was broke. He tried to rent a car but his credit card was declined; he tried to get a floor pass to the convention hall but failed. While he and his wife were earning more than $250,000 a year, his debts were high and his credit cards were loaded up in part with expenses from a failed campaign. Within a year, Michelle was pregnant with their second daughter, Sasha, and Barack was seriously contemplating leaving politics to make money or work in the nonprofit world. He deferred any decision long enough to see the Democrats regain control of the state senate, and for the United States Senate seat to look winnable.

A fear of failure and a vaulting ambition were the twin forces that drove Obama onward and upward. "Neither ambition nor single-mindedness fully accounts for the behavior of politicians," he wrote. "There is a companion emotion, perhaps more pervasive and certainly more destructive, an emotion that, after the giddiness of your official announcement as a candidate, rapidly locks you in its grip and doesn't release you until after Election Day. That emotion is fear. Not just fear of losing—although that is bad enough—but fear of total, complete humiliation."

His reaction to the failure of the Rush race was, after little more than a year of regrouping, to fire up his ambition once again. His friends were not convinced by his dedication to the Illinois state senate, yet they were also taken aback by the swiftness of his rebound. "I knew he would not last in the state senate very long. I knew the unique combination of leadership qualities that Barack has would push him to greatness. They always have," recalled his friend Valerie Jarrett. "Barack has this kind of a—what's the way to describe it?—restless spirit."

Obama's rebound was as analytical as it was ambitious. He didn't just want to move on. This time around, he studied the numbers, especially the approval ratings of the Republican incumbent, Peter Fitzgerald. He thought about the rest of the potential field, and his own position with African American voters. He identified that one of his key strengths was his ability to raise money. It was a cold calculation, not an impulsive, instinctive decision based on his idealistic self-image and his supreme self-belief. Still, when he asked to meet a handful of confidants at the home of Marty Nesbitt to talk about his plans one summer evening in 2002, his friends weren't convinced.

"So, dude, you just lost this race to Bobby Rush, what are you going to do now?" asked Nesbitt.

"Well, I think I'm going to run for the United States Senate," Obama replied.

His friends burst into raucous laughter. "Come on, man," said Nesbitt.

"No, no, no," Obama insisted. "I'm going to run for the United States Senate. No politician with Fitzgerald's approval ratings has ever been reelected. So we know it's not going to be him. I probably can't win if Carol Moseley-Braun runs, so the first thing we need to have happen is that she needs to decide not to run, because African Americans will be loyal to her even though she won't have a chance to win."

As his friends listened more closely, Obama explained what he needed from them: money. "If we raise $5 million, I have a 50 percent chance; $7 million, I have a 70 percent chance; $10 million, I guarantee you I can win, if you can raise that much." His friends thought it was difficult, but not impossible. Besides, he was their friend. "If that's what you want to do, man," said Nesbitt, "OK."

Nesbitt was far more than a fund-raiser; he was trusted and a true believer—just the sort of friend Obama needed to reaffirm his self-belief and turn his vision into reality. Soft-spoken and easygoing, Nesbitt was a successful businessman who ran an airport parking company. He was also supremely charming and well connected, having managed the real estate interests for the Pritzkers, who own the Hyatt hotel group and are one of the wealthiest families in the country. Nesbitt first met Obama through Michelle's brother, Craig, and their beloved game of basketball. As a high school player in Columbus, Ohio, Nesbitt was talent-spotted by Princeton's basketball coach, who invited him to watch their next game against Ohio State University. A freshman dominated the game, scoring twenty-nine points. His name: Craig Robinson. Six years later, Nesbitt was at the University of Chicago's business school, where one of the first people he met was Craig, who was also studying there. When Michelle and Barack started dating, Obama joined Nesbitt's basketball game and the two couples soon bonded over games of Scrabble. Nesbitt's wife, Anita, who worked as an obstetrician, counted Michelle as one of her patients. She delivered Malia and Sasha, turning her into some sort of miracle maker for Obama, who mentioned the feat whenever he introduced her to newcomers. For her part, Anita enjoyed a running joke about Obama's potential to become president. Shortly after Malia was born, she started giving him birthday presents with a presidential theme. One year she gave him a presidential watch with his face superimposed on it. Another year she bought him a presidential board game, taping his photo alongside the nation's leaders. Obama laughed off her presents, including Chris Rock's movie *Head of State.* It was an outlandish joke rooted in something real: Anita was deeply impressed by him, and he was not short of ambition.

The Senate race was an endurance test. Initially the underdog against a better-funded Democrat, Obama rose from the field as the frontrunner grew entangled in his own divorce papers. But without the threat of failure, Obama seemed to lose his drive. His friends had raised all the money he wanted. His TV ads had aired late but proved highly effective, and his poll numbers were rising. He was poised to win the nomination and was ideally placed to become the next United States senator from Illinois. Yet he seemed lackluster, disinterested, and distant from the contest. Something wasn't right. Valerie Jarrett called him and asked him to meet for lunch at one of his favorite Chicago gyms, the East Bank Club. "Uh-oh," he said, "the principal is calling me in."

When they sat down, he jumped right in. "What's wrong?" he asked.

"Your heart isn't in it. What's *wrong* with you?"

Obama pushed back, insisting that everything was OK, right up to the moment when he started to tear up. "I miss my girls," he said. "I don't want to be the kind of father I had." Then he snapped himself out of it. "I'll work it out," he promised. "I'll be OK."

Obama's ambivalence and detachment could be a strength in politics and even in his personal life. It hardened him against failure, protecting him from the pain of defeat, or an absent father. But it also served to isolate him, pushing away those who could sustain him, as he strove to succeed. The price of political success seemed a certain sum of personal failure.

Jarrett was no ordinary friend; she was uniquely positioned to understand his moods and his moves, whether upbeat or down, personal or political. She had been a mentor to Michelle Obama and quickly grew into a close friend. She also had close links to the Nesbitts: her father was a medical professor who mentored Marty's wife, Anita. Born in Iran, Jarrett had lived there until she was five years old, and she later lived in London for a year. Each summer she would travel from East to West Africa while her father researched disease across the continent's tribes. "Part of my initial appeal to Barack was the fact that we had both lived outside the country and viewed it through the lens of someone who could put it in a proper context," she said. "We could appreciate how extraordinarily wonderful America is, but also see that there's a world outside the United States." Jarrett could connect with Barack and Michelle, and she had a long pedigree in Chicago politics. Her grandfather was chairman of the Chicago Housing Authority, and she later ran a real estate management company that was the court-appointed receiver for the housing authority. She seemed to live at the intersection of policy and politics, and had a loyal friend's view of the Obamas. She was a natural sounding board when Obama hit a wall, as he often did, or struggled with a decision. When his self-reliance failed to come up with a solution, Obama often turned to a handful of friends, singular among them Valerie Jarrett.

The testing of Barack Obama was harsh but mostly out of sight in the first several months of his presidential campaign. To the outside world, he had vaulted into the top tier of candidates in early 2007, beating Hillary Clinton in early fund-raising and drawing a vast amount of media attention. But in private, the experience was painful, frustrating, even miserable. He missed his family, felt exhausted by his schedule, detested the repetition of events, and disdained the superficial debates and media attention. "He was shocked and depressed for the first four to six months," said David Axelrod, his chief strategist and friend. "He was like a man thrown into ice-cold water. If it wasn't for the money, we'd have been finished at the start, because the money gave us street cred. It was a shock: the fatigue, the intensity of it."

Obama was failing the test, and he knew it. As much as he had tried to understand what a campaign would be like, he had no idea how intense the attention would be. Every word, every gesture, every step was analyzed and scrutinized. "It's like a public colonoscopy," he told his friend Nesbitt. "It's more rigorous, more in-depth than I ever imagined." Technology made the examination even more painful. Every commentator's opinion was instantly and widely available, and the candidate couldn't help himself. "All of a sudden, you have access instantaneously to what everyone has said or written about you," Nesbitt said. "There was a point in the process where he decided that he had to limit how much of the press stuff that he paid attention to."

For those who warned him of the misery of a presidential campaign, there was an I-told-you-so feeling. Obama did not concede he might have been wrong to run in the first place. It was obvious from his attitude, his ambivalence. "Honestly, those first few months were really tough," said David Plouffe, the bluntest adviser in the early sessions about whether to run. "You can tell someone how brutal it is, but until you do it. . . . You get out of the first blush of excitement over the announcement. You're running around raising a lot of money, spending a lot of time in the early states, never seeing your family. I think there were times when he wondered if he made the right choice to run." Obama's senior aides had a running joke with him. You're in the middle of the lake now, they said. Gotta swim. But did he really want to go swimming? He was comfortable with his life and with himself; he didn't need to prove himself by winning the nomination. His traveling aides tried an alternative tack, as they spent several hours a day with a downbeat candidate. "Well, boss, isn't there anything that makes you feel good about being out campaigning?" asked Robert Gibbs, his communications director, on one flight to Iowa in May.

"Nothing," said Obama.

There was an awkward silence that followed, broken only by his body man, Reggie Love.

"If it's any consolation," said Reggie, "I'm having the time of my life."

Obama's remedy was cerebral, intellectual, detached: to study his own situation and divine some prescription for himself. "He challenged himself: I'm going to figure out how to be a good candidate, and that is the thing about Obama. You get a sense that he can do anything he puts his mind to," said Axelrod. "There's no problem too tough to solve, including, 'OK, I'm not a good candidate but I'm going to become one.' He observes and watches others and it was a remarkable thing to watch."

He needed to be a quick study. Even as his fund-raising was ahead of Clinton's, his personal performance lagged far behind. At a health care forum in Las Vegas just a month after he announced his presidential campaign, Obama and Clinton spoke back-to-back to an audience of progressives and service union members. Where Clinton spoke with conviction and earned an enthusiastic reaction, Obama meandered through platitudes and dull policy statements to little avail. He knew she had dominated the event and diminished his stature. "She looked like a president and I didn't," Obama told his aides afterward. "I'm not a very good candidate right now, but I will learn to be a good candidate. Just give me a little time here."

To escape the inanity of campaigning, Obama wanted more policy time, as if behind-the-scenes conversations with his aides would help him through the test. So his schedule changed to add more conference calls and meetings on energy policy or health care. "I think it was kind of restorative for him," said Plouffe.

Obama struggled to find a campaign style he was comfortable with, or even to communicate that style to his staff. His performances in the first TV debates were faltering, tentative, and unimpressive. Having stepped on the national stage in February 2007 with a big-bang announcement, he debated two months later with a whimper. At his first full debate, hosted by MSNBC in Orangeburg, South Carolina, Obama was asked how he would change the nation's military stance after another 9/11-style attack on two cities. "Well, the first thing we'd have to do is make sure that we've got an effective emergency response, something that this administration failed to do when we had a hurricane in New Orleans," Obama began. "And I think that we have to review how we operate in the event of not only a natural disaster, but also a terrorist attack. The second thing is to make sure that we've got good intelligence, A, to find out that we don't have other threats and attacks potentially out there, and B, to find out do we have any intelligence on who might have carried it out so that we can take potentially some action to dismantle that network. But what we can't do is then alienate the world community based on faulty intelligence, based on bluster and bombast."

Obama may have been right on the policy, but he was wrong on debate strategy. Bluster and bombast beat out emergency planning and global alienation. Both John Edwards and Hillary Clinton promised swift retaliation, and Clinton cited her own experience of 9/11.

Several answers later, Obama tried awkwardly to revisit his weak response by pivoting on a question about his personal efforts to protect the environment. After talking briefly about tree plantings, his daughters, and energy-efficient lightbulbs, he added these late, head-wrenching lines: "One thing that I do have to go back on, on this issue of terrorism. We have genuine enemies out there that have to be hunted down. Networks have to be dismantled. There is no contradiction between us intelligently using our military, and in some cases lethal force, to take out terrorists, and at the same time building the sort of alliances and trust around the world that has been so lacking over the last six years." Behind the scenes, Obama's aides knew their candidate was failing and admitted it was due to his own mind-set. "He had three debates in the general election of the Senate race," said Robert Gibbs. "Part of it is him not doing a lot of sixty-second-answer debates in the past. But part of it is that this is somebody who I think prides himself on believing that not every problem that we haven't solved in the past three decades can necessarily be solved naturally in a sixty-second answer."

The frustrations were mutual between the candidate and his staff, and neither side was content or confident with the other. In early June, his research and communications teams produced a press release that excoriated the Clintons for their support for Indian businesses and India's interests, tying their rivals' fund-raising to the poisonous issue of outsourcing jobs. The release was headlined "Hillary Clinton (D-Punjab)'s Personal Financial and Political Ties to India." "The Clintons have reaped significant financial rewards from their relationship with the Indian community, both in their personal finances and Hillary's campaign fundraising," it began. "Hillary Clinton, who is the co-chair of the Senate India Caucus, has drawn criticism from anti-offshoring groups for her vocal support of Indian business and unwillingness to protect American jobs. Bill Clinton has invested tens of thousands of dollars in an Indian bill payment company, while Hillary Clinton has taken tens of thousands from companies that outsource jobs to India. Workers who have been laid off in upstate New York might not think that her recent joke that she could be elected to the Senate seat in Punjab is that funny."

Obama found the press release even less funny. A few days later, he told reporters that it was "a dumb mistake," taking responsibility for it while also admitting that he had not reviewed the release. In private, he was furious with his own staff. "For a start, it was wrong," he told me. "If you're going to do that kind of thing, get it right. But my roommates in college were Indian and Pakistani, and I had very close friendships with them. I had to go and call some of my best friends and explain why my campaign was engaging in xenophobia. That was the most angry I've been in this campaign. I called people and said, 'If you are even going close to the line, you better ask me first.'" That morning, he woke early on a rainy day in South Carolina to read the story of the Punjab memo in the *New York Times*. He was tired and cranky for the long drive to a small town called Greenwood, where a small lady, a political activist, revived his spirits with an old civil rights chant: "Fired Up! Ready to Go!" For the remainder of the election, he would retell the story of how a simple chant lifted the mood between him and his staff.

The stress of a flatlining campaign began to wear down some of Obama's closest relationships. He was angry with David Axelrod for suggesting changes to his tired stump speech. By early summer, after several months of riffing off his announcement text, Obama's speech had grown unwieldy. "There were times when he was irritated," said Axelrod, "because he was out there killing himself and we were saying, 'Do you know, seventeen minutes into your speech you use this paragraph and it would be better if it were in the subjunctive.'" Obama's response was that they didn't know what it was like to be onstage. "Guys, it ain't easy out here," he replied.

The dispute was serious enough that they needed mediation from Marty Nesbitt. When Nesbitt talked to Obama, his friend was dismissive and annoyed. Nesbitt was surprised at how Obama seemed to doubt Axelrod's motives. "This dude loves you, man," Nesbitt said. "So you can't be reading there's another agenda, other than doing the right thing. You can be pissed, but you know Ax does not have an agenda except for your best interests. Disagree with him if you want. Tell him he's wrong, but you know he has no other agenda." Obama looked up at his friend and stopped his griping. Axelrod adored his boss enough to forgive him for the angry reaction and the dispute. "Part of being a candidate is that you're being poked and prodded and examined and scoped every minute of every day, and not just by your aides but by the press as well, and the political community. Anyone in their right mind would find that a little bit irritating, and he's certainly in his right mind," he said. "And part of it is that he wasn't going to be a trained-seal act. He needed to buy into what he was saying and he needed to feel it."

The stress and pressure encroached deep into the campaign in 2007, even as they held fast to their strategy of building patiently in Iowa. The national poll numbers were stuck almost twenty points behind Hillary Clinton, and his friends and donors thought he should spend some of his cash pile on national TV ads. The idea was nagging on Obama's mind, even as he knew that he had an Iowa-only strategy. "Tell me again why that's a bad idea," he asked his campaign manager, David Plouffe. By late summer, Obama asked Plouffe to run some numbers for him. One friend had suggested he could move his national polls by buying ads on African American TV shows. Plouffe did the math: if they doubled his support among African Americans, they would move all of one and a half points in the national polls. At around 13 percent of the population, there just weren't enough black voters to make a difference across the country. Plouffe was deeply troubled that Obama didn't seem to believe with all his heart that there was simply no alternative to beating Clinton in Iowa. He would wander around headquarters lamenting the candidate's lack of commitment. "He doesn't own Iowa yet," Plouffe said time and again. Obama felt the bad press was depressing morale and he needed to lift them back up. "Everybody is being questioned and the news is bad every day because the press is stuck in that groove, where they're looking for stuff every day that reinforces the story," he told me. "That creates tensions among staff. People can lose focus. People need to feel confident that we're going to pull this thing off."

The candidate took his regular summer escape in Martha's Vineyard, but his life and his campaign were stuck in the doldrums. For eight days, he vacationed in the East Chop corner of the island, along with Jarrett and Eric Whitaker, another close friend and doctor. The friends were like an extended family: Whitaker had also found a mentor in Jarrett's father, was a classmate of Nesbitt's wife, and later met Obama while playing basketball at Harvard. On the island together, they went on bike rides, whiled away days on the beach, and shared cookouts. Even with his Secret Service detail, nobody seemed to notice that Barack Obama was on the beach. His friends cared little for campaign talk, saying nothing about the election until he brought it up on their penultimate day, when he sat down with Michelle and Jarrett. Obama had spent every hour of the day with his wife and daughters, a blissful escape from his endless weeks of speeches in Iowa and fund-raising in big cities. Now he was heading back to a life of frustration. His donors were growing restive, he was bored with his own stump speech, and his poll numbers were stagnating at a double-digit distance behind Clinton's. He was concentrating on Iowa, but even there he was trailing in third place. African American voters were still wondering whether he was black enough, and the political pundits wondered whether he was finished. "He couldn't point to anything other than his instinct and his commitment to his strategy to prove that this was on the right track," said Jarrett. He knew what he wanted to say but he wasn't breaking through. Even inside his own campaign, he felt that his own voice wasn't being heard. What he really wanted was to have a seat at the table when he was traveling the country, and he wanted Jarrett to be that presence. She agreed, but later in the day she noticed he was unsettled again.

"You've already left, haven't you?" she said. "Where are you? You're not here anymore. You were so much fun. Now you have this distant look in your eye. Vacation's over?"

"Vacation's over."

September was more gloomy, even with Jarrett on the road alongside him. On Labor Day weekend, the *New York Times* set the tone of the media coverage in a story based on "interviews with dozens of Democrats"—a newspaper version of a focus group that was easily skewed by the sample or the reporter's views. The story stated that voters felt Obama lacked experience while Clinton was the most qualified to be president. In Iowa, Obama's crowds were small and Clinton seemed to have the momentum. "It wasn't good," said Jarrett. "He wasn't happy. He was working hard and feeling like he was losing traction. He'd been the underdog for a very long time at this point." Obama seemed restless; he wanted to improve his performance and his position. "How can I communicate better? How can I get people to see what I'm trying to show them?" he asked Jarrett. "How can they get to know me a little faster?"

The candidate's impatience was nothing compared with that of his donors. By October, many of his national finance committee—his biggest fund-raisers—were growing more vocal in their criticism of the candidate and their anger toward his aides. They wanted to know why nobody knew Obama yet, in spite of all the money they had raised. What did he have to show for all those millions? What was the point of a grassroots organization if it didn't close the gap in the polls? The candidate and his senior staff thought the only answer was to take the fund-raisers to Iowa, to show them firsthand what the strategy looked like on the ground. Some fund-raisers thought the session was a bad idea; the mood was sour and it was still a long way from the caucuses. Perhaps they could have a greater impact by meeting closer to the vote?

The concerns were well founded. Obama flew out of Chicago with Plouffe and Jarrett on the day a new *Des Moines Register* poll showed him trailing in third place, seven points behind Clinton and one behind Edwards. "It was not an opportune time to hold a finance committee meeting," admitted Plouffe. The conversation on the flight to Iowa was blunt. "They're really angry down there," said Jarrett. "They're grumpy. They're frustrated. Just be prepared: you're walking into the lion's den."

Obama himself was frustrated at his own failings. "I have to figure out how to connect with them," he said. "I'm not connecting with them. It's a safe and I've almost got the combination of how to get it open."

His donors were mostly clueless about Iowa and the campaign's strategy. Many had no idea about how a caucus worked, how it was different from a primary, and how voters had to stand up and be counted in a room with their neighbors. Jarrett herself had never been to Iowa and never seen a caucus. Few had any concept of the community-organizing model that they were helping to pay for. For a couple of days, they joined the ground game, knocking on doors and making phone calls from campaign offices. They attended caucus training sessions, but instead of pretending to vote for candidates, they debated the merits of rival breakfast cereals. They had staff briefings on strategy in Iowa and the other early states. For the high-rolling crowd, more used to cocktail parties and cutting large checks, it was a novel experience to be treated like a young volunteer.

Gathered in a Des Moines museum, the fund-raisers were still unhappy when the candidate walked in to talk to them. The newcomers to political fund-raising were still anxiety-ridden about the campaign's prospects. Some of the veterans of past campaigns felt they were struggling, but no more so than John Kerry had four years earlier. For his part, Obama knew that he had to project a combination of sympathy and confidence to turn them around. "I know you guys are unhappy," he began.

I know you've been down here knocking on doors for me. You've given me money. You believed in a candidate that in all likelihood would never win. Yet you were there for me early on. But I never told you this was going to be easy. Guys, if you thought this was going to be easy, you must not have been listening to me. This was always an underdog campaign but it was based on the idea that we had to create a new kind of politics and that means you guys need to stick with me and have confidence that we've got a game plan and we're executing it. I want to remind you of the fact that even though I gave a great speech back in 2004, I'm running against the most powerful person in the Democratic Party who has name recognition everywhere. I was the unlikely one, remember? This is supposed to be hard. But I just want you to know that I'm going to be there. If you need me, grab my hand. I'll hold your hand. I'll support you through this. This is going to be a tough, tough battle. If you stick with me, and you have confidence in me, I promise you I will not disappoint you.

Whenever he retold the story of how he got fired up and ready to go, Obama liked to say it showed the power of a single voice to change a room, a city, or a nation. In Des Moines in early October, in front of his donors, Obama changed a room and he changed himself. He knew it was now or never, and rose to the moment. "He had to excel at that point," said David Plouffe. "It was just getting closer."

He began to work harder, to focus on Iowa like his political life depended on it. He asked to make more calls, not less, as he had sometimes complained before. He followed up with his staffers in Iowa about the state and local officials whom he had courted earlier. Were they for him or not? He wanted to talk to the hundreds of precinct captains who would control the caucus process. "He was beginning to own it," said Plouffe. "He really wanted it and got it: 'That precinct captain could determine my fate.' You can talk till you're blue in the face, as I did. But it doesn't matter until the candidate gets it. I'm not sure Hillary Clinton ever got to that point." The harder he worked in Iowa, the more he revived his spirits. There was a drive and confidence on the ground, among his young organizers and volunteers, that made him believe again. "Our staff in Iowa was remarkable," he told me. "They were like this island unto themselves. It was almost as if they didn't read the newspapers, other than the *Des Moines Register,* the *Sioux City Journal,* and the *Cedar Rapids Gazette.* That's all they cared about. They were so focused and it was invigorating to go into Iowa and see them. Because even as all these reporters were saying how we were toast, you'd go into this office and there was so much energy and so many volunteers, and people working so hard, that you thought, 'You know what? These kids might just pull us over the top.'"

Obama was cracking the combination safe of a presidential campaign. The sensation of failure in that first year, along with the real failure of New Hampshire, unlocked something deep within. Perhaps it bared "the steel in his spine" that Joe Biden witnessed as a rival candidate in the year before the primaries began. Or perhaps it simply played into the almost classical myths of a presidential contest: the political equivalent of the labors of Hercules or the travels of Perseus. The notion that somewhere in the snows of New Hampshire, or the cornfields of Iowa, there are tests of strength and wit, or a many-headed monster to slay. Either way, the summer doldrums taught him the importance of self-improvement and holding his team together, no matter how intense the outside pressures. And the defeat of New Hampshire taught him the power of demonstrating his toughness before the next round of failure. "We really hadn't gone through the rigors of a campaign that would prepare us for the next phase," he told me.

The next phase was indeed another failure. But a failure that—unlike New Hampshire—served to underscore their broader strategy. Nevada had never staged an early presidential contest, and its caucus system was amateurishly organized and often chaotic. The campaign tried to replicate its Iowa strategy out west, but Vegas wasn't Des Moines and the rural areas looked like barren lands. An hour east of Reno, in the small town of Fallon, a young organizer tried to use the old Iowa methods to rev up the large crowd in a junior high school. He had only shown up a few days after Iowa's caucuses, barely a week earlier. But when he asked how many of the two thousand supporters had caucused before, just four hands went up. A sign on the wall said Yes We Can, but when someone tried to start the chant "Fired Up! Ready to Go!" it fizzled like the audience wave that followed. Obama had won the support of the Culinary Workers Union, a major force in the hotels and casinos of Las Vegas. But that was in a city whose business traded in celebrity, and there were no Democrats more famous than the Clintons. "This is so fucked up," said David Axelrod in a gym in Reno, the day before the Nevada vote. "I don't mean to diss caucuses like the Clintons, but we don't know who is going to show up. We know how many pledges we have, but who knows?"

On caucus day, Obama started his morning backstage at the Mirage, a few hours before voting was to start at several hotel locations on the strip. Through a plain door on the gaudy casino floor, down a long hallway, the candidate was searching for votes somewhere between Uniform Central—where the employees picked up their vaudeville work clothes—and Risk Management. He posed for pictures in the staff cafeteria and walked through the kitchens, past giant sixty-quart stockpots of clam chowder and minestrone soup that bubbled and splashed across the wet floor. In Iowa, he talked at length with teachers about No Child Left Behind, and with farmers about intensive hog farming. In Vegas, he talked football at the Mirage, saying he was supporting the Green Bay Packers because he liked Brett Favre, its legendary and aging quarterback. "Brett Favre is almost as old as me," Obama said. "I have to root for him. You got to root for the old guy."

Democracy, Vegas-style, was a scrimmage. At the Bellagio, next door to Obama's favorite hotel on the strip, Caesars Palace, the caucus was unruly before anyone entered the vast ballroom with its chandeliers and floral carpet. Along the marble-tiled hallways, Clinton supporters staged a noisy chant, prompting charges of intimidation from Obama volunteers. Workers stood in their uniforms, holding boxed lunches branded with their casino names on the side. Inside the ballroom, the workers split along political and racial lines. On one side, a group of mostly African Americans wore Obama stickers; on the other, Clinton's supporters were mostly Latino women. Reporters were penned inside a rectangle at some distance, but the rival groups still managed to chant at the TV cameras. Onstage at the front of the room, in front of a bloodred velvet curtain, supporters jumped up and started waving signs at each other. An Obama supporter ripped up a Clinton sign. "It's organized chaos," said one Bellagio employee. But it looked more like disorganized chaos. In a room of 495 voters, just 10 were for Edwards and they faced a screaming contest as the rival groups tried to peel them away. Some tugged at their arms and jostled, while several Clinton supporters drifted out of the room. "Please don't leave," said the state party official trying to chair the chaos. Standing at the back, Obama's foreign policy adviser Greg Craig looked at the scene in horror. He held both hands to his blanched cheeks as the results came in: 271 to Clinton, 191 to Obama. A huge roar rose from the Clinton side of the ballroom, and several of her supporters began dancing.

The show played out across Nevada, as both sides alleged multiple irregularities and assorted wrongdoings. Doors were locked early, before voters could enter, and caucus chairs were seized by partisan volunteers who intimidated their rivals. Democracy was indeed a mirage in Nevada. Obama lost the caucus but won more delegates by beating Clinton in rural areas. Even in defeat, his campaign proved they had a strategy to win the nomination: by winning delegates, not headlines.

The defeat in New Hampshire, less than two weeks earlier, had already steeled the candidate and his campaign against other setbacks.

"I'm not saying I wanted it to happen that way, because by that time we were already exhausted," Obama told me of his first failure. "There was this sense that the math here could play itself out, that this was a long slog. But there was immediately in my heart this sense of 'You know what? This is a useful corrective.' And it made the whole team more sober and more realistic, but just as determined." Nevada was where the long slog began. "I think the proudest moment of my campaign is us slogging through after that disappointment," he said. "And then losing Nevada, at least the popular vote, but drawing that small satisfaction of getting more delegates. That's the point where Plouffe, the mad mathematical genius, sort of really made clear this whole fact that it's all about the delegates. It was coming out of Nevada where I think everybody figured out this could be long, and it's going to be a delegate fight, and we better plan this out in those terms."

There were other stumbles and disappointments, both personal and political. But Obama had already grown into a patient and disciplined renegade, just like Gandhi, sitting serenely beside his spinning wheel, in Obama's beloved photo. Nothing seemed to shake him after his personal crisis of the first summer in Iowa and the dramatic defeat in New Hampshire. He had a strategy that required a singular focus and some tweaking, but little more. He had an enormous reserve of self-belief that required hard work and humility to temper. But that wasn't hard to find in failure. Obama stuck to his strategy on Super Tuesday, losing several big states like California and New York, but securing more delegates overall by winning smaller states—like Georgia and Idaho—by huge margins. He grew into a methodical insurgent.

Sometimes, the strategy failed him. A month later, in Ohio, Obama spent far too much time and money hunting votes and delegates among an older Democratic population, where Clinton was far stronger. Texas had a large concentration of younger voters and an arcane system of both primary and caucus votes that Obama's team mastered to secure more delegates. A win in either state could have delivered the psychological knockout blow to finish the contest. Instead he lost both. Waiting for him on the other side was the long, six-week contest in Pennsylvania, where the demographic makeup of Democrats—older and whiter than in most other states—was an almost impossible challenge. "Not winning Texas was a real letdown," said David Plouffe. "Something that we mishandled, because we should have focused much more on Texas than we did on Ohio. We should have just said, You know what, we're going to go two-thirds, one-third. That was one of the darker nights of the campaign." The next morning was even darker, as Plouffe and Obama shared a van ride with Michelle, who threatened not to return to the campaign trail until they had come up with a new strategy. "Not a very nice ride," Plouffe recalled with a nervous laugh. "I think she was pissed at both of us. He and I were partners there."

Obama himself was deeply disappointed, but his reaction back at headquarters in Chicago remained calm and measured. He toured the cubicles of gloomy younger staffers, urging them to keep their chins up, then walked into a conference room for a postmortem with his senior staff. He was carrying a handwritten list of observations about what went wrong and what went right. "I think it might be a good idea to do some focus groups and find out what went wrong," he told his senior staff. "But I'm only interested in finding out what we can do better. I'm not interested in assigning blame. I want to figure out what lessons we can learn and not make the same mistakes again." The candidate wanted to talk about how they had burned through their resources—their time and money—and held too many rallies rather than more human-scaled events. He had a list of things he wanted to do: to give speeches on race and faith, and sit down for an exhaustive interview on his relationship to his indicted donor Tony Rezko.

He started by critiquing his own mistakes, then went around the table asking each staffer for their input. "We rise or fall together," he said. "I'm not pointing fingers at any single person because we all share responsibility." Encouraging his aides to speak up, he called on Dan Pfeiffer, his deputy communications director, for his thoughts. Pfeiffer was suffering from a high fever and had barely slept the night before. "Frankly, sir," he said through his haze, "I think Hillary worked harder." Speaking more bluntly than normal, he said she had staged more events and looked like she wanted to win. The candidate bristled. Through the rest of the meeting, he prefaced his comments by repeating Pfeiffer's thoughts. "Well, Pfeiffer says I'm not working hard enough," he said.

At the end of the two-hour session, he stood up and began to walk out. Then he turned around, looked at the somber faces of his senior staff, and added one more thing. "I'm not yelling at you, and I'm not screaming. Although for twenty million bucks for two primaries, and the results we got, I could," he said, laughing. "But I'm not."

Failure gave him the time to correct himself and his organization, and it gave voters the time to see if he was for real. Obama needed the long primary season as much as the voters, no matter how painful and protracted it was. "Some people suggested we get into the race late as a surprise, but it would never have worked because there were so many questions about this guy," said Plouffe. "People began to see him as a nominee and as a president. I think the people of Iowa needed a whole year to kick the tires, as he'd say." The candidate's friends urged him to remain patient. Nesbitt had just read a book called *The Social Atom* by a physicist who saw mathematical patterns in social behavior, especially how people copied success in others. Nesbitt thought his friend had a viral effect that simply needed time to overwhelm the Clintons. "I just think it's a matter of physics," Nesbitt told Obama as the primaries wore on. "That's the question. But there's no way for us to really know the answer except to play it out."

Obama's early failures became part of his defensive shield, a guard against complacency and a tool that could help him attain victory. Later, as the general election drew to a close, and Obama seemed assured of success, he warned his crowds not to kick back. On his final trip to New Hampshire in mid-October, the candidate stood onstage at a large farm market in Londonderry. Behind him were the last orange and red leaves of the New England fall; in front of him were giant crates of pumpkins and big bags of apples. Yet his thoughts were still focused on last winter. "For those who are getting a little cocky, I have got two words for you: New Hampshire," he said to scattered chuckles. "I learned right here, with the help of my great friend and supporter Hillary Clinton, that you cannot pay too much attention to polls. We've got to keep making our case for change. We've got to keep fighting for every single vote. We've got to keep running through the finish line. This election is too important to take anything for granted. The future *you* seek, the future we seek for our children, is too important to let up now. The time for change has come!"

FIVE

BARACK X

Obama awoke in Atlanta and headed for church. It was the Sunday before Martin Luther King Day, and less than twenty-four hours since his defeat in Nevada. After the warmth and excess of Las Vegas, Atlanta was an abrupt change: a bone-chilling morning after a rare snowfall. Gone was the gaudy glare of Caesars Palace and the Bellagio. Now he was driving past Thelma's Rib Shack and Cruisin' Fried Chicken, past four beauty parlors, two funeral homes, and one Masonic supplies store, to a modern redbrick church with a huge white, vaulted interior. This wasn't any old house of worship. It was the new sanctuary of Ebenezer Baptist Church, close to the original church where King preached, a block away from his place of birth and across the street from his final resting place. "Martin Luther King Jr.," read the signs on the street, "A Day On Not A Day Off."

Inside, in front of the large organ pipes, the choir—mostly older men and women, almost all wearing kente cloth scarves—sang the hymn known as the African American national anthem: "Lift every voice and sing / 'Til earth and heaven ring / Ring with the harmonies of liberty." The choir included a soloist who sang at Dr. King's funeral forty years ago; in the audience, as she was every Sunday, sat King's elder sister, Christine King Farris. Barack Obama, carrying his Bible, walked toward five heavy wooden chairs cushioned with purple velvet. Beside him was

Raphael Warnock, Ebenezer's young pastor who had worked at historic churches such as Abyssinian Baptist Church in New York and Sixth Avenue Baptist Church in Birmingham. The pastor looked out at the overflow crowd and smiled. "I think somebody came to have church today," he said. As the choir sang more hymns, and the bell ringers performed, the candidate closed his eyes in what was either deep prayer or a light sleep.

"I've got a feeling that you might want to hear somebody else," Warnock began, "but I am the pastor of the church. I will preach if I want to." So he preached about Hebrews 11, the chapter about faith in things unseen. And he spoke of King's speech on the eve of his assassination, of reaching the mountaintop and seeing the promised land. "I just dropped by this morning to say maybe forty years after his death, it's time to claim the promise. Maybe there's something about forty years," he explained, invoking the children of Israel wandering the wilderness. "After going around and around and around the same old mountain, maybe it's time to finish the job. Maybe it's time to claim the promise. I don't know about you, but I'm tired of going around and around and around the mountain."

Warnock seemed to sense that biblical references might not move his congregation to vote for the candidate seated next to him. So he introduced Obama with something more personal. He wanted them to hear all the candidates, because so much was at stake, but this candidate was special. "We had to fight, bleed, and die just to be able to vote. Now we can select presidents. And now with credibility and intelligence and power, we can *run* for president," the pastor said to cheers and hollers. "So I know where I stand. This is Ebenezer. Giants have stood here. So we don't take this pulpit lightly. We invited this brother because he's committed and brilliant. He has a spiritual foundation. And he is the embodiment of the American dream, regardless of whether you are a Democrat, Republican, or an independent, when you think about the long history of America, Barack Obama makes us proud. All Americans. All Americans. All of us proud that this brother can run. Because of Dr. King, he is here. Because of Dr. King, he is here. And that ought to make all Americans, all Americans, proud."

More than an hour after the service began, and after yet another hymn, the candidate stepped up to the pulpit. He was now the leader of the Joshua generation of the post–civil rights era, and he told the story of Joshua at Jericho's walls. The lesson of Jericho, he said, was that of the early days of the civil rights movement: to march together. "Because before Memphis and the mountaintop; before the bridge in Selma and the march on Washington; before Birmingham and the beatings; the fire hoses and the loss of those four little girls; before there was King the icon and his magnificent dream, there was King the young preacher and a people who found themselves suffering under the yoke of oppression," he said. "And on the eve of the bus boycotts in Montgomery, at a time when many were still doubtful about the possibilities of change, a time when there were those in the black community who not only mistrusted each other, but mistrusted themselves, King inspired with words not of anger, but of an urgency, a fierce urgency, that still speaks to us today: 'Unity,' he said, 'is the great need of the hour.' Unity is the great need of the hour. Unity is how we shall overcome."

The church echoed softly with the sounds of *yes* and *uh-huh*. He didn't need to say that he, too, was a young African American leader, not yet an icon, who faced mistrust from the community. He didn't need to say that he spoke not of anger, like some older politicians, but of urgency—a fierce urgency—and unity. He was drawing a line between King and himself, between the civil rights movement and his campaign, between African Americans and other minorities, between blacks and whites.

Other candidates might come to Ebenezer to pander on the Sunday before Martin Luther King Day, but not this one. He set down a challenge to anyone who wanted to join him, including his audience at Ebenezer. "It's not easy to stand in somebody else's shoes," he warned, to echoes of *no* from the pews. "It's not easy to see past our own differences. We've all encountered this in our own lives. But what makes it even more difficult is that we have a politics in this country that seeks to drive us apart—that puts up walls between us." His target included his own community and its strains of homophobia, anti-Semitism, and anti-immigrant prejudice. But he was also speaking about his own party and its primaries. "Every day, our politics fuels and exploits this kind of division across all races and regions, across gender and party," he said. "It is played out on television. It is sensationalized by the media. Last week, it crept into the campaign for president, with charges and countercharges that served to obscure the issues instead of illuminating the critical choices we face as a nation. . . . We can no longer afford to build ourselves up by tearing each other down. We can no longer afford to traffic in lies or fear or hate. It is the poison that we must purge from our politics, the wall that we must tear down before the hour is too late." Instead of overcoming segregation, the Joshua generation needed to overcome more subtle divisions of racial prejudice and divisive politics.

His campaign wasn't just a way to get him elected president; it was a way to bring people together. And they were coming together by sharing stories, finding common ground, imagining themselves in another's shoes: the way he had organized in Chicago and legislated in Springfield. The candidate ended with a tale of unity from his own campaign, about two supporters who were sitting down to exchange their personal stories—the organizing principle behind his remarkable effort to recruit thousands of volunteers. "There is a young, twenty-three-year-old white woman named Ashley Baia who organizes for our campaign in Florence, South Carolina. Ashley has been working to organize mostly black folks. She's been doing it since the beginning of the campaign, and the other day she had set up a roundtable discussion where everyone around was telling their story about who they were and why they were there," he said.

Ashley's story was that when she was nine, her mother got cancer and lost her job. To save money to pay for medical bills, Ashley ate mustard and relish sandwiches for a year. So Ashley told her roundtable that she joined the campaign to help millions of children like her, whose families had no health care. Ashley went around the room getting everyone to share their stories. "And finally at the end of this discussion, they come to this elderly black man. He's been sitting there quietly the whole time, hasn't been saying a word," Obama explained.

And Ashley asks him why is he there. And he does not bring up a specific issue. He does not say health care or the economy. He doesn't talk about the Iraq war; he doesn't say anything about education. He does not say that he was there because he likes Barack Obama, or he's proud of the possibility of the first African American president. He simply says to everyone in the room, "I am here because of Ashley. I am here because of this young girl, and the fact that she's willing to fight for what she believes in. And that reminds me that I still have some fight left in me, and I'm going to stand up for what I believe in." Now by itself, that single moment of recognition between that young white girl and that old black man, that's not enough to change the country. By itself, it's not enough to give health care to the sick, or jobs to the jobless, or education to our children. But it is where we begin. It is why I believe that the walls in that room began to shake at that moment.

To his critics, this was just a bunch of Kumbaya. The Gullah spiritual from South Carolina was fine for church, but did it have any place in politics? For the candidate and his supporters, the answer was simple. When it came to racial politics, the power of the shared story, of walking in another's shoes, was strong enough to recruit volunteers and move a crowd. Obama was doing something more powerful than running for president. He was inspiring and narrating a new chapter of the great American civil rights story. He was no longer separate because of his immigrant father or his education. He was the organizer in chief of a new movement and the icon of the campaign.

At the end of his speech, the congregation linked arms and sang "We Shall Overcome." Obama walked outside to greet another couple of hundred supporters listening to him on a single loudspeaker on that frigid day. He walked across the street, lay a wreath at the grave of Martin Luther King and Coretta Scott King, and left for South Carolina.

It was easy to forget how unusual Obama's message was for a presidential candidate, until you recalled an earlier candidate who had just suffered his own thumping loss in New Hampshire and traveled to another religious institution at the start of his South Carolina campaign. Eight years earlier, after losing his New Hampshire primary by nineteen points, George W. Bush staged his first event in the South at Bob Jones University in Greenville, South Carolina. At the time, the evangelical university imposed rules against interracial dating and had a long history of issuing anti-Catholic statements. Speaking inside the auditorium lined with a deep red carpet, Bush made no reference to either controversy. He didn't call for inclusion or mutual understanding; he didn't challenge the prejudices of his own audience. At a press conference afterward, reporters asked if he agreed with the university's racial policies. "No," he answered simply. As he put his arm around his wife, Laura, he explained more generally, "It's a different world down here. It's a state that embraces conservative values."

* * *

No matter what happened later, Obama was never assured of a warm embrace by African Americans, or any other kind of American, based on race alone. He shared little with his own community by way of family history, geography, and political style. His memoir revolved around something and someone not present in his childhood: his African father and his African American identity. Even that was a partial view, obscuring the role of his mother and grandparents: the white family that raised him. He was obviously black, yet he grew up with a white perspective. He was American, yet he grew up with an international perspective. He was a Democrat who sought to understand the Republican perspective. He was a moderate who spoke the language of radical change, and a progressive who spoke in moderate tones.

Given his novelty on the national stage, it was easy for his opponents to raise doubts about his identity. Given his race, it was even easier. Voters could only guess at the true nature of any politician and how they would perform once in office. But how could they guess at the true nature of this African American politician? He fit no template of other black figures. He didn't sound like Jesse Jackson or Al Sharpton—there was no rush to play the racism card—yet he spoke compellingly about civil rights. He wasn't an entertainer, an actor, or a sports star, yet his celebrity was widespread.

For many supporters, the X factor was attractive, even inspiring. Obama represented a new generation, a break with the past in black and white politics, and a chance to heal the nation's wounds, whether racial or political. For many others, the X factor was unsettling, threatening, bound up with the dark side of racial politics. He was radical, foreign, Muslim, black. He hated America like his pastor, the Reverend Jeremiah Wright, or wanted to bomb its government like his acquaintance Bill Ayers. He was a modern-day Malcolm X.

It was all too easy to stoke up those latent fears in some Americans. As early as mid-March 2007, only one month after Obama launched his campaign, Hillary Clinton's senior strategist, Mark Penn, identified what he called a "lack of American roots" as a key weakness that could sink Obama. "All of these articles about his boyhood in Indonesia and his life in Hawaii are geared towards showing his background is diverse, multicultural and putting that in a new light," Penn wrote. "Save it for 2050. It also exposes a very strong weakness for him—his roots to basic American values and culture are at best limited. I cannot imagine America

electing a president during a time of war who is not at his center fundamentally American in his thinking and in his values." Penn's advice was
to use the word *American* as much as possible and include the flag in as
many ways as possible.

Obama's multiple identities unsettled people on all sides, starting
with the group that should have been his base: African Americans. The
early questions raised by some black liberals were little different from the
ones raised at the end by white conservatives: who is Barack Obama and
does he share our views? They wanted to know where his allegiances lay,
and whether he was really serving another set of interests. The questions
began at the very beginning. On the day Obama launched his campaign
in Springfield, Illinois, Tavis Smiley of PBS was staging his annual State
of the Black Union conference in Hampton, Virginia. Onstage, Cornel
West, the bombastic Princeton professor, was eviscerating the new candidate.

> Look, Obama is a very decent, brilliant, charismatic brother. There's
> no doubt about that. The problem is, is that he's got folk who are
> talking to him who warrant our distrust. Precisely because we know
> that him going to Springfield the same day brother Tavis has set this
> up for a whole *year*—we already know then that him coming out
> *there* is not fundamentally about us. It's about somebody else. He's
> got large numbers of white brothers and sisters who have got fears
> and anxieties and concerns, and he's got to speak to them in such a
> way that he holds us at arm's length enough to say he loves us, but
> doesn't get too close to scare them up. So he's walking this
> tightrope, you see what I mean? So my attitude is this: my criteria is
> the same. I don't care whether you're running for office, or running
> down the street. My criteria is fundamental. I want to know how
> deep is your love for the people? What kind of courage have you
> manifested in the stances that you have? And what are you willing to
> *sacrifice* for? That's the fundamental question. I don't care what
> color you are. You see, you can't take black people for granted, just
> 'cause you're black.

A few days later, West's phone rang in his office, shortly after class
had ended. It was Barack Obama. "I just want to clarify things and give
you a sense of where I stand," the candidate said. Obama talked about
justice and freedom in the modern era, about his record in Springfield of

expanding health care and helping ex-prisoners move back into the community. "Now there are going to be a number of things I disagree with you on," he warned.

"That's fine," said West. "There will be a number of things I disagree with you on. You're running for president and I'm out there telling the truth. But my fundamental concern is this Shakespeare line: 'to thine own self be true.'"

West wanted to know how Obama would extend the legacy of Martin Luther King Jr. But he really wanted reassurance about how the candidate was different. He was troubled by a line in Obama's breakthrough speech at the 2004 convention in Boston. "Through hard work and perseverance, my father got a scholarship to study in a magical place, America, that shone as a beacon of freedom and opportunity to so many who had come before him," Obama had said.

"That's a Christopher Columbus experience," West told him. "There are some wonderful people in the country. But it has a dark side and a light side. It's hard for someone who came out of slavery and Jim Crow to call it a magical place. There's nothing wrong with that. You've got to be true to yourself, but I have to be true to myself as well. It's a different perspective. Someone like myself must learn from first-generation voluntary immigrants. And voluntary immigrants must learn from people like myself."

A few weeks later, they met at the Mayflower hotel in Washington, D.C., where they talked about the state of the campaign. West was critical of Obama's aides, especially David Axelrod, questioning their progressive credentials. West had preferred John Edwards and his fight against poverty. Until he spoke to the author Toni Morrison, who reminded him that Obama had not been running for president as long as Edwards. What West wanted to hear was some bold talk about racism, like Jesse Jackson or Al Sharpton. He never heard it, yet he still came away satisfied. "He has a different style to Reverend Sharpton and Reverend Jackson, but he wants to speak about racism in his own way, and it can be effective," he said later. Obama reassured West enough that the firebrand signed up to his campaign as an unpaid adviser.

Cornel West was not unique. Whether the community suspected his allegiances or his alien perspective, the result was the same: Obama was lagging Clinton by twenty-four points among black Democrats in the fall before voting began. The candidate blamed his poor polling on his status as a newcomer. "I have not been in national politics very long," he told me in his Senate office. "But for many people I was an unknown commodity, so as certain stories circulated about me or what my priorities were or where I came from, not surprisingly people were willing to give credence to some of those assumptions. So with Cornel, it was just a matter of calling him up, introducing myself, and having a conversation. In some ways, that's a metaphor for what this campaign is about. Me introducing myself and having a conversation and trying to cut through the noise that's created by political opponents, or media that's looking for a good story, or my own fumbles and gaffes."

That was not the full story and he knew it. There was a temptation to set aside his background and identity as he tried to become a presidential candidate. In his announcement speech in Springfield, he barely referenced racial challenges in America, talking only of the historic achievements of Lincoln and the civil rights movement. Even then, he placed them in a uniquely patriotic context. "We welcomed immigrants to our shores, we opened railroads to the west, we landed a man on the moon, and we heard a King's call to let justice roll down like water, and righteousness like a mighty stream," he said. West was imploring him to remember what made him different, while his campaign to date had been focused on finding common ground. The challenge of doing both was a demanding one, as the candidate admitted. "This is a very improbable candidacy, it's fair to say," Obama told me, slowing down his words to measure every phrase with precision. "And for me to win, it's important that those qualities that got me into politics in the first place, those values that led me to become a community organizer or a civil rights attorney, a passion for justice and fairness, that those attributes come through. And if I start sounding like everybody else, if I'm just another Washington politician, then there's no reason for people to choose me as opposed to people who have been in Washington longer and play that particular game better than I do. So maintaining my voice through this process is critical. And it can be a difficult task. There are a lot of forces at work designed to homogenize candidates and there's a premium placed on risk avoidance and not making mistakes. What I'm trying to do is say what I think and not be governed by a fear of making mistakes. But that means I will make mistakes."

★ ★ ★

West was correct in at least one part of his analysis: Obama viewed America as something of an astonished immigrant. He shared the Columbus experience, remembering vividly his first trip to the continental United States around his eleventh birthday. He and his immediate family—his mother, grandmother, and two-year-old sister—spent three weeks traveling across the country by bus and car. His mother didn't drive, and his grandmother had cataracts. So the young Barry, as his family called him at the time, sat in the front seat with his grandmother when it got dark outside. Staying at roadside hotels like Howard Johnson's, they drove from Seattle to Montana, where he saw a buffalo and asked to get out. He walked up to the huge animal and got within twenty feet of it, before his mother screamed at him, "Barry, get back in the car." Another motorist, in his mid-twenties, stopped and tried to get closer; the buffalo charged and almost trampled him. Later he saw snow for the first time, and again stopped the car to run out. "It was all muddy, but I made a snowball," he recalled.

They drove south toward Arizona, taking in Wyoming along the way. "You realize how amazing this country is," he said. "I think Americans take it for granted. But we ended up driving across Yellowstone and it's amazing." Then they journeyed across to Kansas, where his mother grew up, and east to Chicago, where he would ultimately raise his own family. "We went to the Field Museum and I saw shrunken heads, one of them with red hair," he said. "I was eleven years old. I thought it was really cool."

His perspective on America was a wide-eyed one, the result of a childhood in Indonesia and Hawaii. Even in his conflicted teenage years, Obama grew up with a certain innocence: Hawaii was an island insulated from many of the worst racial problems. Yet he was also distanced from more positive influences, from community and mentors. Inside his family, he was both protected and isolated as he grew aware of his own racial inheritance. He was deeply alienated at times, yet he never fully rebelled from the adults who raised him, even as he sought out others who could fill the gaps in his own story. With his mother away from home, doing fieldwork in Indonesia, and his father totally absent from his life, Barry lived with his grandparents but kept himself apart. "Away from my mother, away from my grandparents, I was engaged in a fitful interior struggle," he later wrote. "I was trying to raise myself to be a black man in America, and beyond the given of my appearance, no one around me seemed to know exactly what that meant."

Basketball helped, along with his hoop-playing buddies and some of his grandfather's friends. Stanley Dunham played cards and drank with several older African American men, and by chance one of them fitted squarely into the pantheon of African American writers he was exploring. Frank Marshall Davis was a largely forgotten figure in Hawaii, but he was once a leading black activist and writer of the 1930s and 1940s—a contemporary and friend of Richard Wright, Margaret Walker, Langston Hughes, and Paul Robeson. Growing up in Kansas, Davis was nearly lynched by a group of schoolchildren when he was just five years old. As an adult, he worked as a journalist and poet, and was a strong advocate for racial justice in Chicago. His political writings, on civil rights and labor issues, made him the target of a McCarthyite denunciation by the House Un-American Activities Committee. He later moved to Hawaii with his second wife, who was white.

By the time the young Barry met Davis, he was an eccentric but engaging figure, sporting a large Afro, inviting all comers into his run-down home in Waikiki to talk, drink, and listen to jazz. "I was intrigued by old Frank, with his books and whiskey breath and the hint of hard-earned knowledge behind the hooded eyes," wrote Obama. It was around this time that Obama started exploring black literature—Wright, Hughes, DuBois, Baldwin, and Malcolm X—as he wrestled with what he called the anguish and doubt of African American identity.

Then, one day, a racially charged argument erupted between his grandparents over a black panhandler who scared his grandmother. His reaction was to bridge the divide: to agree with his grandfather that his grandmother's racial attitudes were troubling, and to empathize with his grandmother's fears. Internally, however, he felt torn. "Never had they given me reason to doubt their love; I doubted if they ever would," he wrote. "And yet I knew that men who might easily have been my brothers could still inspire their rawest fears."

Obama sought out Davis for advice, visiting with the poet, sharing some whiskey, and retelling the story about the panhandler. Davis told him that his grandmother was right to be scared, that his grandfather didn't really know the African American mind, and that "black people have a reason to hate." In an instant, at least in his memory, Obama understood that he was on his own in life, distant even from the people he loved most. "The earth shook under my feet, ready to crack open at any moment," he wrote. "I stopped, trying to steady myself, and knew for the first time that I was utterly alone."

Utterly alone but not wholly divorced from his family. Davis did not teach him to hate, but to understand both sides: the fear and the loathing. In that sense, he sounded like a more pessimistic version of Obama's mother. For it was his mother who taught him the importance of seeing the world from the perspective of others, albeit with a Kumbaya idealism that was born in a pre-1968 world. "She was a sixties teenager and in the early sixties it was a time of unabashed, pretty simply etched idealism," said Obama's half sister Maya. "Why can't we just get along? There's real beauty in that, but I don't think it necessarily recognizes and understands the real complexities of bridge building. She certainly felt like at the core everybody was the same. She believed in equality, that every culture and religion had something important to contribute." Obama found his mother's idealism both endearing and annoying, especially as he grew more independent and withdrawn as a student in New York. It was at Columbia that Obama turned his back on his childhood name of Barry and reverted to his birth name of Barack. And it was in New York where his mother took him to watch the Brazilian movie *Black Orpheus*—one of her favorites shortly before she met his father. Obama's reaction was one of almost teenage embarrassment: he became irritated by her simplistic views of race, and distanced himself even more.

Obama had to figure out his identity for himself, and the solution came partly from within his family, and partly as a reaction to his family. In that sense, he was like any other older teenager and young man—but for the complexities of his family life and racial identity. "In many ways, in terms of male role models, Barack was on his own," said Maya. "I think he had to forge his own path. He got pieces from Gramps and his own father, and he may have gotten pieces from my father. But I think in the end he had to decide for himself what it means to be a man. There were few people that he could go to for satisfying answers to his questions about identity and race. It wasn't until he went to New York and transferred to Columbia at the age of twenty that he began to make stronger strides toward understanding what it meant to be a black man in American society."

Obama wanted to correct his mother's liberal idealism, to teach her a lesson about how he was different and about the realities of modern life for African Americans. "I do remember that there were some years where I think I was trying to find my own place and rebelling or pushing away from her and my grandparents in the way that teenagers do, probably even up until my first couple of years in college," he told me. "She was coming back to the States and now she's got a black teenager who is identifying himself more with the African American community. And she suddenly notices that the African American community isn't feeling warm and fuzzy about race relations. That there are tensions that she'd missed out on because she was living in Indonesia in the black power era, the busing, after the civil rights movement turned sour—or the movement itself didn't necessarily turn sour but the view of the civil rights movement got much more complicated. Both the views of blacks and whites. And I remember her feeling saddened by the anger that she sensed in parts of the African American community."

In spite of their differences, Obama also shared his mother's idealism of the civil rights movement. He saw community organizing as an extension of the movement, as well as a chance to find his own place in a culture to which he never fully belonged. He would lie in bed at night dreaming of the movement as a community of activists staging sit-ins and marches, in "a series of images, romantic images, of a past I had never known."

Looking back, long after his mother passed away, he was ready to acknowledge her inspiration. "With respect to my mom and idealism, I think there's no doubt that there's an idealism that my mother passed on. And I'm glad for it," he told me. "If we can't aspire to something better, then why get into politics?"

In his unresolved racial identity, Obama found a political philosophy and purpose in life. He could remake a community in his own image and finally find a place to call home. "Through organizing, through shared sacrifice, membership had been earned," he wrote. "And because membership was earned—because this community I imagined was still in the making, built on the promise that the larger American community, black, white, and brown, could somehow redefine itself—I believed that it might, over time, admit the uniqueness of my own life."

Perhaps the most important passage in his memoir is Obama's reconciliation with his feelings toward his father, after reading what remains of his papers in the Obama family homestead in Kenya. In tears by his father's grave, marked only by yellow bathroom tiles, Obama imagines that he understands how his father failed by holding himself apart. He realizes how his life as an African American is deeply entwined with his father's alienation as a modern African. It is a profound moment of self-understanding and a powerful example of self-projection. "Oh Father, I cried. There was no shame in your confusion. Just as there had been no shame in your father's before you," he wrote. "No shame in the fear, or in the fear of his father before him. There was only shame in the silence fear had produced. It was the silence that betrayed us. If it weren't for that silence, your grandfather might have told your father that he could never escape himself, or re-create himself alone."

Obama learned—in Kenya, New York, and Chicago, and in writing his book—that he could only re-create himself with the help of others. "The pain I felt was my father's pain," he concluded. "My questions were my brothers' questions. Their struggle, my birthright." Self-sufficiency was only half the solution; community and reconciliation made the vision and the person whole. The only irony was that he could only finish writing the book while away from America entirely: in Bali, Indonesia, where his mother went when she left him in Hawaii.

His strategy to solve his personal struggles had some political application. When confronted by racial issues, Obama could always reach back into his personal experience. Not because his experience was entirely similar to that of the white or black Americans who raised questions about him, but because he found it powerfully effective to seek common ground, to form a community, to re-create himself with the help of others. "There's no doubt that my background is not typical of the African American experience to the extent that there is a typical African American experience. And I would dispute by the way that there's a monolithic experience," he told me. "But there's no doubt that mine is unusual. What I wrote about in that last chapter of *Dreams from My Father* was how being in Africa I discovered a whole series of parallels between what he had gone through and what young blacks in this country go through: what W. E. B. DuBois wrote about one hundred years ago, the sense of displacement, the sense of being on the outside, the anger that is bred from oppression and passes its way from generation to generation, the need to overcome that anger or at least to channel it in productive ways, as opposed to having it eat you up inside. So in that sense, here's an example where I might disagree with Cornel West a little bit. Is there a particular life experience that African Americans have that is passed on generationally that is a little rawer, a little nearer the surface, than the West Indian immigrant or my father? Yes. But is the fundamental experience of not being included similar? Is the passion for justice and equality similar? I think it is."

His questions about identity and belonging taught him powerful lessons about synthesis and compromise. Not the harmony of a Benetton ad, but a search for shared stories, a staking out of common ground. That was what he tried to do with his memoir, across continents and the lost years of his youth. It was what he set out to do in Chicago, in street-level politics and the black community, where he first tried his hand at writing. And it was what he wanted to do on a national level with his presidential campaign. "I was very explicit," he told me on his campaign plane. "There's a section in the book where I talk about going around and listening to people and then discovering that everyone has a story that was sacred to them. And those stories tied in with my own. And that was always the intention with the book, to try and locate my own experiences, that on their face seem pretty odd and atypical, within the larger American story. That's what we are doing with our speeches and that's to some degree what I think this campaign is about and what America is about: people from diverse backgrounds and unlikely places finding a common culture and a common set of values and ideals that make them American." It's unclear how much of this perspective was clear to him at the time he was a young man, and how much became clear as he wrote his book in his thirties, just before entering politics. But for all the emotional turmoil of his racial questions, Obama emerged with the personal skills and the political tools that would help build his career and his campaign.

If you can find common stories and values across social and racial lines, then finding common ground across the political aisle is hardly the most daunting challenge of your life. As a state senator in Illinois, not long after the publication of his largely overlooked memoir, Obama chose to set himself apart from the black Chicago caucus and befriended white conservative Republicans and downstate Democrats. Those friendships helped him later, when he immersed himself in two racially charged debates over new legislation—one on reforming the state's deeply flawed death penalty, the other on racial profiling.

Using personal charm and his ability to find common ground, Obama worked hard to win support for a measure that required police to videotape interrogations and confessions. He convinced conservatives that it was in their interests to strengthen public confidence in the criminal justice system and the death penalty. Those arguments won over the most unlikely supporters, including Ed Petka, a former prosecutor whose energetic pursuit of the death penalty had earned him the nickname Electric Ed. "My experience tells me we have a better chance of making progress on these issues when we can ground them in a broader appeal to American aspirations and values rather than when we're simply shouting racism and trying to guilt people into getting things done," Obama told me. "That doesn't mean that there aren't times for some righteous anger. But I strongly believe that Americans want to do the right thing. If you can show them that racial profiling is neither a smart way to fight crime, nor is it consistent with our values as Americans, you can get the bill passed. . . . What I think is important is trying to see the world through the eyes of people who don't agree with you. If I can imagine myself in their shoes, it means I can answer their objections."

Within the confines of Chicago's feud-filled politics, those tactics succeeded politically but hurt him personally. His fellow black Democrats were often unhappy with his compromises and his status. They questioned his understanding of what it meant to be a black teenager on a street corner in Chicago, facing the constant harassment of police officers. Much of those suspicions were present when Obama challenged Bobby Rush for his congressional seat in Chicago in 2000. His rivals wondered out loud whether Obama was some sort of racial decoy. Donne Trotter, another state senator who also challenged Rush, told the *Chicago Reader*, the city's alternative newspaper, that Obama was a fraud who was funded by the city's rich white liberals. "Barack is viewed in part to be the white man in blackface in our community," he said. "You just have to look at his supporters. Who pushed him to get where he is so fast? It's these individuals in Hyde Park, who don't always have the best interests of the community in mind."

It was true that Obama drew on early and vocal support from Chicago's liberal elite. Bettylu Saltzman, one of the doyennes of Democratic politics in the city, recalled meeting Obama in 1992 when she was working for the Clinton campaign and he was registering new voters. "I said, 'He's going to be the first black president of the United States.' He was thirty years old and I was so impressed with him. I don't even remember why he was in the office." Obama's fan base among Lake Shore liberals like Saltzman seemed to distance him further from the South Side, where he had worked as an organizer. For his part, Rush questioned the elitism of Obama's education, and rejected his compromise position on police misconduct. "Barack is a person who read about the civil rights protests and thinks he knows all about it," Rush said. "I helped make that history, by blood, sweat, and tears."

Obama believed that race was far less a factor in his defeat than class. "I have to say that aspect of the race probably has been thoroughly over-hyped," he told me seven years later. "People are trying to fit that into a narrative that isn't entirely there. Were there moments during the campaign where the suggestion was the Harvard-educated Hyde Park law professor wasn't keepin' it real? Yes. Did that have any significant influ-ence on the outcome of that race? No. There were not moments during that campaign where I anguished, 'Oh my goodness, is my black authen-ticity being questioned?'" Yet his ability to speak the language of racial politics was a factor that added to his struggles in that campaign. Obama told the *Chicago Reader* that it was time to find common ground with other racial groups in the city, not hold them apart. "It may give us a psy-chic satisfaction to curse out people outside our community and blame them for our plight," he said. "But the truth is, if you want to be able to get things accomplished politically, you've got to work with them." He may have been right on the substance, but it wasn't clear how talk of psy-chic satisfaction would help him get elected.

To some of his oldest friends, Obama's inability to copy old-style racial politics was an enormous asset when he later ran for Senate and then the presidency. Jerry Kellman, his mentor as a community orga-nizer, said Obama was taken aback by racial politics in his days as a street-level activist and was ill equipped to appeal to people as an African American. "He wasn't good at trading on his race to advance himself. He was an awful ethnic politician, and thank God," Kellman told me a month before the general election. "He's going to be elected president because he lost that congressional race. He did not run a good race, and he's not good at ethnic politics. I don't mean black politics; it's the same thing in Italian and Irish politics, the notion of who you are. That began to emerge in community organizing. His gift is diversity. Not just diver-sity of race and people, but of holding different ideas together and un-derstanding how they relate."

Obama could connect easily with different groups of voters, and that proved vital in his Senate race, when he had to appeal to a far broader group of voters. "One of the things I noticed about him right away when I started working with him was his extraordinary ability to be comfort-able in any venue," said David Axelrod. "We'd be in deep southern Illinois, in a place closer to Little Rock than Chicago, and he would do extraordinarily well. He'd say, 'These folks are just like my grandparents from Kansas,' and talk about how his grandfather was in Patton's army. He can go into an inner-city church and understand their experience. And he can go into a tony suburban area and understand them, being a Harvard Law guy."

To Obama's friends and family, the questions posed about his racial identity or his readiness for presidential power seemed to echo their own experience. For years, they had struggled to overcome the notion that this wasn't their time, or they weren't quite ready for their elite schools or high-flying careers. They had encountered the refined racism that could not conceive of a person of color in a position of leadership. And they had overcome the defensive crouch that kept African Americans down, adjusting their hopes lower, just in case of defeat or disappointment. Obama's presidential run was not just a test of his ability to cross the lines that divided voters. He was breaking the rules about what a black candidate could aspire to, and what black voters should believe of themselves and their country.

His skills and experience were not unique to Barack Obama. They were shared by many of his friends and a far wider generation of well-educated, professional, younger African Americans. Like Obama, they faced challenges to their identity and allegiances as they moved up the social scale thanks to their schooling and their careers. Craig Robinson experienced the same questions about what it means to be black, or even more simplistically, black enough. "Not only have I heard him talking about it, but it happens to any of us who have had to fit into different cultures," said Craig. "It's happened to all of us who have gone to Ivy League schools and worked in corporate America: doing things a certain group feels you shouldn't be doing. We are all—not just white people— we are all comfortable with something we're familiar with. People prefer people who are more like them, not less like them. Do I think the fact that Barack can balance all these different cultures helps him? Absolutely. It's not negative. It's just the way our society works." To Obama, the Robinson family was typical of the success that African Americans, and the nation, needed to celebrate and embrace: a working-class family that had sent both children to Princeton. "Michelle's family tells a story that is pretty powerful," he told me in Iowa early in the campaign. "And that describes about two-thirds of the African American community, which in a generation has been able to participate in American life in a way that their parents couldn't imagine. That's good news. The question is how do we bring that next third along, which is going to take a little more work but it's not something we should feel is unattainable."

The doubts about his racial identity and his viability as a candidate were really an expression of the self-doubts of the community. At least, that was the view of Barack and Michelle Obama, as they turned the conversation back on skeptical African Americans. The doubts offered a chance to talk about self-improvement, to reach collectively and individually for something higher. "To me it's a statement of the things we are struggling with in society," Michelle told me on a car ride through Iowa just four months into the campaign. "It's a good indication that we're still trying to figure this stuff out for ourselves, which is why potentially Barack poses this interesting dilemma for people. Because we are still a country that puts people in boxes. This is what it means to be black. This is what it means to be Republican. This is what it means to *be*. And Barack kind of shakes up those notions because his life has crossed so many different paths. He grew up in Hawaii but he was indeed a community organizer. He became very entrenched and rooted in the black community on the South Side. He is very much a black man, but he is very much the son of his mother, who is very much a white woman. He grew up with white grandparents. So Barack is who he says he is. I say that time and time again. There is no mystery there. His life is an open book. He wrote it. And you can read it. And unlike any candidate he has really exposed himself, pre–political ambition, so it's a book that is kind of free from intent. It is the story of who he is. I guess the only thing is, why are people confused? Their confusion isn't about Barack; it's about *us*. What does all this mean to us as a country? And I think it's a good reflection, because when it's all said and done, to me we are not that different from each other."

That confusion was most obvious, in those early months, inside a community that seemed conflicted about the Clintons, about who Obama was, and about where their own loyalties lay. "We as a black community are struggling with our own identity," said Michelle. "What does it mean to be black? You see it in issues of music and movies. I think our community struggles to make sure that the world understands who we are because when you're in the minority sometimes it seems that there's only one representation of you to the world. It's limited. So I think the black community struggles with what that means. We see what is shown of us on TV but we also know that is not the full picture. So what is the picture? We're figuring it out. It's a conversation that needs to take place."

Yet at the start of the campaign, it was unclear whether the country, or the African American community, was ready to move the conversation on from the racial politics of the 1960s. It was even less clear how much the candidate wanted to move on, or how much he wanted to claim its legacy for himself—especially when he still had so much to prove against the Clintons.

Close to the anniversary of the 1965 Selma-to-Montgomery march, when police attacked peaceful protesters walking across the Edmund Pettus Bridge, Obama and Clinton both traveled to Selma to talk at nearby churches and walk once again across the infamous bridge. Speaking from the pulpit at the Brown Chapel AME Church, the starting point for the march, Obama portrayed himself as part of the Joshua generation, the successors to the Moses generation of the movement. He told how his grandfather's experience in colonial Kenya, where he was a cook and worked as a so-called houseboy, was no different from life in segregated Alabama. And he told how his parents had met and had a child in part because of Selma. "Something stirred across the country because of what happened in Selma, Alabama, because some folks are willing to march across a bridge. So they got together and Barack Obama Jr. was born. So don't tell me I don't have a claim on Selma, Alabama. Don't tell me I'm not coming home to Selma, Alabama," he said. "I'm here because somebody marched for freedom. I'm here because you all sacrificed for me. I stand on the shoulders of giants. I thank the Moses generation; but we've got to remember, now, that Joshua still had a job to do." He was right: there was still much work to do, and his speech was well received. The only problem was that his parents met, married, and separated before the march from Selma began.

He wanted to encourage voters to move on, while also paying his respects to a movement he had dreamed about while lying in bed. So the weekend in Selma grew into a story of correction, to be retold over and over on the campaign trail. This was not a tale of the candidate correcting himself, but of him setting others straight. Selma, he argued, wasn't just about his own community. "When I got back to Washington after celebrating that day, some people said, 'That was a powerful celebration of African American history,'" he told supporters across Iowa. "I said, 'No, that was a celebration of *American* history.'"

He also wanted his own community to move beyond the politics of race. When asked about those who challenged his black identity, Obama suggested the debate was archaic. "Most of those problems or issues were resolved when I was eighteen, nineteen, twenty years old," he told me, as a matter of fact, three months after his Selma speech. "The fact that they have resurfaced in this presidential campaign says more about the country, I think, than it says about me. It has to do with, I think, America still being caught a little bit in a time warp. Sort of the narrative of black politics is still shaped by the sixties and black power. And the truth is that's not, I think, how most black voters are thinking. I don't think that's how most white voters are thinking. I think that people are thinking about how to find a job, how to fill up the gas tank, how to send their kids to college. I find that when I talk about those issues, both blacks and whites respond well."

Yet the narrative of black politics was one he could not fully escape. The truth was that he was not part of the civil rights generation, but he owed that generation a huge debt. After the interview had ended in his office, he offered an answer to a question that was unposed. "I think there's a temptation to posit me in contrast to Jesse or Sharpton and the thing I'm constantly trying to explain is that I'm a direct outgrowth of the civil rights movement; that the values of the civil rights movement remain near and dear to my heart," he said preemptively. "To the extent that I speak a different language or take a different tone in addressing these issues is a consequence of me having benefited from those bloody struggles that those other folks had to go through. To suggest that I'm pushing aside the past in favor of this Benetton future is wrong."

It fell to Michelle, the South Sider not the Hawaiian, to speak more forcefully about racial politics as they were unfolding in the presidential primaries. Two months before the first votes in Iowa, she traveled to Orangeburg, South Carolina, to confront the self-doubts and internal turmoil within the community. Speaking with an earnest passion, she told of meeting Coretta Scott King, who told her not to be afraid because God was with her and her husband. And she drew a direct line between the widow of Martin Luther King Jr. and other great African American heroines: Sojourner Truth, Harriet Tubman, Rosa Parks, and Shirley Chisholm. "These were all women who all knew what it meant to overcome," she said. "Who kept marching even when their feet were sore, who kept organizing even when their backs were aching, and sat down at the front of the bus when they were sick and tired of going to the back. These were all women who cast aside the voices of doubt and fear that said, 'Wait, you can't do that, it's not your turn, the timing isn't right, you see the country just isn't ready.' That's what they were told. And because they listened to their own voices and cast aside that cynicism—because they refused to settle for the world as it is, and insisted on reaching for the world as it should be—this nation marched forward."

The world as it is and the world as it should be: Obama's words in the church basement when she first fell for him as he trained a group of community leaders. She was inspired by him, by great African American women, by her family, and by the voice of self-belief inside her. After all, she explained as she leaned into the microphone, she was told to forget her dreams, as a girl trying to break out of the South Side of Chicago. "From classmates, and friends even, who thought a black girl with a book was acting white. From teachers who told me not to reach too high because, see, my test scores were not good enough. And from well-meaning but misguided folks who said, 'No, Michelle, you can't, you're not smart enough, you're not ready.' Those who said success isn't meant for little black girls like me from the South Side of Chicago." If all that sounded presumptuous—if it was grandiose to tie herself and her husband's campaign to the fight against Jim Crow and slavery—well, that was her point. Who was to say what claim was too grand, or which candidate was unready?

As for those in the community—and there were many—who said her husband could never win, Michelle portrayed them as either fearful or downtrodden by generations of racism. "Now, I know folks talk in the barbershops and beauty salons, and I've heard some folks say, 'That Barack Obama, he's a nice guy, but I'm not sure *America's* ready for a black president.' Well, all I can say is we've heard those voices before," she continued. "Voices that say, 'Maybe we should wait. You know, you can't do it. You're not ready. You're not experienced.' Voices that focus on what *might* go wrong rather than what's possible. And I understand it, I do. I know where it comes from, this sense of doubt and fear about what the future holds. I call it like that veil of impossibility that just keeps us down and keeps our children down—keeps us waiting and hoping for a turn that may never come. It's the bitter legacy of racism and discrimination and oppression in this country. A legacy that hurts all of us."

Some people were like the aunt or grandmother who bought new furniture but put plastic on it to protect it, never fully enjoying it, out of their own misplaced fear. "Sometimes it seems better not to try at all than to try and fail," she explained. "Sometimes that's how it feels. But we have to remember that these complicated emotions are what folks who marched in the civil rights movement had to overcome all those decades ago. It's what so many of us have struggled to overcome in our own lives. And it's what we're going to have to overcome as a community if we want to lift ourselves up."

While he was sitting in a Birmingham jail, Martin Luther King Jr. wrote an open letter to several liberal clergymen who criticized his approach of nonviolent resistance and preferred to confine the struggle to the courts. It was April 1963, two years before the Selma march and two years after Obama was born in Hawaii. "For years now I have heard the word 'Wait!' It rings in the ear of every Negro with a piercing familiarity," he wrote. "This 'Wait!' has almost always meant 'Never.'"

King was talking about segregation, justice, and equality. A generation later, the Obamas were talking about self-belief, role models, and their presidential campaign. As challenges, they were not nearly as formidable as the foes King had faced. But they were still powerful forces that could hold down African Americans. The notion of confronting those forces could remake racial politics in America, opening the eyes of both black and white Americans to new possibilities. It could also help Obama get elected: after all, this wasn't just a campaign, this was history in the making. He wanted to find common ground with African Americans and all Americans, because it was good for the country and good politics, too. That meant placing himself at the heart of a uniquely American story that stretched from the founding fathers to the Civil War to the civil rights movement. It required him to take control as the narrator of a new chapter that only he could write; not the Clintons, not Bobby Rush and Donne Trotter, not even Cornel West. Obama could recreate the country, just as he had re-created himself. It only required him to win the nomination first. Obama had not broken the law, like King; he had only broken its unwritten political rules, its social conventions. He could afford to be a less threatening renegade, but he might end up as a more powerful one, too.

* * *

Race started to roil the contest on the last full day of the New Hampshire primary, when the political world was convinced that Hillary Clinton was heading for defeat. In Dover, New Hampshire, one of Clinton's supporters introduced the New York senator by raising the fear of assassination. "Some people compare one of the other candidates to John F. Kennedy, but he was assassinated," said Francine Torge. She noted that it was Lyndon Baines Johnson, not the idealistic orator, who passed the civil rights laws. Clinton herself extended those comments after the event in an interview with Fox News. "Dr. King's dream began to be realized when President Johnson passed the Civil Rights Act," she said. "It took a president to get it done."

The threat of violence was not academic. Sparked by racist e-mails to Obama's Senate office and his outsized crowds, Congress had requested Secret Service protection for Obama earlier than for any other presidential candidate in history, eight months before any votes were cast.

The impression among Obama's aides was that Clinton was belittling both King and their candidate. Their sensitivities were only heightened the same day when Bill Clinton dismissed the premise of the Obama campaign— its positive image, its media coverage, and its position on the war in Iraq. Later, the controversy intensified when one of Clinton's prominent African American supporters tried to justify her remarks. Speaking in Columbia, South Carolina, Robert Johnson, the founder of Black Entertainment Television, decided to compare his candidate's record on race with Obama's youthful drug use. "As an African American, I'm frankly insulted that the Obama campaign would imply that we are so stupid that we would think Bill and Hillary Clinton, who have been deeply and emotionally involved in black issues when Barack Obama was doing something in the neighborhood—and I won't say what he was doing, but he said it in his book—when they have been involved," he said. As if that weren't belittling enough, Johnson said Obama was trying to behave like Sidney Poitier in *Guess Who's Coming to Dinner.* "And I'm thinking, I'm thinking to myself, this ain't a movie, Sidney," Johnson continued. "This is real life."

By the time the comments were processed and reprocessed, there was a full-blown debate about race, the Clintons' psychology, and the nature of the Obama campaign. A few days later, James Clyburn, the highest-ranking African American in Congress and one of the most influential voices in Democratic politics in South Carolina, warned that the Clintons were distorting the history of the civil rights movement. "We have to be very, very careful about how we speak about that era in American politics," he said. "It is one thing to run a campaign and be respectful of everyone's motives and actions, and it is something else to denigrate those. That bothered me a great deal."

Within days, voters began to ask Obama direct questions about race for the first time in a year on the campaign trail. At a town hall meeting in Carson City, Nevada, close to Lake Tahoe, one supporter took the microphone to say, "Let's get down to brass tacks here. We've never elected a black man to run this country." The gym hushed to a stillness.

"Yeah, that's a good point. I've noticed that," Obama joked.

"So how is it that you're going to address that issue, and overcome that issue?" asked his white questioner.

The candidate seemed unfazed. "Well, look, I think it's a wonderful question and I'm glad you asked it," he said, before explaining how people had predicted that Illinois would never elect a black senator named Barack Obama. Now, he pointed out, he was ahead of all his Republican rivals in the polls and was gaining more independent and Republican support than his Democratic opponents. "I don't want to sound naive," he said. "Will there be some folks who probably won't vote for me because I'm black? Of course. Just like there will be some people who won't vote for Hillary because she's a woman, or won't vote for John Edwards because they don't like his accent. But the question is, can we get a majority of American people to give us a fair hearing? And I believe we already proved it. Folks said we couldn't win in Iowa. We, I think, have moved forward as a country in a significant way."

The real test of whether the country had moved on—and whether African American Democrats would embrace Obama—would come in the next round of voting, in South Carolina. On the morning of Martin Luther King Day, with the candidates readying for a debate in Myrtle Beach sponsored by the Congressional Black Caucus, James Clyburn grew more direct about Bill Clinton. "I think they would say in Gullah Geechee country, he needs to chill a little bit. I hope he understands what that means," he said, referring to African Americans in the state's low country. "He is revered in many sections of the African American community, and I think he can afford to tone it down."

The candidates themselves wanted little to do with the radioactive debate about dubious motives and suspect phrasing. CNN's moderators repeatedly attempted to get the candidates to engage with one another on race. "I've spoken with a lot of African American voters in South Carolina this week, and a lot of them say that electing a black president, that this would change the way whites see African Americans and the way African Americans see themselves," said CNN's Suzanne Malveaux. "Do you think that this is a valid consideration for voters in determining who's president?" John Edwards said it wasn't for him to tell African Americans how to vote. Hillary Clinton dodged the question. And Barack Obama challenged the media's focus on race, saying voters wanted change. "I'm not entirely faulting the media because, look, race is a factor in our society. There's no doubt that in a race where you've got an African American, and a woman, and John," he said, as the audience chuckled, "there's no doubt that that has piqued interest. But I guess what I'm saying is I don't want to sell the American people short."

The moderators came back for a second attempt, asking if Bill Clinton was indeed the first black president, as the novelist Toni Morrison had said, "Well, I think Bill Clinton did have an enormous affinity with the African American community, and still does. And I think that's well earned," Obama said. "I have to say that, you know, I would have to, you know, investigate more of Bill's dancing abilities, and some of this other stuff, before I accurately judge whether he was in fact a brother."

Obama could afford to be generous. His tone with the community seemed effortless, and the crowds responded in kind. Hours before the debate, in Columbia, he joined a march from Zion Baptist Church to the state capitol, where the NAACP was holding a rally opposite the spot where the Confederate flag still flies on the capitol grounds. All three candidates were expected to march, but only Obama joined in the chaotic procession. The Secret Service agents were overwhelmed by the crowds, and could only scream at bystanders or push photographers onto the sidewalk. On the steps of the capitol, where the candidates were now together, Lonnie Randolph, president of the state NAACP, was telling how the chant "Fired Up! Ready to Go!" began on a South Carolina march to bring down the Confederate flag two decades ago.

Obama's support in South Carolina allowed him the room to deliver some tough love in a way that no other Democrat or Republican could do. In front of a boisterous crowd in a Kingstree school, he promised to spend more money on education, but warned that parents—especially African Americans—needed to step up. "I could put all the money in the world into our schools, but if parents aren't willing to parent, there's only so much we can do," he said. "If you're a parent and not telling your child to turn off that television set and put the video game away and do your homework; if you think when they come home a C is OK. . . . A C is not OK. If that child is getting a C, you better tell 'em you better start getting a B. And once they got a B, you tell 'em you better start getting an A. I want to speak to all people here, but I'm speaking especially to the African American community and young people out there. Education is not a passive activity; if we were putting as much time into books as we were into sports, as we were into music. . . . I'm just telling the truth."

Some of the most influential political pundits thought it was over for Obama. The pendulum had swung one way after Iowa, then back again after New Hampshire. Now they were convinced it was too late for him in South Carolina, no matter whether he won or lost. Dick Morris, Bill Clinton's former strategist and now a Hillary hater on Fox News, penned a widely debated column suggesting that Obama would win in South Carolina but lose the nomination as a result. "If blacks deliver South Carolina to Obama, everybody will know that they are bloc-voting," he wrote. "That will trigger a massive white backlash against Obama and will drive white voters to Hillary Clinton." Reporters pressed the candidate on the notion that he was becoming the black candidate, despite his best efforts to transcend racial politics. "Are you concerned that the Clintons are trying to portray you as the black candidate, and if so, is that a problem for your campaign?" asked one wire reporter.

"I have consistently run my campaign but more importantly conducted my job as a public official based on the idea that we are all in it together," Obama replied. "That black, white, Hispanic, Asian, all of us share common dreams, common fears, common concerns. Everybody wants this economy stronger. Everybody wants to bring troops home as quickly as possible. Everybody wants energy independence and security. Everybody is looking to ensure that the next generation can go to college. It's been because of that approach that I think we've been able to attract support across the board."

That kind of talk convinced few in the press, who set their own expectations of what constituted victory for Obama and what South Carolina meant for his prospects. One poll, released the day before the primary, showed Obama getting just 10 percent of the white vote in South Carolina, and a headline lead of eight points over Clinton. Some of the most influential journalists in the field suggested Obama could lose the contest outright in the state, and had already lost the race debate. "Hillary Rodham Clinton has won in South Carolina," declared

Ron Fournier of the Associated Press. "No, not Saturday's primary—though it's no longer outside the realm of possibility that Clinton will defeat Barack Obama here. What she has won in South Carolina is the larger campaign to polarize voters around race and marginalize Obama (in the insidious words of one of her top advisers) as 'The Black Candidate.'"

The Black Candidate spent the afternoon playing basketball at the YMCA in downtown Columbia. "We played on the day of the election in Iowa, but not in Nevada and New Hampshire," he told me. "So let's hope it's lucky today."

He didn't need the luck; it was indeed out of the realm of possibility that he would lose. A few hours later, at Columbia's concrete convention center, several thousand of his supporters filled a victory site and cheered as CNN showed the results of the exit polls. When the screens showed Obama winning 24 percent of the white vote, the crowd started chanting "Race Doesn't Matter!" Obama's final margin of victory was a thumping twenty-nine points. The polls were even more mistaken and misleading in South Carolina than they were in New Hampshire.

The candidate was in no mood to declare victory. Indeed, he extended his ambition from merely winning the nomination to transforming the nation's politics and its mind-set. "It's a politics that uses religion as a wedge and patriotism as a bludgeon, a politics that tells us that we have to think, act, and even vote within the confines of the categories that supposedly define us, the assumption that young people are apathetic, the assumption that Republicans won't cross over, the assumption that the wealthy care nothing for the poor and that the poor don't vote, the assumption that African Americans can't support the white candidate, whites can't support the African American candidate, blacks and Latinos cannot come together. We are here tonight to say that that is not the America we believe in," he declared, to chants of "Yes We Can." "I did not travel around this state over the last year and see a white South Carolina or a black South Carolina. I saw South Carolina. Because in the end, we're not up just against the ingrained and destructive habits of Washington. We're also struggling with our own doubts, our own fears, our own cynicism."

As Barack and Michelle Obama left South Carolina, they took with them two lessons. The first, for the candidate, was personal. "It was a terrific victory," he told me. "What was particularly gratifying was the solid white vote we got in the face of a bunch of polls and commentary that said we were going to get 10 percent." In spite of the pundits, he had proved himself among black and white voters alike; it turned out he was both black enough and white enough to win. "It feels good," he told his friends that night.

The second lesson, for his wife, was even more personal. She felt like she had seen her own past, and perhaps changed the future for another generation. Traveling around the country, she would tell the story of a ten-year-old girl she met in a beauty parlor in South Carolina.

"Mrs. Obama, I want to tell you something," the girl told her. "Do you realize when your husband becomes the next president of the United States, it will be historical?"

"Why yes, I understand that. What does that mean to you?"

"It means I can imagine *anything* for myself." The girl started to cry, and so too did the candidate's wife.

"It broke my heart," she said later. "This little ten-year-old understands it. She knows that she has been living in a nation where she's already five steps behind. She doesn't have the resources or the support. She will not be able to compete. But she also knows she is *so* much better than this nation's limited expectations of her. She knows that she is worthy and able to succeed and to give and to strive and to dream. So all she has are dreams. The one thing I know is what that little girl feels like. Because she could have been me."

If African American voters harbored any remaining doubts about Obama, they were gone after South Carolina. The next day, the candidate flew to Birmingham, Alabama, where Martin Luther King Jr. had sat in jail and Bull Connor had set the dogs and fire hoses on schoolchildren forty-five years earlier. Inside a downtown arena, before thousands of mostly African American supporters, Artur Davis, a young congressman who also excelled at Harvard, was introducing the candidate. Davis's district stretches from Birmingham to Selma and the old plantations of the so-called Black Belt. Standing onstage, Davis said he wanted to talk to the older folks in the arena.

"If somebody in this room who was in Birmingham, Alabama, in 1963, if somebody in this room who was here for Bull Connor, who was here for George Wallace, wherever you are," he said, "did you ever think somebody who looks like me would be standing on this stage presenting somebody who looks like Barack Obama and talking about the presidency of the United States of America? Could you have *believed* it, ladies and gentlemen? Could you have *believed* it?"

Sitting on the riser holding the TV cameras and press photographers, David Axelrod choked up with emotion. But onstage, his candidate was still savoring the sense of vindication. "All the pundits and all the press said, 'Oh, South Carolina is different. The South is the South. It's inexorably divided. There's no chance that Obama's message of unity, of coming together, can work. If you get black votes, then you can't get white votes. If you get white votes, you can't get black votes.' The notion was that we were locked in our past and we could not create a different and better future for America," Obama began. "And then last night came. And people from every walk of life stood up and they said, 'Yes We Can.' The time for change has come. We're going to write a new chapter in the South. We're going to write a new chapter in American history."

Obama's dream of unity lasted all of seven weeks. It survived his strong showing on Super Tuesday and a string of eleven victories across the country in February. But then his King-like vision was rudely awakened by another image of racial politics from the 1960s: the indignation and condemnation that white Americans came to fear in Malcolm X.

On March 13, ABC's Brian Ross broke the story of the sermons of Obama's pastor, the Reverend Jeremiah Wright. "With his powerful voice and his strong words, Reverend Wright can be a mesmerizing presence," said Ross. Mesmerizing and grotesquely compelling. Wright's sermons were openly on sale at Trinity United Church of Christ, but somehow overlooked by reporters and the campaign's research team. The pastor swaggered and strutted across the stage, as he delivered several sermons that were provocative, inflammatory, and sometimes simply unhinged. The first clip showed a 2003 sermon in which Wright condemned the country for its treatment of African Americans. "The government gives them the drugs, builds bigger prisons, passes the three strike law and then wants us to sing God Bless America," he said. "No, no, no. Not God Bless America. God *Damn* America. That's in the Bible. For killing innocent people. God Damn America for treating its citizens as less than human." Ross spliced that clip together with a quote from Obama saying he didn't think his church was particularly controversial. Wright was shown condemning what he called "the US of KKK A," and he mocked Republican African Americans, calling Condoleezza Rice

"Cond-amnesia." Finally, with a flourish, there was Wright's post-9/11 sermon. "We bombed Hiroshima. We bombed Nagasaki. And we nuked far more than the thousands in New York and the Pentagon, and we never batted an eye," he roared, his arm sweeping to his side. "We have supported state terrorism against the Palestinians and black South Africans and now we are *indignant,* because the stuff we have done overseas is now brought right back into our own front yards. America's chickens," he said, turning on his heels and circling his hand above his head, "are coming *home . . .* to roost." The chickens were coming home to roost, which was reminiscent of Malcolm X's answer to a question about President Kennedy's assassination: that white violence had taken one of its own leaders.

Now Wright was Obama's roosting chicken. The *New York Post* called him "Obama's Minister of Hate" while the *Washington Post* more prudently called him a "Preacher with a Penchant for Controversy." Cable TV behaved more like the *Post* in New York than the one in Washington. All day the networks played Wright's sermons on the kind of endless loop they reserved for historic pictures like the collapse of the World Trade Center towers.

While cable gorged on Wright's indignation, Obama was consumed with an old controversy. He was scheduled to clear the air with Chicago's newspapers over his ties to the indicted (and now jailed) property developer Tony Rezko, who had helped Obama extend his yard by purchasing a neighboring lot. When Obama's aides asked to postpone the session, the *Tribune* threatened to print a scathing editorial on the Rezko affair. They had no choice but to go ahead. The candidate was buried in intensive prep work for his Rezko interrogation with his lawyer and senior aides, while all around in campaign headquarters, his staff were watching Wright destroy his presidental hopes on TV.

Sitting down with the Chicago papers, Obama inevitably faced questions about Wright. The *Tribune* wanted to know if the preacher's comments were similar to those of Geraldine Ferraro, the former vice presidential candidate, who had told her local paper that Obama was "very lucky" to be black. "If Obama was a white man," she said, "he would not be in this position." Ferraro wasn't racist, Obama said; she was just wrong. Wright, however, was more complicated. "He's like a member of the family; he's like your uncle who says things you profoundly disagree with, but he's still your uncle," he explained.

The fact that he's retiring and we've got a young pastor Otis Moss coming in, means that people should understand the context of this relationship. That this is an aging pastor who's about to retire and that I have made and will make some very clear statements about how profoundly I disagree with these statements. I don't think they are reflective of the church. They're certainly not reflective of my views. I do think there is an overlap [with Ferraro] in the sense that there is a generational shift that is taking place and has constantly taken place in our society. And Reverend Wright is somebody who came of age in the '60s. And so, like a lot of African-American men of fierce intelligence coming up in the '60s, he has a lot of the language and the memories and the baggage of those times. And I represent a different generation with just a different set of life experiences, and so see race relations in just a different set of terms than he does, as does Otis Moss, who is slightly younger than me. And so the question then for me becomes what's my relationship to that past? You know, I can completely just disown it and say I don't understand it, but I do understand it. I understand the context with which he developed his views, but also can still reject unequivocally.

That kind of nuance had been fine in February, but it was lost in March. The TV clips overwhelmed any kind of explanation, especially the notion that Wright was some ancient relic of another decade. The pundits wanted to know what Obama knew of the sermons and why he failed to quit the church. Each new airing of a sermon seemed to inflame the questions. Was Obama secretly the same kind of radical anti-American as his pastor? What was the real relationship between the still largely unknown candidate and his supposed spiritual mentor? "I'll be honest with you," he told the *Tribune* reporters.

This is somebody who I've known for 20 years. I basically came to the church and became a member of the church through Trinity and through him. He's the person who gave me the line "the audacity of hope." He is somebody who is a former Marine, a biblical scholar, has taught and lectured at major theological seminaries across the country and has been very widely regarded and admired. And, you know, he hasn't been my political adviser; he's been my pastor. And I have to say that the clips that have been shown over the past couple of days are deeply disturbing to me. I wasn't in church during those sermons. The things he said and the way he said them, I think, are offensive. And I reject them, and they don't reflect who I am or what I believe in. In fairness to him, this was sort of a greatest hits. They basically culled five or six sermons out of 30 years of preaching. That doesn't excuse them, and I've said so very clearly. But that's not the relationship I had with him. That's not the relationship I had with the church, and if I had heard those kinds of statements being said, if I had been in church on those days, I would have objected fiercely to them and I would have told him personally. When some of these statements first came to light was right around when I was starting to run for president. He was a year away from retirement and the church itself is a pillar of the community and a well-regarded, well-known church.

Obama released a statement to the left-leaning website the Huffington Post, condemning the sermons as "inflammatory and appalling." His aides wanted to raise the morale of their own supporters and thought the website would help spread their message rapidly, through e-mail. But the condemnation was hastily drafted, between prep sessions for the Rezko interviews, and it was only a placeholder. Writing in longhand on a legal pad, the candidate explained that he had first heard about the statements at the start of his campaign, when he had condemned them at the time, but decided not to leave the church because Wright was on the verge of retirement.

That was not entirely true. The first reporting of Wright's sermons came in a *Rolling Stone* story published just before the launch of Obama's campaign in Springfield. The story described Trinity as a "black nationalist" church and quoted Wright as saying, "We believe in white supremacy and black inferiority and believe it more than we believe in God." Obama did not condemn the comments publicly. Instead his aides insisted that the story was inaccurate, and the writer had wrongly attributed quotes to Wright. The story disrupted Obama's announcement plans: Wright was supposed to deliver the invocation at the start of the event, but instead prayed privately with the Obama family. Obama called Wright the evening before his event, to talk about the *Rolling Stone* story. "Fifteen minutes before Shabbos I get a call from Barack," Wright told the *New York Times.* "One of his members had talked him into uninviting me." Wright said the candidate had told him, "You can get kind of rough in the sermons, so what we've decided is that it's best for you not to be out there in public." Obama asked his research team to examine all of Wright's sermons for more fire and brimstone, but the work was never done. They were swamped with basic research on the candidate's life, his opponents, and more pressing stories. He was only fortunate that the sermons did not emerge on TV in the days before the Iowa caucuses.

A few months after his announcement, the candidate downplayed the idea that there was any distance with his pastor, even though he felt annoyed and upset by Wright's taking his complaints to the *Times*. "It was a blip," he told me. "I think that was a pretty simple story. We were doing our announcement and a story came out in which he was sort of singled out as being more radical than he was. Given that we knew we had given five hundred press credentials that day, I didn't want him placed in the position where he had to defend himself or the church without any kind of backup or knowing what he was going to get into. I would have done the same thing for my sister or a coworker. So I guess it's conceivable I might have been overprotective and probably didn't anticipate that he might feel hurt by it. So we had a discussion about it and everything is fine at this point."

Maybe that was true at the start of his campaign. But Obama's friends were always expecting the worst from Wright at some point; they just didn't know it would come in the form of an endless cycle of Wright's sermons on national television. "He's a very charismatic guy and his speaking style is one where he uses provocative extremes to get to his ultimate point," said Marty Nesbitt. "So you know that if you go back and look at all of his stuff and play a segment of anything, because he likes to be provocative and he likes to be funny, you just know there's something out there somewhere that may surface. I'm not a member, but I have been to Trinity plenty of times. I didn't hear any of the stuff that ultimately made its way onto the news. But I have heard plenty of things where you think it's interesting for a pastor to use that phrase or say it that way. My sense was that there was some Reverend Wright risk, so it was not a surprise. But the way it just got beat, the way the media just looped it over and over and over and over again, surprised all of us. I mean, it was brutal."

Set against his provocative language, Wright's work in the community was what Obama valued: his social ministry with prisoners, his drive to test for HIV/AIDS. Yes, he was risky, but this was a black church on the South Side, where the congregation heard and saw far worse than anything Wright could say or do. "The black church is like a kitchen table," said Valerie Jarrett. "And there are things people say around their kitchen table that they'd never say in polite society. It's because you feel safe and can express your biggest concerns or fears. And part of how this church made people feel comfortable coming in was to almost state things in the extreme and then that legitimizes any other emotion that people walk in the door with. Because you're almost stating things in the absurd. And if I'm absurd, you're a little less absurd. You feel like OK, you can come here and almost be willing to confront the worst things that have happened to you in the course of the week."

Obama felt personally conflicted by race, religion, community, and friendship. He was tied to Wright in so many ways that it seemed impossible to break fully free. He had indeed come to his faith through Wright and Trinity, but his faith was more complex than a set of spiritual beliefs. Through Wright and Trinity, he had come to terms with his identity, his place in the world and the African American community. The process started out of political expediency: he was trying to organize church leaders, and not unreasonably those pastors wanted to know which church he belonged to.

But he was also attracted to the unusual combination that was Trinity and Wright. Trinity was a black church in a white denomination, the United Church of Christ. It had a largely working-class congregation and a reputation for being a home to yuppies. Then there was the beguiling, charismatic figure of Wright himself: proud enough to brag about building a new sanctuary at their first meeting, humble enough to know that life at Trinity would survive long after he did. Wright had built Trinity out of the ashes of the black church in the post–civil rights era. He was deeply influenced by James Cone, who wrote *Black Theology and Black Power* in 1969, two years before he took control of Trinity. "For me, the burning theological question was, how can I reconcile Christianity and Black Power, Martin Luther King Jr.'s idea of nonviolence and Malcolm X's 'by any means necessary' philosophy?" Cone wrote. Wright was an intellectual and an activist, a Ph.D. in the history of religion, who knew Tillich and Niebuhr as well as street talk. "It was this capacious talent of his—this ability to hold together, if not reconcile, the conflicting strains of black experience—upon which Trinity's success had ultimately been built," Obama wrote.

What attracted Obama to Trinity and to the church? In a word, roots. Trinity was committed to keeping its community rooted. Obama was intrigued by the church's "Black Value System," which included "a disavowal of the pursuit of middleclassness"—the notion that if you were successful, you were no longer part of the community. At a time when he was leaving Chicago for the ivory tower of Harvard, this was no abstract concern. He talked to black professionals who had "a feeling, at once inchoate and oppressive, that they'd been cut off from themselves." Trinity helped them overcome those feelings. So when Obama sat down at Trinity to hear Wright's sermon "The Audacity of Hope," he found the voice that pulled it all together: his voice and Wright's, his feelings and the audience's, his story and black history. He imagined seeing other churches and congregations, the people of the Bible and Chicago, his family and his community. He wrote:

> In that single note—hope!—I heard something else; at the foot of that cross, inside the thousands of churches across the city, I imagined the stories of ordinary black people merging with the stories of David and Goliath, Moses and Pharaoh, the Christians in the lion's den, Ezekiel's field of dry bones. Those stories—of survival, and freedom, and hope—became our story, my story; the blood that had spilled was our blood, the tears our tears; until this black church, on this bright day, seemed once more a vessel carrying the story of a people into future generations and into a larger world. Our trials and triumphs became at once unique and universal, black and more than black.

Trinity was the place where Barack married Michelle and they baptized their daughters. But its role in Obama's religious and political life was vague: a presence, but not a pivotal one. In some ways he approached religion like his mother, as an anthropologist, revering the ritual and spiritual power of faith without fully immersing himself. In describing his mother's spiritual life, he sounded like he was talking about his own doubt-filled, inclusive approach. "I think she believed in a higher power. She believed in the fundamental order and goodness of the universe," he told me. "But I think she was very suspicious of the notion that one particular organized religion offered the one truth. So, in that sense she was a skeptic about our interpretations of the meaning of life or what that higher power was." Still, he was more committed to a single religion than she was, according to his sister Maya. "She understood that he had spent some time with the churches on the South Side of Chicago, and for him being Christian meant he could really see what it was to be Christlike, in the sense of sort of being a balm to help heal the world," Maya told me. "I think he took that quite seriously, and she understood why that was important to him. She didn't feel the same need, because for her, she felt like we can still be good to one another and serve, but we don't have to choose. She was, of course, always a wanderer, and I think he was more inclined to be rooted and make the choice to set down his commitments more firmly."

More firmly but not all that frequently: Obama started married life by going to Trinity twice a month, then "less frequently" when his daughters were born. Once he was running for Senate, Obama went to church to connect with voters more than his community of faith. "There was quite a big chunk of time, especially during the Senate race where, you know, we might not have gone to Trinity for two, three months at a time," he told me. As for his interaction with Wright, he seemed more like a social friend than a spiritual adviser, as he was often portrayed in the media. "I cannot recall a time where he and I sat down and talked theology, or we had long discussions about my faith," he explained on his campaign plane one summer afternoon. "You know, if I met with him, it was after church to have chicken with the family and we would have talked stories about our family. But certainly he strengthened my faith."

With those admissions, he might have been trying to minimize his relationship with his radioactive pastor. Or he might have been admitting that he had overstated his attachment to the church and his faith. After all, he wrote a chapter on faith in his political book, *The Audacity of Hope*, but it was one of the shortest chapters in the volume. Its lesson was simply to call on progressives to shed their antireligious feelings—not to find Christ, but to find common political ground.

In fact it was the very inclusive nature of Trinity and the United Church of Christ that was a powerful attraction for the candidate. He seemed totally at home in the almost hippie atmosphere of the United Church of Christ's annual convention, its general synod in Hartford, Connecticut, soon after he launched his campaign. Instead of the radical screeds of Jeremiah Wright, a pastor wearing kente cloth led a prayer by strumming a steel-string guitar and singing a Spanish-language song, "Gracias por la Luz." After a recital by a youth orchestra, there was another blessing that also praised a vaguely New Agey concept: "We give thanks for the light. Let it shine." Instead of "God Damn America," the arena sang "America the Beautiful" before the UCC president, the

Reverend John Thomas, walked onstage wearing a Hawaiian lei around his neck.

Wright himself appeared at the synod with a taped address, as an introduction to Obama. (He could not attend because he was officiating at a wedding in Chicago.) Wright told of his long relationship with Obama before describing the senator as "a man who believes that Muslim, Jew, Christian, atheist, nonbeliever, black, white, Indonesian, African, South American, Chicano, Native American, Aboriginal, Australian, all are God's children and can live together and work together fruitfully and productively on God's earth because God does love the world, which includes all people. That is the Barack I have known for twenty years. I would say to him today the same thing I said to him the day he was elected: keep on being that Barack Obama. You are God's child. We love you." In other words, "to thine own self be true."

Being true to yourself was only half the clichéd advice in *Hamlet*. Before that, there are another couple of lines that Obama seemed to struggle with: "Give every man thy ear, but few thy voice; Take each man's censure, but reserve thy judgment." There was plenty of censure after Wright's sermons hit cable TV but Obama could reserve his judgment no more.

He had long wanted to give a speech on race, thinking it was inevitable that he should address the subject at some point during the course of the election. In fact, he first wanted to deliver a race speech in October, as his own campaign faltered. But his political aides thought the speech was a bad idea at the time. "A lot of folks cautioned that he had run such a transcendent race that maybe it wasn't such a good idea to introduce race," said Valerie Jarrett. "He had always thought that he was uniquely qualified to lead a conversation on a topic that is so sensitive, but where he could at firsthand appreciate the different perspectives. But there wasn't really a necessity to do it, so it just didn't get done." Now there was a necessity to do or say something beyond his initial statement to the Huffington Post. After all, the tapes were playing endlessly on television and the public outrage was only growing.

Sitting at dinner with Jarrett and Eric Whitaker, Obama phoned the other missing member of his closest group of friends, Marty Nesbitt, for advice. "You're going to find out how much equity you have with voters right now, because this is ridiculous," Nesbitt said. "But it's a blessing in disguise." Even Obama found his optimism excessive. When he stopped laughing at the other end of the phone, Nesbitt tried to explain. "This is why people support you," he continued. "They want to get past these issues. They want to come together. Remember your convention speech in '04? That's what this is really all about. What has happened is the media and these circumstances have created a hurdle that only you can clear. It's a blessing because if you can clear this hurdle, it confirms what your followers and your constituents hoped that you could deliver. It's not going to change our friendship or change who you are as an individual. Either you're the guy who can get elected, or you're not the guy who can get elected."

Obama called his senior staff and said he needed to go beyond the initial statement. "Guys, I don't think that's enough," he told them. "I want to give a speech on race. From a political standpoint, this is a moment of great peril and requires more than the typical political response. But I have got a lot to say about this and I think it requires a thoughtful speech. It's a speech that only I can write. Either people accept it or they won't, and I may not be president."

It was Friday night, and Obama wanted to deliver the speech by Tuesday. He was campaigning all day Saturday and shooting a TV ad on Sunday. When his senior staff asked exactly when he was going to write the speech, he said, "Don't worry. I know what I want to say."

On Saturday night he spoke to his speechwriter Jon Favreau to lay out a sketch of the speech; the next night he took Favreau's outline and started writing after he put his daughters to bed. By three in the morning, he had finished half the speech. Five hours later, he was en route to Pennsylvania for a full day of campaign events. At 10:00 p.m. on Monday night, he retired to his hotel room to write the second half of the speech that he would deliver the next morning. By 2:00 a.m. on Tuesday, he had e-mailed the speech to his senior staff. David Axelrod knew of no other candidate who could have written such a complex and subtle speech under such pressure. "This is why you should be president," he e-mailed his boss in the middle of the night.

The story started on TV, and it was fueled by cable coverage, so it was only natural that the big speech was a made-for-TV moment. There seemed to be more cameras and reporters than invited guests inside the small auditorium at the National Constitution Center in Philadelphia. Bundles of plastic cables stretched through the hallways, into the fire escape, and outside to the street full of satellite trucks that beamed the speech live across the nation. Inside, Obama's aides tinkered with the podium and paced around nervously, knowing the morning's newspapers had billed this moment as the make-or-break point for their campaign. The tension was so great that the introducer, former senator Harris Wofford, forgot whether it was day or night. "Are you as happy as I am to be here tonight?" he asked to a smatter of applause. The audience looked less than happy, and it was only midmorning.

Without his usual campaign music, Obama walked onstage with four Stars and Stripes on either side of his podium. Reading each word carefully from his teleprompters, he started with the widest possible panorama—of the founding fathers writing the Constitution, the slave trade, the Civil War, and the civil rights movement. At the end of his condensed history of race in America, he arrived at his own campaign and himself: his search for common political ground, which he suggested was rooted in his family story of mixed races and geography. "It's a story that hasn't made me the most conventional candidate," he said. "But it is a story that has seared into my genetic makeup the idea that this nation is more than the sum of its parts—that out of many, we are truly one."

It was a profoundly patriotic speech that sounded nothing like Wright's condemnation of America. Still, when he came to address his former pastor's comments, he denounced him but would not disown him. Wright represented his roots, after all. "I can no more disown him than I can disown the black community," he explained. "I can no more disown him than I can my white grandmother—a woman who helped raise me, a woman who sacrificed again and again for me, a woman who loves me as much as she loves anything in this world, but a woman who once confessed her fear of black men who passed by her on the street, and who on more than one occasion has uttered racial or ethnic stereotypes that made me cringe. These people are a part of me. And they are a part of America, this country that I love."

The speech was an exercise in bridging the divide: he recounted the racial resentment of both African Americans and working-class white folks. But what separated him from Wright was what also separated him from Cornel West: his optimism about America. "The profound mistake of Reverend Wright's sermons is not that he spoke about racism in our society. It's that he spoke as if our society was static; as if no progress has been made; as if this country—a country that has made it possible for one of his own members to run for the highest office in the land and build a coalition of white and black, Latino and Asian, rich and poor, young and old—is still irrevocably bound to a tragic past," he explained. "But what we know—what we have seen—is that America can change. That is the true genius of this nation. What we have already achieved gives us hope—the audacity to hope—for what we can and must achieve tomorrow." He ended by recounting the story he had told in Ebenezer Baptist Church in Atlanta, of Ashley Baia, his young white organizer in South Carolina. By the end, many of his friends—including Marty Nesbitt, who seemed so nonchalant about whether he cleared the hurdle or not—were in tears.

His ability to see both sides of the race debate was not a political act; it was personal. Two days later, flying on his campaign plane, he told me how his mother had prided herself on seeing all sides of the racial spectrum. He felt the same way, even as he tried to distinguish himself from her. "Actually this week, with the whole Wright thing, was very personal to me because I understood it on both sides in a very visceral way," he said. "I know the sadness and the sense of pain and hurt that my mother would feel from a sense that blacks were painting whites with a broad brush. Because I actually remember her saying to me once, 'I don't feel "white." That's not my identity.' And I remember wanting to make sure that she understood that me embracing an African American identity in no way meant that I wasn't affirming or embracing her." As a young man, Obama felt annoyed by his mother's idealism about racial politics and the civil rights movement. But in his middle age, he had come to value her sense of hope. "As I grew up, and became clear about who I was," he explained, "then that part of her that was in some ways always innocent for most of her life is part of what I appreciate deeply about her."

If the candidate felt positive about America's potential, he and his senior staff felt the opposite about the news media. "It was the moment that everybody had been waiting for, because race is like catnip for journalists and this spilled a whole bag of catnip in front of them," recalled David Axelrod. "It was a feeding frenzy."

Running through Obama's Philadelphia speech was a harsh critique of the media. "At various stages in the campaign, some commentators have deemed me either 'too black' or 'not black enough,'" he said. "We saw racial tensions bubble to the surface during the week before the

South Carolina primary. The press has scoured every exit poll for the latest evidence of racial polarization, not just in terms of white and black, but black and brown as well." He laid down an explicit challenge to the media to deal with race as something other than political sport, and to change its coverage of the election. "We can tackle race only as spectacle—as we did in the OJ trial—or in the wake of tragedy, as we did in the aftermath of Katrina—or as fodder for the nightly news," he said. "We can play Reverend Wright's sermons on every channel, every day, and talk about them from now until the election, and make the only question in this campaign whether or not the American people think that I somehow believe or sympathize with his most offensive words. We can pounce on some gaffe by a Hillary supporter as evidence that she's playing the race card, or we can speculate on whether white men will all flock to John McCain in the general election regardless of his policies. We can do that. But if we do, I can tell you that in the next election, we'll be talking about some other distraction. And then another one. And then another one. And nothing will change."

For the media, nothing had changed. Racial conflict was still a compelling train wreck that attracted gawkers to the Web, TV, newspapers, and magazines. Coverage of the six-week-long Pennsylvania primary was dominated by race, and Obama's ultimate defeat only seemed to confirm the wisdom of that coverage. Never mind that Pennsylvania was home to one of the oldest Democratic electorates in the country and Obama had consistently failed to attract as many older voters as Hillary Clinton. On the night of Obama's defeat in Pennsylvania, Ron Fournier of the Associated Press wrote an analysis of "the five reasons why Clinton is still alive. Five ways he'd be vulnerable in November." The first of those was race. "The jury is still out on whether a black man can overcome America's original sin and be elected president," he wrote. "An AP-Yahoo News poll found that about 8 percent of whites would be uncomfortable voting for a black president. The actual percentage is probably higher because voters are shy about admitting a racial prejudice to pollsters." Despite a late series of campaign swings by his white opponent in the fall, Pennsylvania voted for a black president by ten points in the general election.

Almost every outlet indulged in racial stereotyping. *Newsweek* ran three Obama cover stories in the month after the Pennsylvania primary, and all three included heavy racial components. The series started with a cover entitled "Obama's Bubba Gap" and ended with "Obama, Race and Us," which was an open letter from one of its most senior, and white, writers on how the candidate should deal with race. "The good news is that you have all but won the nomination," the letter began. "The bad news, if we are willing to face reality, is that the country—some parts of it, anyway—may not be ready to elect a black president of the United States." The magazine constructed a poll designed to flush out racist voters, configuring a set of questions (the "Racial Resentment Index") to identify those who disliked the civil rights movement and affirmative action. Among those racist Democrats, Clinton's lead over McCain was an unsurprisingly huge fifty-nine points. What was even more shocking was that racist Democrats also favored Obama over McCain by a healthy eighteen-point margin.

Many journalists and commentators were not that different from Reverend Wright: they seemed unable to accept that America was in the process of change, or that white voters might not vote as a bloc on matters of race. Around the same time that *Newsweek* printed its memo to Obama, polls showed that 68 percent of voters believed America was ready for a black president. In 2000, that number was just 38 percent. Well before he clinched the nomination, Obama had already changed racial attitudes across the country, at least when it came to the presidency.

What he could not change was the definition of white attitudes. Underneath most analysis of Obama's problems lay a curiously narrow idea of what constituted the white vote. Appalachian voters in Pennsylvania, West Virginia, and Kentucky seemed to rank more highly than white voters elsewhere. For instance, on the same night as he lost Kentucky by thirty-six points, Obama won Oregon by eighteen points. According to exit polls, Obama won every group of white voters in Oregon except for those sixty years and older, whom he lost by one point. He won voters earning less than $50,000 a year and he won voters without a college degree. Some pundits suggested that Obama lost states, like Pennsylvania, where there were black and white populations living close together. Yet in Oregon and West Virginia, there was the same, minuscule proportion of African American voters. In fact there was ample polling to show that gender and age were bigger obstacles to voters than race.

It was impossible to tell if journalists were fascinated by race because it sold well, because of their own personal attitudes to race, or because they were perhaps—like Wright—stuck in another decade. In any case, there was little discussion about why white voters were behaving so differently across the country. Instead, the long weeks of April and May were consumed by photo-op campaigning and racially tinged stories in the national media.

The final debate of the primaries seemed to capture the stagnation of the coverage. A month after his speech on race, Obama found himself in another hall inside the National Constitution Center in Philadelphia. Only this time, he was next to Hillary Clinton, and in front of ABC's Charlie Gibson and George Stephanopoulos. Just before the broadcast began, Clinton demanded a change to the format: instead of sitting down, she insisted on standing behind podiums. Then came the one-track questions. The third question was about Reverend Wright, as was the fourth, which included this from Stephanopoulos: "Number one, do you think Reverend Wright loves America as much as you do? And number two, if you get the nomination, what will you do when those sermons are played on television again and again and again?" Before going to a commercial break, the candidate had to explain why he wasn't wearing a flag pin, and why he was associated with Bill Ayers, the former 1960s radical.

After losing Pennsylvania by nine points, Obama sat down with his senior staff to look at how they planned to win the next two big contests, in Indiana and North Carolina, in two weeks' time. The polling in North Carolina showed him with a solid lead, but the lead in Indiana seemed to switch with each new poll. One factor, however, remained constant: Reverend Wright was planning his comeback tour, a media blitz including TV interviews and a speech at the National Press Club in Washington in April. Obama's aides felt sick at the prospect and could only relieve their nerves with some gallows humor. Sitting in Chicago, listening to the campaign's plans, David Plouffe detailed the challenge they faced. "Everyone needs to be clear," he said. "At least nine of the next thirteen days, Jeremiah Wright is going to be the news." They would barely have a week of campaigning after Wright's return.

It was time to talk directly to Wright. Over the next week, Obama's friends at Trinity tried to talk their pastor out of his comeback tour. But by now the church was deeply divided between Obama supporters and Wright supporters, and the conversation was going nowhere. So the candidate decided to go see Wright himself in secret, in Chicago. First came the dance over where to meet: one intermediary suggested a neutral location, but Obama said he was happy to go wherever Wright wanted. They ended up talking at Wright's home, and Obama tried to adopt the tone of a concerned friend giving advice. He did not want to tell his former pastor what to do, but he did want to nudge him in the right direction by making him aware of what was about to happen. Wright wasn't heading for vindication; he was heading for vilification.

"Look, you're a pastor, you have your own role to play," Obama said. "But I can tell you how politics in the cable and blog age works. Here's what you need to anticipate: that it's going to be a media circus. But obviously, you need to do what you need to do."

Wright felt embattled and wanted to tell his side of the story to the rest of the world. He thanked Obama for his opinion, but looked and sounded like the aggrieved party.

It was indeed a circus, and Wright was the clown trying to tame the lions. He lectured his National Press Club audience on the history of the black church, hammed up his answers for the cameras, and harangued the moderator who relayed the audience's first question about America's chickens coming home to roost on 9/11. "Have you heard the whole sermon?" he asked. "Have you heard the whole sermon?" When the moderator said she had heard most of it, he snapped back, "No, no. The whole sermon. Yes or no? No, you haven't heard the whole sermon? That nullifies that question. Well, let me try to respond in a nonbombastic way. If you heard the whole sermon, first of all, you heard that I was quoting the ambassador from Iraq. That's number one. But, number two, to quote the Bible, 'Be not deceived. God is not mocked. For whatsoever you sow, that you also shall reap.' Jesus said, 'Do unto others as you would have them do unto you.' You cannot do terrorism on other people and expect it never to come back on you. Those are biblical principles, not Jeremiah Wright bombastic, divisive principles." In other words, they weren't his comments; they were his Christian beliefs.

Obama was campaigning in North Carolina as Wright was performing on national television. Inside headquarters in Chicago, his staff stood open-jawed as they watched. "Every time you thought it couldn't get worse, it did," said his deputy communications director Dan Pfeiffer. As soon as the spectacle finished, the candidate called Valerie Jarrett for her take.

"It's really bad, and I think you've got to watch it," she said cautiously, not willing to tell him to dump Wright completely.

"What did he say?" asked Obama.

"I'm going to paraphrase it for you, but I don't think there's any substitute for you watching it yourself."

As reporters inundated his aides with new questions, the candidate read only snippets of Wright's comments before taking off from Wilmington, North Carolina. At the bottom of the airplane steps, he took six minutes of questions about an event he had not yet seen. "He does not speak for me," the candidate said of his ex-pastor. "He does not speak for the campaign."

That night, when he got to his hotel, Obama finally watched the full video on cable. He was shocked and angry. Obama felt he had been selfless in Philadelphia, respecting his pastor, the church, and the community. Now he believed that Wright only cared about himself.

The next day, after a regular town hall event in Winston-Salem, the candidate called a news conference behind the stage where he had just rallied his supporters. "I have spent my entire adult life trying to bridge the gap between different kinds of people," he began.

That's in my DNA, trying to promote mutual understanding, to insist that we all share common hopes and common dreams as Americans and as human beings. That's who I am. That's what I believe. That's what this campaign has been about. Yesterday, we saw a very different vision of America. I am outraged by the comments that were made, and saddened over the spectacle that we saw yesterday. You know, I have been a member of Trinity United Church of Christ since 1992. I have known Reverend Wright for almost twenty years. The person I saw yesterday was not the person that I met twenty years ago. His comments were not only divisive and destructive, but I believe that they end up giving comfort to those who prey on hate and I believe that they do not portray accurately the perspective of the black church. They certainly don't portray accurately my values and beliefs. And if Reverend Wright thinks that that's political posturing, as he put it, then he doesn't know me very well. And based on his remarks yesterday, well, I may not know him as well as I thought, either.

With that, he said his relationship with Wright would never be the same again.

His senior aides feared their presidential campaign would never be the same again, either. "To me, that was the most perilous point in the campaign," said Robert Gibbs. "That easily could have been the end." A week later, on the night before the primaries, Obama's musical hero Stevie Wonder played an outdoor set for a huge crowd of twenty-one thousand supporters in downtown Indianapolis. It should have been a magical moment, as Wonder played the campaign's unofficial theme, "Signed, Sealed, Delivered." Instead, it rained through the event and the candidate's pep rally. Later at the hotel bar, David Axelrod was unusually miserable. The last night of the campaign's internal tracking polls showed their support collapsing, and he feared the same in North Carolina. He blamed Wright, and the rehashing of the affair when Obama appeared on NBC's *Meet the Press* a day earlier. When he delivered news of the final Indiana tracking poll to the candidate, the reaction was one of personal pain about his former pastor. "How could someone I knew, someone I trusted, do this to me?" Obama said.

The next morning, as the candidate's closest friends and aides ate breakfast, the mood was almost funereal. "Let's hope for the best," said Jarrett, trying to be cheerful. They anticipated losing Indiana by seven or eight points, and winning North Carolina by the same margin. The candidate himself stepped into a coffee shop next to the hotel lobby, where he spotted some voters whom he could press for their support. How was it looking to him? As bad as Axelrod suggested?

"It is what it is," he told me. "Listen, we've had a month, two months of bad stuff. It's kind of hard to change the storyline."

In private, with his friends, he indulged in some misery-filled humor. "If I lose this, can we still hang out together? I could give speeches. I could earn at least as much as Bill Clinton," he said. "And we could all just hang out together." Sure, they said. As long as he spent all his money looking after them.

Obama won North Carolina by fifteen points, lost Indiana by just one point, and beat Reverend Wright once and for all. His victory was long and hard fought, in part because he took a renegade's path toward race and politics. When Wright erupted, a more conventional candidate might have cried racism and rallied his black base; yet he chose instead to explain and educate. When Wright reemerged, a less disciplined candidate might have dug in; yet he scarcely hesitated to cut his former friend loose. Through it all, Obama demonstrated that he was different, but not scary; new, but not naive; cool under intense pressure, and cold-blooded enough to win.

Race would never entirely disappear from the election, but it would morph into different shapes and debates about the candidate's identity and his loyalties. In spite of his bombastic pastor and a bomb-throwing media, the voters seemed to care more about the content of his character and his economic plan than the color of his skin. Obama's dream had survived, but only just.

SIX

GAME CHANGER

The YMCA in Columbia, South Carolina, has seen better days. Outside, it looks like a grand edifice of red brick and pale stone in what counts as the city's downtown. Inside, its carpeted hallways lead you to a gym where the wooden floors are hiding several dead spots. Bounce a ball on one and it barely rises above your ankles. That isn't the only challenge on this cold winter's afternoon, as the candidate gathers with some friends, aides, and Secret Service agents to shoot hoops. "Watch him go left," warns one agent. "He'll switch from the right, with a crossover bounce and a drive. Push him right." Sure enough, when he's not calling the plays, the candidate drives to the basket or stops short for a jump shot. He measures the strengths and weaknesses of newcomers, often telling them to their face what they are capable or incapable of. It's the kind of sweaty, wheezing, physical game of hoops that middle-aged men can barely muster. The agents are built for blocking and tackling, not running fast breaks. But it's hard to say what kind of shape the candidate is in, hidden under a baggy gray T-shirt and gray sweatpants. After all, even the younger staffers have grown flabby after a year on the campaign trail. His body guy, Reggie Love, trots on one supposedly fast break, and the candidate gets mad with the former Duke player. "You play like that for Coach K? He'd kill you," he shouts.

Obama liked to say it was his lucky game. Shooting hoops on election day was one of the fistful of charms in his pocket, the trinkets thrust upon him along the campaign trail. He had played in Iowa, but not in New Hampshire, so there must be some lucky connection. But basketball was more than just another turn of fortune's wheel. It was like his daily workout: a way to focus, to be centered, to connect with himself and what he was trying to do in life, in politics, and on the court. Whether he was on or off the ball, he controlled the game. He could be self-confident to the point of arrogant, cool under fire, or fade into the background as the consummate team player. When he couldn't keep up with the faster players, he could always try to psych them out by shouting "Boo" when they took an outside shot.

Basketball was a strategic challenge, not just a physical one. Walking off the court on Super Tuesday in early February, inside the luxury East Bank Club in Chicago, the candidate had played solidly but not outstandingly. But he was upbeat as he surveyed the day's primaries across the nation. "You know, I feel good," he said. "When we're doing what I think we should be doing, when the campaign is working the way I want it to be, it makes me calm. Just like Iowa. We didn't do that in New Hampshire and it didn't make me happy. It upsets me when I'm not playing my game. But right now, we're playing our game." It turned out he was right: he eked out a surprising edge in the day's primaries and caucuses, winning more states and slightly more delegates than the top-ranked Team Clinton.

Basketball was so much more than a game. It was his childhood dream to join the NBA, and he chose his first college in Los Angeles partly because of a vague promise that he might play there. As a teenager, he played with the ball his father had given him as a Christmas present. That ball helped him to find another family on court, "where a handful of black men, mostly gym rats and has-beens, would teach me an attitude that didn't just have to do with the sport," he wrote. "That respect came from what you did and not who your daddy was. That you could talk stuff to rattle an opponent, but that you should shut the hell up if you couldn't back it up. That you didn't let anyone sneak up behind you to see emotions—like hurt or fear—you didn't want them to see." It was on court that he said he made his closest white friends. And many years later, it was on court that he made friends in Chicago, and even passed the test of his future brother-in-law, who could *really* shoot hoops. Craig Robinson, a former star forward at Princeton and later head coach at Brown and Oregon State, was assigned the family task of judging his game and his character. "You can tell a lot about people by the way they play," he told me, "and you develop relationships with guys based on whether they don't shoot the ball every time they come down the court. He wasn't selfish and he's a hard worker."

Politics was no pastime for Barack Obama, but it tested him in similar ways to his beloved basketball. The campaign challenged his character and his strategy. To win, he needed to demonstrate what kind of game he could play. Was he a high-minded purist who never threw an elbow? Could he keep his cool while his opponents tried to rattle him? Was he all hope and no fight? It wasn't easy to do both: to run a principled campaign that inspired the young and the jaded, while also playing the contact sport of street politics. He could try to balance them out: playing gracefully and sticking to his positive message, then turning more aggressive when he got fouled. But what really guided him were two factors that were neither positive nor negative. First, he was deeply competitive and wanted to win. Second, he wanted to be a game changer, someone who could turn the contest on its head. Someone like Michael Jordan, who could switch from being an individual star to a team player and back again. Or someone from his personal list of heroes: Lincoln, FDR, Gandhi, King, Picasso, John Coltrane. "When I think about what binds them together, I'm enamored with people who change the framework, who don't take something as a given, but scramble it," he said. "So Gandhi being able to say what looks like weakness can be a strength and Picasso mastering realism and then flipping it." They were all renegades who had broken the rules only after mastering them in the first place. Obama's challenge was to play enough of the old game to prove his mettle, and enough of the new game to change the framework of American politics. If successful, he was writing the playbook for not just his presidential campaign but also his time in the White House.

In the early months of his campaign, his weaknesses looked like plain old weaknesses, not Gandhian strengths. As his polling numbers stagnated through the fall of 2007, and he lagged far behind Clinton, the pundits were of one mind: Obama needed to attack Clinton or drop out. "Every time he goes at her, or tries to, in kind of a hesitant way, it's a glancing blow," said Chris Matthews on MSNBC. "It never seems to land, the blow. He doesn't seem to know how to throw a Sunday punch. . . . He better go after her. And if he doesn't go after her, he has got to get out of the way, or he will get knocked out of the way." Even some of the candidate's closest supporters urged him to go negative, but he refused. In late October he met for dinner with some old Washington friends who advised him to go on the attack. "That's not the way I want to win," he told them. "We're not going to get personal. We're not going to kneecap anybody."

His staff could be forgiven for confusion: the candidate would call a foul according to a standard that only he could fully understand. He was furious when his campaign had tried to get personal with a memo attacking the Clintons for their ties to Indian businesses. He wanted to compete, but not too fiercely; he wanted to win, but not at all costs. "I think it was Justice Stewart during an obscenity case, when they asked him what obscenity is, he said, 'I know it when I see it.' I know where I think you cross the line into the dark side of politics," he told me after a campaign rally in New Hampshire. "I have no problem contrasting my policy positions with others'. I don't mind others drawing contrasts with my policy positions."

Early on, the contrasts were drawn for him, and they were far more personal than political. Maureen Dowd of the *New York Times,* a modern-day Dorothy Parker, suggested that Michelle Obama was belittling her husband for talking about his dirty socks and his failure to make the bed. "Many people I talked to afterward found Michelle wondrous," she wrote. "But others worried that her chiding was emasculating, casting her husband—under fire for lacking experience—as an undisciplined child." Looking back, the Obamas later found the notion amusing. But in the immediate aftermath, Michelle stopped talking about his domestic shortcomings. "Somehow I've been caricatured as this emasculating wife," she told me with a laugh, as she drove in an SUV through Wisconsin. "Barack and I laugh about that. It's just sort of like, 'Do you think anybody could emasculate Barack Obama?' *Really,* now." Even the candidate conceded that his wife could be more aggressive and outspoken than he was on the campaign trail. "The one thing that maybe Michelle can do that I can't do," he told me, "is that she can probably go after people who go after me more forcefully, just as the angry spouse. Whereas I have to be more diplomatic, I think, than she does about some of these issues." Maybe she could get away with being defensive as his wife. Or maybe she was just more engaged in the game than he was, and couldn't stand the thought of defeat. Michelle shunned team sports in spite of her athletic physique—a decision she ascribed to bucking expectations, but her husband suggested had more to do with her distaste for losing. "She's too competitive. She hates losing," he told me. "We can't even play cards. She can't stand me winning."

At the heart of the effeminate caricature was a contest he cared little for, or simply failed to comprehend: the TV debate. As a Senate candidate, his debate performance was dismal. He found that his rival, Alan Keyes, could easily get under his skin by questioning his sincerity, especially about religion. "In the three debates that were held before the election," he wrote, "I was frequently tongue-tied, irritable, and un-characteristically tense." For all his supposed cool and self-confidence, Obama could be rattled and impatient, especially if he took the contest personally. At one point he even confronted Keyes physically, poking him in the chest when they exchanged words at a parade on Indian Indepen-dence Day.

As a presidential candidate, Obama showed little anger. In fact, any emotion would have been better than his languid, lackluster demeanor of those first debates. His responses rambled around the subject, rarely touching on any talking point or any of his rivals. It was as if he didn't understand or didn't care for the rules of the game: to dodge difficult questions and pivot the answers into an assertion of strength or, even better, an assault on an opponent. Standing onstage as one of eight can-didates, jamming serious policy questions into sixty-second answers, seemed like a waste of time. "The whole format, with all those people, and you just have a couple of minutes to distinguish yourself," said his speechwriter Jon Favreau, "it was so phony to him."

Obama wanted to explain issues, not score points; he wanted to compromise, not debate. "I came in, and still do, with a very conversa-tional, professorial style. I think of these things as conversations, and they're not," he told me. The challenge was not just one of language; Obama was working from the wrong political playbook. "These debate formats are not a natural form of communication for me," he explained to me on his campaign plane. "Partly because the way I think about pol-icy, and the way I think about governance, and the way I think about in-teracting with people generally is to find out what it is that they're thinking, to give them a sense of what I'm thinking, and then try to syn-thesize and try to find what is the truth that lies between people. Now that's an enormous strength when you're negotiating a complex piece of legislation. My natural instinct is not to try to beat the other person down, but rather to understand their point of view and make sure they under-stand my point of view, and then see if we can find common ground. Well, that is completely contrary to what a debate is about. That may be why I never became a trial lawyer. Or that was never attractive to me.

And that's really a skill that is much more akin to what a trial lawyer does." There was already one outstanding trial lawyer onstage: John Edwards. And he was doing a far better job of scoring points against Clinton.

By early August 2007, with his campaign stuck in the doldrums, Obama had reached his limit, which was already relatively low. In his prep session for the next debate, at Drake University in Des Moines, he was grouchy. He seemed to hate debate prep even more than the debates themselves. He had no clear strategy and no single message. His staffers, standing in as rival candidates, were ruthlessly trashing him and everything he stood for. "Everyone was beating the hell out of me," he told me later. The whole thing seemed pointless.

"This thing isn't on the level," said Favreau, who was helping with the prep.

"Yeah," said Obama, breaking into a chuckle. "*None* of this is on the level."

"You've got to *play*," Favreau explained, as the tension eased. "You've got to *act* like it matters."

It was something of an epiphany for Obama. Suddenly he could see the superficial game for what it was. For the first few minutes of the debate, ABC's George Stephanopoulos went around the stage inviting the other candidates to take a swing at Obama, asking them if he was ready to be president. Obama watched the spectacle, ready with a comeback line from his communications director, Robert Gibbs. "Well, you know, to prepare for this debate," he began, "I rode in the bumper cars at the state fair." As his fellow candidates laughed at the joke, Obama finally got it: none of this really was on the level. From the moderator to the other candidates, it was all playacting. "This was performance," Obama later told me. "It wasn't a conversation. What I mean by performance is you've got to have a pithy sound bite, that nobody is interested in your lengthy explanations of the complexities of the situation. This isn't a law school class, and you've got a time limit to stop having such a long windup so that you never get to your answer. I guess the way to describe it is that you are a four-hundred-meter runner and suddenly they put you in the hundred meter and it takes you a while to figure out: what is this race about?"

The race he wanted to win was the one that focused on him. If he was just one of the pack, the contest hardly interested him. But this ABC debate focused on him and was worthy of a counterattack, where he could at least hit his rivals from a position of moral strength. "Barack is a very good counterpuncher," said David Plouffe. "So from the very first moment, he was kind of on the griddle and he responded well. Some of these other debates with eight candidates, it would take him some time to warm up and he'd have to fight his way in."

By the fall of 2007 he was on the griddle all day, every day. It was just where he needed to be to lift his game. "Barack is competitive and he's a prime-time player," said his Senate chief of staff, Pete Rouse. "He performs best when the pressure is on and the stakes are high." Now the pressure was higher than ever, and the candidate's competitive spirit kicked in.

Four days before his next debate in Philadelphia, Obama sat down with the *New York Times* and accused Clinton of failing to tell the full truth about her positions. He tried to stick to his self-image of a more positive and principled politician. He said he was not trying to "kneecap the front-runner, because I don't think that's what the country is looking for." But this wasn't just a contrast in policy positions; it might not be obscene, but he still failed the Justice Stewart test. On Social Security, Iraq, and Iran, Clinton was hiding her true self, he suggested. "I don't think people know what her agenda exactly is," he said. "Now it's been very deft politically. But one of the things that I firmly believe is that we've got to be clear with the American people right now about the important choices that we're going to need to make in order to get a mandate for change, not to try to obfuscate and avoid being a target in the general election."

He was indeed more aggressive at the debate, and he was more fortunate, too: he got several assists from his rival candidates and the moderators, NBC's Tim Russert and Brian Williams. In the first response of the show, Obama promptly attacked Clinton by accusing her of dishonesty, flip-flopping, and being a pseudo-Republican. "I'm running for president because I think that the way to bring about that change is to offer some sharp contrasts with the other party," he said. "I think it means that we bring people together to get things done. I think it means that we push against the special interests that are holding us back. And most importantly, I think it requires us to be honest about the challenges that we face. It does not mean, I think, changing positions whenever it's politically convenient. And Senator Clinton, in her campaign, I think, has been for NAFTA previously. Now she's against it. She has taken one position on torture several months ago, and then most recently has taken a different position. She voted for a war, to authorize sending troops into Iraq, and then later said this was a war for diplomacy."

What followed was accurately described by the Clinton campaign as a pile-on. Edwards accused Clinton of Orwellian double-talk; Dodd and Biden attacked her for voting for a saber-rattling Senate amendment against Iran; Edwards again questioned her honesty on Iraq policy. Russert and Williams grilled her for never saying she opposed the war in Iraq, for her lack of executive experience, for hiding her White House records, and for her position on Social Security. Clinton withstood the pressure until close to the end, when she tripped herself up in two answers about driver's licenses for illegal immigrants. First she suggested she was supportive of them; then she claimed she never said such a thing. Dodd, Edwards, and then Obama jumped on her contradictions. She had just demonstrated what they were attacking in the first place. "Well, I was confused on Senator Clinton's answer," Obama ventured. "I can't tell whether she was for it or against it. And I do think that is important. One of the things that we have to do in this country is to be honest about the challenges that we face."

The only challenge Obama couldn't face was the one Russert raised next with Dennis Kucinich, the Ohio congressman running yet another vainglorious campaign for president. Was it true that he had seen a UFO over the home of actress Shirley MacLaine in Washington State? Kucinich said he had, but insisted that so too had Jimmy Carter. Russert refined the question for Obama, saying the three astronauts on Apollo 11 believed in life beyond Earth. Did he? "You know, I don't know. And I don't presume to know," he said before executing a perfect pivot on the debate stage. "What I know is there is life here on Earth. And that we're not attending to life here on Earth. We're not taking care of kids who are alive and unfortunately are not getting health care. We're not taking care of senior citizens who are alive and are seeing their heating prices go up. So, as president, those are the people I will be attending to first." It might have been an easy question compared with illegal immigration, but the substance was less important than the style. He had learned how to play-act as a presidential candidate.

In his own retelling, Obama preferred a revisionist account of the moment when he crossed the line to the dark side. He chose to remember the moment he resisted the pressure to attack, rather than the moment he decided to play the game and win. After all, he had been less aggressive than either John Edwards or Tim Russert. And he only tiptoed across the line: there were no attack ads on TV or radio, just a few well-placed suggestions of dishonesty and two-faced posturing.

Having flashed some steel, he later seemed to enjoy the notion that he was too soft to win; it made him sound more principled. A few days before the caucuses in Iowa, where voters prefer their candidates to sound "Iowa nice," Obama remembered how he had refused to attack his rival. In a hot crowded ballroom inside the Marriott hotel in Coralville, he chuckled as he told a crowd of around fifteen hundred supporters about his favorite editorial cartoon. It showed him on a big-screen TV as Tigger from *Winnie the Pooh,* bouncing on his tail with a big smile as he tried to hug Hillary Clinton. A bubble over a TV viewer read: Obama in Attack Mode . . . "When we were down in the summer, and folks were writing us off, they said, 'Oh he's got to go negative. He can't keep up with this positive campaign. If he wants to catch up, he's got to kneecap the front-runner, do a Tonya Harding on her. Whack!' That's what they said. You know that. You remember. They were all writing me off, saying, 'He's too nice. He can't win.' But you know what? We didn't change course. We kept on running a positive campaign. We pointed out our differences, but we rejected the slash-and-burn tactics that Washington is so accustomed to." Not slash and burn, more like slice and dice.

The candidate was learning to keep his cool when he was trying to rattle his main opponent. In place of the heat of his encounters with Alan Keyes, he found he could achieve more with a psy-op strategy by staying just above the fray, while reaching down whenever needed. It helped him take the measure of his rivals, while also throwing them off their game. In mid-December, less than a month before the first vote in Iowa, he saw his opportunity. He was traveling to Des Moines for yet another debate and was getting ready to board his plane at the same time as Clinton was boarding hers, at Reagan National airport. Clinton asked to talk to Obama and she apologized for comments by her New Hampshire cochairman. Billy Shaheen had suggested that Republicans would exploit Obama's self-confessed drug use if he won the nomination. Such comments had no place in her campaign, Clinton assured Obama, and Shaheen would resign. But Obama was not satisfied: he felt it was part of a pattern, which included an e-mail forwarded by a Clinton volunteer in

Iowa suggesting that he was Muslim. Clinton grew agitated, waving her arms and poking her finger at him, as she hurled his own negativity back at him. Wasn't he the one who just called her disingenuous for saying she couldn't release her own White House papers? Wasn't it his donor David Geffen who accused her and her husband of lying with ease? Instead of responding with anger, Obama tried to chill his rival, placing a hand on her arm. Clinton recoiled from the gesture, which seemed either patronizing or restraining or both. Obama boarded his plane with a new sense of wonder. "I never saw that look of concern in her eyes before," he told his senior aides. "I think we can win this one."

The contest wasn't just being played out in Iowa or New Hampshire; it wasn't just taking place through TV ads and debates. It was taking place in the minds of the candidates, as a test of will and character. Reporters and voters were searching for a sign of strength or weakness, an insight into whether the candidates had what it takes to become commander in chief. Some of that was superficial: the spectator sport and pop psychology of presidential politics. But some of it was meaningful, too: how else could the voters decide who was ready to become president? There was no training program, no perfect résumé, no guaranteed guide to how they would perform under the high ceilings of the Oval Office. There was just the stress test of a presidential campaign. And if you could stress your opponent a little more than usual, maybe they would fumble or stumble. Maybe you could inject just enough doubt to make their supporters think again.

The tarmac encounter was just a prelude. By the time voting began, it was Bill, not Hillary, who was losing his temper. In the closing days of Iowa, Obama was arguing in every stump speech that he was the political equivalent of Bill Clinton in 1992: inexperienced, perhaps, but the only force for change. "You can have the right kind of experience and the wrong kind of experience," Obama would quote Clinton at every stop. "Mine is rooted in the real lives of real people, and it will bring real results if we have the courage to change."

Clinton struck back a week later, in the closing days of New Hampshire, when a Dartmouth College student made a fleeting reference to the issue of judgment. "Since you raised the judgment issue, let's go over this again," Clinton said as he tossed his index cards onto the podium to engage in some classic finger-wagging. "That is the central argument for his campaign: 'It doesn't matter that I started running for president less than a year after I got to the Senate from the Illinois state senate. I am a great speaker and a charismatic figure and I'm the only one that had the judgment to oppose this war from the beginning. Always, always, always.'" Clinton argued that his wife's vote to authorize war was not in fact a vote to go to war. Then he claimed that Obama had sailed through fifteen debates without getting questioned about his voting record on Iraq, which was similar to his wife's. "Give me a break. This whole thing is the biggest fairy tale I have ever seen," he said, before accusing the Obama campaign of smearing him just like Kenneth Starr, his nemesis in the Monica Lewinsky affair. "The idea that one of these campaigns is positive and the other is negative—when I know the reverse is true, and I have seen it and I have been blistered by it for months—is a little tough to take. Just because of the sanitizing coverage that's in the media, doesn't mean the facts aren't out there," he concluded. The next day, Obama could only offer sympathy to the former president. "I understand he's feeling a little frustrated right now," he told reporters at a Dunkin' Donuts in Manchester.

The mind games began in earnest in Nevada. Both had won surprise and substantial victories: Obama in Iowa, Clinton in New Hampshire. Soon after his shock defeat in New Hampshire, Obama was flying to northern Nevada and taking stock with his friend Marty Nesbitt. "I think if we keep up at our current pace," he said, "we'll finish up a respectable second." Nesbitt agreed. He knew that his friend wanted to change the course of the contest, but sensed that he didn't know how.

The next day, the candidate started with a high-minded tone in front of reporters on the issue of race. "I have been a little concerned about how the tenor of the campaign has been going over the last few days," he began. "Over the last couple of days, you have seen a tone on the Democratic side of the campaign that is unfortunate. I may disagree with Senator Clinton or Senator Edwards on how to get there, but we share the same goals. We are all Democrats. We all believe in civil rights. We all believe in equal rights. . . . I don't want the campaign to degenerate into so much tit for tat, back-and-forth, that we lose sight of why all of us are doing this."

The principled position did not last long. A few hours later, Obama was sitting down with the editorial board of the *Reno Gazette-Journal*. Whether intentional or not, he launched a new round of tit for tat when he started to mess with the minds of his biggest rivals. First he downplayed Bill Clinton's position in history. "I think Ronald Reagan changed the trajectory of America in a way that, you know, Richard Nixon did not. And in a way that Bill Clinton did not. He [Reagan] put us on a fundamentally different path because the country was ready for it," he said, leaning back in a black leather chair. Then he wrote off Republicans as outdated, a group that was once "the party of ideas" but was now stale with its obsession with tax cuts. Finally he looped back on the generational shift that he represented. "Some of it is the times. And some of it is maybe a generational element to this partly, in the sense that I didn't come of age in the battles of the sixties. I'm not as invested in them," he said without naming those classic sixties warriors who led the Clinton campaign. "So I think I talk differently about issues. And I think I talk differently about values and that's why I think we've been resonating with the American people. And by the way, when I say this sometimes it's interpreted as I don't think anybody who's a baby boomer should be president. That's not what I'm saying. What I'm saying is I think the average baby boomer has moved beyond a lot of the arguments about the sixties, but our politicians haven't." He didn't think the Clintons and their generation should be excluded from the presidency; he just suggested they were stuck in a mind-set that was outdated and out of touch.

What followed was a mixture of high-stakes goading and opportunism. Bill Clinton seized on Obama's comments and twisted them into more than just a personal slight; they became, in his mind, a betrayal of the entire party. "Her principal opponent said that since 1992, the Republicans have had all the good ideas," Bill said of his wife's rival in Pahrump, Nevada. "So now it turns out you can choose between somebody who thinks our ideas are better or the Republicans had all the good ideas." Obama's comments grew more and more personal for Clinton over time. Two days later, in New York, he extended his line of thinking. "He said President Reagan was the engine of innovation and did more, had a more lasting impact on America than I did," he declared. "Which [will] be costly maybe down the road for him because it's factually not accurate." Compared with her husband, Hillary Clinton sounded subdued. She reworked Obama's comments to suggest that he supported the privatization of Social Security and an end to the minimum wage.

At first, Obama's team seemed unsure how to respond to a former president who remained enormously popular with the party's voters. But when they responded, the counterattack was forceful. "He's basically been on the attack for several weeks," said David Axelrod. "That's his role: saying things that she can't or he shouldn't. In the last few weeks

he has become increasingly intemperate and there's been a lot of statements coming from him that are just flat-out distortions. I admire him as
a former president but we're not going to stand by and let Senator
Obama's voice or record be distorted by anyone." That meant responding to the attacks with surrogates like former senator Tom Daschle, who
lamented how the former president had squandered the respected status
of his postpresidency. Each counterpunch reinforced the broader thrust
about honesty and openness. In defending the candidate, Obama's campaign was attacking the truthfulness of the Clintons. And in defending
himself, the candidate was demonstrating that he could take the punches
of a presidential contest.

He was turning weakness into strength, and echoing some of his heroes. In Sumter, South Carolina, he defended his comments on Reagan,
called for honesty in politics, and connected both with the chain e-mails
smearing him as a secret Muslim. "So don't be confused when you start
hearing a whole bunch of this negative stuff," he told a lively, mostly
African American audience. "Those are the same old tricks. They're trying to bamboozle you. It's the same old okie-doke. Y'all know about
okie-doke, right? It's the same old stuff. Just like if anybody starts getting
one of these e-mails saying, 'Obama is a Muslim.' I've been a member of
the same church for almost twenty years, prayin' to Jesus, with my Bible.
Don't let people turn you around because they're just making stuff up!
That's what they do. They try to bamboozle you." Someone in the
crowd shouted out "Hoodwink!" "Hoodwink you," the candidate chuckled. "Try to hoodwink you. All right, I'm having too much fun here." He
and the crowd were echoing one of Malcolm X's most famous, and fictional, speeches—polished up and performed by Denzel Washington
in Spike Lee's movie—when he rails against politicians for pacifying
black voters in Harlem. "I'm gonna tell ya like it really is. Every election
year, these politicians are sent up here to pacify us. They're sent here, set
up here by the white man. This is what they do," the movie version of
Malcolm X says, whipping up the crowd. "I say it and I say it again: You
been had. You been took. You been hoodwinked. Bamboozled. Led
astray. Run amok."

It was an engrossing spectacle, watching two Clintons take on their
renegade rival. Yet as the traveling circus moved on in South Carolina,
Obama seemed more than just a hapless victim. When Hillary Clinton
revived the controversy about Reagan and Republican ideas at their next

debate, Obama was ready with his own opposition research: Clinton had herself praised Reagan in similar terms in a new book by NBC's Tom Brokaw. "These are the kinds of political games that we are accustomed to," Obama said wryly, before raising the subject of her husband's attacks.

"Well, I'm here. He's not," she said.

"OK, well, I can't tell who I'm running against sometimes," he quipped as the crowd applauded.

Not only were the Clintons playing games with the truth; they were ganging up on him. The next day, reporters wanted to know if the Clintons were becoming an obsession for Obama. "Are you allowing President Clinton to get in your head?" asked Jeff Zeleny of the *New York Times* after one rally in Greenwood, South Carolina.

"I am trying to make sure that misstatements by him are answered. Don't you think that's important?" Obama said with an irritated tone and a grin.

Zeleny persisted shouting over the barrier that separated him from the candidate, who had not fielded reporters' questions in almost a week.

"Come on, Jeff, don't try cheap stunts like that. You're better than that." After autographing some supporters' campaign signs, Obama walked back to Zeleny. "My suspicion is, I think, that the other side must be rattled if they're continuing to say false things about us," he added.

The counterattack seemed like a less aggressive way of going negative than a first strike in a debate. Never mind who fouled first, or how much he enjoyed rattling the other side. What mattered was winning the contest. "We had to figure out how to deal with a former president who was just lying, engaging in bald-faced lies," he told me later.

But what about his singular focus on the Clintons rather than hope or change? People said Bill Clinton got into his head.

"Yes, but I got into *his*," he said with a broad smile.

Obama liked to see himself as a playmaker, a point guard who could direct the game and outsmart his opponents, moving the ball to his teammates, or driving to the basket as needed. Control and timing were key, and he used both to great effect through the course of the election.

Sometimes that meant strategic delay. Just before the Iowa caucuses, John Kerry called Obama's aides with some big news. He had been going back and forth on whether to endorse the outsider, and as the party's last presidential nominee, his decision would have a big impact. Now he was ready to step into the spotlight again and break with the Clintons.

Obama's aides were torn. They wanted the legitimacy and credibility that Kerry would bring. But the goal in Iowa and beyond was to bring in new voters, and Kerry was hardly a new factor in politics. Obama and his aides debated the endorsement on New Year's Day in a high school locker room after an early-morning rally. "That isn't who we are," said Mitch Stewart, their Iowa caucus director. "We're not the D.C. people. We've got this far without them. Let's close it." Obama asked his other aides and they nervously agreed. "I'll call him," he told his team. "Hard decision," said David Plouffe. "Nine out of ten campaigns would have made the other decision. It was not unanimous, but we all got to the same place in the end."

Instead they deployed Kerry two days after their defeat in New Hampshire. Speaking in South Carolina, where he had launched his own campaign four years earlier, Kerry said timing was everything. "Martin Luther King said the time is always right to do what is right," he declared. Except when Obama's timing turned out to be better than his own. "Kerry's endorsement ended up being much more meaningful to have it right after New Hampshire," Plouffe said. "It put the wind back in our sails right away."

Obama repeated the feat two days after his victory in South Carolina, only to greater effect. In theory, the contest was equally balanced: he had won two states, while Clinton had also won two. In practice, he took control of the game with a far bigger endorsement from two generations of Kennedys: Senator Ted Kennedy, his son Patrick, and his niece Caroline, the last member of President Kennedy's immediate family. Every Democratic candidate had aspired to carry the torch of the Kennedys, and some, like Bill Clinton in 1992, had made the connection explicit. Now the Kennedys themselves were making the claim, and confronting the Clintons, too. "There was another time, when another young candidate was running for president and challenging America to cross a New Frontier. He faced public criticism from the preceding Democratic president, who was widely respected in the party," said Ted Kennedy. "Harry Truman said we needed 'someone with greater experience' and added: 'May I urge you to be patient.' And John Kennedy replied: "The world is changing. The old ways will not do. It's time for a new generation of leadership.' So it is with Barack Obama. He has lit a spark of hope amid the fierce urgency of now."

Even the cool-blooded candidate was overwhelmed by the moment, in front of a roaring crowd of students at American University in Washington, D.C. "It was the first time I got emotional," he later told me. "I actually choked up. It wasn't just the endorsement. It was the young people out there. You could see that it was something similar to what had happened all those years ago." The Kennedys' endorsement dominated the news for most of the week that separated South Carolina from Super Tuesday, ensuring national coverage for a candidate who was still only vaguely known across the country.

The contest was not just about getting into the heads of his rivals; it was about keeping his own head when all about him were losing theirs. While his mood swings were limited, the news swings were not. Expectations were raised and dashed from the beginning, and the candidate rapidly learned that he needed to bury his emotions even deeper if he wanted to win. The pendulum movement began with his record-breaking fund-raising in 2007, then swung back when he failed to take an immediate poll lead. "That created what has turned out to be the classic dynamic of this entire campaign, which is the press overreacting in one direction and then overreacting in another," he told me on the campaign plane one morning. By the time he reached Iowa, he was already tuning out the noise. One day late in the caucus campaign, as his bus rolled through the state, he grew annoyed at the sight of David Axelrod and Robert Gibbs jumping up and down as they read the latest polls on their BlackBerrys. The candidate turned around from watching TV and banished them from his sight. "I don't know what you're reading, but I want you to read it away from me," he said. "Go to the back of the bus and read it there." The candidate began to avoid the press commentary and urged his friends to do the same. "He started scolding me for reading too much of this stuff and watching too much cable TV," said Marty Nesbitt. "He said, 'I don't know why you guys torture yourself with that stuff.'"

Soon after Super Tuesday, when it became clear that the contest would run for several months, Obama sounded so chill that he barely seemed to care about the outcome of the contest. He spoke as if it didn't matter whether he left the life of presidential politics altogether. "I'll be fine. I'll spend time with my children," he told me at the front of his campaign plane.

Would he just go back and teach constitutional law?

"Yeah. I don't have to do this," he said as if running for president were just a seasonal job. "Of course, I really want to beat them now. They've annoyed me. But I could do something else. I'm not sure she could."

Could he really walk away from the grassroots movement he had built, from all the emotion and adulation that was so evident on the campaign trail?

"Oh, I'll campaign for her if she's the nominee, for sure," he added casually.

There was an obvious ambivalence, which wasn't entirely coherent. He was nonchalant about defeat, yet he desperately wanted to win. He was self-confident enough to consider walking away, yet so annoyed with his rivals that he felt driven to succeed.

Sometimes it was hard to know where the Zen mood ended and the complacency began. At times he could feel too self-assured about his own abilities and accomplishments. After eking out a narrow victory in delegates on Super Tuesday, Obama began an extraordinary run of eleven straight wins through the rest of February. Each week brought more victories, more delegates, and more momentum. But for all the euphoria, there was little new in the Obama campaign. Instead of declaring the contest all but finished, the candidate repeated his speeches and rallies. Winning became strangely dull. "We had this enormous run through February, where we win eleven straight, and at that point all cylinders are clicking," he told me. "That's when we're having these huge rallies and filling every auditorium. My speeches are, I think, full of energy and people. We're just on a roll. But that's eleven victory speeches, thirty huge rallies. Everything gets stale after a while. So at a certain point it starts losing its spark, its freshness."

When his campaign tried to regain its spark and go on the offensive, it was Clinton who seemed invigorated. She viewed aggressive campaigning as "the fun part" of an election, while he delegated the fun to his subordinates and preferred to counterpunch only when forced to do so. When one of his less honest campaign mailings surfaced in Ohio, it was Clinton who triumphed. In a state reeling from the loss of manufacturing jobs, Obama's team suggested that Clinton was a strong admirer of the NAFTA trade deal. "Hillary Clinton believed NAFTA was 'a boon' to our economy," read one mailing over a picture of the padlocked gates to a factory. In fact, the word *boon* was a *Newsday* reporter's summary of her previous statements. Clinton took the mailing and waved it to the cameras in Cincinnati. "Enough with the speeches and the big rallies and then using tactics that are straight out of Karl Rove's playbook. This is wrong, and every Democrat should be outraged," she said. "So shame on you, Barack Obama. It is time you ran a campaign consistent with your messages in public. That's what I expect from you. Meet me in Ohio. Let's have a debate about your tactics." In New Hampshire, Obama had failed to say a word about the Clinton mailing that attacked him for supposedly being weak on abortion rights and choice. Six weeks later, Clinton would make no such mistake.

Now it was her turn to transform weakness into strength. Clinton's flame seemed to burn brighter, leaving the impression that her campaign was very much alive. When she won in Texas and Ohio, at the start of March, her upbeat tone matched the latest results and she savored the victory. Obama seemed to withdraw from the fight and rarely trumpeted his victories. "I was really annoyed with the press," said Valerie Jarrett. "Because he kicked butt. And he didn't get credit for it. Then he has Texas and Ohio. The spotlight was on those two and it just erased everything he had done, race after race after race after race. Probably it was our fault. We should have celebrated those wins more than we did. Each one of those should have been an Ohio. We didn't do that. Maybe we were a little gun-shy. If Clinton had won all those races, it would have been over."

Obama had good reason to sound gun-shy even if he didn't feel that way inside. After his defeat in New Hampshire, he was wary of declaring victory or changing his game plan. "They are tenacious candidates and a tenacious campaign," he said after touring the livestock and farm machinery at Houston's rodeo on election day. "She's going to push as hard as she can. As they said, they are deploying the kitchen sink strategy and seeing what works. Our job is to stay on our game and keep playing our game."

In fact, he changed his game after losing Texas and Ohio. He cut back on his big rallies, as Clinton had urged him to. He engaged in smaller events, with lots of photo opportunities. And his campaign ended up trading attacks and counterattacks with their counterparts on Clinton's side. He was occupying a middle ground between positive and negative campaigning, and succeeding at neither. By the time he reached North Carolina in late April, he conceded that he was off his game. "I've got to admit, I haven't always seen our philosophy that we started with in the last couple of weeks. Sometimes folks are throwing stuff at you and you start reacting," he told a crowd of eighteen thousand fans at the University of North Carolina in Chapel Hill. "And I told my staff the other day, 'You know, I don't want to be goaded into something. The press likes to ask: Is he tough enough, is he hitting back? I want us to remember what got us into this race.' When you start bickering, when you start arguing, when you're worried about superdelegates, when you're worried about tactics, when you're worried about winning, you forget about what the campaign is all about. This campaign is not about me. This campaign is not about Hillary Clinton. This campaign is not about John McCain. This campaign is about *you*. It's about your struggles. It's about your hopes. It's about your dreams."

The next morning the candidate thought his game was good enough to play with the UNC Tar Heels team that had just reached the final four of the NCAA tournament. The campaign wasn't about him, but this was one of his dreams all the same. After all, he was in good shape and played regular pickup basketball, and the cameras would love it. He posed for a group photo with the kids who were less than half his age, and spent the next five minutes sprinting up and down the court. "These guys are a lot better than me," he said to one of the team's coaches. He hit one outside shot, and later executed a flashy behind-the-back bounce pass. Then he started missing his outside shots and his signature drive to the basket. His lungs were heaving as he subbed himself off and collapsed in a chair. "Old man wants to stop," he wheezed.

He had to play, and win, on his own terms. Not by mimicking Clinton's style, or by succumbing to his supporters' passions. He would compete by remaining detached, by thinking strategically and outsmarting his opposition. The paradox of being Barack Obama meant that he could understand Clinton even as he was determined to vanquish her. One day on the campaign plane, his aides were attacking

Clinton for looking angry when she denounced his NAFTA mailings. Obama turned on his staffers. "You have no idea how hard it is," he said. "I know how hard it is and I can understand how she feels. She's been at this a long time. She's a great public servant and the new guy comes along, totally unanticipated, and changes the scene. I can see why that would be irritating."

In the media, the contest always looked like a grudge match. Obama supposedly snubbed Clinton when he failed to shake her hand as they gathered in the House chamber to listen to President Bush's final State of the Union address. It might have looked like a snub: Obama turned away from Clinton as she shook hands with Ted Kennedy, who was standing next to him. But looks could be deceiving. Obama explained that he had only turned away to answer a question from his other seatmate, Claire McCaskill. Besides, he had waved to Clinton just a few moments earlier. His true position was conflicted: he was somewhere between public hostility and a warm embrace.

Most of his supporters felt far less charitably toward Clinton. On the night of Super Tuesday, a crowd of his closest friends and supporters in Chicago started to boo as the Clintons appeared on one of the TV screens in the Hyatt hotel ballroom where Obama was to speak. A few minutes earlier they had chanted "Yes We Can!" Suddenly they were chanting "No She Can't!" There were similar feelings among a far smaller group of friends on his plane on the night he lost the Pennsylvania primary. Clinton rarely called to congratulate Obama on his victories, and Obama's friends felt he should return the snub. Obama hesitated for a moment, then picked up the cell phone. "Congratulations on your victory," he said. "See you in the next state."

On the night he clinched the nomination, many of the same friends watched Clinton's speech alongside the candidate in a bar inside the Xcel Energy Center in St. Paul, Minnesota. Several of them grimaced as Clinton refused to concede the contest, even as her rival picked up enough delegates to win. "This has been a long campaign, and I will be making no decisions tonight," she said, and urged her supporters to go to her website and "help in any way that you can." Obama's friends turned to look at him for some flicker of a reaction to this latest snub, or at least for a clue to his response. But he looked inscrutable, even as Clinton's supporters urged her to take the contest to the convention by chanting "Denver! Denver! Denver!"

In fact he had come to admire Clinton's spirit, and looked forward to an easier opponent and an easier battle. "I've always understood the enormous expectations that she carried with her and the fiercely competitive nature of her and the fact that she cares passionately about these issues. My respect for her is undiminished," he told me in the bar. "There's no doubt that in some ways the general election will be easier for me psychologically, just because it's harder to have a contest inside the family."

That night, Obama called Clinton to congratulate her on her symbolic win in South Dakota, and to suggest they might want to meet and talk some time soon. Where and when was her choice. He even sat down with a group of some of her supporters to tell them he knew personally how they felt. "I understood that they were as inspired by her candidacy as some of my supporters were inspired by mine," he said later. "They're not alone in drawing inspiration from her campaign. My own daughters now take the possibility of a woman being president for granted in a way that they might not have, had she not run."

How could he set aside the rancor so quickly? Maybe because he had proved himself worthy of the big leagues. Maybe because he was ambivalent about the game in the first place: he wanted to win, but didn't need to win. Or maybe because it made no sense to dunk the ball after the final buzzer. He wanted to unify the party and help his own chances of victory in November. And he wanted to return to his natural philosophy of finding common ground. Once victory was assured, he had little interest in the combative approach that helped him to win.

The day after praising Clinton for inspiring his daughters, Obama met with his archrival in the Washington home of Senator Dianne Feinstein. The press was locked on his campaign plane, taxiing along the runway when the news broke. Feinstein showed them into her living room, gave them each a glass of water, and left them while she worked upstairs. Two aides sat in a nearby study, and the two former opponents were alone. Clinton started by congratulating Obama on his victory and the former rivals got down to business about campaigning together. "We talked about how we could move forward and work together and win in November," recalled Obama. "I thought she handled the conversation very gracefully."

Clinton had readied a team of lawyers, led by Cheryl Mills and Bob Barnett, to work on the details of what he might do for her campaign and what she might do for his. She suggested Obama ask his own aides to negotiate with them. But on one issue, Clinton would not negotiate: she was only going to submit to a vetting if she was assured of the vice presidency. After eighteen months of campaigning against each other, she felt that Obama knew all there was to know about her. It was a reversal of the normal pattern for a vice presidential candidate: the vetting typically happened before the selection, not the other way around. To Obama's inner circle, that was a clear way for Clinton to disqualify herself from serious consideration. Not because of the presumptuous nature of her position, but because there was no way that she could pass the vetting, especially on her husband's personal and political life in his postpresidency.

After an hour, they emerged from the living room and called up to Feinstein to say they were finished. "Good night," Feinstein said. "I hope you had a good meeting." They laughed and left.

The negotiations that followed were far from smooth. Obama had no team of lawyers ready to go and Clinton had few functioning campaign staff beyond her lawyers. When Obama's aides wanted to issue a joint statement after the meeting, they could find nobody to approve the language on Clinton's side. Obama called David Plouffe to set up a meeting, and Plouffe ended up reading the lawyers the language of a bland press release that evening. A few days later, Clinton's lawyers flew to Chicago for a four-hour meeting at the Hilton hotel. Much of the conversation was logistical about joint campaign events, staff, and mailing lists. But what they couldn't resolve was the issue of Clinton's campaign debts of $23 million. Clinton had lent her own campaign $11 million, which she did not expect to be repaid, leaving $12 million owed to vendors and consultants.

Despite the displays of harmony and gracious talk between Clinton and Obama, their aides and supporters remained bitterly divided. Obama's inner circle believed that Clinton had racked up the debt to tear down their candidate when it was obvious she had no path to win. "My belief is that they had a discussion after Indiana and North Carolina, in which they said, 'If we stick in this race the debt is going to be astronomical,'" said Plouffe. "And they decided, 'Well, Obama is going to have to deal with it.'"

For their part, Clinton's friends were angry that Obama refused to e-mail his entire list of supporters to ask them to donate cash to pay off her debts. In fact, Obama's team took the trouble to investigate whether such a move would work. Their conclusion: such a request would backfire. "Even if we had wanted to, we couldn't," said Plouffe. "If we had done an e-mail for her, we would have raised less than a quarter million and had hundreds of thousands of people unsubscribe. We did research on this. It wasn't just animus, because the animus was fading. People just thought it was an inappropriate thing to ask from us."

Obama and Clinton seemed more comfortable in the role of peace-makers than their staffers or supporters. Some of Clinton's backers bris-tled at the sight of Obama hiring Patti Solis Doyle, the campaign manager she had fired several months earlier, as chief of staff to the un-chosen vice presidential candidate. Others were struggling to stomach the mood among Obama's supporters. Ed Rendell, the Pennsylvania governor who was one of Clinton's biggest boosters, was finding it so hard to show public support that an Obama supporter sent him a can of Kool-Aid with a campaign sticker on it and a note telling him to drink up. The next day, at a fund-raiser for his state party in a downtown Philadel-phia restaurant, Rendell opened the can, poured it into a glass of water, and shared it with his special guest, New York governor David Paterson. "Now I feel that Senator Obama is the most wonderful person ever to have lived in the United States of America," Rendell oozed before the crowd of 150 donors. "The smartest, most sensitive, most decent and honorable man. Now I understand what you guys have been feeling for the last six months."

Three weeks after sitting down at Feinstein's home, Obama and Clinton flew together on a Midwest Airlines plane from Washington, D.C., to Manchester, New Hampshire. Sitting in seats 2A and 2B, they chatted earnestly about the country's divisions and how to unite the na-tion in the general election. Even their wardrobes spoke of peace and harmony: his tie matched the shade of her pantsuit, the shade of powder blue found on the helmets of United Nations peacekeepers. They trav-eled by bus for ninety minutes to a joint rally in the small town of Unity, chosen not just for its name but for the fact that they had both won pre-cisely 107 votes there in January's primary. En route they shared stories about the bad food they had eaten on their world travels; and how Obama used his Apple laptop to videoconference with his daughters, while Clinton had only just worked out how to use a BlackBerry. Obama wanted to hear about the Clintons' experience of raising a daughter in the White House, and she told of their efforts to protect Chelsea's privacy.

At the outdoor event in a field, on a summer's afternoon where the air was stiflingly humid, she praised his grace; he praised her grit. She talked about her four decades of public service; he talked of his two. "I'm proud we had a spirited dialogue," Clinton said, and the crowd chuckled at her understatement. "That was the nicest way I could think of saying it. But it was spirited because we cared so much." Obama thanked Clinton for teaching his daughters that anything was possible. "They can take for granted that women can do anything that the boys can do," he said. "And do it better. And do it in heels. I still don't know how she does it in heels." Thunder rumbled in the dark clouds behind the trees, no more than a few miles away. It rained a little, then cleared; the air felt thick, but the static was gone.

Obama wanted to change the rules of the game, not just break them. He planned for a general election where he could control the game, its pace and its style. He had a renegade's sense of risk, but each gamble was measured, and each gambit designed to dominate or undermine his adversary. Some would involve compromises to policy or the politics of hope. But he had long since reconciled himself to the petty pace that creeps in on a presidential campaign. He could always mix the positive and the negative, and he could always restore hope later. For now, he needed to win.

The conflict between high-minded principle and low-minded politics was there from the beginning of the general election campaign. The day after beating Clinton and clinching the nomination, Obama took a congratulatory phone call from his Republican opponent. "I'm looking forward to a civil, substantive debate on the issues," Obama said. McCain agreed, before pushing his proposal to hold several town hall meetings together. "We're definitely interested in going beyond the traditional three presidential debates," Obama replied. "Our staffs will communicate. We're going to try to work something out." They even found common ground by sharing a joke about their unlikely victories: if you had asked the pundits a year ago whether it would be an Obama-McCain general election, they agreed there would have been few takers.

But the next day, talking to reporters onboard his plane, Obama made it clear he was ready to do whatever it took to win. When asked if he would stay within the limits of public funding for the fall, he described the election as a political cold war. "We're not going to unilaterally disarm," he said, pointing to heavy fund-raising by the Republican Party. "I'm not underestimating the challenge we have ahead," he explained, as he surveyed the battlefield. "John McCain is a strong candidate and the Republican Party is accustomed to winning presidential elections. They're not going to give up without a fight. I'm going to have to bring my A-game and I'm going to need the best teammates possible to win."

Obama would not accept McCain's rules. The day after he secured the nomination, McCain's campaign manager, Rick Davis, called to make a formal offer of town halls stretching all the way to the official debate season. David Plouffe told Davis the idea sounded appealing, but Clinton had yet to concede the contest. "You've been kicking around there for three months," he said. "We still have a lot of healing to do here." His formal response came soon after: two town halls, not ten. To Obama's team, that was a big concession in a compressed time frame, for a candidate whose first and last debates through the primaries were horrendous. But McCain's team rejected the counteroffer and told the press before responding to their counterparts in Chicago. "Screw these guys," said Plouffe. "They can't be trusted."

Instead Obama started his A-game with a single decision that changed the rules of the contest completely. It was the biggest strategic move since Obama decided to run for president in the first place, and it may well have changed presidential campaigns for years to come.

Back in January, after the first four states of the primary season, Obama's finance chair, Penny Pritzker, started to plan further ahead than any normal campaign staffer. Pritzker was not a political animal, but a successful business executive with an MBA from Stanford and an economics degree from Harvard. Her fund-raising operation had been a huge success, raising unprecedented sums first from wealthy donors, then from small Internet donors. Now there was a real prospect of winning the nomination and moving into the next phase: the general election. At business school she had learned to go through the planning exercise of a decision tree, and by Super Tuesday she pushed the campaign to do the same. What if they took public financing? That would limit their overall spending to $84 million and leave additional fundraising and spending to the national party. What if they didn't? That would force them to raise an unknown sum, build a different campaign structure, change the candidate's schedule to include far more money events, and reconfigure their relationship with the Democratic National Committee. For the next six weeks, Pritzker worked with Julianna Smoot, who led the finance staff, to narrow down the issues for the candidate and his senior aides. David Plouffe had to draw up budgets for the general election while his candidate was still battling Clinton through Pennsylvania and the upheaval of Reverend Wright's performance. "It forced a planning exercise that I don't know would have been undertaken at that point," said Pritzker.

The great unknown was the political cost to breaking free from public cash. David Axelrod undertook some research, but the calculation was always more instinctive than a focus group or poll could pinpoint. What complicated the decision was a simple questionnaire, one of several filled out by staffers for interest groups around the country. Back in November 2007, the Midwest Democracy Network—a group of twenty public interest groups in the region—succeeded in pressing the Obama and Edwards campaigns to state their positions on campaign finance, voting rights, and government reform. When asked if he would give up private money to take public finance, Obama replied, "Yes. I have been a longtime advocate for public financing of campaigns combined with free television and radio time as a way to reduce the influence of moneyed special interests." The answer cited a letter he wrote to the Federal Election Commission at the start of the campaign, asking if he could raise private money but keep the option of returning it if he agreed to a deal with the Republican nominee to accept public cash instead. "If I am the Democratic nominee," his campaign wrote, "I will aggressively pursue an agreement with the Republican nominee to preserve a publicly financed general election."

Now Obama's senior aides were proposing a complete reversal, based on political advantage, not a principled position. Plouffe was angry they had ever boxed themselves in with any public statement. "We mishandled this from the very beginning," he said later. "We should have just said we would want to retain it as an option, which is really what we thought. Some kid screwed up a frickin' questionnaire. We never said yes in public. I was furious that we filled out the damn questionnaire, much less screwed it up. But that's campaigns." Inside campaign headquarters in Chicago, Obama's staffers were conflicted. Many believed that public finance, no matter how obscure an issue, was part of Obama's appeal in reforming the political system. Pritzker's team began to look at whether they could raise enough private money but impose their own limits on donations to something less than the legal maximum of $2,300. But there was no way to reach their budget goals in that case. Besides, Plouffe thought the suggested compromise was a wimp-out. "I had no tolerance for that," he said. "Either you're doing it, or you're not, OK?"

As they studied the feasibility of breaking free, Obama started to hedge his public position, saying it would be "presumptuous" to lock himself in. In private, he was warm to the idea in his conversations with Pritzker. "Can we do that?" he asked her. "Is it smart?"

Pritzker was daunted by the notion of raising $75 million in the first year of the campaign; now she was proposing several times that figure in a fraction of the time. But her argument to Plouffe was less about the money than his management. By taking public money, he would have to abide by rules that separated additional fund-raising and spending at the national party's headquarters. "You're really good with a strategy and being in control," she told him in early February. Plouffe agreed, and so did the candidate.

When Obama made his final decision, soon after he won the nomination in June, the media reaction was intense. "It's not an easy decision, especially because I support a robust system of public financing of elections," the candidate said in a video message on his own website. "But the public financing of presidential elections as it exists today is broken, and we face opponents who have become masters at gaming this broken system." He was the first candidate to turn down public finance since the post-Watergate laws of the 1970s, and the editorial boards hated it. "His effort to cloak his broken promise in the smug mantle of selfless dedication to the public good is a little hard to take," wrote the *Washington Post*. For all the editorial outrage, the polls showed no impact: voters had no idea which candidate was taking public money, and more than 70 percent of them did not care about the issue.

Obama's team did little to hide the expediency of their decision. Their attempt to negotiate with their counterparts was desultory: Obama's lawyer met with McCain's for forty-five minutes to discuss what he called the broken finance system, among other issues. The way Obama's aides saw it, McCain had been running a general election campaign using private money since he locked up the nomination in March.

Their argument was not based on fairness; it was based on effectiveness. They faced hostile advertising from outside groups like the National Rifle Association and National Right to Life. And they wanted to build a vastly expensive grassroots operation across the nation, expand the number of battleground states, and spend millions on TV advertising to get their candidate known. Above all, the money allowed Obama to look like he was reconciling principle with politics, by running upbeat and critical ads at the same time. "Being out of the system, we're able to basically be up on our perch," said Plouffe. "We've got our positive track. We've got our negative track on McCain. We've got the ability to deal with whatever nonsense negatives are running. It's strategically really important." By breaking the traditional fund-raising rules of presidential politics, Obama could rewrite the playbook of the general election: of where he campaigned, what kind of organization he could build, and what tone his advertising took.

The same day as he reversed himself on fund-raising, Barack Obama found himself sitting beside John McCain inside Holy Trinity Church in Georgetown. It was the funeral service for Tim Russert, the preeminent political journalist in Washington. At the request of the Russert family, the two rivals sat together. Obama asked after McCain's family, and they both discussed Ted Kennedy's deteriorating health. The small talk over, they faced a more pointed message from the pulpit, where Russert's son, Luke, urged them to "engage in spirited debate but disavow the low tactics that distract Americans from the most important issues facing our country." To Obama, it sounded like Russert was echoing the language of his own campaign.

There was a good reason why Obama wanted to change the rules, and it wasn't just because of idealism: he and his team were poor players of the old-style game of campaign politics. They had little aptitude for or interest in winning the daily or hourly news cycle, which the pundits had elevated to the most important task of any presidential campaign. There was something self-engrossed about the media's analysis: that one of the key measures of a campaign's performance was how well it influenced the media. To Obama's senior aides, the media looked like a childlike creature who was easily distracted and suffered from a painfully short attention span. Even at the start of the general election phase, the candidate was struck by how the press ignored the real disputes between himself and McCain, and preferred instead to cover manufactured ones. "We have some very big differences between myself and John McCain," he told me. "I don't think on our side at least this has gotten personal. There's a sharp difference in approach on everything from energy policy to health care policy to education and the war in Iraq. And there's no doubt that there's going to be a vigorous debate back and forth. I don't think there's anything wrong with that. The truth is that most of what we spend time talking about is positive. It's just you guys don't report on it."

Over the previous twenty-four hours, the news cycle was dominated by a dispute over how to deal with Osama bin Laden in the unlikely event that he was captured alive. The story began with Obama praising the Nuremberg trials of Nazi leaders as a model for dealing with bin Laden. He said he didn't want to turn bin Laden into a martyr and argued that America could gain support for counterterrorism by following international conventions. Within hours, the Republican National Committee and the McCain campaign were attacking Obama for supposedly backing off an earlier pledge to seek the death penalty for terrorists like bin Laden. The candidate himself was surprised that the media would take the bait. "What you report on is today's suggestion that I would not apply the death penalty to Osama bin Laden, according to McCain's foreign policy chief, and us responding that's demonstrably not true. And that is the news *you* guys want to make. My discussion that I had in the city colleges about how we are going to get kids higher education funding gets nothing."

It sounded like a traditional candidate's complaint about the press ignoring the day's intended message and hyping an unplanned debate on a different topic. But the press was not entirely to blame. For much of the first two months of the general election, the candidate's message was simply drowned out by the louder message from the other side. They worked harder to shape press coverage and relied on the conservative echo chamber.

The biggest exception was Obama's foreign trip to the Middle East and Europe, when he dominated the coverage for a full week with glowing pictures and reports about his diplomatic skills. On the short flight from Berlin to Paris, the candidate seemed content with being in full control. "There was a point where we just got too focused on the skirmishes with the McCain campaign," he told me as he finished a simple lunch. "But this week I really felt like we were hitting the right tone, staying on what we wanted to do, while still defending ourselves."

That self-contented mood did not last long. Running against the Clintons, he enjoyed flipping the dynamic of the primary contest. But on his return home from his foreign travels, the McCain campaign immediately turned the strength of his successful trip into a critical weakness. "He's the biggest celebrity in the world," said the female narrator over a TV ad showing pictures of Obama's huge rally in Berlin, followed swiftly by pictures of starlets Paris Hilton and Britney Spears. "But is he ready to lead? With gas prices soaring, Barack Obama says no to offshore drilling and says he'll raise taxes on electricity. Higher taxes, more foreign oil: that's the real Obama." The ad was an instant hit on cable TV: an irresistible mix of politics and young female stars. It was also the McCain campaign's first serious attempt to define the character of Obama, who remained ill defined for many voters. Obama's aides fielded endless questions about whether the foreign trip had in fact been a blunder. "We've let them take over the narrative," David Axelrod lamented. "And we've got to get it back."

Obama wasn't for higher taxes or foreign oil. But he was against the kind of campaigning that the celebrity ad epitomized. Fighting that kind of politics was far more palatable to him than fighting the character of his rivals. In the primaries, Obama had always found it easier to counterattack rather than initiate an attack; easier to challenge Clinton's tactics as part of his crusade to change Washington. Now McCain was slotting into the same template. "I think he's a little annoyed by the lies and the distortion and he thinks that's something that is fundamentally wrong with our political process," said Marty Nesbitt. "Sometimes when you get the playground bully, if you're the peacemaker, sometimes you've got to knock the bully out if you want to bring peace to the playground. I think he's struggling with striking that balance. He's got to slay the dragon to get America's political process back on the right track. He's got to defeat this death spiral of political dirty tricks and distortions that have come to consume the process. He's very annoyed by that." In his own mind, he was cleaning up the game, not fouling the other side.

The celebrity ad turned into an opportunity for a game-changing reversal. McCain was a hard opponent to define as part of the old political culture because he had frequently crossed partisan lines. But the celebrity ad looked and sounded like old-style negative politics, so Obama's team took the celebrity theme and threw it back at their rivals. "For decades, he's been Washington's biggest celebrity, John McCain," the male narrator said over clips of McCain on TV chat shows. "And as Washington embraced him, John McCain hugged right back. The lobbyists: running his low-road campaign. The money: billions in tax breaks for oil and drug companies, but almost nothing for families like yours. Lurching to the right, then the left, the old Washington dance, whatever it takes. John McCain. A Washington celebrity playing the same old Washington games."

By the late fall, almost six in ten voters believed McCain was running an unfairly negative campaign, compared with just four in ten at the end of the summer. McCain's support among his base of independent voters never recovered. David Plouffe credited the celebrity ad for their new strategy. "We just didn't have the jujitsu of saying, 'We've got all these big problems, all this guy wants to do is attack, aren't you tired of that?' We couldn't have said that in June, July, and most of August. We tried, but people wouldn't accept it," he said. "It was really a remarkable shift. Then it became available to us. The reason McCain has paid such a high price for it is because people expected so much more from him."

Just like the mind games with the Clintons in the primaries, the criticism of McCain had an added benefit. Obama's team believed they were rattling McCain and throwing him off his game. "Did we ever say we're going to do this to get under his skin? No," said Plouffe. "Would we say, Boy, we got under his skin? Um, yes. We know that saying he was running a historically negative campaign did that."

Selecting a vice president is more than just a campaign decision; it is the only presidential-style decision of the entire race, a moment that shows what kind of judgment a candidate possesses. It can shape a general election and the administration beyond, if successful. In public, Obama's approach was methodical; in private, he was also deeply competitive. "I'm a strong believer in doing this in a careful, deliberative way, outside of the day-to-day political pressures that inevitably start up during this kind of thing," he explained on a plane journey two days after securing his party's nomination. "There's no decision that I'm going to make that's going to be more important before the November election. I intend to do it right. And I'm not going to do it in the press."

The candidate was doubly strategic: about the needs of his campaign and those of his future administration. But of the two, he was more immediately concerned with winning. "Barack's focus was on someone who would help him win the election," said Pete Rouse, his senior aide. "His view was, 'If this person doesn't help me win the White House, it's kind of a moot point.'" That meant analyzing his own weaknesses as well as those of his opponent, to find someone with stature who could fill the gaps. He was poor at attack politics, and needed someone to take the fight to McCain. He lacked experience, and needed someone who knew Washington and the world. He had struggled in the primaries with the white, working voters of the old Rust Belt states. In sum, he needed to play offense and defense at the same time. "Given the fact that he's positioned as a different kind of candidate, running to change Washington, he couldn't afford to take a big risk on his VP pick," said Rouse. "By definition, you're restricted to finding someone who isn't an outside-the-box candidate."

Obama was cautious, thorough, and detached. He wanted no surprises and set up a selection committee to vet the candidates and make recommendations. He relied on Caroline Kennedy, who became a good friend after her early endorsement, and Eric Holder, a Washington friend and former deputy attorney general in the Clinton era. A third member, Jim Johnson, came on the recommendation of John Kerry and promptly quit as controversy swirled around his time as CEO of the mortgage-market giant Fannie Mae.

But Obama was unhappy with the shortness of the short list. "The one thing that came out, and he said that a lot, was how frustrated he was to have such a limited pool of people from which to choose," said Rouse. The short list boiled down to Senators Joe Biden and Evan Bayh, and Governors Tim Kaine and Kathleen Sebelius. Obama was pragmatic enough to consider the notion of Hillary Clinton as his veep. But she refused to be vetted unless she was assured of the job. Besides, the candidate was uneasy not only about her impact on his polling among independent voters but also about her husband. "If she helps us politically we ought to look at it," he told his senior aides. "But I'm concerned about Bill Clinton being a loose cannon."

The view inside Obama's inner circle was that he was always leaning toward Biden. "My guess is he ended up where he started out," said Valerie Jarrett. "He thought he was going to end up having the right combination. Biden filled in where there might be some doubt and also wasn't vulnerable where Barack was vulnerable. He couldn't hurt him the way Kaine or Sebelius or Bayh could." None of the other three could help him with the issue of foreign policy experience, and Bayh had the added drawback of living in a state where a Republican governor would appoint his replacement.

David Axelrod and David Plouffe intuited the same about Obama's leanings, at least until the final phase of the pick. Biden could be a verbose campaigner with little discipline once his mouth was open, and Bayh seemed like a safer choice. Still, Obama didn't tell his committee about his feelings or influence them in their decision. By the end of their process, Kennedy and Holder both came down for Biden, without reservation.

There were many doubts about Biden among Obama's closest advisers. Did he really want the job? Had he put aside the tension that used to exist between them? Biden was chairman of the Senate Foreign Relations Committee and he was disdainful of the new senator from Illinois. "In the Senate, Obama and Biden weren't particularly close," explained Rouse. "Biden took pride in his Senate seniority and broad experience in public life, and he seemed to view Barack as somewhat of an impatient pretender. Obama was not one to stand on pretense. Those perceptions changed when they got to observe and know each other so intensively on the campaign trail in 2007."

Instead, Obama grew close to the senior Republican on the committee, Dick Lugar, working closely with him on securing conventional weapons and unconventional materials in the former Soviet bloc. Biden's respect for Obama grew during his own failed presidential campaign, but he made no public blessing of Obama, even after the primaries ended. Instead Biden and Obama would talk on the phone about foreign policy at regular intervals, although it wasn't clear whether Biden was trying to build a relationship or show off his superior knowledge. After all, as a rival candidate he had diminished Obama both as an African American—calling him "smart, clean, and articulate"—and as a possible commander in chief, saying he wasn't experienced enough to take the top job.

When they finally sat down to talk through the job, in a secret meeting in a Minneapolis hotel in early August, Obama wanted to test Biden. "Barack wasn't sure that Biden wanted to do it," said Plouffe. "And Biden did a good job of saying, 'I do.'" The two former rivals clicked. Biden didn't want a portfolio like Al Gore; he wanted to be consulted as a confidant and adviser. For his part, Obama liked Biden's political advice and wanted to hear more. He was interested in his experience passing legislation, including the 1994 crime bill, and could see him as a help in the White House. "As self-confident as he is, Barack isn't threatened by accomplished people or their intelligence," said Rouse. "He is very interested in what other people think."

Obama unveiled his vice presidential candidate on the same site in Springfield, Illinois, where he launched his campaign eighteen months earlier, in front of the old statehouse. The contrast between the two days was extreme. The weather was as hot on that late-August day as it was cold on the announcement day in February. The crowd was twice the size of the one that showed up at the start of the campaign, reaching an estimated thirty-five thousand people. Instead of warming themselves with hats and scarves, they fanned themselves with Pepsi cups, which they had ripped open. And while Obama preferred to stay above the fray, his aides were celebrating a team player who never minded a personal foul or two. "He'll have a fist in the face of John McCain every day," said Robert Gibbs, "and he adds a level of gravitas as well." It looked like the season of the renegade was drawing to a close. At the side of the stage stood David Wade, the new press secretary to Biden. He was wearing a gift from his old boss, John Kerry: a tie with dozens of little flip-flops on it.

The candidate lived for the NBA finals feel of the big moment. He loved raising his game for when it really counted. In fact, he added to the thrill of the moment by cranking up the pressure: by starting prep late and by pumping up expectations. The bar was already set high for his acceptance speech. He needed to top his last convention speech, the one that had set him on this trajectory toward the presidency. But that wasn't enough. He decided to do something that Kennedy had last pulled off with his New Frontier speech at the Coliseum in Los Angeles: to move his convention in Denver from the indoor Pepsi Center to the outdoor Invesco Field, home to the Denver Broncos. The official reason was to allow more people to watch the speech in person, recruiting and organizing thousands more Colorado voters for the ground game in a critical battleground state. The unofficial reason was that the candidate and his senior staff loved the gamble of it all. "I think as a campaign, we were always best when we were on the high wire. Always," said David Plouffe. "It helped us kind of regain a little bit of that insurgent feel."

There's a difference between vertigo and insurgency, and Obama's speechwriter Jon Favreau simply felt sick about the convention. The day before Obama left for his summer vacation in Hawaii, Favreau met with the candidate, Axelrod, and Gibbs to talk about the acceptance speech for the first time. Obama talked at length about all the people he had met on the campaign trail and to lay out some guidelines. "I want to put my life story in there," he said. "Because when I see that woman who sleeps three hours a night, I think of my mother. It's got to tell a story. All my speeches tell a story. And we've got to make the choice in the election—the choice between me and McCain. You've got to know what I'm for policywise, and you've got to know what he's for. We've got to lay out my agenda. Not in a wonky way, but it can't be an election-night speech." For Favreau, that was already a sprawling wish list, and he was determined to keep the speech as short as possible.

"I'm going to write in Hawaii," the candidate continued, "but you should write, too. We don't want to do parallel tracks. But do you have enough?"

Compared with the trickle of time he normally had with the candidate, this was a fire hydrant. "I came to this meeting thinking I wouldn't have enough," Favreau said, "but you've given me so much in this meeting that I think I can do it."

What followed was three weeks of speechwriting hell; of self-torture and 4:00 a.m. alarms. "I'm going to lose it," Favreau told his friends. "I'm going to quit." Holed up with his speechwriting team of Ben Rhodes, Adam Frankel, and Sarah Hurwitz, Favreau spent a week working on a first draft. When Axelrod read it, there was silence for the first six pages. On page seven, he said, "I like this paragraph." Favreau was burning inside. "It's not quite there," Axelrod concluded. "It's fine for now, but we should see what Barack thinks."

The candidate was also dissatisfied. "I don't know if the story is quite there," he said in a brief phone call. "Produce something else and send it back to me."

The second draft did not fare much better. "You know what," the candidate said, "I'm going to write now."

Obama took a hotel room at the Park Hyatt in Chicago and worked for three nights, starting at 8:00 or 9:00. It was a world away from the simple task of writing his convention speech four years earlier, when he dashed off his words in one sitting while watching a basketball game on TV. Now, writing in longhand and then typing on his computer, he was toiling past midnight and under intense pressure. On Monday at 1:00 a.m., just three days before he would walk onto Invesco Field, he e-mailed his version of the speech. "I wrote this," he started unnecessarily. "It's too long, but this is the story I want to tell. We need to just cut this down."

The next morning, on his campaign plane, it was suddenly his turn to sound like the anxiety-ridden writer. "What do you think?" he asked Favreau and Axelrod.

"It's long," they chimed.

"I know it's long, but you guys are going to cut it," he said. "It's good, right?"

His aides said yes, but it was Monday already. On a short flight to Iowa, they started circling places to cut, especially his long section on foreign policy.

The next day, the candidate looked at the newly shortened speech and was still unhappy. "We're close but there's something we need to hang it all together," he told Favreau. "A theme."

Soon after Hillary Clinton delivered her speech in Denver, Obama walked into Axelrod's hotel room and stayed until one in the morning while they thrashed out his idea for a theme: America's promise. "Can you get me a draft by the time I land in Denver tomorrow night?" the candidate asked. Favreau pulled yet another all-nighter and delivered a new version the next day, just twenty-four hours before showtime. "I think we're there," the candidate said. "We just need to cut a little more." That night, Obama sent his speechwriter to bed early, despite his protests that he had to deliver his speech the next day. "We have plenty of time," he said, before turning to the rest of the writing team. "I'm so proud of Favs," he told them. "All of you guys, go to bed. Let's all go to bed and we'll wake up tomorrow and figure it out."

Just four hours before he walked onstage, Obama practiced his speech for the first time. He was barely on page three when there was a knock at the door of his hotel suite. It was room service. Obama answered and walked back carrying a plate.

"Who ordered the Caesar salad?" he asked. Axelrod admitted it was his, and the candidate laughed with his aides: nothing was more important than feeding his strategist's stomach.

The speech was the epitome of hope: a mile-high conception of politics, not the low road of the campaign. The word *promise* featured in the final text more than thirty times. And when the candidate reached his reference to Martin Luther King, he could go no further. "It is that promise that forty-five years ago today brought Americans from every corner of this land to stand together on a Mall in Washington, before Lincoln's Memorial, and hear a young preacher from Georgia speak of his dream," he said as he choked up.

"You know what? I've got to stop," he said, as he walked around the suite. "This is kind of a big deal."

Three hours later, they were done tinkering and rehearsing after two run-throughs. "I like this," Obama said.

The big deal on cable TV was the kind of manufactured controversy that intensely annoyed Obama and his staff: the staging at Invesco Field, which the early reports suggested was similar to a Greek temple. Republicans loved the description, calling it the Barackopolis, a temple to Obama's self-love. In fact, much of official Washington is inspired by classical architecture, including the Capitol, the presidential memorials, and the White House. American democracy has never been modest about its self-image, or shy about claiming its place as the successor to the classical age. For anyone familiar with the nation's capital, the visual echoes of the set were clear. It was a mixture of the colonnade of the Rose Garden, with its backlit windows suggesting Obama's next workplace, and the Lincoln Memorial, where Martin Luther King Jr. had spoken. By the time the candidate saw the set, the most excessive touch was the columns around two flat screens at either end of the stage, a grandiose way to frame a giant TV.

But just twenty-four hours earlier, those elements seemed positively modest. In its original form, the set was far more theatrical. Behind the candidate's podium, in place of the backlit windows, was a neon-lit horseshoe leading to a 160-inch plasma screen. Purple runway lights ran along the edges of the stage. Jim Margolis, Obama's chief ad maker, could only think of one thing: *Deal or No Deal*. "You guys have got to be kidding me," he said when he regained control of his jaw. "I really appreciate all you guys are doing. But all that stuff has got to be out of here before he does the walk-through tomorrow. All those runway lights: out. The light surround: out. Plasma screen: out. And get me thirty flags. Put flags all around him." The intention was to make Obama look presidential, not like a TV celebrity.

The next day, when the candidate saw the more tasteful set for the first time, his aides joked that they had another source of inspiration. "We know how much you love Caesars Palace," quipped David Axelrod. Obama stepped up to the podium to test his teleprompters. The text onscreen was his speech from the last convention in Boston. It was just four years since he stepped onto the national stage. He ran through two minutes, and the stage crew applauded in the empty stadium.

More striking than the set was the weather: clear blue skies, with bright sunshine and no humidity on the day of the big speech. The crush to enter the stadium was so great that many people overheated in the long lines outside. Those who weren't suffering were phoning voters for the campaign in one giant, snaking phone bank. Onstage, the musical acts began, including Stevie Wonder playing "Signed, Sealed, Delivered." Backstage, where the sound of the stadium was nothing more than a faint echo, the candidate was greeting ten supporters who won a competition to peek behind the scenes on the big night. "Have a great time tonight," he told them, as if the night was their entertainment, not his moment of testing. A crew from CBS's *60 Minutes*, looking far more frazzled than the candidate, trailed him as he turned back to his private holding room.

His wife emerged first with their daughters as "Born in the USA" echoed through the stadium, now masked by the dim light of dusk. Then came the candidate. His face lightly powdered with makeup, he was ready to go onstage.

He walked out of his holding room to shake hands with his staffers and walk onto the field. "It looks like fun out there," he told me, savoring the prospect of the spotlight. "All right. Let's do this thing."

From the bright white cinder-block hallway, he passed through a small white door into a hot, dark tunnel. The walls and ceiling were gray tarp and there was blue carpet underfoot. It was a Secret Service cocoon to shield his movements, penetrated only by the roars of eighty-four thousand people. The tunnel turned a sharp corner and opened the steps to the stage.

Inside the stadium a biographical video told his life story, while the candidate slowly paced up and down the back of the stage. "I was in love with him," Michelle said on video, and the crowd sighed. Overhead a helicopter buzzed, while Barack closed his eyes. On-screen, he remembered his mother passing away. Backstage, he held his right arm across his chest and propped his left hand on his chin. He was getting in the zone, pushing the distractions out of mind, withdrawing into himself, digging for focus. "One person's struggle is everyone's struggle," he said on video. "We need to recognize ourselves in each other. . . . That's the country I believe in. That is what's worth fighting for." Then a burst of primary-night rock, U2's "City of Blinding Lights," and the flash of thousands of cameras. A signal from a stagehand, an upward tilt of his head, and he was striding out toward a field of Stars and Stripes and signs saying CHANGE. He thought he had his game under control until he saw sixty thousand cameras flashing at him. It was only then, in a brief moment of pause, that he realized the magnitude of what he was doing.

Standing to the left of the stage, Favreau watched the speech looking unusually nervous and formal, in a blue pinstriped suit. He held his arm across his chest, just like his boss, as he watched him settle into a steady pace. He only relaxed after the crowd responded to several applause lines, when the candidate condemned President Bush's concept of an ownership society: "What it really means is, you're on your own," Obama said.

Moments later, he slapped down McCain's celebrity ad by recounting the sacrifices of his mother and grandmother. "I don't know what kind of lives John McCain thinks that celebrities lead," he said, "but this has been mine." The crowd rose to its feet and Favreau allowed himself a little smile.

Sitting in the audience was Michelle Obama and their daughters, who wanted to know when their father would be finished and why they had to stop banging their flags on the floor. Overhead, the skycam scanned across the delegates, snapped forward and pulled back. Behind the candidate, a large flag drifted in and out of the camera shot with the gentle flapping of the breeze.

The balance between positive and negative, between patriotic promise and political attack, was almost impossible to maintain. Even as the candidate pledged not to attack McCain's character, he demolished his campaign's slogan. "What I will not do is suggest that the senator takes his positions for political purposes. Because one of the things that we have to change in our politics is the idea that people cannot disagree without challenging each other's character and patriotism," he said, casting himself once again as the referee of fair and foul politics. "The times are too serious, the stakes are too high for this same partisan playbook. So let us agree that patriotism has no party. I love this country, and so do you, and so does John McCain. The men and women who serve in our battlefields may be Democrats and Republicans and independents, but they have fought together and bled together and some died together under the same proud flag. They have not served a Red America or a Blue America—they have served the United States of America. So I've got news for you, John McCain. We all put our country first."

He ended with an understated reference to Martin Luther King Jr. and an overstated use of pyrotechnics. Fireworks burst from the top of the stadium, confetti showered into the air, and streamers exploded from the top of the classical set. Pieces of red, white, and blue confetti drifted down from the sky like the flakes of an Iowa snowstorm. The Obama and Biden families walked onstage for the crowd and the cameras. As he waved for the last time, just before he turned to walk off the set, he glanced at the crowd with the same wan expression he had at the moment he choked up in rehearsal.

Backstage, the mood was as giddy as the days after Iowa. "He nailed it," declared Axelrod. "When we left the hotel, he was very happy with it and very moved. When he's in this mood, you know it's going to be very good." The hallway was full of friends, family, politicians, and celebrities. John Legend and will.i.am wandered by, before Stevie Wonder walked down.

Obama emerged from his holding room to a burst of applause. "The great thing about him and so many of his big speeches is if he gets his rhythm going, the speech kind of flows," said Gibbs. "When you run for this office, more than any other, you can't hide and you can't depend on others to go that last little bit. We can only go with him for so long. You have to climb that last hundred feet to the summit by yourself."

What did the candidate think of his own performance?

"Not bad," he told me with a smirk.

Almost everything the candidate had learned about the game over the last eighteen months was tested in the next two. He needed to stay cool while under pressure, foul his opponents strategically, and inspire his supporters incessantly.

The first test came the next morning, as his motorcade rolled out of town on a clear bright morning under a big blue sky. The new Democratic nominee drove through downtown Denver, then a manufacturing district where the workers took to the sidewalk to applaud and wave, through the suburbs and the prairie to the distant airport. Before he reached his campaign plane, news broke that McCain had picked Sarah Palin, the unexpected, untested Alaska governor, as his running mate. Obama's staffers could barely contain their disdain about McCain's poor judgment and Palin's lack of experience. "Are you kidding me? Unless we mess up or the race is overtaken by external events, this election is over," said Pete Rouse, who previously worked in Alaska government. At the airport David Plouffe shared his instant opinion with the candidate. "This is just not going to wear well," he told his boss. "It is a stunt."

Palin was on a list of ten possible candidates drawn up by Obama's aides before the convention, but she didn't make the cut when they narrowed down the list. Everything pointed to Joe Lieberman, the self-styled independent Democrat from Connecticut. Palin was unexpected, but also a strange pick in polling terms. Lieberman represented a bipartisan revolution in Washington. Palin instead reinforced a maverick brand that needed rebuilding. The only problem was that voters had little idea what the word meant. In Obama's internal polls, 19 percent of voters described Obama as a maverick, compared with 17 percent for McCain.

In public, Obama's aides felt constrained by their recent battles with Hillary Clinton and were unsure how women would react to their new opponent. The campaign issued two press statements: one belittling her experience, the other congratulating her on breaking a political barrier for women. When the candidate and his own running mate stopped for questions in Pennsylvania—inside a biodiesel plant fueled by chicken shit, no less—they kept their comments respectful and even positive. "She seems like a compelling person," Obama said, "obviously a terrific personal story."

Palin did not return the favor. Her acceptance speech at the Republican convention trashed Obama for supposedly demeaning small-town America and for what she caricatured as his self-indulgent, unpatriotic campaign. "I guess a small-town mayor is sort of like a community organizer, except that you have actual responsibilities," she began. "This is a man who can give an entire speech about the wars America is fighting, and never use the word victory except when he's talking about his own campaign. But when the cloud of rhetoric has passed, when the roar of the crowd fades away, when the stadium lights go out, and those Styrofoam Greek columns are hauled back to some studio lot, when that happens, what exactly is our opponent's plan? What does he actually seek to accomplish, after he's done turning back the waters and healing the planet? The answer is to make government bigger, and take more of your money, and give you more orders from Washington, and to reduce the strength of America in a dangerous world."

For two weeks, Democrats panicked as a half-dozen polls showed McCain taking his first sustained lead of the election. The polls and Palin's aggressive tone renewed questions about Obama's stubborn desire to balance positive and negative politics. Obama and his inner circle brushed their anxieties aside. Far from being a sign of strength, Palin looked like an admission of weakness. "They forfeited their core message of experience," said Plouffe. "I was so stunned by that, and it struck me that they were a lot more concerned about their base than they had let on." The polls backed up those gut instincts. Before the Democratic convention, Obama was ahead by one point in the campaign's polling of the battleground states; by September 11, a week after the Republican convention, the polls were tied once again. While Palin energized the Republican base, the critical polls kept moving toward Obama. Two weeks after his successful convention, McCain was down four points in the battleground polls.

The candidate believed that the Palin pick was a mark of how rattled his opponents were. The only surprise was how the media became obsessed with her and how easily journalists were distracted from the real contest between him and McCain over big issues like the war and the economy. The distractions culminated in a manufactured dispute over the meaning of the phrase "lipstick on a pig." Obama had used it to describe McCain's promise of change; McCain's campaign insisted it was a sexist insult to Palin. For two full days, the phrase was debated in the media—more than an entire election's worth of coverage of Social Security, China, or New Orleans. "It was basically sort of a Hail Mary pass," Obama told me on his campaign plane as the polls turned back in his favor. "They were just flailing. It was sort of like, you've got to do *something*. And it's amazing that it worked. Something happened in the press that was really strange. I've never seen it before. Just the degree to which everybody got sucked up into this weird vortex."

His friend Marty Nesbitt shared with him an e-mailed photo, which summed up their collective response to weak-kneed Democrats. It was a picture of the candidate delivering his convention speech, with the caption "Everyone Chill the Fuck Out. I Got This."

Obama chuckled. *"Exactly,"* he said. "That's exactly how I feel."

In the meantime, Obama's own veep pick was living up to his promise to keep a fist in the face of their opponents. In early September, Biden was offended about a story pushed by conservative operatives about his daughter getting into trouble with the police. When Biden's staff suggested he issue a statement, the veep pick brushed them aside. "Hell, no," he said. "I'm going to call John myself." McCain refused to take his call, annoying Biden even more. Then, on the anniversary of the 9/11 attacks, Biden was with Obama in New York, where the candidates were readying for a forum on public service at Columbia University. There Biden walked up to McCain's staff to ask where the Republican nominee was. McCain's aides said he could not be disturbed, but that did not inhibit Joe Biden. He walked up to McCain's door and thumped on it. "John McCain," he shouted. "It's Joe Biden. The next time I phone you, take the damn call."

Palin's vortex was not entirely destructive. On the downside, the campaign spent two weeks fighting media questions about how they would deal with Palin. "It was a tough couple of weeks just because the ferocity of the press attention was such," said Plouffe. "Our view was once this settled down, this was going to be an unhelpful choice for McCain because it was clearly a political choice." But on the upside, Palin provided a huge boost to Obama's already record fund-raising. Worried supporters started to send more cash and those resources allowed the campaign to develop an extraordinary strategy. "She was a big multiplier," said Plouffe. "We were going to have a big September no matter what. But she probably was worth at least $20 million, $25 million, I would guess."

For all the negativity surrounding Palin, she effectively funded some of the most positive TV commercials of any presidential campaign in modern times. It was the late surge in cash that paid for a thirty-minute prime-time program, which Plouffe wanted to slot in between the final debate and the general election. The first of its kind since Perot's infomercials in 1992 and 1996, the show cost $5 million to produce and air, and told the stories of regular voters in battleground states, as well as Obama's personal story, before switching seamlessly to a live rally in Florida. One in five homes in the top TV markets, representing more than 33 million Americans, watched the show on NBC, CBS, Fox, and cable channels. The infomercial made no attempt to attack or criticize McCain.

The prime-time show was a tough call to make and a difficult moment to execute. One of the toughest issues was whether to switch to the live rally at the end. As the candidate readied himself for the final debate of the election, his aides held a late-night conference call to decide whether to go ahead with the live TV. Jim Margolis, Obama's senior advertising strategist, wanted the live segment to show some immediacy, to inspire voters to action. But he warned there was a big risk involved: if they overran, the networks would just cut them off the air. The candidate was nervous about whether the timing would work, while Axelrod was noncommittal. David Plouffe didn't much care about the nerves. "We've been taking risks ever since we started this," he said, "so what the fuck? Let's take one more risk."

Still, Margolis fretted about the timing of the live component, especially as the first speaker was the impossibly verbose Joe Biden. Biden needed to end his remarks with a forty-five-second introduction of the candidate. "If you are behind, we're going to get you to where you need to be with forty-five seconds to go," he warned the vice presidential candidate. "And if you are ahead, we've got to stop and wait. And you can talk about whatever you want to talk about."

"Well, what if I, you know—" Biden hesitated. "Sometimes I go a little long."

"Sorry, we're going to be right there at the introduction. You just got to be there at the right time."

On the night, Biden was as undisciplined as ever and lagged way behind. Margolis pushed the prompter ahead, losing several pages at a time, to hit the time cue with forty-five seconds to go. As he walked off-stage, Biden shook his head and smiled. "Man, if I had known these guys were this good," he told his aides, "I'd have dropped out much earlier."

In spite of all his pregame nerves, Obama hit all his marks flawlessly, without pause, as the cameras switched live to his national broadcast. "I told you," he deadpanned to his senior aides as he walked offstage. "Nothing to it. What were you guys worried about?"

In the primaries, Obama had struggled to balance positive and negative campaigning. But in the general election, it was far easier to find his equilibrium. "We've never been guided by the ends justifying the means," said David Axelrod. "The ends don't justify the means. There have to be limits to what you're willing to do. Going against that, you don't bring a knife to a gunfight." Obama wasn't Eliot Ness in the movie The Untouchables, chasing down Al Capone in 1930s Chicago. But he did lay down the law at times inside his own campaign, when he felt they were bringing a gun to a knife fight. He was deeply unhappy with a long Web ad that raised McCain's involvement in the Keating Five scandal of the savings and loan crisis. Plouffe wanted to deploy the thirteen-minute commercial when McCain's team launched a long-expected personal attack, as they did in early October, when Palin accused Obama of "palling around with terrorists." Obama was upset about the ad, telling Plouffe—who ordered up the attack—that he did not approve.

Yet he was torn between the ball game he dreamed of playing and the one he needed to play to win. Even his friends thought it was time for him to get scrappy. Marty Nesbitt believed the election was now a pickup game of three-on-three. "No matter how good you are, it's going to be close," he said. "They're going to do whatever it takes to keep it close: 'We'll clutch and grab and hack and push and kick and scratch and bite to keep him from scoring.'"

Even in the final days of the election, the candidate pointedly refused to hack back. Flush with cash, Obama's campaign expanded the battlefield as election day approached. They took out TV ads in Georgia and North Dakota—where they had previously pulled out—and in McCain's home state of Arizona, where the polls now suggested the race had narrowed to between one and four points. On his regular late-night conference call, the candidate was skeptical. "Is this for real? Do we really stand a chance in Arizona?" he asked. When he heard about the polls, he relented but set down a clear marker. "Well, put up a positive ad, then. Nothing negative. We're not going to keep a boot on his throat," he said.

His aides pushed back, wanting to go in for the kill. "No," he insisted. "I feel strongly about this. We're not going to do that in Arizona." Obama ended up losing Arizona by almost nine points.

For the most part, his campaign understood the kind of balance he was trying to strike. In the final days, Obama's team managed to target Palin with an attack ad that felt like anything but. There were none of the dark undertones of the classic negative hit: no sinister voice or music—only a sound track of guitar and piano that was faintly upbeat, along with written quotes from John McCain about his lack of economic expertise. McCain suggested that he might have to rely on a vice president for such knowledge. His choice? Sarah Palin, winking at the camera. You might never know that you had just watched a double hit on McCain's poor judgment and Palin's poor résumé.

Obama emerged from the general election with his hope intact because he found a strategy that was neither too hard nor too soft. He also reconnected with his burning desire to win. There were several times when he wanted to ease back, when the election seemed a little too easy or a little too comfortable. Instead, the late rise of Sarah Palin and the panic that she triggered among some Democrats combined to drive him toward the finish line. "He always steps up his game when it's on the line," said Pete Rouse. "We would joke internally that you knew things were going well when he complained about his schedule, asked for more time to work out, or wanted to come back to Chicago from the road an hour earlier. We got a little bit of that after the convention, but then Palin and McCain surged. He was back at it, highly focused, and didn't complain at all. He was working his tail off. He raises his game depending on the level of the competition."

After twenty months of campaigning, he knew himself well enough to preempt his own mistakes. "Every time we've gotten in trouble in this campaign," he told NBC's *Today* show just two weeks before the election, "it's because we stopped trying to play ball-control offense." When he was in control of the ball, he could reshape the game to play to his strengths. He could raise more money than anyone in history and spend it on new kinds of commercials. He could play offense, defense, and common sense. He could master the old game of politics and be a renegade who changed it into something new.

On a long flight from New Mexico to Florida, late in the general election, I asked him about something that his friends know well: that he only really engages in the final minutes of the fourth quarter.

He smiled broadly and nodded in recognition: "Gimme the ball."

SEVEN

ALIEN

On the night of the last primaries in June 2008—after sixteen months of triumphs and failures, of public swooning and media feeding frenzies, of his growth as a candidate and his graying in early middle age—Barack Obama flew with some of his closest friends and aides to St. Paul, Minnesota. He had secured his party's presidential nomination and the symbolism of his travel was clear. It was time to move on, literally and psychologically, from the public and private obsession with Hillary Clinton. He would speak to his supporters and the nation onstage at the Xcel Energy Center, the site of the Republican convention. No matter what happened there in three months' time, he was ready for their attacks and could fill out their arena with a crowd that jammed the space from floor to ceiling. His familiar blue and white banner, promising Change We Can Believe In, was almost lost amid the red, white, and blue. Four large Stars and Stripes draped down from the upper balcony, while a fifth flag hung down from the roof.

Behind the stage, along a winding hallway past the press room and a bar where his friends and family snacked, the candidate and his wife were sitting down with the head of the Secret Service. Life would change as a nominee, even though he had experienced their protection for the last year. The Obamas emerged from their room as if the security talk had lifted their mood. Walking down the hallway, he read out an e-mail from his brother-in-law Konrad Ng in Hawaii, who graciously and respectfully declined the vice presidency. Konrad said he was sure the search would yield an equally qualified candidate. Obama turned the corner to see his friends and family in the bar, which sported an unusual fishing theme. There was a boat on one side and several plastic fish affixed to the walls, including a giant muskie over the bar itself, a large and elusive beast that can eat ducklings.

Change had come to Barack Obama, but he clung to some constancy. "Of course, people are very nice to you," he told me. "I would like to think some of it is heartfelt. You get calls from people who you weren't hearing from right after Pennsylvania or before Iowa. But here with this crew," he said, gesturing to his friends and family, "everybody here is the same. That's why they are in this room, because they don't change. If I lost, they would love me just as much." They were the people who knew him best, before politics and Chicago, before he even dreamed of this moment.

So how was he feeling inside?

"You know me: steady," he explained. "The only thing that will choke me up is calling my grandmother. I'll be calling her later."

Wasn't his grandmother even steadier than he was, a woman of few words?

"That's exactly why she moves me."

Looking back, after the initial shock of losing in New Hampshire, he felt that the primaries had played themselves out according to plan. "Once we had a sense that we would go all the way, then yes, the dynamic was what we expected. With the exception of Maine, which we won, and Indiana, which we lost because it was right after the Wright stuff, every state was exactly as Plouffe predicted sixteen months ago," he said. "There are just some built-in demographic and structural issues, and when you have an extraordinary candidate like Hillary who can still raise $20 million or $30 million after losing eleven straight and can sustain a race, it's going to be pretty much what you expect."

His expectation of the general election was just as clear. "We know what the race is going to be," he said, standing at a high round table opposite a flat-screen TV. "The Republicans can't compete with us on the issues so what they are going to do is to make me into a scary guy. They will use Wright and Ayers. But if the American people know me and my story and Michelle, then I think we'll win."

Ahead lay the scary caricature of the general election; for now, he was standing in the comfort zone of family and friends. As they walked to the holding area backstage, his friends were light-headed with excitement, recalling their tears at his announcement in Springfield. Michelle Obama held her arms around her husband's waist before he walked onstage, and they chuckled together. Onstage, the candidate dedicated the moment to his grandmother, "who helped raise me and is sitting in Hawaii somewhere right now because she can't travel, but who poured everything that she had into me, and who helped to make me the man I am today."

But he also wanted to ready the crowd for the battle ahead, and the prospect that his opponents would try to redefine the man he was today. Was he the devoted grandson of an elderly Kansas woman or a partially Muslim alien with a soft spot for terrorists? "What you don't deserve is another election that's governed by fear, and innuendo, and division. What you won't hear from this campaign or this party is the kind of politics that uses religion as a wedge and patriotism as a bludgeon," he said. "What you won't see from this campaign or this party is a politics that sees our opponents not as competitors to challenge, but enemies to polarize, because we may call ourselves Democrats and Republicans, but we are Americans first. We are *always* Americans first."

He was undoubtedly American first, from the moment he burst onto the stage in Boston decrying the separation of red and blue America. But he was also a deeply unconventional American, in birth, upbringing, and friendship. His approach to foreign policy was shaped as much by personal as professional experience. In his view, his international exposure made him more informed about the world, even if it made him less of a conformist with the foreign policy establishment. "It's widely disdained by our opponents as little qualification, but the fact that he has lived overseas and lived in a place like Indonesia, which has a large Muslim population, and has traveled widely, has given him a particular familiarity with the way others see us," said David Axelrod. "We Americans tend to be very focused on the world as we see it, and a little bit limited in trying to understand how others see us." Obama spent his life trying to understand how others see him, and that effort informed his foreign policy as much as his domestic politics.

To his opponents, his life overseas was much like his middle name: another cause for derision or suspicion. They were constantly trying to make the case that Obama was un-American and unfit to lead: that he was somehow too different to be trusted, too new to know anything. Some of his most outspoken critics sharply limited their definition of the

American character: Obama was unpatriotic for failing either to wear a flag pin on his lapel or to put his hand over his heart for the national anthem. The debate took a ridiculous turn, and the candidate—no matter how superficial he judged the issue—could not entirely escape. He later took to wearing the flag pin after supporters, including one disabled war veteran, kept thrusting them in his palm. As for his hand-on-heart behavior, he explained that his grandfather had taught him to put his hand over his heart for the Pledge of Allegiance, not the anthem. His rivals did not learn the same protocol. At the Harkin steak fry in Iowa in 2007, he was photographed as the only candidate with his arms down while the anthem played.

In some ways the candidate possessed a thin Washington résumé in foreign affairs. He had spent only two years on the Foreign Relations Committee by the time he launched his presidential campaign, although it was two years' more experience than that of a Texas governor who rose to the presidency six years earlier. Hillary Clinton was at least familiar with military affairs from sitting on the Armed Services Committee, even if she was less involved in diplomacy. But committee assignments were never the real test for a presidential candidate. If they were, Joe Biden and Chris Dodd—both veterans of Foreign Affairs in the Senate—would have been front-runners for the Democratic nomination. No question, Obama lacked formal experience. Instead, what he brought was a worldview that gave him insight into one of the most intractable problems of the so-called war on terror: why some nations seemed hostile toward the United States and more favorable to radical critics and even terrorists.

Obama's worldview was formed early in his life, not just by living abroad but by the conscious effort of his mother. Ann Dunham was an internationalist at heart, and she raised her son to feel the same way. "She clearly saw me as part of a global citizenry," he told me. "And I think if you had asked her, she would have said, 'He's part me, he's part his father, he's part Indonesian, he's part Hawaiian.' She was somebody who very much embraced the idea of a cosmopolitan identity. And I'm sure that's what she would have encouraged in me as well."

Indonesia was the formative experience for him as much as for his mother, and she later built a life and career there after he returned to Hawaii. In the sprawling, chaotic capital of Jakarta, the young Barry Obama immersed himself in a boy's life of soccer, street food, and an eclectic culture of mixed religions and ethnic groups. "Indonesia was a fascinating place for a young boy," said his sister Maya. "I know that Mom talked about the fact that he would go off with the village kids and play soccer and come back with gaping wounds and make her worry." He would eat from roadside stalls, enjoying satay (grilled skewers), *nasi goreng* (fried rice), and *soto* (chicken noodle soup). His stepfather would take him out for *bakso bola tenis*, a broth with meatballs the size of tennis balls. And the culture was just as exotic and complex as the cuisine. He watched *wayang*, the shadow puppet theater, and listened to the music of gamelan groups, mixing xylophones with gongs, flutes, and strings. He knew the stories of the Mahabharata, from the country's Hindu past, and he sat through both Catholic and Islamic studies in his two elementary schools. Later, he would visit his mother in Jogjakarta in central Java, where he would often visit Borobudur temple, a giant Buddhist pyramid with intricate statues and relief carvings.

His experience of Muslim life was limited, even at his state school where he had religious studies once a week. "Indonesia wasn't only a moderate Muslim country, it had an explicitly secular constitution. But the culture itself was so laden with Hindu, animist beliefs that it just didn't encroach upon the culture," he told me. "I remember there were two girls in the whole school who wore headscarves. Nobody wore headscarves on the streets. I mean, women were driving on Vespas and when you went out into the villages they were all taking baths in the river. So it was much more similar to probably growing up in Bombay than it would have been to what it was like growing up in Saudi Arabia."

What lingered with him, especially after his return to the American life of Hawaii, was the sense of raw poverty, the chasm that lay between the masses and the wealthy and well connected. Many presidents have seen grinding poverty at home, but few have witnessed it overseas. "It was the first place he was really exposed to real poverty and real inequity and got a sense of the fact that there are lots of things that you can't take for granted, that there are people with real needs. And I think that recognition really only became jarring in the relative comfort of Hawaii," said Maya. Indonesia's poverty taught him, at an early age, to empathize with those at the very bottom of the third world, rather than ignore them or push them aside like the expats his mother disdained.

It also taught him to savor the advantages that came with his American identity. "It made you appreciate America in a way that you might not otherwise appreciate," he told me. "Some of it is the surface stuff: the paved roads and the lights on the buildings. When you go back to

Hawaii, TV for more than three hours a day. The things you would expect a kid to find appealing. But some of it was deeper than that. The sense of poverty in Indonesia and the inequality was something you never saw in America. You now see it unfortunately in places like Manhattan. But growing up in Hawaii was probably similar to growing up in a lot of small towns or even medium-sized cities in America. Where the banker's kid went to school with the police officer's kid. There was a sense that everybody was middle class, that everybody had a chance. So you go to Indonesia and you've got generals who've got a fleet of cars, servants, and a big mansion. And you've literally got beggars outside on the streets. There was a sense even as a child that there was this fundamental unfairness when compared to what was happening in America."

The result was a set of international experiences that reaffirmed his personal quest back home: the need to be curious about others, to close the gap between cultures, and to find a common point of contact. "I think that he has his experience not as a representative of government but as a man in search of answers," said Maya. "These are very important experiences, not just in Indonesia, but through other parts of the world, talking to a mother who lived in a dozen countries. I think they function as a very important layer for him and help him to generate empathy and work with multiple perspectives simultaneously. They help him to help other people to find common ground."

Empathy was the common theme of the rolling conversations between mother and son about the state of the world. Sitting on the beach or taking a walk, they would talk about her work with women in Asia or about American politics and philosophy. These were the foundations for a political philosophy that was distinctly American, centrist and internationalist: he was not red or blue, black or white, Kansan or Kenyan, expat or native. For Obama, America was neither a melting pot nor a mosaic, but something much more comforting. "I think the best analogy I've heard is sort of a gumbo," he told me on his campaign plane. "It's not a thin soup. It's got these big chunks of stuff in it. But those things are seasoning each other. It's not tomato soup. It's something thick."

He carried his international outlook with him to college, where he gravitated toward foreign students at Occidental College in Los Angeles, before transferring to Columbia in New York. He mixed with an exotic group, finding that the outsiders formed a natural bond with minorities. "It was interesting because the international students also identified with the African American students," he told me. "So there was sort of an amalgam of foreigners, African Americans, Latinos, sort of the misfits all kind of congregated together a little bit. There were a couple of punk rockers, some political leftists." Obama moved easily between the misfits, sitting with African Americans in the cafeteria one day, then with the foreigners another day. Among his close friends were a small group of Pakistani students, including Wahid Hamid and Hasan Chandoo. Obama and Hamid shared a strong work ethic instilled by their families and their limited finances. "We developed a mutual respect," Hamid said. "Even though he was from Hawaii and the United States, we were both there to try and make it in America in some way." Together they shared a weeklong driving vacation along the West Coast, down to Mexico and up to Oregon, visiting friends in a beat-up red Fiat coupe that was too small for the six-foot-plus Obama.

Those friendships proved critical to his understanding of Muslim politics, which would much later shape his position on the so-called war on terror. His friends helped him understand the complex religious and ethnic politics between Sunni and Shia, rich and poor, in a country that would be at the center of the battle against al Qaeda. His mother worked in India, Bangladesh, and Pakistan in the late 1980s, and he visited her there, touring sights like the Taj Mahal. But it was on an earlier trip to Pakistan, with Hamid and Chandoo, when his insight deepened. Chandoo's family was wealthy, well connected, and international: his father was born in Rangoon, Burma, and his mother was from Bombay, India. Hamid's family was more middle-class, and they both counted Karachi as their family home.

For a few weeks Obama lived with their families, met their friends, and explored the busy city in the midst of Ramadan with its daytime peace and nighttime festivities. They played basketball on bare cement strips outdoors and ate the spicy food that Chandoo had introduced him to at Occidental, a taste Obama had first acquired in Indonesia. Indeed, he found that Pakistan often evoked memories of Indonesia, especially the yawning gap between rich and poor, the powerless and the powerful. "It reminded me of some of the tensions in Indonesia in the sense that you had at that time a military government," he told me. "You had a lot of problems with corruption, a lot of unemployed young men on the streets, a very wealthy ruling class that was plugged into the international economy but that in some ways wasn't woven into the larger economy of Pakistan. So there were a lot of trends that were similar to what I saw in Indonesia and what I would later see in Kenya."

It was a side trip to the farmlands of the interior, not far from Karachi, that would make the deepest impression. In Hyderabad, staying with one of Hamid's friends, he was shocked to see a life that had barely changed in centuries. For the historic Talpur family in Sindh province owned not just the land but also effectively its peasants, who toiled amid the sugarcane and mangoes. The Talpurs lived in comfort compared with their peasants, with running water and electricity, but their village home was still rudimentary when it came to plumbing. They lived a simple but comfortable life, eating fresh-killed chickens for dinner and the fruit and vegetables from their land. They also lived a blissfully superior life, arguing that their peasants would be lost without their rule. Obama probed their attitudes, and met their laborers, with a respectful but inquisitive approach. Although a Muslim country, Pakistan maintained some remnants of the Indian caste system. Some of its landowners retained feudal authority, even though their counterparts in India had lost much of their power a half century earlier. "You had untouchables who were still functioning as indentured servants, effectively. And the equivalent of feudal lords who still were essentially the law of the communities in which they lived," he told me.

Among the peasants was a Pakistani of African origin, the descendant of slaves brought by Arab traders from East Africa to the western coast of the Indian subcontinent many centuries before. He had worked the Talpur land for many years as an indentured servant, just like the tobacco farm laborers of the American South, barely removed from the status of a slave. He was a direct link to an earlier slave trade, before Europeans took slaves to the Caribbean and North America. His ancestors may have even come from land in modern-day Kenya, the home of Obama's father.

The trip to Pakistan, as well as his international friendships and his early childhood in Indonesia, gave him a touchstone for his foreign policy. Instead of a typically wonkish approach, focusing on pure government power, Obama understood the need to reach those beyond the elites. "What it tells me is that the most important aspect of our foreign policy is not simply our relations with the rulers of these countries, but also our appreciation and understanding of the challenges and the hardships and the struggles that ordinary people are going through there," he told me. "Because in a country like Pakistan, if we are not thinking about that untouchable that's working in the fields, or the young man who is a day laborer in Karachi, and we think that interactions with the Oxford-educated Pakistani in parliament somehow gives us an insight into the country, we can be really mistaken and can make a series of misjudgments."

He concluded that Pakistanis needed to understand that the United States wanted to improve their quality of life, not just the security of Americans. And his interactions with Karachi families made him realize that there were alternatives to Washington's traditional reliance on strongmen like President Pervez Musharraf, who had grown from a military dictator to an international partner after the 9/11 attacks. "One of the other things that I was clear about when I traveled there was that there is a sizable middle class and a tradition inherited from partition that believes in rule of law and believes in a government that is accountable to the people," he explained. "So our willingness to put all our eggs in the Musharraf basket without understanding this other tradition, and without understanding that our choice in a place like Pakistan is not simply military dictatorship or Islamic rule, led us to make a series of miscalculations that has weakened our fight against terrorism in the region."

Above all, his experiences in Indonesia and Pakistan taught him something that President Bush only fully came to comprehend several years after he invaded Iraq: there was a deep and complex divide between the Sunni and Shia traditions of Islam. Hamid was Sunni, while Chandoo was Shia, introducing Obama at an early age and in a personal way to the historic rivalries and the powerful regional dynamic between Iran and Iraq. While his friends did not engage in religious argument, they helped explain the forces that would lead directly to a brutal civil war. Obama understood that it would never be easy to reconcile Iraq, or transform it into a peaceful democracy, after invasion and occupation. "Both as a consequence of living in Indonesia and traveling in Pakistan, having friends in college who were Muslim, I was very clear about the history of Shia-Sunni antagonism which had defined the war between Iraq and Iran, and which was the fault line of a lot of tensions inside of Pakistan," he told me. "And so this notion that somehow we were going to be able to create a functioning democracy and reconcile century-old conflicts I always thought was a bunch of happy talk from this [Bush] administration."

The result was the speech an Illinois state senator, with no Washington experience in foreign policy, delivered to a group of antiwar protesters in downtown Chicago in 2002. It was two weeks before Congress voted to authorize the invasion of Iraq, a period of intense political pressure in the run-up to the midterm elections that year, and little more than a year after the attacks of 9/11. Some polls showed that a broad majority of Democrats approved of military action to remove Saddam Hussein. Others suggested that Democrats were evenly divided on the war: liberal Democrats opposed the invasion, while moderate Democrats supported it in equal measure. The political calculation was not clear for Democratic officials across the country, including an aspiring Chicago politician who was preparing to enter the party's crowded primary field for the United States Senate. So when Barack Obama took the microphone at Federal Plaza, the text of his speech rolled up in his right hand, he was taking a significant gamble. Behind him stood a protester with a placard saying War Is Not an Option. Yet he started by distancing himself from the pacifists nearby. He was not antiwar, he explained; he supported the American Civil War, the Second World War, and the war in Afghanistan. "What I am opposed to is a dumb war. What I am opposed to is a rash war," he declared. "What I am opposed to is the cynical attempt by Richard Perle and Paul Wolfowitz and other armchair, weekend warriors in this administration to shove their own ideological agendas down our throats, irrespective of the costs in lives lost and in hardships borne." He condemned Saddam as a brutal man who butchered his own people, but insisted that the Iraqi dictator could be contained until he lost power.

Obama's views of an invasion were based not just on the rashness of the war but on its impact on a region he seemed to understand better than many Democrats in Washington. While he rejected the neoconservative happy talk, some of his Pakistani friends did not agree with him. Chandoo, a supporter of the war in Iraq, thought that Saddam's demise would throw Iraq into turmoil at some point and inevitably suck in American forces. Hamid, his Sunni friend, opposed the conflict. Still, Obama correctly predicted the impact of the war on Iraq, al Qaeda, and the broader region. "I know that even a successful war against Iraq will require a U.S. occupation of undetermined length, at undetermined cost, with undetermined consequences," he said. "I know that an invasion of Iraq without a clear rationale and without strong international support will only fan the flames of the Middle East, and encourage the worst, rather than best, impulses of the Arab world, and strengthen the recruitment arm of al Qaeda. I am not opposed to all wars. I'm opposed to dumb wars."

As his unlikely campaign began, Obama's early opposition to the war—and the unconventional experience that lay behind it—was a boon. Five years after his speech in Chicago, the vast majority of Democratic voters were adamantly opposed to the war in Iraq and anything that smacked of President Bush's foreign policy. He was alone among the top three candidates in having opposed the war from the outset, which frustrated his rivals immensely. The Clinton campaign suggested Obama had back-tracked on his antiwar position in 2004 and beyond, saying he was all talk and no action. In fact, Obama had chosen not to lead the antiwar effort in Washington because he wanted to stick to his early Senate strategy of staying out of the national limelight and placing Illinois first.

Instead the candidate's real vulnerability lay in his lack of formal for-eign policy experience. While his judgment on Iraq was sound, his polit-ical touch was sometimes entirely absent. Some parts of diplomacy are less about policy than walking through the minefield of international and domestic politics. At the first Democratic debate of the election, in Orangeburg, South Carolina, Obama was asked to name America's three most important allies around the world. His answer: the European Union, NATO, and Japan. Never mind that the EU is not a single ally and NATO is a multinational alliance. By mentioning the EU before NATO, he walked headlong into Europe's rivalries, especially the failed efforts to establish a coordinated approach to foreign policy and defense. His an-swer completely ignored North and South America, as well as the Middle East. It took the moderator, NBC's Brian Williams, to remind him that he had failed to mention Israel.

Three months and several debates later, in Charleston, South Car-olina, Obama wandered into another thicket of politics and protocol. Re-sponding to a question from a YouTube contributor, Obama sounded confident but he seemed to ignore the detail of the query: In the spirit of the 1977 visit of Anwar Sadat of Egypt to Israel, would he agree to meet without preconditions with the leaders of Iran, Syria, Venezuela, Cuba, and North Korea, within the first year of entering the White House? "I would," Obama began without hesitation. "And the reason is this: that the notion that somehow not talking to countries is punishment to them—

which has been the guiding diplomatic principle of this administration—is ridiculous. Now, Ronald Reagan and Democratic presidents like JFK constantly spoke to the Soviet Union at a time when Ronald Reagan called them an evil empire. And the reason is because they understood that we may not trust them and they may pose an extraordinary danger to this country, but we had the obligation to find areas where we can potentially move forward." Clinton immediately rejected her rival's position, saying she did not want to be used as propaganda. "I will use a lot of high-level presidential envoys to test the waters, to feel the way," she said. "But certainly, we're not going to just have our president meet with Fidel Castro and Hugo Chavez and, you know, the president of North Korea, Iran, and Syria until we know better what the way forward would be."

Obama's aides, sitting in the staff room, feared they would spend the next several days cleaning up the candidate's comments. On a conference call the next morning, they were debating how to phrase a memo to explain how Obama's position was in fact close to Hillary Clinton's. Robert Gibbs, traveling in a car with the candidate, stopped the conversation. "Barack would like to say something," he said.

"Look, guys, this is ridiculous," Obama said. "We shouldn't be afraid of this. I want to have this debate. We talked to Stalin. We talked to Mao. The idea that we can't talk to someone like Ahmadinejad is ridiculous. It's just typical D.C. conventional wisdom."

His staffers were taken aback. They retooled the tortured logic of the memo and turned it into an aggressive defense of the candidate's statement. "It was a real teaching moment for us," said Dan Pfeiffer, one of the campaign's press secretaries at the time. "It was the first time we saw Obama relish the fight. For the next five-day period we saw a side of him and a side of ourselves that was very important for the long run." The dispute pitted the renegade candidate—willing to throw out not just Bush's approach but also the diplomatic dance surrounding presidential talks—against the establishment candidate with her White House sensibility and stature. By the end of the week, Obama had dug himself in, turning the moment of weakness into a tale about self-confident diplomacy. He reached for a line from Kennedy's 1961 inaugural address, placing it at the heart of his stump speech: "Let us never negotiate out of fear, but let us never fear to negotiate." Campaigning in Iowa, he portrayed himself as a fearless leader, not a rookie candidate. "I was called irresponsible and naive because I believe that there is nobody we can't talk to," he told one rally. "We've got nothing to fear as long as we know who we are and what we stand for and our values." By the late fall he described his position, which he had arrived at in haphazard fashion, as "aggressive personal diplomacy."

It was a neat move of political jujitsu, turning an opponent's attack into an opportunity for counterattack. There was, however, the small logistical problem of arranging five presidential meetings with rogue leaders in his first year as president. Quite aside from his own schedule, there was an enormous amount of preparatory work that would need to take place—preparations that might easily tip into preconditions. As the primaries drew to an end, Obama's foreign policy team began to rework his answer to stretch the timing of any meetings and emphasize that there would be groundwork before any talks. "Engagement at the presidential level, at the appropriate time and with the appropriate preparation, can be used to leverage the change we need," said Susan Rice, one of his closest foreign policy advisers. "But nobody said he would initiate contacts at the presidential level; that requires due preparation and advance work." It was hard to know where preparation ended and preconditions began. Even with a more open approach to direct talks, any presidential meeting could be derailed by the failure to agree on a clear agenda.

Obama's command of foreign policy was critical to his chances of winning the presidency. But there was no clear way to measure whether he had crossed the bar of looking and sounding like a commander in chief. In many ways, his renegade-like readiness to break with the past and challenge conventional wisdom—whether planned or not—made it much harder for him to look presidential. So much of the back-and-forth on foreign policy hinged less on policy than appearances and emotions. A week before the Iowa caucuses, the candidate declared that his experience of living overseas meant more than the niceties of diplomatic ceremonies that greet a First Lady or a member of Congress. "My experience is grounded in understanding how the world *sees* America, from living overseas and traveling overseas, and having family beyond our shores. It's that experience, that understanding, not just of what world leaders I went and talked to in the ambassador's house, who I had tea with, but understanding the lives of people like my grandmother who lives in a tiny village in Africa without running water and without heat, that's been decimated by AIDS and malaria," he told supporters in Coralville. "That's the experience that helped inform my opposition to the war in Iraq. That's the kind of experience that's rooted in the real lives of real people. And that's the kind of experience that Washington and America needs right now." The tea-drinking put-down prompted a rapid response from Madeleine Albright, the former secretary of state, who insisted that Clinton had been to refugee camps and orphanages "where tea is not the usual drink." Instead of debating their timetables for withdrawal from Iraq, the campaigns were arguing over beverages sipped overseas.

Clinton struck back in style, if not in substance, with her own series of personal attacks, suggesting that Obama was too inexperienced to keep the nation safe. In fact, her own foreign policy résumé largely consisted of ceremonial travel as First Lady—with one exception: a tough speech on women's rights at a UN conference in Beijing. If their contest boiled down to speech making, Obama had something more relevant to brag about: opposing the war in Iraq. Laura Bush had traveled extensively as First Lady, but nobody suggested that she was qualified to be commander in chief. Clinton resorted to padding out her résumé by suggesting that she had dodged sniper fire on a First Lady trip to Bosnia with her teenage daughter, Chelsea.

Those pesky details did not interfere with the most powerful ad of the primary season. "It's 3:00 a.m. and your children are safe and asleep," said the movie-trailer voice over pictures of children tucked in bed with their toys. "But there's a phone in the White House and it's ringing. Something is happening in the world. Your vote will decide who answers that call. Whether it's someone who already knows the world's leaders, knows the military. Someone tested and ready to lead in a dangerous world." The ad ended with Clinton picking up the phone by the soft light of a table lamp.

Few of the world's leaders whom Clinton had met as First Lady were still in power eight years after she left the White House. Nevertheless, the ad dominated the news, and Obama was left to debate Clinton's tactics. "We've seen these ads before. They're the kind that play on people's fears to scare up votes. Well, it won't work this time. Because the question is not about picking up the phone. The question is: What kind of judgment will you make when you answer?" he told a small group of veterans at an American Legion post in Houston, Texas. "We've had a red-phone moment. It was the decision to invade Iraq. And Senator Clinton gave the wrong answer. George Bush gave the wrong answer. John McCain gave the wrong answer."

There was a direct link between Hillary Clinton's attempts to scare voters about Obama and John McCain's attempts to do the same in the general election. In many ways, she laid the foundation for the later scaremongering. After the 3:00 a.m. TV ad and her victory in the Texas and Ohio primaries, Clinton staged a press event in Washington with several military officers beside her. "I think it's imperative that each of us be able to demonstrate we can cross the commander-in-chief threshold, and I believe that I've done that," she asserted. "Certainly, Senator McCain has done that, and you'll have to ask Senator Obama with respect to his candidacy." That attack crossed the line of decorum for many Democrats, including Obama himself. A month later, in Pennsylvania, the candidate was still smarting at the notion that Clinton would trash him compared with a Republican. But when encouraged by reporters to return the compliment, Obama declined. "I know that sort of conventional textbook politics means that unless you completely demonize the other side, you are showing weakness. I don't believe that," he told reporters in a Philadelphia diner on the morning of the Pennsylvania primary. "But I think Senator Clinton suggesting that she and John McCain are the two people qualified to be commander in chief is probably something that could end up coming back to haunt us in November."

For some with long memories, Obama's break with the past on foreign policy was a reminder of the last Democratic icon. Ted Sorensen, JFK's special counsel and speechwriter, heard clear echoes between Kennedy and Obama in the debate about experience and judgment. When Kennedy delivered a speech condemning western support for French colonialism in Algeria, he was roundly criticized—just as Obama was criticized for his position on seeking to talk with hostile countries, especially in the Muslim world. "There were those in foreign policy circles—in the Democratic and Republican Parties—that said it was a naive and inexperienced move on Kennedy's part," Sorensen told me. "He was a lot younger when he started running than Obama is now. LBJ would make remarks like, 'What has Kennedy ever done except write a couple of books?'" Such criticism came to a head during the U-2 crisis in 1960, when the Soviets shot down an American spy plane over their territory and captured its pilot, Gary Powers. "Kennedy said since we had obviously violated Soviet airspace without asking their permission, he thought it was regrettable. Johnson thundered in one of his campaign speeches, 'Do you believe in apologizing to the Soviets?' Of course, the crowd shouted, 'No!' But you and I are talking because Kennedy resolved the Cuban missile crisis. Stepping back from the brink of world-wide destruction because he was willing to communicate and, dare I say, negotiate with the Soviet Union."

There was a peculiar irony to the notion that Obama could not handle foreign affairs or talk to world leaders. As the primaries rolled along, the candidate immersed himself in a unique international crisis, in real time, doing something that most presidential candidates can only dream of: a personal, presidential-style intervention in foreign affairs. His actions were all the more curious because he never tried to exploit his role in a campaign ad, a set-piece speech, or a sharp put-down in a TV debate.

The crisis erupted in the closing days of the Iowa contest, when Kenya staged its general election in late December 2007. The sitting president, Mwai Kibaki, was declared the winner, but there was widespread international agreement that the election was rigged against his challenger, Raila Odinga. Kenyan politics and society were shaken to their tribal foundations, as Odinga's minority Luo tribe rioted against the ruling majority Kikuyu tribe. Kenya, one of the most stable and relatively comfortable countries in Africa, was suddenly witnessing young mobs, lynchings, curfews, and soldiers on the streets. Hundreds died as the political leaders squabbled over the election results and the notion of a power-sharing deal.

Kenya's bloodshed was especially personal for Barack Obama. Traveling with him on his campaign bus as Kenya burned was his sister Auma, who had recently moved from London to Nairobi and now feared for her return and her family's safety. The crisis was almost a case study in his unconventional foreign policy experience. Obama had met with President Kibaki during his chaotic African tour fifteen months earlier, when the young senator confronted the older African leader about corruption, tribalism, and freedom of the press. "It's a lot easier when you go to a country and just exchange pleasantries," said Scott Gration, a retired air force general who accompanied Obama to Africa and later became one of his foreign policy advisers. "But he took up these big issues, including corruption, and did it in a way that was respectful and emphasizing the way forward." Drawing on his family experiences in Kenya and Indonesia, Obama publicly condemned corruption on his African trip and continued to do so on the campaign trail in his first major foreign policy speech of the election. "The corruption I heard about while visiting parts of Africa has been around for decades, but the hunger to eliminate such corruption is a growing and powerful force among people there," he told the Chicago Council on Global Affairs. "And so in these places where fear and want still thrive, we must couple our aid with an insistent call for reform."

Behind the scenes, as he grappled with John Edwards's late surge in Iowa and Hillary Clinton's comeback in New Hampshire, the candidate was talking to officials in Washington and Nairobi. He wanted to know if he could be helpful and supportive in trying to stabilize the situation. That meant working alongside the Bush administration even as he was railing against its foreign policy at every campaign stop. "It was Senator Obama who made the decision that despite the pressures of political business, this was more important," said his foreign policy adviser Susan Rice. "If there was something he could do to help, he would do it. But he didn't want to be a loose cannon. He could have easily picked up the phone or knocked out a statement. But he thought it was more important to coordinate closely with the administration on how he perceived the situation and how they perceived it." He asked Secretary of State Condoleezza Rice for her assessment of what was happening on the ground, and whether he could help by intervening. He talked to the U.S. ambassador to Kenya, Michael Ranneberger, and Archbishop Desmond Tutu, who was also in Kenya at the time.

The result was an unusual moment in the often bizarre history of the Iowa caucuses: a presidential candidate in Davenport recording a statement for Voice of America radio on the aftermath of elections eight thousand miles away. He spoke to the opposition leader, Odinga, who came from the same Luo tribe as his own family, urging him to stick to the democratic process and meet with Kenya's president without preconditions. He pressed him to halt a mass rally and avoid escalating the violence. President Kibaki, however, proved much more elusive: Obama's calls went unreturned. The president did not seem to want to talk to any American official.

Obama's political team was nervous about anything unpredictable in the final days before Iowa. How could they calculate the impact of Kenya's crisis? Would it remind voters of his foreign background? Could it backfire if the crisis worsened and Obama was seen to take sides with his father's Luo people? Those concerns did not interfere with the candidate's approach. The political staff did not press the foreign policy team to back off or shift their strategy. When it came to foreign affairs, especially a violent crisis with a personal impact on Obama's family, they knew better than to play politics. They told reporters about his phone calls, but they never placed it front and center as they debated his foreign policy expertise with the Clinton and McCain campaigns.

By the time the candidate himself spoke about the crisis at length, in South Carolina, the press was fixated on the racial and psychological drama of the Clintons. The candidate mentioned Kenya briefly in his opening remarks at one session with reporters, saying the country was "an anchor for the region," but he was asked no questions in return. He later called into a Kenyan radio show and wrote an op-ed column for the *Daily Nation,* one of the country's largest newspapers. By the end of January, as the violence continued, Obama began to have concerns that the Bush administration was stumbling. "Historically Kenya has not fallen into this sort of ethnic bloodshed and I think everybody in that country has to pause and think very carefully," he said when I asked if the administration could be doing more. "Kofi Annan is there and I hope the administration is very actively supporting his efforts. But ultimately, the leaders of Kenya really have to stand up and say irrespective of the election outcome, this is something that we really have to put an end to." The strategy of the former UN secretary-general proved successful. A month later, Kenya's rival leaders signed a power-sharing agreement, and a coalition government emerged in April, just before Obama lost the Pennsylvania primary.

While his personal experience helped shape his foreign policy, it also opened him up to some of the most potent political attacks. To some voters and politicians, his international family—even his overseas travel—served to make him exotic, foreign, mysterious, suspicious. There were also the obvious matters of his Kenyan Muslim name, and the color of his skin. Indeed their obvious nature only made them more compelling to those who were already distrustful of this renegade. He was a rule breaker who emerged disconcertingly quickly from another culture or another party. What was his true allegiance and his true identity? If you never trusted him in the first place, the answers were ugly indeed.

The most insistent argument was an anonymous e-mail, or series of e-mails, distributed widely with the same core question: "Who is Barack

Obama?" The answer was a long and rambling diatribe of anti-Muslim sentiment mixing half facts and whole lies. "Probable U.S. presidential candidate, Barack Hussein Obama was born in Honolulu, Hawaii, to Barack Hussein Obama, Sr., a black MUSLIM from Nyangoma-Kogel, Kenya and Ann Dunham, a white ATHEIST from Wichita, Kansas," read one e-mail. "Obama's parents met at the University of Hawaii. When Obama was two years old, his parents divorced. His father returned to Kenya. His mother then married Lolo Soetoro, a RADICAL Muslim from Indonesia. When Obama was 6 years old, the family relocated to Indonesia. Obama attended a MUSLIM school in Jakarta. He also spent two years in a Catholic school. Obama takes great care to conceal the fact that he is a Muslim. He is quick to point out that, 'He was once a Muslim, but that he also attended Catholic school.'"

Obama was never a Muslim, and he attended a public elementary school in Jakarta. His father was an atheist, not a Muslim; his stepfather was anything but radical; his mother was a spiritual woman who subscribed to no single religion. In any case, the candidate himself was a practicing Christian who married in church, baptized his daughters, and swore his oath of office on a Bible. And he never described himself as a Muslim.

No matter. The virus was coursing through an electronic bloodstream. When *Insight* magazine described Obama's school in Jakarta as a madrassa, the story was picked up by Fox News, the *New York Post,* and endless blogs. It was also easily debunked by CNN, which sent a reporter to visit the supposed madrassa and found a nonreligious public school instead. A year later, the notion that the school was Muslim was still finding its way into respected publications like *The Economist.* Flying on his campaign plane in March 2008, the candidate picked up the magazine to point out a letter correcting the oft-repeated error. "There's a letter once again from the ambassador, a former ambassador," he told me. "And he says, 'You give the wrong impression that it was a Muslim school. It was a state school.' Literally it was no different than the Catholic school that I attended. In fact it was probably less explicitly religious than the Catholic school I attended because at the Catholic school you would start every day with a prayer." There was little Obama could do except talk regularly about the e-mails at election stops, or rebut the rumors on the campaign's website. He printed flyers that stressed his Christian faith. One small handout in South Carolina listed his church as one of just five biographical bullet points alongside the names of his daughters.

The personal smearing quickly tipped into the pretense of a policy dispute, especially among Jewish voters who were concerned about Israel's precarious security. The candidate's failure to cite Israel as an ally in his first TV debate may have heightened Jewish anxieties. But a more likely explanation was his short Washington résumé, his name, the Muslim-baiting e-mails, and the color of his skin. Obama's opponents had few obvious qualms about stoking those anxieties and prejudices. Clinton's supporters and sometimes her staff pointed out her strong support for Israel and suggested Obama was suspect on the issue. Ann Lewis, a senior adviser to Clinton and leading surrogate for her campaign, told one conference call with Jewish leaders that Obama's chief foreign policy aide was Zbigniew Brzezinski, who was Jimmy Carter's national security adviser. Brzezinski held no such position with the Obama campaign, but that wasn't the point. His reputation was toxic among American Jews because he endorsed a book blaming the pro-Israel lobby for the country's foreign policy failures. The mere mention of his name was code for anti-Israel and anti-Semitic.

The candidate felt as bemused by the attacks as he was frustrated by their tenacity. After all, in his failed campaign for Congress in 2000, he faced criticism that he was too *close* to Jewish supporters. Now he faced precisely the opposite charge, even though his senior strategist was Jewish and so was his finance chair. "I think there's still some concern because those concerns have been continually stoked," he told reporters on his plane in late February.

Whether it's through these e-mails that suggest I'm a Muslim and have attended madrassas and was sworn in with my hand on the Koran. Scurrilous e-mails that were untrue. Whether it was an article that was in *Newsweek* recently indicating the degree to which Clinton supporters have questioned my positions on Israel. I think it's very clear why there have been problems. It's part of a series of political strategies. Not all of them necessarily, by the way, the result of the Clinton campaign. I have no idea where those e-mails are coming from. And so we've had to continually correct them. But the fact of the matter is that we won the Jewish vote in places like California. Where there are large Jewish populations, we more or less split with the Clinton campaign. Some of my strongest supporters are members of the Jewish community. I have the rock-solid support of the Jewish community in Chicago, the group that knows me best. Nobody has ever been able to point to a statement that I've made or a position that I have taken that [is] contrary to the long-term security interests of Israel.

His opponents tried to find those statements and positions, but they came up with little. That did not stop the personal attacks masquerading as policy debates. Well before Obama clinched the nomination, John Mc-Cain suggested that the Palestinian terrorist group Hamas wanted to see Obama win. Talking to conservative bloggers, McCain ignored Obama's condemnation of Hamas and his refusal to negotiate with the group. "I think it's very clear who Hamas wants to be the next president of the United States," McCain said. He was referring to a recent radio interview by a Hamas adviser who expressed his desire to see Obama win the election. "I think that people should understand that I will be Hamas's worst nightmare," McCain asserted. "If Senator Obama is favored by Hamas, I think people can make judgments accordingly." Later, the Republican National Committee issued a series of Israel-focused press releases, the first of which questioned why Obama continued "to mislead the American people on his record on Israel." The RNC's main exhibit was a blog item from the *Politico* that suggested "a real, if kind of inchoate, skepticism" about Obama at a conference of the pro-Israeli group AIPAC. Kind of inchoate it surely was. The press release also cited Obama talking about Palestinian suffering and his readiness to meet with the Iranian leader.

If the attacks were intended to weaken Obama's position among Jewish Americans, they succeeded. Howard Gutman, one of his biggest fund-raisers, felt compelled to write to a rabbi in the Washington, D.C., area who was planning to deliver a sermon condemning Obama's speech on race in Philadelphia. When the candidate visited synagogues, his local supporters assured the audience that they could trust him. Steve Rothman was one of several endorsers at a Philadelphia synagogue in mid-April, where the New Jersey congressman insisted that the candidate understood the preeminent position of Israel. "Israel will always be," he said, thumping both fists on the table in front of him, "an irreplaceable ally of the United States of America which Barack Obama has committed himself to defend. What kind of person is Barack Obama? I'm from Jersey. Would *I* support somebody who wasn't a stand-up guy? Would I support somebody whose words meant nothing, who was untested?

After all, I worked with the Clintons as a congressman in my first years, my neighbor is Senator Clinton. I *know* them, yet I have chosen Senator Obama to support." Such excessive displays were only undercut by the low-key performance of the candidate himself, whose energy levels never quite matched those of his most fervent Jewish backers. Outside, his volunteers handed out pins saying the candidate's name in Hebrew script.

He was ready for combat in any synagogue, and he needed to be. Inside a large reception hall at the B'nai Torah synagogue in Boca Raton, Florida, in May, he tried to defuse the fears about his name. "Let's be honest," he began, answering the very first question of his town hall meeting. "Part of what raises concerns is you've got a black guy named Barack Obama. So people say, 'He's got sort of a Muslim-sounding name, we don't know what's going on.' So let me just clear up what's going on. My father was from Kenya, and Barack actually, interestingly enough, means the same as Baruch—it means one who is blessed. The reason that's interesting is it's the same Semitic root, the same source." His absent father was agnostic, and his mother was from Kansas, he explained. They both called him Barry, but he wanted to acknowledge his heritage as he got older. Besides, he said, his audience shouldn't worry about his name. "You had a prime minister named Barak in Israel," he pointed out. "It should be pretty familiar to this audience."

If the fears weren't founded on his name, they were built on some other dark suspicion. A few minutes after explaining his name, he was asked to identify his "close personal friends" who were "solemnly pro-Israel and antiterrorist." As the crowd jeered the questioner, the candidate said he wanted to respond. "I have to be very cautious about this because you remember the old stereotype about somebody says, 'I'm not prejudiced. Some of my best friends are Jewish.' Or somebody says, 'I'm not prejudiced. Some of my best friends are black.' So I hesitate to start listing them out." Then he proceeded to list several of them: Penny Pritzker, his finance chair; James Crown, his Illinois cochair; Lee Rosenberg, a close friend on the executive board of AIPAC; Abner Mikva, his political mentor and a former White House counsel. It had come down to this: a list of Jews to testify that he was no terrorist sympathizer.

Of all the frustrating and elusive foes, the Muslim-Jewish axis was the most challenging. It was everywhere and nowhere. He could do as little to stop the e-mails as he could to change his name. He countered with the facts but he was fighting against innuendo, not statements; against prejudice, not reason. He wanted to beat this shadowy opponent, so he went after the propagators and perpetrators. At least he could put a face on them, even if they weren't fully responsible. He could try to elevate the election debate and reform the nation's politics, before it consumed his campaign. There was Sean Hannity and Fox News: the people he expected to assist in swift-boating him, just as they had helped to trash the distinguished Vietnam record of John Kerry four years earlier.

For a moment it looked like there was an opening, a sign of weakness. Rupert Murdoch, the spiritual leader and owner of Fox News, made surprisingly positive comments about Obama at a *Wall Street Journal* conference in California. "You've got a candidate trying to put himself above it all so he's not the average politician. And he's become a rock star. It's fantastic," Murdoch said. "He has other problems. He may not carry Florida because the Jewish people are suspicious of him, and so are the Hispanics. He's got problems there. But he'll probably win Ohio. Who knows? If it's a close election, you could start adding different states and so on, and he'll probably win." Murdoch said McCain was his friend but he was "unpredictable" and didn't understand the economy. "I want to meet Obama," he said. "I want to know: is he going to walk the walk?"

If anything, the relationship between Fox News and the Obama campaign worsened after Murdoch's glowing review. Fox was pushing a new scurrilous rumor that Michelle Obama had used the word *whitey* from a church pulpit alongside either Reverend Wright or Louis Farrakhan. It didn't much matter. Nor did the source: the Republican hitman Roger Stone, who claimed to have a hand in every scandal from Watergate in 1972 to the Willie Horton ad of 1988 and the staged protest that helped stop the Florida recount in 2000. The candidate was angry and so were his trusted aides and friends. David Axelrod called Roger Ailes, Fox News' president, to complain. The result: Ailes agreed to keep Stone off the air. When a news reporter for another outlet asked the candidate about the rumor, he laid down some ground rules. "There is dirt and lies that are circulated in e-mail, and they pump them out long enough until finally you, a mainstream reporter, asks me about it. And then that gives legs to the story," he said, measuring his words carefully on his campaign plane. "This is the same kind of nonsense that we started with the madrassas, in which CNN had to fly to Jakarta to disprove it. And, frankly, my hope is that people don't play this game. It's a destructive aspect of our politics right now."

A few days later, inside the grand old Waldorf-Astoria hotel in Manhattan, Rupert Murdoch and Roger Ailes, two of the biggest propagators of destructive politics, were sitting face-to-face with the candidate. The one they had portrayed as Reverend Wright's disciple, the husband of a racist black woman, and the former student at an Indonesian madrassa. Obama asked Murdoch about his father and his rise to power; Murdoch responded with little humility by offering him advice on how to lead the world. Then he got up and switched seats with Ailes. Obama's tone shifted abruptly. How could he get a fair shake from Fox when it was so determined to smear him as a scary alien, black Islamic radical? Obama asked him what political issues concerned him. Ailes replied that he only cared about America's "sovereignty and security." He also cared about something more commercial: he wanted Obama on the air, to end his unofficial boycott of Fox News. For his part, Obama wanted Fox to end its unofficial campaign against Michelle.

It looked like they had a deal of sorts. By September, Obama was on Bill O'Reilly's show for the first time, in an interview that was strong enough and long enough for Fox to stretch over several nights for better ratings. "There's a whole bunch of stuff said on Fox about me that is completely biased," the candidate said at one point, when pressed about his relationship with left-wing bloggers. "But I still don't mind coming on your show." A week after Fox taped its interview, Murdoch's *New York Post* rushed out an early, front-page endorsement for the general election. "The *Post* today enthusiastically urges the election of Sen. John S. McCain as the 44th president of the United States," the story began. "McCain's lifelong record of service to America, his battle-tested courage, unshakeable devotion to principle and clear grasp of the dangers and opportunities now facing the nation stand in dramatic contrast to the tissue-paper-thin résumé of his Democratic opponent, freshman Sen. Barack Obama." The deal with Murdoch and Ailes was over. "We got screwed," admitted Axelrod.

Besides Fox News, there were others who personally offended the candidate by toying with the Muslim caricature to scare voters away. Chief among them was the most prominent Jewish politician in the nation, and a former friend and ally: Joe Lieberman. Obama knew that Lieberman was a close friend of John McCain's, but he also expected a touch of respect and friendship, too. After all, Obama had campaigned for Lieberman in his primary contest in 2006, against intense opposition from left-wing bloggers. While he wasn't expecting his support, Obama was at least expecting some decency. Instead, Lieberman frequently attacked his position on Iran and Israel at Republican fund-raising events, and on McCain's campaign conference calls with reporters. He wondered out loud why Hamas was supportive of Obama's candidacy. And he only halfheartedly tried to stop the rumors that Obama was Muslim. Campaigning in Florida, Lieberman had answered a question about Obama's supposedly Muslim faith by saying, "Obviously one's religion is a matter of choice. Everything I knew said he was Christian." *A matter of choice.* It sounded like Obama had chosen to be something, anything, at different times. *Everything I knew.* That left everything he didn't know. "Of course, the most important thing is that Senator Obama said it's just not true," Lieberman explained, without ever saying himself that the rumors were just not true. They were weasel words that left the door open to doubt while seeming to close it.

The candidate engaged in some face-to-face persuasion. On the Senate floor together for a budget vote in June, Obama guided Lieberman to a corner to talk privately. It looked like a repeat of his tarmac chat with Hillary Clinton the previous year: Obama used his height advantage to place a reassuring and controlling hand on Lieberman's shoulder, while Lieberman jabbed his finger back. Obama reminded Lieberman that he had campaigned for him in 2006 and refrained from criticizing him when he ran as an independent in the general election. Now Lieberman was questioning his ability to be commander in chief, his support for Israel, and even playing with the rumors about him as a Muslim. "I thought we had a friendship," said Obama. "I'm disappointed with the approach that you've taken in the campaign. I have no problem with you supporting McCain. But for you to be the attack dog, to insinuate that you're not sure about my religion but you took my word for it—it's disappointing." Lieberman disputed that he had ever done such a thing. Noticing reporters straining to hear from the gallery overhead, they ended the interchange with a smile. Both senators said publicly the conversation was about "politics." Lieberman's staff denied there was ever any mention of the Muslim rumors, but the candidate stuck to his account. "I wasn't chastising him the way it was reported," he told me later. "But you always hope for the best in people. It's always nice if, after encouraging someone to do the right thing, that actually has a result."

There was one more strategy to pursue. He had to demonstrate his undying patriotism for the United States, and his unwavering commitment to its ally Israel. He went to a cavernous room inside Washington's convention center to speak to the pro-Israeli group AIPAC. "Before I begin," he said, standing on a stage with fake Roman columns behind him, "I also want to mention that I know some have been receiving provocative e-mails that have been circulated throughout the Jewish communities across the country. And a few of you may have gotten them. They're filled with tall tales and dire warnings about a certain candidate for president. And all I want to say is—let me know if you see this guy named Barack Obama, because he sounds pretty scary. But if anybody has been confused by these e-mails, I want you to know that today I'll be speaking from my heart, and as a true friend of Israel. And I know that when I visit with AIPAC, I am among friends. Good friends. Friends who share my strong commitment to make sure that the bond between the United States and Israel is unbreakable today, unbreakable tomorrow, unbreakable forever." He told of his great-uncle helping to liberate part of the Buchenwald concentration camp, and of traveling to Israel to see homes destroyed by Palestinian rockets. He even committed to an "undivided" Jerusalem, prompting sustained applause for the notion that Palestinians could not share Jerusalem as their capital, or take control of their own part of the city.

There was a downside to excessive displays of public affection. The line about an undivided Jerusalem was a blunder, which escaped the vetting of his entire team of senior foreign policy aides. The next day the candidate was forced to backtrack on his own clear statement. "Obviously, it's going to be up to the parties to negotiate a range of these issues. And Jerusalem will be part of the negotiations," he told CNN's Candy Crowley, before saying that he was against dividing the city. "My belief is that as a practical matter, it would be very difficult to execute," he explained. "And I think that it is smart for us to work through a system in which everybody has access to the extraordinary religious sites in Old Jerusalem, but that Israel has a legitimate claim on that city." His aides went further in reworking his words. "Obviously, it wasn't optimally phrased," said Susan Rice. "His comments were accurate. But if we had to phrase it again, there would be more language. He meant it's a final status issue and Jerusalem is the capital of Israel, and that in the future it should not be divided as it was after 1948, with barbed wire and checkpoints." That did not qualify as the same kind of applause line. The reworking of his overstatement renewed concerns about his support for Israel, even though he continued to hold a strongly pro-Israeli position. Perhaps the candidate was more effective when he was critiquing Washington's foreign policy consensus rather than pandering to it.

There was one sentiment he could never overstate: his patriotism. It didn't really matter how many times he said he loved his country, or how obvious the setting: for someone with his name and smears, there were never enough Stars and Stripes. Less than a month after clinching his party's nomination, the candidate traveled to the Truman Center auditorium in the former president's hometown of Independence, Missouri. Standing onstage with four flags behind him, he drew a line against the personal attacks before he could be swift-boated on his own identity. "Throughout my life, I have always taken my deep and abiding love for this country as a given. It was how I was raised; it is what propelled me into public service; it is why I am running for president," he explained. "And yet, at certain times over the last sixteen months, I have found, for the first time, my patriotism challenged—at times as a result of my own carelessness, more often as a result of the desire by some to score political points and raise fears and doubts about who I am and what I stand for. So let me say this at the outset of my remarks. I will never question the patriotism of others in this campaign. And I will not stand idly by when I hear others question mine."

He had spent many hours on the speech, turning in a final version around 2:30 that morning. It threaded together American history with his own family anecdotes: of sitting on his grandfather's shoulders to watch the astronauts come ashore in Hawaii, or listening to his mother read the Declaration of Independence while they lived overseas and witnessed Indonesian military rule. Neither story was an easy point of reference for most voters: few Americans had lived on a Pacific island or could locate Indonesia on a map. Yet the values he expressed were classically, uniquely American.

His biggest applause line came when he quoted Mark Twain, Missouri's favorite son, who wrote, "Patriotism is supporting your country all the time, and your government when it deserves it." The real patriots in Obama's eyes were the dissenters, the critics, the rule breakers, and the renegades. People like Martin Luther King or the whistle-blower at Abu Ghraib, who served a higher ideal of American values. Or a misfit president from Independence, who was unpopular in office and unpolished as a politician.

Truman was beloved by underdog candidates and beleaguered presidents. He had staged an upset victory in 1948 and won historians' acclaim once he left office. John Kerry had campaigned in Independence in 2004, and George W. Bush liked to compare himself to Truman throughout his second term. Yet as he walked out of the Truman Center to head toward Truman's home a few blocks away, the candidate looked anything but beleaguered. A crowd had gathered outside the center chanting "Yes We Can"; around the corner a thirteen-year-old girl started to cry as he approached. He walked past a block of modest bungalows greeting children and seniors through screen doors. One fan gave him her T-shirt; another said his wife thought Obama was a cutie. He toured Truman's home, and as he left, I asked him what he liked about the former president. He didn't cite his comeback victory or his vindication in the history books, as most candidates and presidents do. He just liked Truman as a low-key, fallible, regular American. "He was a man of little pretense," he said. "He was somebody who I think came into the job with enormous humility, didn't have all the answers all the time, made mistakes but constantly stayed focused on how could we make the country safe and better for ordinary people. And that's, I think, what you want out of your president."

Conventional, sane candidates steered clear of foreign affairs as much as they could. They traditionally feared a faux pas and calculated that voters cared little about anything beyond American shores. Why take the risk of plunging into foreign policy when there were so many chances of screwing up? Foreign policy was a test to endure, a set of questions to survive. It took a peculiar kind of candidate — one with a lot to prove and the self-belief to match—to dream up the reckless high-wire act of taking his campaign overseas. After all, when presidents travel overseas they have a limitless budget, endless layers of security, vast logistical support from American embassies, and the full cooperation of their hosts. When candidates travel overseas, they have none of the above. Just a plane, a handful of aides, stratospheric expectations, and a large press pack waiting for a stumble.

This candidate was different. Before clinching the nomination—even before the first votes were cast—he was seriously considering a foreign tour. Obama and his core foreign policy team—led by Susan Rice, Greg Craig, and Tony Lake, three former Clinton officials—were planning a trip in October 2007. The campaign was flatlining in the polls and faring little better with its fund-raising. Yet the candidate wanted to press ahead with the overseas travel and his political teams in Iowa and New Hampshire did not object. His foreign policy team was skeptical about the trip's prospects even as they started drawing up a schedule. But the candidate and his senior staff were convinced that voters wanted to see a president who was admired and respected around the world, unlike the sitting president who drew his biggest crowds on antiwar protests. The decision came in a September conference call when the candidate was sitting on his plane in California, and his advisers were scattered across the country. Obama listened quietly as his aides laid out the pros and cons of the trip, including fears that Bill Clinton might use his contacts to make mischief for them overseas. "I really want to go," Obama concluded. "It would be a great thing to do. But on balance, let's not go now." Traveling as a candidate would be great; traveling as a nominee would be historic. Greg Craig jumped in: if he went to Germany, he could get a crowd of five thousand people.

"I'll go when I'm the nominee," Obama said calmly, "and I'll get thirty thousand."

He was still three months away from winning the Iowa caucuses and it was several months since he had attracted such big crowds at home. The pundits were writing him off and his fund-raisers were openly challenging his strategy. Yet he fully expected to win the nomination and travel across the world by the following spring, in another six months. If you were going to break the rules of presidential campaigns, you'd better have the self-confidence to see it through.

Instead it was the maverick John McCain who first staged a foreign trip in March, once he clinched his party's nomination. McCain took more senators than press with him on his travels. And he attracted the most attention for a painful moment on camera when he claimed that Iran was training al Qaeda in Iraq, rather than al Qaeda's sworn enemies, the Shia militias. Standing at the ancient citadel in Amman, Jordan, McCain was only corrected by a stage whisper from his traveling buddy Joe Lieberman.

Obama would have to wait another four months to get a chance to prove he could master the foreign policy brief and draw a crowd. At the same time, his own foreign trip, in the middle of a presidential campaign, would expose him to another test: could his team pull off the logistical challenge of taking a candidate and his entourage overseas?

The candidate was fortunate with his staff. His advance team was young but they had compressed a career's worth of experience through the long primary season. His foreign policy staffers were trusted aides from his Senate office: Denis McDonough and Mark Lippert, who had recently returned from Iraq, where he served as a navy intelligence officer. Having won the nomination, Obama could also call on any number of foreign policy experts from the Clinton years.

However, elections were poor times to sound nuanced about policy. Two weeks before flying overseas, he restated his commitment to withdrawing troops in a safe and secure way. "We're planning to visit Iraq. I'm going to do a thorough assessment when I'm there," he told reporters standing on the tarmac in Fargo, North Dakota. "When I go to Iraq and I have a chance to talk to some of the commanders on the ground, I'm sure I'll have more information and will continue to refine my policies." His comments set the press into a tailspin as reporters parsed his refined language to suggest that he was backing off his sixteen-month timetable for withdrawal. In fact, the candidate had always allowed some wiggle room for delaying withdrawal.

Meanwhile the Iraqis were also refining their own plans. As Obama prepared to visit Iraq and Afghanistan, the Iraqi prime minister sat down with the German magazine *Der Spiegel*. "U.S. presidential candidate Barack Obama talks about sixteen months," Nouri al-Maliki said. "That, we think, would be the right time frame for a withdrawal, with the possibility of slight changes." In a single interview, the Iraqi leader wiped out McCain's main argument against Obama on Iraq: that he was naive and stubbornly fixed on a timeline, which did not take into account the facts on the ground. McCain was left to argue that his rival had failed to visit Iraq since before the surge of additional troops, and never visited Afghanistan.

Both situations would change in a matter of days. The candidate toured Afghanistan and Iraq with no press and two senators by his side: Republican Chuck Hagel and Democrat Jack Reed. But the pictures that emerged, courtesy of the Defense Department, were priceless. The candidate sank three-point shots on a basketball court in Kuwait and shared jokes on a helicopter flight with the commander of U.S. forces in the region, General David Petraeus. By the time Obama arrived in Amman, Jordan, to meet up with his newly refurbished plane and the press, the trip was already a runaway success.

Obama delivered his first press conference on the same ancient citadel where McCain had confused the Shia power of Iran with the Sunni group al Qaeda. McCain had stood in front of the ruined columns of a temple to Hercules, suggesting little more than the end of empire or a tourist jaunt in the Mediterranean. On the same location, Obama's handlers positioned their candidate in front of the concrete jumble of a modern Arab city, with Amman's steep hills sprouting low-rise homes behind him. A brisk wind billowed dust across the citadel and suspended several kites in midair, held still by hidden hands on the slopes below.

For almost an hour in the searing sunshine, the candidate fielded questions from network TV correspondents. He praised McCain for caring for the safety of the American people. He praised the troops behind the surge, and he praised Petraeus. But he made it clear that he was already trying to think like a president, and that sometimes meant disagreeing with the general. He wanted to shift the military focus away from Iraq and back to Afghanistan, which he called without irony the central front in the war against terrorism. "In his role as commander on the ground, not surprisingly, he wants to retain as much flexibility as possible," Obama explained of his disagreement with Petraeus. "What I emphasized to him was, you know, if I were in his shoes, I'd probably feel the same way. But my job as a candidate for president and a potential commander in chief extends beyond Iraq."

Barely perspiring in a dark woolen suit, he was buzzed by several flies but stumbled only once, when he confused Israel with America. "Let me be absolutely clear. Israel is a strong friend of Israel's," he declared. "It will be a strong friend of Israel's under a McCain administration. It will be a strong friend of Israel's under an Obama administration. So that policy is not going to change." As stumbles go, it was better to promise excessive support for Israel than to confuse the Sunni and Shia.

After Obama left the citadel, Chuck Hagel retreated to a shady corner under some vine leaves to wait for his driver. The decorated Vietnam veteran and friend of McCain was once considered a presidential contender in his own right. Now he lamented the scale of the international challenges facing the next person living in the White House, and the way the policy debate had grown so partisan. "There's no military solution in Iraq. There wasn't a military solution in Vietnam or Algeria. We've got to get deeper and broader into this. The next president, whether it's McCain or Obama, they're going to have to get into this on January 20," he explained. "The next president is going to have to forge a consensus to govern in this country, in America, and that's going to include a bipartisan foreign policy. The next president is going to have to bring everybody together because these issues are so big, so deep, so wide, the president can't govern and he can't speak for America unless he has got a foreign policy that has some consensus."

For all the risk taking of the trip, much of the journey was designed to demonstrate that the candidate could master the safe ceremonies of diplomacy. In Jerusalem, he shook hands with the Israeli president, Shimon Peres, under an olive tree, then went inside his residence to drink tea and heard his book recommendations. He met with the Palestinian president, Mahmoud Abbas, in Ramallah, then he helicoptered to see the Israeli town of Sderot, a target of Palestinian rocket fire. It was a perfectly balanced day. He started the day talking to the Israeli opposition leader, Benjamin Netanyahu, and ended it by talking to the country's prime minister, Ehud Olmert.

The obligatory trip to Yad Vashem, the searing Holocaust museum, promised to be more political theater. He wanted to wear a light, tan suit under the broiling July sun, but his aides insisted on a dark woolen suit with a flag pin in the lapel, and an undershirt beneath it all. He toured the museum and laid a white wreath in the dark Hall of Remembrance.

But then he ventured outside, to sign a guest book beside a memorial to an orphanage director, and he slipped back into the realm of a writer who could do more than repeat his scripted lines. He wrote a long inscription, stopping only to mop the sweat from his brow, then shared some thoughts with the reporters beside him. "I'm always taken back to the core question of humanity that the Holocaust raises," he said after he finished writing. "That is on the one hand man's great capacity for evil. But on the other hand our capacity to join together to stop evil and to speak out in one voice. So despite this record of monumental tragedy, this ultimately is a place of hope because it reminds us of our obligations and responsibilities and hopefully creates a better future for our children and our grandchildren. My main goal for my next visit is to make sure that my daughters are with me." An Israeli journalist shouted a question about how he would avoid "a second Holocaust" at the hands of Iran. But the candidate mopped his brow again, and said it would be wrong to hold a press conference at Yad Vashem.

Instead he left his sentiments in the pages of the guest book. "Let our children come here and know this history," he wrote, "so they can add their voices to proclaim 'never again.' And may we remember those who perished, not only as victims but also as individuals who hoped and loved and dreamed like us, and who have become symbols of the human spirit."

The next morning, before dawn and before leaving Israel, he placed a white yarmulke on his head to visit the Wailing Wall, the western wall of the Second Temple. With a clear moon in the dark sky above, he listened to a rabbi read Psalm 22 ("My God, my God, why hast thou forsaken me?") and placed a note in the cracks of the wall, amid all the other prayers scratched on scraps of paper and stuffed into the gaps between the stones. A heckler yelled, without explanation, "Obama, Jerusalem is not for sale! Obama, Jerusalem is not for sale!" As he turned to leave, a yeshiva student grabbed his prayer note from the wall and later handed it to the press. "Lord—Protect my family and me," he wrote. "Forgive me my sins, and help me guard against pride and despair. Give me the wisdom to do what is right and just. And make me an instrument of your will."

Obama flew to Berlin not knowing whether he would find pride or despair in the German capital. It was the public highlight of the trip, complete with an outdoor rally in the heart of a continent that had shunned President Bush. Berlin was the big gamble. An outdoor event in Berlin in July could mean rain or cold weather, just as easily as blue skies and sunshine. The German press estimated that Obama could attract a crowd of between 10,000 and 500,000. And the campaign's expert organizers had little idea what to expect of the crowd, either. Back home, they could guess at the likely size of an audience because around three-fourths of attendees registered through the campaign's website. In Germany, there were no online registrations to speak of.

Flying blind, the campaign struggled to pick a venue. German officials suggested sites that could hold just a couple of thousand people, but Obama's staffers wanted to aim higher. The advance team asked for permission to stage events at several sites, including the Brandenburg Gate, where President Reagan had called on Mikhail Gorbachev to tear down the Berlin Wall. But when the German chancellor, Angela Merkel, expressed her opposition to the idea, the campaign struck it off their list of options. They had no formal cooperation from the U.S. embassies overseas and needed all the help they could get from foreign governments. A dispute with the German leader would not be helpful, even if there were suspicions that the Bush administration had influenced Merkel's opposition. Instead Obama's aides settled on the Victory Column, a little more than a mile through the Tiergarten park from the Brandenburg Gate itself. The crowd could gather in front of the column, or stretch down the street to the gate.

As his plane landed Obama could see a larger jumbo jet on the tarmac with a red carpet outside and an honor guard. It belonged to Nouri al-Maliki, his newfound ally, who had just received a full departure ceremony. If Obama was going to receive a hero's welcome, it was largely because of Bush's decision to invade Iraq.

German security staff strained to catch a glimpse of Obama, not the Iraqi leader, through every window overlooking the runway. As he drove from the airport, Obama and his aides saw that the streets were full of Germans watching his motorcade en route to his hotel. More crowds pressed around the front and back doors of the hotel. "I think there will be some people there tonight," the candidate deadpanned.

His Secret Service detail was expecting a crowd of between 30,000 and 40,000 at the Victory Column. But as the sun set on a clear summer's day in Berlin, the steady flow through the Tiergarten was building to something five times that big. As the candidate took to the platform, a throng of 200,000 stretched a mile in front of him to the Brandenburg Gate. It was larger than any audience gathered by President Bush; his biggest crowd was 130,000 people in Tbilisi, Georgia, where someone threw a grenade at the stage.

Obama was merely a presidential candidate and his Berlin speech reflected his unique background. "Tonight, I speak to you not as a candidate for president, but as a citizen—a proud citizen of the United States, and a fellow citizen of the world," he said to cheers. "I know that I don't look like the Americans who've previously spoken in this great city. The journey that led me here is improbable. My mother was born in the heartland of America, but my father grew up herding goats in Kenya." A woman in the crowd started ululating, and the candidate grinned as he recognized the sound of celebration across the Middle East and East Africa.

After the speech, the candidate was quietly satisfied. "It went pretty well," he told his friend Marty Nesbitt, at home in Chicago, as a matter of fact. "It was about 200,000 people." Back at his hotel, Obama's cautious foreign policy aides were excited that they had pulled off such a huge event with so little support. But on cable TV, the pundits immediately began to question whether it was wise for Obama to describe himself as a citizen of the world when so many questions remained about his own patriotism. For the candidate himself, such criticism was simply ignorant of the history of American presidents. Reagan had used the same phrase at the United Nations, and Kennedy had said something even more international, and more famous, in Berlin itself. "Do they not realize what 'Ich bin ein Berliner' meant?" he asked me in disbelief.

There were different rules for the rule breaker. If he didn't fail by drawing small crowds or stumbling over policy, he could always fail by being too popular or too idealistic. David Axelrod was finishing up a late breakfast opposite the Brandenburg Gate when he started reading the judgment of the conservative *New York Times* columnist David Brooks. "Obama has benefited from a week of good images. But substantively, optimism without reality isn't eloquence," Brooks wrote. "It's just Disney." Just Disney, Axelrod smoldered. Not a diplomatic blunder in sight, and a crowd of 200,000 Europeans. And Brooks thinks it's all Disney?

If the campaign didn't trip over foreign logistics, there was always the Bush administration to help out. When Obama tried to visit wounded troops at the Landstuhl military hospital, the Defense Department objected. He could visit as a senator with Senate staff, but not as a presidential candidate with campaign aides. Obama offered to leave his campaign plane and press behind, but that was not good enough. Military officials objected to Scott Gration, the candidate's senior military adviser and a retired air force general, who was neither campaign staff nor Senate staff. Obama's inner circle was pissed. Without proof, they detected the hand of the McCain campaign or the Bush White House, or merely embarrassed Pentagon officials who regretted the priceless pictures of the candidate in Iraq and Kuwait. Obama himself wanted nothing to do with the mess and backed down. He could rewrite the rules of a presidential campaign, but not those of a stubborn Defense Department.

He felt fatigued as he flew to his seventh country in the space of a week. Almost as soon as his plane took off for the short flight from Berlin to Paris, he was asleep. He awoke just in time to eat lunch before landing, but still looked and sounded groggy as he scooped some wild rice into his mouth. If he felt happy with the trip or the size of the crowds, he didn't show it. How could he stay grounded when 200,000 Europeans had just showed up to hear him speak as a candidate?

"Because most of them can't vote in a U.S. election," he told me, laughing. "My overriding mood during the course of this trip is a sober one. When you look at the very difficult problem of Iran, the very difficult problem of Afghanistan and Pakistan, continuing difficulties in Iraq, the challenges of Middle East peace, the next president is going to have his hands full. And that's before you start talking about climate change, the economy, relationships with Russia, China, and North Korea. The point is, it doesn't take much to puncture any euphoria you may feel because of a speech you've given."

Even before his return, some conservatives were attacking him for the supposed narcissism of his campaign and the way it was focused on his own story. That rankled him: McCain could campaign on his life story, but he—as a newcomer—couldn't tell his own?

"They just don't like the fact that I get so many people showing up to hear me talk," he told me. "And so few show up for McCain."

As his plane landed in Paris, he was feeling constrained. Back in March, as the primaries dragged on, he likened himself to a dancing bear. "They let me out of my cage. I do my dance," he told a handful of reporters. "They let me back in my cage. They feed me occasionally. They let me work out. And every once in a while I break loose, before they get the tranquilizers." Now the bear wanted to break loose. He was heading into Paris and the prospect was tantalizing.

"Can I go to a museum?" he asked his aides. "Or go for a walk in the Jardin du Luxembourg?"

His advisers looked confused. "You want to go for a run?" asked Phil Gordon, his Europe expert.

"Or maybe just a stroll," the candidate bargained.

He would get neither. Just a fast drive past the balconies and *boulangeries*, the cafés and the boutiques, and that rarest of sights in recent years: crowds of curious Parisians anxious for a glimpse of an American politician. Then the gilded bear cage of the Élysée Palace, the home of President Nicolas Sarkozy.

It was the French president who looked like he needed some tranquilizers when he emerged with the candidate for a press conference. He had already told *Le Figaro* newspaper that he always thought Obama would win the nomination, unlike his supposedly expert foreign policy advisers. Now he was so pneumatically, maniacally happy to be next to Obama that he all but endorsed him. He compared himself to Obama: both of them had immigrant parents and a funny name, too. NPR's Don Gonyea asked Sarkozy if he was indeed endorsing Obama, and whether he had conferred with his friend President Bush for his opinion. At which point, the candidate reached over to restrain his new French friend with a hand on his shoulder, and Obama's aides looked intently from the sidelines.

"First of all," the candidate interjected, "I'm going to warn my dear friend President Sarkozy to be very careful about that question." When Obama finally allowed Sarkozy to speak, the French leader was barely restrained. "It's the Americans who choose the president, not me. You Americans," he began. "Good luck to Barack Obama. If it's him, France will be very happy. If it's another, France will be the friend of the United States of America." At this stage of the trip, the greatest risk Obama faced was an overly affectionate French president.

The dancing bear didn't even get to sleep in the City of Lights. By midnight he was in London, to prepare for a final morning of meetings with past, present, and possibly future British prime ministers. After breakfast with Tony Blair, he traveled to Downing Street to see Gordon Brown, then on to Westminster for a sit-down with the conservative leader David Cameron. He finally succeeded in getting his stroll outdoors with Gordon Brown in the gardens behind Downing Street.

At this, his last stop, he sounded less like a candidate than a weary, worldwise leader-in-waiting. Obama's aides confided that they preferred the energy of the up-and-coming Cameron compared with the dour and dreary Brown. But the candidate himself pointed out that power was a burden in itself. When asked if Obama had any advice for the beleaguered Brown, the candidate said, "Well, I don't have advice for Prime Minister Brown. I will tell you that you're always more popular before you're actually in charge of things. And then, once you're responsible, then you're going to make some people unhappy. That's just the nature of politics. And these things go in cycles. Even during the course of this campaign, there have been months where I'm a genius and there are months when I'm an idiot. At least, if you read the newspapers."

On the flight back home to Chicago, Obama's staff were toasting a successful high-wire act. The Secret Service agents were delighted that they had experienced no security incidents through eight countries, with minimal support. And after a week of almost total domination of the news cycles back home, the campaign's political brains were ready to look ahead. There was just one nagging question: why were the polls so tight after such a good run of news over the last week? "Because America doesn't know who Barack Obama is," said David Axelrod. "Because he's so new. Because they'll take every last chance to kick the tires. They won't make up their minds until the very end."

McCain's campaign tried to deflate the tires with a sharp ad about Obama's celebrity, and the commercial was successful inside the Beltway.

Washington's pundits turned on Obama's strategy, declaring the trip a dismal failure, the equivalent of John Kerry windsurfing in Bermuda shorts.

Inside Obama's inner circle, there were no regrets. They thought the celebrity ad ignored the voters' main concerns, and there was minimal movement in the polls. Axelrod told the foreign policy team that the trip wasn't designed to move the needle one way or another; it was intended to allow the candidate to go toe-to-toe on foreign policy against McCain in the fall. Sitting back in Chicago for the entire trip, David Plouffe agreed. "It was a huge asset for us, a huge asset," said the campaign manager. "People got to see him on the world stage. The trip was executed perfectly."

The high-wire strategy succeeded better than anyone predicted: by the general election, foreign policy fizzled as an issue. The subject that fueled the candidate's rise through the start of his campaign was the war in Iraq. By mid-September, it ranked as only the fourth biggest priority for voters, barely above health care, and a long way behind job creation. That shift was partly the result of the worsening economy, and partly the result of the improving security situation in Iraq itself. But it also reflected the dynamic between the two candidates. McCain held a narrow single-digit lead over Obama on foreign policy, far behind the huge lead Bush commanded over John Kerry four years earlier.

As the TV debates approached, those numbers gave Obama's aides the confidence to ask for a late change in topics. Instead of debating domestic policy in the first encounter, Obama wanted to talk about foreign affairs. "We just wanted foreign policy first because it was seen as McCain's strong suit," said Plouffe. "There was some risk there and we thought we'd get rewarded for it on foreign policy."

Obama's confidence was not just based on poll numbers. He worked harder at the debates than any other event in the long campaign, especially compared with his impatient and desultory prep during the primary season. In August, shortly before leaving for his vacation in Hawaii, he promised his senior staff to do far better than he had against his Democratic rivals. "I understand this is a very serious process and I'm going to take it very, very seriously," he told his debate team in Chicago. "I know what my role is. I have to do better in the debates. But you guys have to pick up your game, too."

They picked up their game and took to the road. A small group of aides met secretly with Obama in several different states ahead of the debates, flying separately from the candidate to avoid press attention. They waited for him at his hotel to work through his briefing books for several hours at the end of the day, refining his positions on world affairs and honing what he wanted to say in the debate. By the time he reached his first debate camp in Clearwater, Florida, Obama had mastered his briefing books and requested additional material.

Obama's debate staff was meticulous. Inside a century-old resort hotel—once luxurious enough to welcome Al Capone but now half deserted and dilapidated—his team built a full-size mock-up of the debate stage. "We wanted him, when he went into the actual debate, to feel like he had been there before," said Robert Gibbs. On the substance of foreign policy, he seemed fluent and focused. But he still needed to iron out two stylistic problems with his debate coach Michael Sheehan. First, when he wanted to look serious, his facial expression could often appear angry rather than concerned. Second, he often cocked his head to listen to his rivals, which left him looking snootily down his nose. Obama learned to look serenely at McCain and to keep his head on the level.

Obama more than held his own during the first debate in Oxford, Mississippi. He took the attack to McCain on Iraq, even on the question of the successful surge of additional troops, which McCain advocated and Obama rejected. "You talk about the surge," he said, as he turned directly to his rival. "The war started in 2003, and at the time when the war started, you said it was going to be quick and easy. You said we knew where the weapons of mass destruction were. You were wrong. You said that we were going to be greeted as liberators. You were wrong. You said that there was no history of violence between Shia and Sunni. And you were wrong." McCain's response was a constant refrain through the debate: that Obama was naive or didn't understand the world. The problem for McCain was that Obama spoke confidently and in complex terms about world affairs, and had done so through the entire foreign tour. The accusations of naïveté or ignorance failed to ring true. One poll showed that Obama won the first debate by a twelve-point margin, while his numbers on national defense and foreign affairs were almost identical to McCain's. Another poll asked voters to say one word to describe the candidate during the debate. For Obama, "confident" was the most popular, with "presidential" in fourth place. For McCain, "experienced" was the most popular, with "presidential" trailing last, in twentieth place.

Naive was a better way to describe the foreign policy comments of McCain's vice presidential pick, Sarah Palin. Obama made foreign policy look easy, weaving together his policy expertise with his personal experience overseas. Palin made it look like hard work, and her comments were toe-curlingly superficial. The Alaska governor suggested to ABC's Charlie Gibson that she gained insight into Russian affairs because she could see Russia from Alaska, and she had trouble defining the Bush doctrine. She tried to draw on her personal experience of foreign affairs, but she sounded almost incoherent. When CBS's Katie Couric asked her if she had ever negotiated with the Russians, Palin explained, "We have trade missions back and forth, we do. It's very important when you consider even national security issues with Russia. As Putin rears his head and comes into the airspace of the United States of America, where do they go? It's Alaska. It's just right over the border. It is from Alaska that we send those out to make sure that an eye is being kept on this very powerful nation, Russia, because they are right there, they are right next to our state."

With or without Sarah Palin, McCain's attack on Obama's inexperience rang hollow in a year when experienced officials had driven the world into a recession and a deeply unpopular war. The same strategy had been deployed before against a young, hopeful Democrat, as Al Gore pointed out on the night he endorsed Obama. "The other party seems to think that age and experience are factors that will work in their favor during this campaign. But our shared experience as a nation tells us otherwise," Gore said at a raucous rally in Detroit.

I remember when one prominent Republican wondered out loud whether the Democratic nominee, and I quote, "really was grown up enough to be president." Another used the phrase, quote "naive and inexperienced." Another said, "The United States cannot afford to risk the future of the free world with inexperience and immaturity in the White House." Who are they talking about? Every single one of those quotations came from the campaign of 1960 when the Republicans attacked John Fitzgerald Kennedy. Richard Nixon's slogan in that campaign was Experience Counts, to which John F. Kennedy responded, "To exclude from positions of trust and command all those below the age of forty-four would have kept Jefferson from writing the Declaration of Independence, Washington from commanding the Continental army, Madison from fathering the Constitution, and Christopher Columbus from ever discovering America."

Obama exuded confidence in foreign affairs and he lacked the fear to cower from the personal smears. But there were limits to his strategy. He pushed back against the rumors that he was a Muslim, but never tried to counter the bigger smears against Muslim Americans. He didn't have the political strength to respond as Colin Powell did, in the final weeks of the election, when the retired general and former secretary of state endorsed him on *Meet the Press*. Powell was deeply troubled by Republicans suggesting that Obama was Muslim. "Well, the correct answer is, he is not a Muslim, he's a Christian. He's always been a Christian," said Powell.

But the really right answer is, what if he is? Is there something wrong with being a Muslim in this country? The answer's no, that's not America. Is there something wrong with some seven-year-old Muslim American kid believing that he or she could be president? Yet, I have heard senior members of my own party drop the suggestion, "He's a Muslim and he might be associated with terrorists." This is not the way we should be doing it in America.

I feel strongly about this particular point because of a picture I saw in a magazine. It was a photo essay about troops who are serving in Iraq and Afghanistan. And one picture at the tail end of this photo essay was of a mother in Arlington Cemetery, and she had her head on the headstone of her son's grave. And as the picture focused in, you could see the writing on the headstone. And it gave his awards—Purple Heart, Bronze Star—showed that he died in Iraq, gave his date of birth, date of death. He was twenty years old. And then, at the very top of the headstone, it didn't have a Christian cross, it didn't have the Star of David. It had a crescent and a star of the Islamic faith. And his name was Kareem Rashad Sultan Khan, and he was an American. He was born in New Jersey. He was fourteen years old at the time of 9/11, and he waited until he [could] go serve his country, and he gave his life.

The candidate never seized the same chance to defend Muslims in America, but he recognized early on the deadly nature of such politics. He wanted to change American foreign policy, for sure. But he also ran against the politics of fear as perfected during the Bush years, at home and abroad.

Before he clinched the nomination, Obama found himself under sustained Republican attack for promising direct talks with Iran. The attacks only intensified when he pointed out that American presidents had negotiated with the Soviet Union, and that Iran was a tiny threat in comparison. So he took his counterattack a step further, arguing that the tough-talking president and his candidate, John McCain, were weaklings. "For all their tough talk, one of the things you have to ask yourself is, what are George Bush and John McCain afraid of? Demanding a country meets all your conditions before you meet with them: that's not a strategy. It's just naive, wishful thinking," he told one town hall meeting in Billings, Montana. "I'm not afraid that we'll lose some propaganda fight with a dictator. It's time for America to win those battles because we've watched George Bush lose them year after year after year. It's time to restore our security and standing in the world."

He then traveled an hour east to Crow Agency, little more than a mile from the monument to the battle of Little Bighorn. There he was welcomed as a hero by Native Americans and adopted into the Crow Nation under a new name, Awe Kooda Bilaxpak Kuuxshish, meaning One Who Helps People Throughout the Land. He walked arm in arm with his honorary Crow parents, Mary and Sunny Black Eagle, as several women ululated in celebration. Onstage, the candidate promised an annual summit at the White House with tribal leaders and a senior White House adviser on Native American affairs. For a candidate whose middle name was Hussein, and who had spent more than a year fighting rumors about his patriotism, he seemed surprisingly breezy.

"I like my new name," he said. "Barack Black Eagle. That's a good name."

When the event ended, his staff played the song "Only in America" as the candidate beamed at the women in traditional costume, and the signs saying Natives for Obama, just a few minutes' drive from the site of Custer's Last Stand.

EIGHT

THE RECKONING

Between the Oval Office and the press briefing room lies the Cabinet Room, dominated by a long, mahogany table and the heavy leather chairs surrounding it. One chair, with its back to the Rose Garden, is higher than the rest and carries a brass nameplate on the back saying, simply, The President. Sitting in the higher chair was the man who liked to call himself forty-three. At opposite ends of the elliptical table were the two men who wanted to become forty-four. The rest of the chairs were filled with congressional leaders, Republicans and Democrats, as well as administration officials. It was two weeks after the collapse of Lehman Brothers bank, in late September. Barely twenty-four hours earlier, John McCain had suspended his campaign to address the financial crisis; the next day, he was scheduled to meet the man at the other end of the table for their first TV debate in Oxford, Mississippi.

President Bush welcomed his guests and promptly turned to his treasury secretary, Hank Paulson, the former chairman and CEO of Goldman Sachs. "Hank, can you give us a readout of the situation?" asked the president. Paulson's diagnosis was dire. In the two weeks since Lehman went bankrupt, Paulson and the Fed chairman, Ben Bernanke, had hit the panic button, pressing a dazed and confused president for billions of dollars to rescue the financial system. The Fed had bailed out the insurance giant AIG, and that was just the beginning. The night before, the president had addressed the nation to sell what amounted to a $700 billion life raft. "Our entire economy is in danger," he warned. Now, without the help of his speechwriters, he tried to instill the same sense of urgency in the politicians around his cabinet table.

"We need a solution that is big enough to fit a big problem," he told them. "We aren't just gonna sit here and watch this thing crater. Here's my test: I'll ask Hank and Ben, 'Will it work?' And if it works, then I'll support it. If it doesn't, we'll keep working."

Bush followed protocol and called on Harry Reid, the Senate majority leader, but Reid deferred to his candidate. "We're represented by Senator Obama," he said. Obama talked at length about the crisis and his daily conversations with Paulson. He said he was ready to act quickly, but also ready to hear alternatives. The president turned to McCain for his input, but he pointedly declined and took a swipe at his rival. "I will wait my turn," McCain told the room. "I have learned to respect seniority."

What followed was anything but respectful. The House Republican leader, John Boehner, made it clear he opposed Paulson's plan and suggested his own smaller alternative. The House Democrats were outraged, while Paulson looked dejected. President Bush seemed helpless to stop the cross fire and pleaded for Paulson's plan. "I'm not going to let this sucker go down," he declared. Obama suggested that the treasury secretary take onboard some of the Republican concerns and amend his plan.

After three-quarters of an hour of heated discussion, McCain had yet to voice his opinion. "It would be good to hear from Senator McCain," Obama interjected. "And then I want to ask Hank a question."

McCain maintained a grumpy silence. "Go ahead," he said. "Ask your question."

Obama asked Paulson a detailed question about insurance, before McCain finally ventured to speak.

"If the senator has quite finished, I want to thank the president for calling this meeting," he began. "I feel like some concerns have already been addressed, like CEO pay, which Hank opposed and now he's moved in our direction." But McCain declined to put forward his own plan or fully back the House Republicans.

When pressed for his opinion of Paulson's plan, McCain said he had not read the proposal, which only ran to three pages. Obama snorted dismissively and rolled his eyes.

The meeting broke up in rancor, and the House Democrats walked across the hallway to the Roosevelt Room. There, Paulson begged on bended knee for the House Speaker Nancy Pelosi to save him.

"Don't fucking blame us," interjected Barney Frank, the chair of the House Financial Services Committee. "It's your fucking party that's doing this. Get them onboard."

Obama intervened to calm the tempers, but he left the White House appalled at the disarray. "If the markets knew what just happened, they would collapse," he told his senior aides. "Take your money and put it in the mattress."

Four days later, the Paulson plan failed to win a majority in the House, against strong Republican opposition and many Democratic defections. The Dow Jones industrial average dropped almost 778 points, its biggest one-day decline since the crash of 1987, wiping $1.2 trillion from the stock market.

The candidate had never seemed so engaged in the entire two-year-old election. It gave him the chance to dig deep into the policy debate and the opportunity to strike at his opponent. He could talk to Paulson as if he were the president-in-waiting, grappling with a crisis as it unfolded. Paulson made no reference to President Bush, suggesting he rarely received any meaningful direction from the White House. He also relayed helpful information about his disagreement with McCain over the AIG bailout, which the Republican candidate initially opposed. Obama's mind was humming: he was talking to his own economic team, taping ads on the economy, approving economic ads against McCain, and devoting much of his stump speech to the same subject. "This is the kind of stuff that he thrives on: policy, politics, and decision making," said his senior aide Pete Rouse. The candidate and his aides liked to think that good policy was good politics. Now they had the chance to put the aphorism into practice.

The only irony was that it often looked like this time might never come. Through the primaries, the candidate struggled to find his voice on the economy, and the pundits confidently declared he would never succeed with voters at the lower end of the economic scale. He was a brainy elitist, they said, and his poll numbers sagged because he failed to connect with downscale Democrats. Just six weeks after launching his campaign, Obama was pigeonholed as the candidate of college grads, along with other losers like Eugene McCarthy, Gary Hart, and Bill Bradley. Ron Brownstein, the influential columnist at the *Los Angeles Times*, observed that there were two types of Democrats—"upscale 'wine-track' candidates and blue-collar 'beer-track' contenders." Using another image altogether, he compared the wine sippers to priests like Woodrow Wilson, pitted against the beer-swilling warriors like Harry Truman. "Hillary Clinton has firmly positioned herself as a warrior," he wrote, since she focused on blue-collar economic anxiety. Obama, in contrast, was a priest who had written two bestselling books and spoke of reform. "Since Obama entered the campaign, the question he's faced most often is whether he is 'black enough' to win votes from African Americans," wrote Brownstein. "But the more relevant issue may be whether Obama is 'blue enough' to increase his support among blue-collar whites." Brownstein would write the same analysis as Obama's campaign stalled in the fall, and again when he lost in Pennsylvania the following year. The caricature was echoed by other respected commentators including Joe Klein at *Time* and John Dickerson at *Slate*. Soon the elitist image was a given on cable TV and in newspaper stories across the country.

As with any good caricature, there was a detail of truth that could be contorted into a dominating feature. On one trip to an Iowa farm west of Des Moines, the candidate spoke about how crop prices were staying flat while supermarket prices were rising. "Anybody gone into Whole Foods lately and see what they charge for arugula?" he asked. "I mean, they're charging a lot of money for this stuff." Arugula at Whole Foods? In Iowa? As reporters pointed out, there were no Whole Foods stores in Iowa, although there was one over the river in Omaha, Nebraska. But the supposedly backwater farmers of Iowa knew plenty about arugula and other fancy foods. Besides the fact that arugula is sold at supermarket chains like Iowa's Hy-Vee, or Safeway stores nationwide, the crop grows in several small farms across the state. Iowa's farmers produce higher-quality food, including Niman Ranch pork, some of the best-quality meat in the country. The candidate himself decided to portray the arugula-eating reporters as condescending to Iowans. "All the national press, they said, 'Oh, look at Obama. He's talking about arugula in Iowa. People in Iowa don't know what arugula is.' People in Iowa know what arugula is," he told one audience in Independence, Iowa. "They may not eat it, but you know what it is."

First came arugula, then came the beer and bowling. Journalists who penned caricatures were only a few steps below candidates who campaigned by photo op. Both served to reduce an election to its simplest level of identity politics. In one dismal stretch in Pennsylvania, Obama sipped Yuengling beer at a sports bar in Latrobe, toured a wire factory for Slinky toys in Johnstown, bought hot dogs at a diner in Altoona, and stopped by some bowling lanes to roll several gutter balls.

"Let me tell you something," Obama said to the disappointed crowd behind him at Pleasant Valley Lanes. "My economic plan is better than my bowling."

A voter in the next lane shot back, "It has to be."

The next day, at the dairy complex at Pennsylvania State Agricultural Facilities, the candidate was asking deep questions about growth hormones in cows when one of the Holsteins decided to take a disconcertingly loud leak. The candidate turned around to look at the remarkable process before returning to his conversation about hormones.

At least he learned how to avoid stepping in it. On a tour of Philadelphia's Italian Market, he tasted some exquisite Spanish ham, *jamón ibérico,* made from pure-bred wild pigs that graze on acorns. At a price of $99.99 a pound, it was delicious but hardly the best way to relate to the nation's struggling workers. Instead he bought a goat's cheese from West Chester, costing a mere $25.99 a pound.

Gourmet ham and cheese turned out to be less costly than the words that emerged from his own mouth. In the middle of the Pennsylvania primary, as he was struggling against Clinton to reach working-class Democrats, he traveled to San Francisco for a fund-raiser. There, he tried to explain why his message of hope and change wasn't resonating in the Rust Belt, and ended up belittling the working-class culture of the very states he needed to win.

Here's how it is: in a lot of these communities in big industrial states like Ohio and Pennsylvania, people have been beaten down so long, and they feel so betrayed by government, and when they hear a pitch that is premised on not being cynical about government, then a part of them just doesn't buy it. And when it's delivered by a forty-six-year-old black man named Barack Obama, then that adds another layer of skepticism. . . . The truth is that our challenge is to get people persuaded that we can make progress when there's not evidence of that in their daily lives. You go into some of these small towns in Pennsylvania, and like a lot of small towns in the Midwest, the jobs have been gone now for twenty-five years and nothing has replaced them. And they fell through the Clinton administration, and the Bush administration, and each successive administration has said that somehow these communities are going to regenerate and they have not. So it's not surprising then that they get bitter, they cling to guns or religion or antipathy to people who aren't like them or anti-immigrant sentiment or antitrade sentiment as a way to explain their frustrations.

Instead of warming to working voters, his analysis was far too cold for comfort. He knew he had blundered at the time, as his "bitter" and "cling" comments looped around cable TV for several days. "I had said something very similar on *Charlie Rose* and I was tired enough where my syntax got garbled," he told me. "But my basic point was that when people have been betrayed economically over and over again, they vote based on things they feel they have more control over, like their way of life, hunting, and their faith. But the two words, the way I had used them and the fact that we were in that time where interpretations are less than charitable, it was just the classic spiral."

Hillary Clinton chose to be less than charitable at an event called the Compassion Forum, discussing moral issues at Messiah College in Pennsylvania. There she said his comments were "elitist, out of touch, and frankly patronizing." To Obama's senior aides, there was something more than a little ironic about Clinton's patronizing line of attack. Bill Clinton had faced the same elitist charge in his first presidential campaign, and since leaving the White House had joined the ranks of the elites by earning tens of millions of dollars in speaking and consulting fees. "Bill Clinton had a similar problem in '92," said David Axelrod. "Because he went to Yale and Oxford, his opposition to the Vietnam War and his nonservice during the war, there was this stereotype that the Republicans tried to foment of him as elitist. It was a big problem and it was cured over time with the help of a film at the convention that gave people a real sense of his true history."

For most of the last year, the candidate had treated the economy as a policy issue, to be discussed in wonkish terms, at a distance—not a personal tale that he could relate to with his own true history. His first economic events were hastily arranged affairs with little attempt to tie them to his own life or his policies. For instance, there was a roundtable discussion about home foreclosures in January, where he listened to stories of woe while sitting in the corporate skybox of an arena in Reno, Nevada. Nobody on the campaign seemed to think there was anything wrong with talking about economic pain inside a room dedicated to executive perks. Nobody had put much effort into the issue, either. There were just two small signs taped to the wall bearing the new slogan Reclaiming the American Dream.

By the time they reached Ohio, Obama's team was out of steam. Their arena rallies had lost much of their impact, and the hope-filled stump speech seemed all too familiar. They decided to play one of the most traditional economic cards: to rail against free trade and, by extension, Clinton's support for the North American Free Trade Agreement (NAFTA). At a titanium plant in Youngstown, Ohio, the campaign engineered several pictures of the candidate walking through a dark, satanic factory floor, past molten metal in hulking crucibles. At the press conference that followed, Obama delivered a sustained critique of Clinton's position on free trade. Two weeks later, the campaign was struggling to explain comments by its economic adviser Austan Goolsbee to Canadian officials about the candidate's position on NAFTA. According to Canadian diplomats, Goolsbee said that the candidate's attacks on NAFTA were "more reflective of political maneuvering than policy," suggesting Obama was faking his anger about free trade. Goolsbee denied the Canadian account, but he still seemed to be minimizing Obama's rhetoric, and the campaign lost precious time parsing out his comments. The NAFTA dispute was the closing act of the primaries in Texas and Ohio, leading several senior Obama aides to conclude they had been suckered into the wrong fight. "We were so tired and wanted to win so bad," said one senior Obama aide. "We were already in the twenty-ninth and thirtieth mile of what we thought was a twenty-six-mile marathon. It was consistent with what he believed about NAFTA, but it appeared like the same old politics. We sacrificed some of what makes us different to try to score a knockout."

The solution was to tell Obama's true history, and he seized the moment to do something he had largely sidestepped. Partly in response to voters' deepening economic fears, and partly to explain away his own "bitter" comment, he began to sharpen his economic message and personalize his pitch. His TV ads started to feature old photos of him walking outside shuttered factories in Chicago, mixed with new film of him on factory floors talking to workingmen. He started sharing more details about his family's modest means, and how his young mother had lived on food stamps for a time. He explained how his first job in politics, as a community organizer, was to deal with the aftershocks of the manufacturing slump of the 1980s. And he told how he and Michelle had struggled until recently with law school loans and credit card debts. The campaign had recently released tax returns showing how their financial rise was both recent and dramatic. In 2004, just two years before deciding to run for president, the Obamas made $207,000—a very low figure for two Harvard Law School graduates. The following year, their income ballooned to $1.6 million, thanks to the book advance and royalties that followed his convention speech. In contrast, the Clintons had earned $109 million since leaving the White House.

His comments about small-town America came to light in mid-April, on a Friday; by Monday he was recalling his first visit to a shuttered steel mill as a community organizer. "It was late in the afternoon and I took a drive with another organizer over to the old Wisconsin Steel plant on the southeast side of Chicago," he told a group of union leaders and managers in Pittsburgh. "And as we drove up, I saw a sight that is probably familiar to some of you. I saw a plant that was empty and rusty. And behind a chain-link fence, I saw weeds sprouting up through the concrete, and an old mangy cat running around. And I thought about all the good jobs it used to provide, and all the kids who used to work there in the summer to make some extra money for college. What I came to understand was that when a plant shuts down, it's not just the workers who pay a price, it's the whole community. I saw folks who felt like their government wasn't looking out for them and who had given up hope. So I worked with unions and the city government, and we brought the community together to fight for its common future. We gave job training to the jobless and hope to the hopeless, and block by block, we helped turn those neighborhoods around." His economic sales pitch was no longer an afterthought or an abstract policy debate, but the very reason he entered political life in the first place. "You can trust me," he said. "Because politics didn't lead me to working folks; working folks led me to politics."

There was real concern inside the campaign that the "bitter" comments were halting and even reversing momentum that had narrowed the contest in Pennsylvania to five points. So the candidate came out swinging—but at John McCain, not Hillary Clinton. At lunch with newspaper executives and editors in Washington, D.C., Obama demonstrated how much easier he found it to campaign on the economy against his Republican opponent. "If John McCain wants to turn this election into a contest about which party is out of touch with the struggles and the hopes of working America, that's a debate I'm happy to have," he said. "In fact, I think that's a debate we *have* to have. Because I believe that the real insult to the millions of hardworking Americans out there would be a continuation of the economic agenda that has dominated Washington for far too long. I may have made a mistake last week in the words that I chose, but the other party has made a much more damaging mistake in the failed policies they've chosen and the bankrupt philosophy they've embraced for the last three decades."

For Michelle Obama, the elitist caricature was personally offensive. The daughter of a municipal worker who had grown up in a one-bedroom bungalow on the South Side of Chicago, she was in no mood to sit back and take their rivals' criticism. "I am a product of a working-class background. I am one of those folks who grew up in that struggle. That is the lens through which I see the world," she told supporters at a high school in Evansville, Indiana, a few days after Obama's "bitter" comments emerged. "So when people talk about this elitist stuff, I say, 'You couldn't possibly know anything about me.'"

The elitist debate was more personal than factual: an attempt to fit the candidate into the template of previous Democratic failures, like Michael Dukakis, Al Gore, or John Kerry. But the numbers suggested a very different picture of what voters believed about Obama, Clinton, and McCain. Polls showed that white working-class voters believed that Obama looked down on them no more than McCain, and slightly less than Clinton. Of the three candidates, he was seen as the least likely to favor the rich. In other words, he was elitist in neither outlook nor politics. Exit polls among the lower-income group—those earning less than $50,000 a year—suggested voting was roughly evenly divided across the country between Clinton and Obama. Indeed, between the primaries in Ohio and Pennsylvania, Obama's performance improved by six points among low-income Democrats, despite the intense debate about his "bitter" comments.

Besides his stray words, the candidate's elitist caricature was built on the results of two flawed pieces of analysis. One was that the results of primaries in Rust Belt states were insightful about a candidate's economic strengths and weaknesses in the general election. To Obama's senior staff, the votes reflected age and gender more than class, and the dynamic of the general election would be totally different. "Who won the Pennsylvania primary in 1980? It was Ted Kennedy and George Bush," said David Plouffe soon after the Pennsylvania primary. "I think the facts completely undermine the assertion about the general election and these blue-collar Democratic voters. We have done very well with blue-collar men in the contests so far, and she has an appeal to white women."

The other flawed analysis focused on the importance of working-class voters in general. The paraphernalia of working-class politics were central to campaign imagery, especially for Democrats: images of the candidates drinking beer or standing on the back of a pickup truck were highly prized. But they were as much of a throwback to campaigns past as the town hall meeting or the whistle-stop tour. Working-class voters had shrunk dramatically along with the manufacturing jobs that sustained them. Low-wage earners were more likely to hold down jobs as restaurant servers or office cleaners than factory workers. By education and occupation, America's voters had changed dramatically over the past sixty years. In 1940, three-quarters of adults over twenty-five lacked a high school diploma. By 1980, that was down to less than a third, and in 2007 it was just 14 percent. Over the same period, white-collar workers doubled as a percentage of the workforce, from one-third to around two-thirds. The remaining white working-class voters steadily abandoned the Democrats after 1968. Bill Clinton split their vote with Ross Perot, but Al Gore lost them by seventeen points and John Kerry lost them by twenty-three points. Obama ultimately lost that group by eighteen points and still won a resounding victory, in part because there was an ever-shrinking pool of such voters.

Obama's later success with the economy had its foundations in the final stages of the primary season. He reacted to successive defeats in the Rust Belt primaries by personalizing his campaign even more. He was convinced that he could, by force of character and the strength of his personal story, win the economic argument against Clinton and McCain. For it was now a three-way contest: McCain was several weeks out of his own primary season and the Republican assumption was that Obama would emerge as the Democratic nominee. After losing the Pennsylvania primary, Obama was staring at two more weeks before the last major states of Indiana and North Carolina, and another six weeks until the final votes in Montana and South Dakota.

He called two of his senior aides to his home in Chicago for a late-afternoon meeting. Instead of being angry or upset, he wanted to talk in practical terms about how to move forward. "You need to take more ownership of your campaign," said Pete Rouse. The candidate responded by starting a nightly conference call at the end of each day with a dozen staffers to plot the way ahead. Until then, the campaign had tried—and failed—to plan its days with a morning call that began at 8:00 a.m. on the East Coast, long after their rivals were already e-mailing press releases. The nightly call would prove critical as the financial crisis unfolded through the fall. "It was really effective through the economic crisis because he, not staff or consultants, was driving the strategy in response to the crisis," said Rouse.

The style of his campaigning changed quickly: he grew more personally engaged in the economic story within days. A week after losing in Pennsylvania, he and Michelle were sitting down for a lunch of Subway sandwiches and potato chips with the Fischer family in a home that was full of close relatives and knickknack angels. Mike Fischer worked at Amtrak and was worried about a new round of layoffs; he didn't want to uproot from his community in Beech Grove, Indiana, to look for a job elsewhere. Their daughter was pregnant and her husband was being deployed to Iraq. The Obamas listened to their worries, suggested a few ideas, and shared stories about their own lives and their own support system. They empathized and humanized themselves along the way, explaining how they relied on Michelle's mother and their network of friends in their own community. "We couldn't be doing what we're doing without Michelle's mother," said the candidate, as if his job of running for president was no different from working for Amtrak.

Winning the economic debate was nothing like working on the railroad. It was less of a long slog than a few moments of opportunity, matched by the desire to reclaim control of the campaign. One of those rare moments came just before the Pennsylvania primary when John McCain suggested an old idea for helping drivers deal with record-high gas prices: a suspension, or summer holiday, for the gas tax. His proposal, announced on the April 15 tax filing deadline, was to suspend the 18.4 percent federal tax from Memorial Day to Labor Day. A week later, Hillary Clinton joined in with a slightly tweaked version of the same gas-tax holiday.

For Obama, the gas-tax suspension was a dumb idea that he had seen fail in Illinois. Instead of passing on the reduced cost, the oil companies simply pocketed the difference. Besides, the gas tax paid for road construction, which was sorely needed in a slowing economy. On a single economic issue, he could run against both McCain and Clinton and re-take control of an election that seemed to be out of his grasp for the last two months. "We had a narrative but we lost our thread trying to close this thing out," David Axelrod said at the time. "We were the fresh challengers against the Battleship Inevitable, the entitled front-runner, and somehow she moved into that position herself. This gives us an opportunity to go back to our narrative. Part of what we're about is we're not going to do politics the way it's always been done. Politics has failed in Washington and it's what we're running against. What she's doing here is right out of the Washington textbook." Axelrod had no time to focus-group or poll-test the message before it was rolled out, as he usually did: his candidate had his own experience and was driving the train. "He thought it was demagoguery and he jumped on it," said Axelrod. "We tested it for four or five nights and our position kept beating hers two to one."

The argument triggered dueling TV ads and photo ops. Clinton attacked Obama for refusing to suspend the tax. To show her concern, she drove to a gas station with a sheet-metal worker on his way to work in a pickup truck, while her own motorcade idled nearby. Obama ran a long, sixty-second ad—cut from a single campaign event at an unscripted rally—condemning the idea as "typical of how Washington works." He changed his stump speech to include the kitchen-table calculation that the gas-tax holiday would save the average family "thirty cents a day, which is less than you can buy a cup of coffee for at 7-Eleven." His aides started referring to "the McCain-Clinton" policy and calculated how many jobs would be lost without gas-tax revenues paying for infrastructure for three months.

Polls showed that a small majority thought the gas-tax holiday was a bad idea. But more important for Obama, a large majority of 70 percent believed the idea was a case of candidates trying to help themselves politically rather than providing relief to average Americans. The argument was good enough to narrow the contest in Indiana, but not good enough to overcome the reemergence of Reverend Wright. Obama lost Indiana, but only narrowly, by one point, and he won North Carolina convincingly, by fifteen points. Perhaps more important than the primary results was the strategy that emerged through those final contests. The gas-tax debate laid out a pattern that would repeat itself in the financial crisis of the fall. Obama could campaign against Washington politics—against its gimmicks, half-truths, and indifference—and promise a presidency that understood and cared about ending the economic pain.

When Obama's high-minded strategy of reform failed to carry the economic argument, he could always fall back on the fudge of compromise. The first economic skirmish of the general election revolved around another energy issue: offshore oil drilling. Two weeks after Obama secured his party's nomination, McCain reversed his longstanding opposition to offshore drilling when he proposed that states should be allowed to decide whether oil companies could explore off their coastline. Obama condemned the idea as a flip-flop and a gimmick, pointing out that McCain had supported the ban when he last ran for president in 2000. "This is yet another reversal by John McCain in terms of his earlier positions," he told reporters on his plane. "We could set up an interesting debate between John McCain 2000 and John McCain 2008. The biggest problem with John McCain's position is that it seems like a classic Washington political solution, which is to go out there and make a statement without any clear evidence that this would result in strengthening the U.S. economy or providing relief to consumers. There's no way that allowing offshore drilling would lower gas prices right now. At best, you're looking at five years or more down the road. And even the most optimistic assumptions indicate that offshore drilling might reduce the worldwide price of oil by a few cents. So this isn't something that's going to give consumers short-term relief and it isn't a long-term solution to our problems with fossil fuels generally and oil in particular."

It was a sound policy argument, but it didn't reflect what the voters were looking for. They wanted action to deal with high gas prices, even in states with coastlines that might be threatened by oil drilling. Saying no sounded like Obama thought that the status quo was fine, or that environmentalists were more important than motorists. "McCain looked like he was being courageous and taking on the Washington establishment," conceded Axelrod, "and we looked conventional." The McCain team called Obama "Dr. No" after the Caribbean-based villain of the James Bond movie of the early 1960s. Public opinion was squarely with McCain on more drilling for oil. The vast majority of voters supported offshore drilling through the summer, reaching as much as 73 percent in June. "They saw it before we did," said Jim Margolis, Obama's ad maker. "Intuitively we didn't understand it and we approached it with a four-year-old, six-year-old mind-set. We didn't do the research. We depended on our gut instead of looking at it in the context of a four-dollar gallon of gas."

Obama shifted his language and his position accordingly. His internal polling showed that drilling was important for voters because they wanted relief, but they also wanted something bigger, more long-term, in dealing with energy and the economy. He justified his reversal by limiting the drilling and saying it would help a bipartisan package of energy reforms. In any case, he did not want to be dogmatic about the environment. Nonetheless it was an expedient move, for Congress's sake and for his own election. "My interest is in making sure we've got the kind of comprehensive energy policy that can bring down gas prices," he told one newspaper. "If, in order to get that passed, we have to compromise in terms of a careful, well-thought-out drilling strategy that was carefully circumscribed to avoid significant environmental damage—I don't want to be so rigid that we can't get something done."

McCain's energy maneuvers did not always succeed. When Obama suggested that motorists could save money by inflating their tires correctly, McCain's aides handed out tire-pressure gauges to mock his proposals. They backed down when McCain conceded that his rival, along with the American Automobile Association, was correct.

Obama took the opposite style of campaign, preferring policy debates to visual gags. Wherever possible, he adopted a pseudo-presidential tone as the economic debate unfolded throughout the general election. He wanted to portray his concerns as being more national than local, more executive than legislative, more policy-driven than poll-tested. He was more than just a candidate; he was a nominee and president-in-waiting. So when he sat down for an early-summer discussion about the economy with several of the nation's governors, his priorities—in style and substance—were clear. His aides chose an elegant white meeting room in the Chicago History Museum, just beyond a display of posters for the 1933 World's Fair, the city's ambitious attempt to lift its spirits out of the Depression with a celebration of science and industry. Inside the meeting room, the candidate was projecting an image of the great unifier. There were state flags and Stars and Stripes along the walls. And there were both Clinton supporters and Obama supporters around the horseshoe table: governors like Janet Napolitano of Arizona, who long supported him, and Ed Rendell of Pennsylvania, one of Clinton's biggest backers, who spent most of the session looking distracted, tired, and bored.

The candidate himself was an earnest student, taking copious notes on a desktop lectern, as the governors urged more spending on infrastructure projects. Indeed, he was almost presidential, sitting behind an oversized new seal, designed by his new media team of young tech-driven staffers. The blue-and-white circle included an eagle and his campaign's Web address, along with a Latin motto: Vero Possumus, or Yes We Can. "Is that presidential enough for you?" David Plouffe quipped at the back of the room. "I think we should sell them for $250 a pop." Three days later, after the guffaws from the bloggers and pundits died down, the seal was no more.

Lost in the laughter was an economic strategy that survived through election day and beyond. Obama wanted to see more rebate checks as a stimulus, more aid to states for health care costs, and he was a strong advocate of far greater government spending on roads and bridges: a Keynesian approach to public works, which Democrats had largely avoided since the Reagan era. Instead of skirting the issue, he used it to beat his opponent over the head. "To create new jobs, one step that I'll take as president is to invest $60 billion in a national Infrastructure Reinvestment Bank," he told the governors. "All of you understand firsthand how badly our roads and our bridges, our water systems, our locks and dams are in need of repair. You know that it's a safety and economic issue. You understand how many jobs this creates. That's why I believe Senator McCain's plan to pay for a gas-tax holiday with transportation and infrastructure funding is an especially bad idea."

The candidate and his senior staff knew there would be one, and only one, battlefield in the general election: the economy. Their certitude was rooted in the only extensive national polling they conducted through the entire election, soon after the primaries were over. All their other polling focused on statewide surveys designed to help them win in the Electoral College. But the single investment in national research gave them the big picture of where and how they had to win. Axelrod brought together his entire media and polling team for the first time to hear the data at his consulting firm's loft-style offices overlooking the elevated track of the El. There were two dozen operatives: a combination of the core group of consultants who toiled through the primaries and newcomers who could add more regional expertise. They would later focus on twenty-two battleground states, which would ultimately shrink to sixteen, as some states, like Washington and Maine, grew more blue, and some, like Georgia and Alaska, grew more red. But for now, the poll of 1,172 voters nationwide at the end of May gave them some clear guidance about the priorities of the general election.

The survey was the brainchild of Joel Benenson, the campaign's chief pollster, a blunt and meticulous New Yorker and former political reporter for the *Daily News*. Benenson used what he called a bake-off between three basic propositions. One was that voters wanted a strong commander in chief to deal with a troubled world; another was that they wanted a leader to turn around the economy in a time of hardship; the third was about changing politics to fix the broken ways of Washington.

When they asked voters to choose between fixing the economy and a strong commander in chief, the economy won by six points among all voters. But among what Benenson called "up for grabs" voters—those most likely to change their vote before election day—the economy won by eleven points. The numbers were far higher than the conventional wisdom suggested at that point, in the early summer, when Obama was facing intense questions about his commander-in-chief credentials against John McCain's.

When Benenson squared the economic argument against the need for change, the economy won again by eight points among the up-for-grabs voters. Even in the final combination, of change versus the commander in chief, the national security argument lost narrowly. "We didn't need a poll to tell us it wasn't going to be about change," Benenson said. "But what we did find out was how much the economy was going to be driving the campaign." Voters were concerned not just about the pure economy of prices and jobs but about the broadest range of pocketbook challenges. "We knew that energy, health care, education weren't just issues in their own silos," Benenson said. "They linked into the economy for voters. Voters saw those as fundamental linchpins of our economic future from both their personal perspective and business."

When the pollster later shared his data with the candidate and other senior advisers, he wasn't surprised. "You know," Obama told him, "voters are always just ahead of the politicians, aren't they?"

Who were the voters who were up for grabs? They had loose party affiliation and were either undecided now or had previously switched their votes between parties. Three-fourths of them were independents, and they hated partisan bickering and negative campaigning. They were independent middle-class women living in rural towns like Bristol, in the southwestern Appalachian corner of Virginia—Obama's first stop after clinching the nomination—or Pueblo, forty-five minutes south of

Colorado Springs—his last western stop of the election. The group included a lot of suburban parents under forty-five years of age, who were slightly more affluent, earning more than $75,000 a year. There were some independent urban young men and women, too. But what knitted them all together was their focus on the economy. Even the war in Iraq, which they opposed, was seen as an economic hole as well as a national security disaster. Together they made up around 18 percent of the electorate—more than enough to decide the presidency.

The national poll suggested that McCain was surprisingly vulnerable in some of his core areas. McCain was selling himself as commander in chief and while there was no challenging him on his military record, the concept was surprisingly elastic and so was the contest. Obama's aides figured that commander in chief was just a title. When they narrowed the questions down to the essential qualities required for the job, their candidate rebounded. The results were out of line with the media image of a president in the Bush era. Being ready to serve as commander in chief ranked at the same level as restoring respect for America around the world, and several points behind general "toughness." Lagging far behind all the other Bush-like qualities was the notion of being patriotic. When the question was about who was ready as commander in chief, Obama was down by eighteen points—a number that was far less than they expected for a war hero pitted against a freshman senator. But that was the same margin Obama *led* McCain on the question of who could restore respect for America.

McCain's main branding as a maverick seemed to resonate only inside the Beltway. Across the nation, Obama was twenty-six points ahead when it came to putting working families ahead of special interests, and he was twelve points ahead on the question of putting partisan politics aside. If a maverick candidate was all about change, McCain was no maverick: Obama led him on the issue of change by twenty-two points.

Obama's own numbers were themselves a reversal of the conventional wisdom at the end of the long primary contest. After several rounds of Reverend Wright and his own comments about the bitter nature of small-town America, the candidate's aides were concerned that voters would see Obama as some kind of alien or unsympathetic figure. Instead, he was leading McCain on the central question: does he share my values? Obama led McCain by eight points, despite McCain's stirring biography and service to his country. "This was one of the things that did surprise us at the outset," said Benenson. "Here was this guy, McCain, who people thought had this incredibly powerful biography, and they thought that it translated into all these other big qualities about him. But it didn't. His campaign seemed to put so much stock in that, but there were so many other things going on with the electorate that they never tended to. They never really seemed to try to connect him with people, to really demonstrate that he really got their lives." When it came down to empathy—whether the candidates cared about people like the voters themselves—Obama enjoyed a twenty-one-point lead at the start of the general election.

At the Democratic convention in Denver, Obama's senior aides sat with Joe Biden to brief him on their findings—and on his mission to reach those up-for-grabs voters. The media commentary suggested that Biden would be deployed to win his fellow Catholic voters, because Obama had struggled with them against Hillary Clinton. But the campaign's polling showed him almost tied with McCain among Catholics. Biden liked the focus for his mission, which included wealthier voters— a group Obama was losing at that time by fifteen points in the battle-ground states.

Biden also liked the campaign's ability to connect and empathize with regular voters. On the second day of the convention, he walked onto a small stage in a theater in Denver, where Michelle Obama was holding a public discussion with several women, including women governors from across the country. A sign on the podium hit the campaign's general election theme in all its up-for-grabs generality: Economic Security for American Families. Biden praised workingwomen, especially single mothers, and he steered clear of anything partisan. And he heaped praise on Michelle Obama for her convention speech, before saying that she, like her husband, had touched a nerve across the nation.

"I ran against him, man," he told the audience to a nervous burst of laughter. "I thought I should be president. I ran like the devil but I tell you what: I watched something. These folks get it. They tapped into a fundamental essence of what the country is: that people don't want you to give them a handout. They want you to give them a chance."

Obama's economic approach combined the wine and beer tracks beloved by the political pundits. His policies emerged from an unusual source for a freshman senator: a personal think tank. As a new senator in

Washington, Obama hired a shrewd and pragmatic policy director, Karen Kornbluh, a senior Clinton Treasury official under Robert Rubin, to help shape his thinking. To that end, Kornbluh organized a series of dinners and briefings with experts and advocates across the policy spectrum. Obama wanted to test his ideas and analysis, hear fresh thinking, and fashion an agenda that would inform his speeches, his new book, and his legislation. One dinner, at the modern French restaurant Bistro Bis close to Capitol Hill, brought together John Holdren, a physicist-environmentalist, Bill Klinefelter from the United Steelworkers of America, and scientists from the Natural Resources Defense Council. Democrats had traditionally found it hard to square the interests of labor and the environment, but Obama wanted to bring the two together. The green movement wanted to protect the planet at all costs; the labor unions wanted to protect jobs at all costs. Now national security needed to be factored in, with Democratic hawks backing the development of alternative energy. With the help of new technologies, government subsidies, and tougher regulation, Obama thought he might be able to meet several goals at the same time, around a dinner table with wine and beer drinkers together.

What emerged were a series of speeches—and a chapter of his book *The Audacity of Hope*—which foreshadowed his campaign promises and his administration's policies. Soon after Hurricane Katrina struck New Orleans, Obama spoke at Resources for the Future, a nonpartisan think tank on energy and the environment. Katrina had demonstrated how a natural disaster could deepen the nation's energy crisis, shutting down Gulf Coast refineries and pushing gas prices even higher. "As usual, the American people are already way ahead of Washington," he said.

Whether it's Galesburg farmers growing the corn that can fuel our cars or the Chicago factory workers making the microchip that lets us plug them in, people across the country have been taking America's energy future into their own hands with the same sense of innovation and optimism that sent the Wright brothers into the sky, led Dr. Salk to a cure for polio, and fueled Henry Ford's confidence that his workers could afford the cars they made. But for too long now, this can-do spirit has been stifled by a can't-do government that seems to think it has no role in solving great national challenges or rallying a country to a cause.

This was not just a laundry list of policies about energy and security; it was an attempt to place the policy options in the middle of a bigger story about everyday Americans. Obama was trying to connect with an audience outside the think-tank world of Washington, and as the campaign polling suggested, it was something voters valued highly. "As we cut through all the talk and the politics in the energy debate, we can see what the debate is really about," he said. "We see the family that thinks twice about what they'll spend at the grocery store this week, because they've been paying forty dollars to fill up the tank for the last month. We see the grandmother who isn't sure how she'll make her Social Security check cover January's heating bill. The autoworker who isn't sure what the future at Ford holds for him. And the mother who sees turmoil in the Middle East and worries that someday her son might have to fight to secure our oil supply. Ultimately, we see a nation that cannot control its future as long as it cannot control the source of energy that keeps it running."

In trying to please everyone and solve every problem, Obama handed his opponents plenty of ammunition. He had just voted for the Bush administration's energy bill because it gave some support to alternative energy. Clinton would later attack his vote as support for President Bush and Vice President Cheney. McCain attacked the same vote for supporting ethanol subsidies and the oil industry. His post-Katrina speech also called for higher fuel efficiency standards, as well as support for American carmakers to produce more hybrid cars—either through direct subsidies or by helping them with health care costs for their retirees. But there was one policy he rejected outright: more drilling. "We could open up every square inch of America to drilling," he said, "and we still wouldn't even make a dent in our oil dependency."

He took the same approach to the Detroit Economic Club, four months into his presidential campaign, in a speech that he regularly cited as an example of delivering tough talk to America's special interests. "I went to Detroit to insist that we have to increase fuel efficiency standards," he said to a group of voters in one early TV ad. "Now, I have to admit, the room got kind of quiet. We can't just tell people what they want to hear. We need to tell them what they need to hear. We need to tell them the truth."

The story got more dramatic with each retelling, as the candidate turned his policy wonkery into political strategy. The only problem was that the room in Detroit was not exactly quiet, as an anonymously edited YouTube video showed. His policies were crafted to help all sides: there were incentives for the industry to change its ways, and those proposals won applause from his audience. Obama could be an independent and innovative politician when he wanted to. He could also act like a politically skillful salesman when he needed to.

Both sets of skills were critical as his campaign skirmished with McCain's team over energy and the economy throughout the general election. McCain started the summer trailing far behind on empathy with voters. That deficit was partly the result of political necessity: he was straddling the line between supporting some of President Bush's policies and acknowledging the deeply disgruntled mood of the voters. Yet he continued to hedge on the economy even after he had secured the Republican nomination.

Soon after Obama's "bitter" comments, McCain attacked his opponent for being "out of touch" before describing an economy that was at odds with the experience of many Americans. "I think if you look at the overall record and millions of jobs that have been created, et cetera, et cetera, you could make an argument that there's been great progress economically over that period of time," he told one TV interviewer. "But that's no comfort. That's no comfort to families now that are facing these tremendous economic challenges. But let me just add . . . the fundamentals of America's economy are strong."

Strong was not how the economy seemed as it slowed and contracted through 2008. McCain sounded like he was cheerleading for Bush's economic policies, and at least one of his advisers compounded the problem. His economic adviser, Phil Gramm, the former Texas senator and economics professor, ridiculed those suffering economic pain in the early summer. Gramm was more than just another figure inside McCain's inner circle: McCain had chaired Gramm's ill-fated presidential campaign in 1996, and Gramm was now cochair of McCain's campaign. He spoke with authority on the economy, yet he dismissed talk of economic decline by saying the country had become "a nation of whiners." He told the *Washington Times* that there were small amounts of economic growth. "You've heard of mental depression," he said. "This is a mental recession." When challenged the next day, Gramm stood by his comments, insisting that the data did not point to a recession. The start of the recession would later be officially pinpointed to six months earlier, at the end of 2007.

Obama jumped on Gramm's remarks within twenty-four hours. It was an opportunistic attack but nonetheless effective, as the candidate tied his own childhood to the troubles facing regular Americans today. First he spoke of his mother's difficulties as a single parent. "I remember when she was young and still getting her degree, struggling to provide for us, worrying sometimes about how she was going to pay the bills while she was raising us and going to school on her own," he told supporters at a school in Fairfax, Virginia. "There were a couple of times when she had to swallow her pride and get some food stamps to make sure that we had enough to eat. So I know how hard it can be for a lot of women out there." Then he went on to attack McCain and Gramm together. "Senator McCain unfortunately doesn't seem to see the problem. He surveyed the Bush economic record and said we had made 'great progress' with the economy. Today one of his top economic advisers, former senator Phil Gramm, said that we're merely in a mental recession. I guess what he meant was it's a figment of your imagination, these high gas prices. Senator Gramm then called the United States 'a nation of whiners.' This comes after Senator McCain recently admitted that his energy proposals—for the gas-tax holiday and drilling— would have mainly 'psychological benefits.' Now I want all of you to know that America already has one Dr. Phil. We don't need another one when it comes to the economy. We need somebody to actually solve the economy. It's not just a figment of your imagination. It's not only in your head."

McCain added to his own troubles a month later when he struggled to answer the simple question of how many homes he owned. "I think," he hesitated, "I'll have my staff get to you." It may have been a gotcha question but for the vast majority of people, it was not a difficult one to answer. "It's condominiums where . . ." he trailed off. "I'll have them get to you." The answer was not easy to pin down. His staff said four; reporters counted seven or eight, while some outside groups said ten. The same day, he told the conservative radio talk show host Laura Ingraham that the fundamentals of the economy were still strong.

Tipped off about the story a full day before it appeared, Obama's team was ready to take full advantage with a powerful ad featuring McCain's gaffe. They had been looking for a way to explain why McCain agreed with Bush's economic policies. Now they had the answer: he was so wealthy that he was totally out of touch. Obama reinforced the message as he campaigned in Virginia again, this time in a wooded picnic area outside a high school in Chester, south of Richmond. "If you don't know how many houses you have, then it's not surprising that you might think the economy was fundamentally strong," Obama shouted into his microphone, feigning shock and surprise. "But if you're like me, and you got one house, or you were like the millions of people who are struggling right now to keep up with their mortgage so they don't lose their home, you might have a different perspective. By the way, the answer is, John McCain has seven homes. So there's just a fundamental gap of understanding between John McCain's world and what people are going through every single day here in America." In southern Virginia, a battleground state rich in up-for-grabs voters, the economic argument was vital for the Democratic candidate. Obama could connect with undecided voters on their top priority while also trashing his rival as being out of touch—in terms of politics, personal values, and perspective.

There was an added benefit to the strategy: it subtly suggested a candidate who was too old to understand the world. At campaign headquarters, David Plouffe insisted they had never discussed the idea of going after McCain on the question of age. But several senior figures working alongside Plouffe seemed to enjoy references to McCain's age and infirmity, while one referred to him simply as "the old man."

Whether age or temperament lay behind McCain's response to the meltdown of the financial sector, his behavior was simply erratic. In the middle of the biggest crisis of the entire two-year-old election cycle, his statements and his behavior were off-kilter. He "suspended" his campaign to return to Washington to work on a rescue package, but stayed in New York City. He promised only to return to the trail when the crisis was resolved, but resumed campaigning well before that point. And he threatened to miss the first TV debate, but showed up all the same. When he finally sat down in the White House to debate the rescue package, he remained silent for most of the meeting. Obama's team collectively and theatrically rolled their eyes at their rival's histrionics. "We'd be saying the same thing if he was forty-two years old," said Plouffe. "The response to the economic crisis wasn't about age at all. It was about impulsiveness."

Obama himself seemed bemused and surprised by McCain's "suspension" of his campaign, coming minutes after a phone conversation in which the candidates agreed to issue a joint statement on the crisis—and defer all talk of halting the election. "Can you believe this? I just got off the phone with him," he told his aides at his debate camp in Florida. "A president has to be able to do more than one thing at a time."

In contrast, Obama savored the opportunity to call economic experts and walk deep into the weeds with Clinton-era officials like Bob Rubin, Larry Summers, and Gene Sperling. Their analysis was shocking. Unemployment could rise into double digits, as high as 10 or 15 percent—levels far higher than the worst of the early-1980s recession. If he weren't such a serious-minded politician in the first place, the dire warnings would have sobered up even the most optimistic candidate. "Obama stepped up his game during the economic crisis and McCain looked lost," said Pete Rouse.

McCain did not help his cause by elevating a single, unvetted voter to become the mascot of his campaign. At their final TV debate in Hempstead, New York, the two candidates debated intensively about their economic plans. Or more precisely, they debated the tax position of one Joe Wurzelbacher, otherwise known as Joe the Plumber. Wurzelbacher turned out to be neither a trained nor licensed plumber, nor was he called Joe (his real name was Samuel). But he was a hero in the conservative media for confronting Obama at a campaign stop near Toledo, Ohio. There he told the candidate that he wanted to buy his plumbing business but faced higher taxes under the Democrat's plans. After a long discussion about Obama's tax proposals, Wurzelbacher asked the candidate if he supported a flat tax. Obama said no, explaining that the rate would need to be too high for average workers, and that richer people (including himself) should pay more. "My attitude is that if the economy's good for folks from the bottom up, it's going to be good for everybody," Obama said. "If you've got a plumbing business, you're going to be better off if you've got a whole bunch of customers who can afford to hire you, and right now everybody's so pinched that business is bad for everybody and I think when you spread the wealth around, it's good for everybody."

Spreading wealth around is one of the fundamental principles of a progressive tax system. The wealthy pay higher rates of tax than the working poor, and those taxes disproportionately help those at the bottom of the economy by paying for government programs. But in McCain's retelling, the phrase became a socialist nightmare. "You know, when Senator Obama ended up his conversation with Joe the Plumber," he said at the TV debate, snatching at his words, "we need to spread the wealth around. In other words, we're going to take Joe's money, give it to Senator Obama, and let him spread the wealth around. I want Joe the Plumber to spread that wealth around. You told him you wanted to spread the wealth around. The whole premise behind Senator Obama's plans are class warfare, let's spread the wealth around. I want small businesses—and by the way, the small businesses that we're talking about would receive an increase in their taxes right now."

Obama calmly tried to explain that almost all taxpayers would get a tax cut under his plan. Only small businesses making more than $250,000 a year would see a tax rise (and even those would only pay more tax if they chose to pay personal income tax, not corporate tax, on their business profits). "I want to cut taxes for 95 percent of Americans," Obama replied to McCain in the TV debate. "Now, it is true that my friend and supporter Warren Buffett, for example, could afford to pay a little more in taxes." At which point, McCain grew even more exasperated. "We're talking about Joe the Plumber!" he declared.

McCain wanted to talk about Joe the Plumber until election day. Speaking to a Miami radio station two weeks later, the GOP nominee was asked if Obama's policies were socialist. "His economic policies are clearly those that have been used by other countries that you could describe as socialist," McCain said. "I mean redistribution of wealth, take money from one group, give it to others, is a fundamental principle of some of these 'socialist' countries. . . . That's what George McGovern wanted to do, that's what Jimmy Carter did, and we're not going to do it." Obama responded with a touch of humor at a huge outdoor rally in downtown Raleigh, North Carolina, just days before the election. "Because he knows that his economic theories don't work, he's been spending these last few days calling me every name in the book," the candidate said as he wound up for the punch line. "Lately he's called me a socialist for wanting to roll back the Bush tax cuts for the wealthiest Americans so we can finally give tax relief to the middle class. I don't know what's next. By the end of the week, he'll be accusing me of being a secret communist because I shared my toys in kindergarten. I shared my peanut butter and jelly sandwich." If Obama and his team sounded relaxed about the socialist line of attack, that was because they had polled and focus-grouped the term down to its underwear. "It's excessive," said David Plouffe. "We've exposed people to the socialism thing in any number of venues and people reject it out of hand. They say, 'I might not agree with him on taxes, but I don't think anybody running for president is socialist.'"

As the attacks rained down, the candidate seemed energized. Unlike his performance during the primaries, he grew more engaged in the economic debate as it dragged on. Inside campaign headquarters, his aides saw a clear difference from six months earlier. "He was intellectually engaged in this challenge because it's so immediate and so complicated and so consequential, both politically and substantively," said Pete Rouse.

The politics of the final stretch were consequential but not entirely accurate. As the recession took hold, the candidates presented an exaggerated caricature of each other and an understated picture of the economy. Obama wanted to turn the United States into North Korea; McCain wanted to hand the federal budget to big corporations. The economy was deteriorating through each week of the closing phase of the 2008 election. Yet neither candidate shared with voters what to expect from a long-term recession, or even depression. Perhaps they were unaware of what was going on in the real economy, or perhaps they feared that such dire warnings were unlikely to win them any votes. The economic debate amounted to neither straight talk nor change we could believe in. The only question was which caricature would lose the day.

The disparity between the needs of a campaign and the needs of the country were painfully obvious in midtown Manhattan on the morning after the New York debate. Even at this late stage of the election, Obama needed cash to sustain his vastly expensive, and privately funded, campaign machine. So he shared his insights with around one hundred high-rolling donors over breakfast under the gilded opulence of the Metropolitan Club, established by the great financier, industrialist, and robber baron J. P. Morgan. Sitting at one of the round tables was James Wolfensohn, the former investment banker and ex-president of the World Bank. Standing along the wall was Richard Parsons, the former CEO of Time Warner and one of the most prominent African Americans in the Republican Party. Each of the guests paid more than $30,000 for their seat. "I don't need to tell the people of New York that we are going through the worst economic crisis since the Great Depression, and families all across America are frightened," the candidate explained to New Yorkers with tens of thousands of dollars in spare cash. "They're frightened about their jobs. They're frightened about their savings. They're frightened about their ability to send their kids to college."

The financial crisis was a real-time test, and the voters formed their judgments of the candidates as the economy ground to a halt. The polls moved within a narrow range for the last month of the election, but the conclusions were clear. Obama had demonstrated that he could be pragmatic and nonpartisan; that he could master policy substance in Washington and street politics on the trail; that he could be calm and cautious in a crisis yet a rule breaker in times of trouble.

Winning a two-year-long election was just the beginning. Now all he had to do was lift the economy out of a deep recession, rescue the collapsed financial system, end two long wars, halt climate change, and fix the nation's health care. There was little that was conventional about the scale of the challenges that awaited him. To tackle them all, he would need the common sense of a political outsider and the sensibility of a Washington insider. For now, the making of a renegade president was complete. Soon it would be time for the president to remake the world.

NINE

TRANSITION

President Barack Obama was sitting alone with his back to an unlit fireplace, leafing through his briefing papers, inside the Oval Office. Over his right shoulder sat a large bronze bust of Martin Luther King Jr.; to his left was a vase of big red tulips, which half obscured him from the sight of anyone walking through the door behind him. His eyes were dark gray, and he rubbed them into their sockets. It was a quiet pause in a relentless schedule, the day after his first address to Congress, and a late night working both sides of the aisle in the House chamber. That morning he announced his third nominee for commerce secretary. Next would come a session with his in-house economics professor, Larry Summers, alongside his treasury secretary, Tim Geithner, plus the Democratic and Republican leaders of the congressional committees dealing with the near-bankrupt financial sector. Later that afternoon, he would talk to the press about overhauling the nation's financial watchdogs. Outside, in the hushed halls of the West Wing, his foreign policy aides were making final changes to a speech he would deliver in just two days: on the long-promised winding down of the war in Iraq, and the return home of most of the nation's troops.

He looked like he had been cramming for an exam all night long. His new workload was punishing and his decisions reached far beyond his sight lines across the Rose Garden, the South Lawn, and the National Mall. The Oval Office was a case study in chaos theory: a flutter of wings could repair a school, lay down a new rail line, shut down a bank, or destroy a home on an Afghan hillside. There was a new budget that shifted taxes to the wealthy and promised the first steps to universal health care. And there were so many billions in stimulus spending that his cabinet secretaries had more money than any of their predecessors in living memory.

He was still a renegade in his outsized ambition and his readiness to break with convention. Yet he also now carried the institution of the presidency. His aides and courtiers paced nervously and talked in subdued tones outside. Protocol dictated that he could only speak through a microphone attached to a stocky blue podium with the presidential seal stuck on front. Having run against Washington as an outsider, he was now running Washington as its preeminent insider. So how much could he really change before the nation's capital changed him?

"I'm the captain of a ship," he told me. "I am not the builder of a ship. So there's certain constraints, in terms of the ship's capacities. I can't transform an old steamer into a nuclear submarine. I can't steer the thing faster than its capacities. And most importantly, I don't control the weather or the oceans. On the other hand, given what the oceans are and what the weather is and what the constraints of the ship are, I can be a better captain or a worse captain. And my job is to be the best captain I can be."

He was not the first president to see himself on the high seas. Kennedy kept a plaque on the same heavy timbered desk, hewn and carved from the oak of the HMS *Resolute* that still dominated Obama's Oval Office. The plaque was the Breton fisherman's prayer: "O, God, Thy sea is so great and my boat is so small."

There was another figure of leadership who sprang to mind, someone whose voyage began from the same place, far from the West Wing and even farther from Cape Cod. Back on the streets of Chicago at the start of his political career, Obama had watched Harold Washington visit his community to open a job center. The city's first African American mayor, Washington was an inspiration for many of his closest Chicago friends and aides. Yet after the mayor drove away, Obama was frustrated with his volunteers, with the slowness of change, and with the icon himself. "More than anything, I wanted Harold to succeed," he wrote.

Like my real father, the mayor and his achievements seemed to mark out what was possible; his gifts, his power, measured my own hopes. And in listening to him speak to us that day, full of grace and good humor, all I had been able to think about was the constraints on that power. At the margins, Harold could make city services more equitable. . . . But beneath the radiance of Harold's victory . . . nothing seemed to change.

I wondered whether, away from the spotlight, Harold thought about those constraints. Whether . . . he felt as trapped as those he served, an inheritor of sad history, part of a closed system with few moving parts, a system that was losing heat every day, dropping into low-level stasis.

I wondered whether he, too, felt a prisoner of fate.

Did President Obama, whose gifts and power measured so many people's hopes, also feel constrained by the system, by the size of government, or even by fate?

"Well, you know, the point I was making was that being an elected official means that you're responsible for a whole bunch of things that are within your control, but that your success or failure ultimately may also hinge on some things that are not in your control," he told me. "In the case of a big city, you know what's happening with tax revenues, what's happening to the employment base. You know, you could be the best mayor in the world in Flint, Michigan, and if the auto industry is collapsing you're going to have problems.

"I think that's true for a mayor. I think that's true for a governor. I think that's true for a president. So I don't think of it in terms of trying to avoid fate; I think of it in terms of understanding what's within my control and what's not within my control. And that's why—so far, at least—I feel pretty calm on the job. We've got these huge problems—not of my making—they're global in scope. My job is to make the best possible decisions given those circumstances.

"And as long as I feel that every day I'm making good decisions, motivated by what's right for ordinary Americans, what's going to create jobs for them and keep them in their homes and give their kids a chance to go to college and have good careers, then I sleep pretty easy at night."

Feeling calm was always Obama's gut check on his own performance. Over the course of the long presidential campaign, he felt best about his efforts when he was playing ball-control offense: when he and his team were executing their game plan. He stuck to his strategic plan as a candidate, and as a new senator in Washington. Now as president, he followed a strategy crafted through the election and transition. It was his executive guide to running the country and shaping the world, and it went beyond his policy briefs to include talking to the world beyond the iron gates surrounding the White House.

"I think that we learned an awful lot about what it takes to put an effective organization together during the campaign," he told me. "I mean, running a huge, multibillion-dollar bureaucracy is obviously different than running a political campaign. On the other hand, the campaign itself was big enough that I had a sense of what worked and what didn't in executing, on the one hand, but also messaging on the other.

"And I think that if you think of the presidency just as a bureaucratic job, then you will not be effective. If you think of it only as a rhetorical, political job, you will not be effective. And I think that our goal has been to say, how do we function as good managers and good stewards of government and reform it and clean it up and make it work and make it tight? But let's not lose sight of the fact that we also have to persuade the American people as to where the country needs to go. And those two things have to work in concert, in tandem, to be effective."

A month earlier he stepped inside the White House for the last time as a guest. He and his family stopped at the Executive Mansion for coffee with the Bushes, while the Bidens chatted with the Cheneys. When he stepped out of the White House to get into the armored presidential Cadillac, the crowds screamed from the Pennsylvania Avenue bleachers, built for the privileged ticket holders who would see the inaugural parade.

Inside the limousine, President Bush shared some final thoughts with his successor. Both were politically astute enough to know that for all the campaign talk against each other, they were now partly reliant on each other. Obama could draw on Bush's experience more easily, and in more relevant ways, than any other former president. And Bush needed Obama's outreach if he wanted any official role in his postpresidency. As they traveled slowly up Pennsylvania Avenue past the exuberant crowds along the route to Capitol Hill, there were signs trashing them both. One group held posters saying Arrest Bush; another held signs proclaiming Obama as the devil.

At the back of the limo, Bush lamented that his final days in office were plagued by friends lobbying him for pardons on behalf of clients or acquaintances. Not the least among the lobbying parties were both Dick and Lynne Cheney, who argued long and hard for a full pardon for the vice president's convicted chief of staff, Scooter Libby. Bush had already commuted Libby's prison sentence, but left standing a fine of $250,000 and four hundred hours of community service. He felt he had done more than enough for someone convicted of perjury and obstruction of justice after leaking the name of a CIA official. Besides, he disliked the pardon system in Texas and he hated it now. "I know there's this unfettered authority," he told Obama. "But there's something wrong with the system where the privileged have the access and the others don't."

Bush was in an expansive mood with Obama's team. Axelrod met the outgoing president at the Capitol and thanked him profusely for helping extensively with the transition. "You're going to have the ride of your life," Bush told Axelrod. "So make sure you enjoy it." Axelrod was already overwhelmed at the sight of the enormous crowds celebrating Bush's departure and Obama's arrival. "The sense of joy and possibility was so palpable," he said. "With so much of our politics lately, people are so divided from their elected leaders. There's so much cynicism and disenchantment. To see people from all walks of life and all parts of the country, and even some people from around the world, made you realize it was not just his moment; it was their moment, too. Something important was happening and they helped make it happen. It was a renewing experience."

The day was nearly as cold as the one almost two years earlier in Springfield, Illinois, when Obama announced his far-fetched attempt to become president of the United States. On the platform outside the Capitol building were his old friends and his close family, alongside senators, Supreme Court justices, and tiered rows of press. Beyond the bulletproof glass, the balcony, and the ticketed seats below, there was the National Mall stretching almost two miles to the Lincoln Memorial. He had jogged there for inspiration as a senator, after dark, where he would read the Gettysburg Address and the Second Inaugural Address. He would imagine Martin Luther King speaking to the mighty crowd around the Reflecting Pool, and think of the faceless, nameless Americans—the slaves and soldiers, the workers and their families—who built the nation.

A few days earlier, he had taken his wife and their daughters to the same place, to read the Gettysburg Address at dusk. Michelle explained

the meaning of the address, especially its promise to work for more justice and equality, when their elder daughter, Malia, piped up, "Yes, how
are we doing on that, Mr. President-elect?" The family turned to the Second Inaugural. Their younger daughter, Sasha, thought it looked long
and wondered if her father had to deliver something similar. "Actually
that one is pretty short," he explained. "Mine may even be a little longer."

"First African American president," interjected Malia. "Better be
good."

The Lincoln Memorial was later the site of the happiest moment of
his inaugural celebrations. Two days before his swearing-in, he sat with
his family and closest friends as Stevie Wonder, U2, and Bruce Spring-
steen headlined a concert to kick off the party. "I didn't have to perform,"
he recalled later. "I was just sitting there thinking about the crowd and
thinking about the music and the setting. And at that point I felt a great
sense of satisfaction about the spirit that our campaign had unleashed.
And it was less about me than it was about how we had helped to trigger
this atmosphere. That was a really good moment."

He closed his eyes just before he emerged in front of the crowd and the
cameras. He was waiting inside a passageway lined with Capitol Hill police and Secret Service agents. Outside was a shimmering, glistening,
pointillist painting. Almost 2 million people covered every blade and peb-
ble of the Mall, all the way to Lincoln, their faces turned toward him or
staring at giant JumboTron screens with his image. He could only turn
his thoughts inward, for a few seconds. "The only moment in which I
think the magnitude of it swept over me was when I was standing in the
little tunnel right before you go out," he told me later. "It was dark; it
wasn't lit. It was sort of like a visual metaphor of 'You're about to be
shot out of a cannon. Here we go.'"

Better be good. The forty-fourth president stepped up, placed his left
hand on Lincoln's Bible, and raised his right hand opposite Chief Justice
John Roberts. "I, Barack Hussein Obama," they echoed each other, as
if they were the most normal names ever uttered on the white marble
steps of the Capitol.

Better be good. Then the Harvard Law graduates stumbled over each
other and the word *faithfully.* Roberts misplaced the word in the oath of

office, and Obama smiled as he recognized the mistake. He knew that they both felt distracted. Roberts repeated the line, this time staying true to the Constitution, but Obama was thrown off balance: he could only recall the official advice to repeat everything Roberts said. But which line to repeat? In the snap of the moment, he chose the original mistake, not the corrected line. It was his first trip off a high-wire act in two years. He survived the Berlin speech, the outdoor convention, and the live prime-time TV show without any obvious stumbles. This one just happened to take place in front of the biggest crowd of them all.

Better be good. The new president had stopped thinking about the moment in all its historic import. He just wanted to do his job and avoid screwing up. "Once I got out on the stage, I was so concerned with saying hello to everybody and hitting my marks and making sure that the prompter was working, and the fact that it was cold," he told me later, "that you couldn't actually absorb it."

It was bitterly cold, but he had no intention of firing up the enormous crowd with his speech. "We remain a young nation, but in the words of Scripture, the time has come to set aside childish things," he said sternly. "Our time of standing pat, of protecting narrow interests and putting off unpleasant decisions—that time has surely passed. Starting today, we must pick ourselves up, dust ourselves off, and begin again the work of remaking America." It was a workmanlike speech, celebrating what he called "the risk takers, the doers, the makers of things"—not unlike the risk takers and doers of his own campaign. He defended the scale of his ambition as essential at a time of crisis. But he also minimized the grand changes ahead as simply pragmatic choices. He portrayed an era that was post-Reagan and post-Clinton, where the debate was "not whether our government is too big or too small, but whether it works." At times, he evoked Bush with a promise to defeat terrorists. At others, he was the anti-Bush, rejecting his predecessor's readiness to rewrite the rule of law. "We reject as false the choice between our safety and our ideals," he said.

Yet his most distinctive lines were brief allusions to the reason so many people, especially African Americans, squeezed onto the Mall to witness the moment of his swearing-in. He foresaw a world with less religious hatred because America had shown the way. "We have tasted the bitter swill of civil war and segregation, and emerged from that dark chapter stronger and more united," he noted, pointing to the unity on display before him, for all the world to watch on television. "This is the meaning of our liberty and our creed—why men and women and children of every race and every faith can join in celebration across this magnificent Mall, and why a man whose father less than sixty years ago might not have been served at a local restaurant can now stand before you to take a most sacred oath."

Those lines were scribbled by Obama over a weekend at the Hay-Adams hotel opposite the White House, shortly before he moved into more presidential quarters inside Blair House, across Pennsylvania Avenue from the Executive Mansion. He had taken a draft crafted by his young speechwriters and rewritten half of it, ending one of the most relaxed writing processes of the last two years. Although the pressure of history was far higher, their goal was to aim low. "We're in a very serious time," said his chief speechwriter, Jon Favreau. "We're always conscious that it's very easy for rhetoric from him to seem big and hopeful and inspirational, just because of the way everything was in the campaign. So a little goes a long way."

Obama had something fairly simple in mind. Just two weeks after the election, he chatted with Favreau in his transition offices in Chicago about the kind of inaugural addresses he admired. "The best inaugurals I think describe very clearly the moment that we're in, and the moment that the country is in at that point," he explained. "And I think if we can describe the moment we're in to people, so everyone can think, 'Yes, that's exactly how this time feels right now,' then I think we can also paint a picture of where we need to go." He wanted the members of Congress behind him to remember why they got into politics. And he wanted the crowds in front of him to go home and be better parents or volunteer more hours in their community. "I want people to leave thinking that the destiny of the country is in their hands," he said.

The newly inaugurated president left the Capitol as the day grew cold and dark, late in the afternoon. The cheering crowds that lined his parade route were fading faster than the pale rays of sun. Bleachers handed over to big donors were almost empty as the temperatures plunged, and staffers invited members of the public to fill them instead. By the end of the day, the forty-fourth president was watching the parade with a few friends and family in the chilly, glass-enclosed viewing stand erected just outside the White House gates.

That night, the Obamas stopped by ten official balls, most of them inside Washington's soulless concrete convention center, surrounded by crowds of supporters desperate to snap their photos. They danced slowly and dutifully to a few bars of "At Last," the signature tune of the blues singer Etta James, reworked and smoothed out by Beyoncé Knowles. Just before the neighborhood ball, where the guests included D.C. residents, Obama stopped for a brief TV interview. "Mr. President," said Robin Roberts of ABC. "Sounds good, doesn't it?"

"You know," replied the president, "it's got a certain ring to it."

They returned to the White House for their first night as president and First Lady. But there was one more party awaiting them: sixty close friends and family enjoying their new home. Michelle was tired after a frigid day in an elegant but insufficiently warm outfit, complete with high heels. She retired to bed, but her husband stayed to talk and pose for photos until three in the morning.

The next day, his first full day as president, he watched Joe Biden swear in his senior staffers inside the blue velvet interior of the White House auditorium. The joy of inaugural day was almost gone. He would later sit down with his economic team and his Iraq team in the Situation Room. But even before those sessions, at something as simple as a swearing-in ceremony, there was sobriety and even tension, as the vice president cracked a joke at the chief justice's expense. "My memory is not as good as Justice Roberts's," he said to scattered laughs and groans from the senior staff. As Biden asked for a copy of the oath on paper, the president stepped forward to the podium and tapped his vice president on the elbow to shut him up. He glared out at his staffers, then turned to the side and stretched a tense smile at his aides. Biden later called up the chief justice to apologize for his joke.

Obama had gone out of his way to avoid blaming Roberts for the bungling of the oath. A few hours later, he would call Roberts back to repeat the oath in the White House Map Room. There were no TV cameras or news photographers present to record the historic do-over; just a handful of reporters and White House staff watched Renegade act with "an abundance of caution," as his counsel put it.

"Are you ready to take the oath?" asked the chief justice.

"Yes, I am," the president said. "And we're going to do it very slowly."

* * *

The transition was a contradiction: a mixture of the heady glee of New Hampshire and the deliberate caution of Iowa. There was the overconfidence that came from winning a stunning victory with the biggest margin in twenty years, bigger than Bill Clinton or George W. Bush. But there was also a degree of uncertainty: a sense that the team that ran against Washington needed to recruit Washington experts if they wanted to achieve their ambitious agenda in what they expected to be a short honeymoon. Those contradictory feelings were heightened by the split personality of the transition itself, divided between its leadership in Chicago and its staff in Washington.

Obama himself was feeling the weight of his new job almost immediately. The evening after the election, he and Michelle invited several close friends over to their home for dinner. There were his Chicago friends—Valerie Jarrett, Eric Whitaker, Marty Nesbitt—along with several of his Hawaii high school friends who had traveled over for the election. "He was more serious than he usually is," said Nesbitt. "There was a lot of stuff on his mind. He talked about what it was all about: being organized and having the right people." But for his friends, and perhaps for Obama, too, there was also a sense of what was about to change for them all. "I'm giving up a good portion of a friendship to the rest of the world," said Nesbitt. "If he had lost, then our friendship would probably not have changed."

In the immediate afterglow of the election, Obama's closest advisers felt far more upbeat about themselves and their boss. Over a breakfast of coffee and oatmeal in Chicago, David Axelrod said he believed his old friend was fully prepared for the Oval Office after the rigors of the long campaign. "I've never been so confident about a person. I just feel he has grown into this role. It's like the two years were a proving ground," he said. "You never know at the start. It doesn't matter who it is. But you just don't know until you expose someone to that relentless pressure. And what we learned about him is how well he handles it. It was just phenomenal. He just does not get unsettled, and the more the pressure, the cooler he becomes. It's like Michael Jordan said, 'When the game gets close and something big is on the line, it all slows down and I see things better.' That's the way he is when it gets tough. It's a unique quality that only big, big game players have." Of course, Obama's inner circle knew there was a difference between campaigning and governing: the decisions were bigger in the White House, but the pressure was more relentless on the campaign trail. "The thing about the White House is that the decisions you make are life-and-death decisions, so in that sense it's more profound," said Axelrod. "But every day is not a campaign day. Every day is not an election day."

In the days after the election, Obama hunkered down in Chicago's sleek black federal building with two senior aides: Axelrod and his new chief of staff, Rahm Emanuel. The two aides were the yin and yang of Obama's political world. Axelrod was soft-spoken and relaxed, an idealist and thematic thinker who liked elegant phrasing and had stayed outside Washington. Emanuel was pugnacious and permanently coiled, a realist and deal maker who shot double-barrel swearwords and had mastered Washington in both the Clinton White House and Congress. He had offered advice during Obama's Senate race, but when Obama approached him for support at the start of his presidential campaign, he declined. "I owe a lot to the Clintons," he told the candidate. "I'm hiding under the desk." Through the primaries, Emanuel was an adviser in the shadows, talking directly to the candidate or his friend Axelrod. By the summer of 2008, several months before the election, Obama had already settled on Emanuel as his pick for chief of staff. He thought he had brilliant political instincts, and liked his hard-charging ability to be decisive and move quickly on multiple fronts. He valued his Beltway experience, as well as his work on the financial rescue package. And he enjoyed Emanuel's readiness to disagree with him, to challenge his approach to politics.

But he also knew Emanuel was not a manager in the style of David Plouffe, the low-key and disciplined leader of his campaign. So Obama set up a top-heavy White House, with three senior advisers almost on a par with the chief of staff: Axelrod, his chief strategist; Valerie Jarrett, his chief loyalist; and Pete Rouse, his chief manager. The top four were meant to balance one another. Axelrod and Emanuel were close friends from Chicago and closely aligned in politics, if not style. But they also ran the risk of dominating the West Wing together. Jarrett and Rouse were there to act as a counterweight, prized for their personal commitment and lower-key presence.

If Obama felt he could control his new team, he was wrong. Early on, Emanuel freelanced into an area where he had little guidance or control, with the tainted Illinois governor Rod Blagojevich. Even Obama's counsel, Greg Craig, could not determine how many times Emanuel spoke to Blagojevich, or when the calls took place. In his first conversation with the governor, Emanuel discussed the merits of various candidates to take Obama's vacated seat in the United States Senate. "In those early conversations with the Governor, Mr. Emanuel recommended Valerie Jarrett because he knew she was interested in the seat," wrote Craig. "He did so before learning—in further conversations with the President-Elect—that the President-Elect had ruled out communicating a preference for any one candidate." Just a week later, Emanuel discovered that his new boss wanted Jarrett to take a position alongside him in the White House.

The official explanation—that Emanuel knew Jarrett was interested in the seat—was only partially true. Jarrett assumed she was heading for the White House, until Senator Dick Durbin approached her to suggest the Senate shortly before the election. Jarrett was conflicted between the independence of a senator's life and her desire to stay close to her friend, the new president, as a powerful and trusted adviser. Most of her friends thought she should go to the Senate, with one exception: Michelle Obama. Emanuel was not conflicted at all: he was unsettled by her personal relationship with the Obamas and wanted her outside the White House. By the Sunday after the election, a few days after naming Emanuel his chief of staff, Obama offered her the White House job with a broad brief covering relations with state and local governments, as well as public outreach. Within a few weeks of working at the White House, the tension between Jarrett and Emanuel had dissipated, as both focused on their overwhelming workloads and learned to appreciate each other's expertise.

At the top of the transition, the president-elect was feeling more secure than his predecessor. Obama's challenge was not Bush's: he was in no danger of watching a powerful vice president hijack his administration. Biden's experience never fazed him; if anything, he was more distracted by his vice president's indiscipline. "He can't keep his mouth shut," said one senior Obama aide. At one session soon after Jarrett pulled out of consideration for the Senate seat, the senior transition team met to discuss cabinet picks. Biden tried to compliment Jarrett after one contribution. "You should be in the Senate," he quipped. After the meeting, as everyone returned to their offices, Obama stopped Biden to warn him not to say anything like that again. "It's not funny," he told him.

Above all, Obama wanted to avoid the mistakes of Bush and Clinton. Compared with Bush, he wanted a stronger central structure and a weaker vice president. Compared with Clinton, he wanted to avoid alienating his own party in Congress, and he wanted to use his first six or twelve months achieving as much as he could. To reach both ambitions, he needed experienced staff. At one meeting with a former senior Clinton official during his transition, Obama asked for one good piece of advice. "Leave your friends at home," said the Clinton official. "Arkansas friends killed Clinton and Georgia friends killed Carter."

Of all his transition choices, none was easier to make, or more complex to execute, than Hillary Clinton as secretary of state. Obama had long wanted his former rival on his team, no matter what his friends and aides said about her aggressive campaign. "The person most positive about Hillary Clinton was Barack," said one senior Obama aide. "He always said, 'She's smart, she's very talented, and obviously a woman with her own following. If it weren't for Bill Clinton raising questions about what he will say, I would want to have her in the administration in a very significant way.'" His staff opposed the idea for the most part, arguing that Clinton would never be truly loyal. But Obama was willing to leave the primaries behind, including his own strong feelings at the time. "I don't hold grudges," he told his aides. "I don't worry about the past. I'm concerned about what happens now. If she can help me and Bill Clinton isn't too much of a liability, we should seriously look at this."

Through their extended struggle for the nomination, Obama learned to appreciate Clinton's consistency. "She's very precise in how she executes her plans and the way she communicates," said Marty Nesbitt. "He values knowing what he's getting. And he's more interested in having a productive team than anything else." Still, Obama was under no illusion about the legacy of the long primary season. During one transition meeting, Obama said he wanted to offer Clinton the diplomatic job. "I'm really interested in pursuing this, but I know she has some hard feelings coming out of this campaign." Emanuel and John Podesta, the former Clinton official who ran the transition, assured Obama that she was over those hard feelings now. Obama smiled and said, "Believe me. She's not over it yet."

His decision to offer her the job of secretary of state came surprisingly early. Well before the end of the primaries, when his staff and friends still felt hostile to her, Obama decided that Clinton possessed the qualities to carry his diplomacy to the rest of the world. "We actually thought during the primary, when we were pretty sure we were going to win, that she could end up being a very effective secretary of state," he told me later. "I felt that she was disciplined, that she was precise, that she was smart as a whip, and that she would present a really strong image to the world. . . . I had that mapped out."

Recruiting and managing a team of rivals would not be easy, and Clinton came with her own set of issues. Chief among them was her campaign debt, which she wanted eliminated before she took the job of secretary of state. Would the president-elect go out and help her to do so? "I'm not begging her to take this job," Obama told his senior aides. "If she wants it, I could help. But I'm not willing to go out in these difficult economic times to do a flashy fund-raiser in California." As it happened, plenty of people in the Senate were begging Obama to offer Clinton the job. Obama's aides believed that many Senate Democrats thought Clinton had extended her presidential campaign far beyond the point where she had lost the election. Her negative advertising wasted Democratic money, threatened to undermine the party's nominee, and suggested that she was disloyal to the party. They were unwilling to offer the junior New York senator a position ahead of her lowly rank, and she stood little chance of becoming majority leader. "There was a lot of encouragement from inside the Senate to get her into this job," said one senior Obama aide. "They wanted her out of there."

Obama's aides hoped that Clinton would not have free rein before or after her formal acceptance of the job. "We'll be very clear about putting people in key spots that the principals will be fine with, but they will be our people," said one senior Obama adviser. "The senior staff at State and NSC [National Security Council] are going to be high-quality people who are our people. There are ways to build in safeguards and controls." Yet Clinton still managed to negotiate more freedom to pick her own staff than any other cabinet official, most of whom were handed White House lists of personnel to choose from. Obama did not seem to care about the subcabinet picks as much as his own loyalists.

As for controlling the uncontrollable Bill Clinton, Obama's aides drew up a series of checks on his fund-raising for both the Clinton Global Initiative and his work on HIV/AIDS across the world. But they really counted on Hillary to be the ultimate safeguard—against both her husband and her own ambition. "It's in her interests to keep him in line," warned one senior Obama aide. Others in Obama's inner circle said the president-elect believed Clinton needed to demonstrate that she was a team player and to shape her own career and legacy. "There are plenty who don't trust her and think she still harbors something," said another senior adviser. "It's still potentially problematic down the road. Barack's thinking on this is that it's not in her interests to mess with us. She can't win that fight internally and she's smart enough that she won't want that fight publicly."

Several weeks into the administration, even Clinton's internal critics believed the relationship was a success. "They have both worked really hard at it," said one senior White House official. "There's a natural affinity and respect that ironically grew out of being opponents. You get to know someone really well after all that."

His national security adviser came out of neither the Obama nor the Clinton camp. If anything, General James Jones was more closely aligned with John McCain. His strength was his experience and his vision for managing—and rebuilding—the sprawling national security apparatus. Having worked in the Middle East for Bush's secretary of state, Condoleezza Rice, Jones realized just how broken the National Security Council was under the old White House. He had Rice's support, but the Pentagon and CIA were nowhere to be found and his work stalled as security envoy between the Israelis and Palestinians. One of his main pitches for the job was his desire to reform the NSC and expand its brief to take in energy and the economy, as well as the traditional areas of defense and diplomacy.

Jones was typical of the kind of character Obama was searching for. He wanted strong principals who could stand up for themselves, and stand up to him. "He likes to mix it up and he has enough confidence in his intellectual strength to do that," said Valerie Jarrett. "It's not Doris Kearns Goodwin's team of rivals. But he is never intimidated by someone who disagrees with him. He wants people to push him." He also wanted his transition staff to come up with a diverse, balanced team, with a mix of experience, geography, and politics. "There were some positions where he considered experience a real strength, that they knew how to do their job, like Carol Browner, who worked on the environment in the Clinton administration," said Jarrett. "But he didn't want to have only people who were part of the Clinton administration. He met a lot of people on the campaign trail who left an indelible impression on him, and he wanted to make sure there were lots of opportunities to help those people. On the other hand, we were not going to just hire people because they were supporters. We wanted to put people in a position where they were going to thrive and perform well."

The result was that at the lower levels, the transition often seemed a fraught and unhappy operation. Loyal staffers and supporters felt slighted by the jobs they were offered and the sight of Clinton backers riding high. Some felt an inflated sense of their own importance, at least in the eyes of senior transition officials. Others were just disappointed by the process. "You give a job to one friend and you know another hundred friends will be unhappy," said a senior transition staffer. "And then that friend is an ingrate within six months."

Obama left Chicago with his family and a handful of his closest friends for their regular winter vacation in Hawaii in late December. It was their first Christmas in Hawaii since he grappled with his decision to run for president. Last winter he was campaigning in Iowa; now he was returning to his home state as president-elect. Even his vacation style had changed. He could no longer stay at the Hyatt hotel on Waikiki Beach; now he rented a private home in the far more low-key and laid-back Kailua. Instead of his campaign workouts with his body guy, Reggie Love, he drove ten minutes to the gym at the Marine Corps base, often with Michelle.

Hawaii was not just a chance for simple pleasures. The day before Christmas Eve, his motorcade left his vacation home in the early afternoon to stop at the First Unitarian Church in Honolulu. There, inside what was once a simple two-story home, he sat through an hour-long memorial service for his grandmother, the woman who poured her all into him but did not live to see him elected president. Afterward, he drove with his family to the highway pull-off on the blustery southeast coast, to the Lanai Lookout. A few months earlier, he had stood on the rocky outcrop to throw a lei into the ocean in memory of his mother. Now he was scattering his grandmother's ashes.

Before moving to Washington, he returned briefly to his family home in Chicago for the last time. Even though Obama had traveled for the last two years, leaving the city was hard for him. He was giving up a way of life, a privacy and normalcy that he prized and had fought to protect through the campaign. On the night of Halloween, with his neighborhood teeming with trick-or-treaters, he decided he wanted to be a normal parent just one more time. It was only four days before the election, but he ignored his staff warnings and chose to walk the two blocks to the home of Marty Nesbitt, for his traditional Halloween party. With his motorcade rolling slowly beside him, he walked into his street holding the hand of his daughter Sasha, who was dressed as a corpse bride. Suddenly a phalanx of photographers jumped out of a waiting bus in front of them. "All right, guys," he said impatiently. "You've got your shot. Leave us alone." The photographers kept on shooting. "Come on, guys, get back on the bus," he insisted. "I'm asking you." He crossed the street, then noticed he was getting chased by a foreign TV crew. Then he and his seven-year-old daughter started to run, his Secret Service agents jogging briskly behind him. The chase reminded him of his recent trip to Hawaii to visit his very frail grandmother for the last time. When he tried to take a walk along the streets where he had grown up, he found himself chased down by photographers and TV crews.

Now he couldn't take a stroll in his own neighborhood and was fighting against the change, while his wife, Michelle, had driven the two blocks with their elder daughter, Malia. "Barack is walking," she announced to the party. "But I told him I didn't want to have anything to do with that." When Obama arrived at the Nesbitts' house for their traditional party with apple cider and a big pot of chili, his friend was pissed at the sight of a large crowd gathered outside. "Why did you walk to my house? Now everyone knows you're in here," Nesbitt said. Every time he tried to talk to Obama, the doorbell rang with another hundred kids looking for candy and the Democratic nominee.

"Man, you still have your anonymity," the candidate said.

"And yours is gone," Nesbitt replied.

Obama looked like he missed it. He had just one simple question. "If I lose this thing, how quickly can I get my life back?"

The answer was never, and the adjustment was hard for the whole family. When he decided to run, his daughters had three questions for him: would they get to see the Secret Service agents in shades, would they have to move, and could they get a dog? "I can help with the dog," he said, "but the other two, I'm not so sure."

On election night he promised to deliver the dog, and they had lived with the Secret Service for more than a year. But in early January they moved to Washington a day ahead of him, to ready themselves for the start of school, leaving the president-elect rattling around their old home for a day. He found it hard to say good-bye to their old life and space. A friend of his daughter Malia dropped off an album of photos of them together. As he flipped through the pages, sitting alone in his empty home, he cried.

Six weeks later he returned to Chicago with his family for a weekend break. As he helicoptered into the center of Chicago, he looked pained at the rush-hour traffic that police had stopped on Lake Shore Drive for his arrival. "We shouldn't have come here in rush hour," he told his aides. "What happened to the days when I could just have my friend Mike pick me up at the airport, and there was no hoopla?"

"You know what, Mr. President?" said his adviser Valerie Jarrett. "You may not be enjoying your new life, but I am."

After a weekend visiting old friends, the Obama family found they had moved on. Even the president's mother-in-law, Marian, who was the most reluctant to move into the White House, agreed. "I'm ready to go back," she said.

Still, the restrictions and isolation of the presidency were a burden on Obama, even as his family and friends adjusted rapidly to the White House. "He would love nothing better than to stroll outside the gate at a moment's notice," said Jarrett. "But that isn't how he rolls nowadays. He misses the interaction with a wide range of people. He doesn't have a cell phone and very few people have his BlackBerry e-mail. And they are very careful about using it."

His first and last order of business was to save business from itself. Reviving the economy, saving jobs, softening the suffering for the unemployed: all were goals of his gargantuan stimulus package. In its earliest calculations, it was five times the initial estimates of the cost of invading Iraq. The final cost, at around $800 billion, was equivalent to all federal spending on the wars in Iraq and Afghanistan, and the wider war on terror, for the entire presidency of George W. Bush. The numbers only seemed normal after the vast sums spent rescuing the financial markets. In terms of size alone, Obama's stimulus looked not just renegade but revolutionary.

Yet the way he parceled out such vast amounts of cash was also markedly cautious. He took an incremental approach on many fronts rather than a big-bang focus on a few specialized areas of spending. There was money for roads, schools, alternative energy, and health care. There was help for state governments, the unemployed, and parents struggling to pay for college. He was trying to please all of the people at least some of the time, and the polls suggested he was winning—at least with Democrats and independent voters. The latter were the ones who gave him victory in the general election and several key primaries. And they were the ones most responsive both to his economic argument and to his promise of ending the old partisan politics. So when the pundits declared his stimulus plans a failure for lacking Republican support, they missed the point. Independent voters appreciated his efforts to reach out to Republicans. As the Senate prepared to vote on the stimulus, independent voters were far more supportive of his spending plans than Republicans, by a margin of twenty-one points.

The cautious, catchall approach suffered in Washington. Republicans savaged the plans by focusing on special-interest spending, including help for the movie industry and family planning. The new White House was slow to respond in kind, either by counterattacking the Republicans or by mounting a sustained defense of their own policies. Public support for the package declined twelve points between January and February.

But the president found his voice again on the road. When it came time to sell his economic plan, he flew for his first out-of-town event to Elkhart, Indiana—a state he won by less than one point, making him the first Democrat to win there since Lyndon Johnson's landslide in 1964. In a town where unemployment had trebled in a year, the president said it was time to end the political games. "We can no longer posture and bicker and resort to the same failed ideas that got us into this mess in the first place—and that the American people rejected at the polls this past November," he said. "You didn't send us to Washington because you were hoping for more of the same. You sent us there with a mandate for change, and the expectation that we would act quickly and boldly to carry it out—and that is exactly what I intend to do as president of the United States."

If he could not win Republican votes, he could at least take on some Republican ideas. He could embody the change in politics he envisioned, not just by reaching out to the other party but also by compromising on his plans and cutting some pet spending projects. He would, through sheer force of will and salesmanship, reinvent himself as a better and bipartisan president—whether Republicans were with him or not.

Republicans, even favorable ones, found his strategy hard to comprehend. Lindsey Graham, the independent-minded Republican senator from South Carolina, took to the Senate floor to lament Obama's turn toward campaign rhetoric as his stimulus package struggled to reach the sixty votes needed to break a filibuster. "Please don't overestimate your ability to persuade people just because you're a gifted orator," Graham said. "What we've done is we've lost a young president's promise to change things." He sounded like the Clinton Democrats of the primary season: the ones who wished Obama were a little softer, a little easier to box into his own rhetoric.

In fact, there was always a compromise at the core of his promise of change. He made no secret of the fact that he was willing to bend his principles to get results, to drop ideology for pragmatism. What he personally believed was that a new kind of honest, people-powered politics would help bring about his policy goals. But it was the policy goals that mattered to him, not the style of politics.

In February 2008, not long after the Super Tuesday primaries, he explained the concept of "change" by checking off all the ways he wanted to fix the broken political system: to reduce the influence of special interests, increase voter participation, and cut through the spin and public relations. But then he explained what he really wanted. "Now, there's another aspect to this, and that's the need to change policies," he told me on one flight to Seattle in the dead of night. "Whether it's fixing our health care system or reversing climate change or making our schools work for all children or alleviating poverty. I have never been a good-government type that's interested in change just because it's somehow morally correct. I have a pretty hardheaded view why we have to make our democracy work. We can't bring about these changes without a more engaged citizenry, and a more accountable and transparent government that allows us to sort through our various differences. . . . It leads to better outcomes. It's often viewed incorrectly as pie in the sky, let's hold hands and sing 'Kumbaya,' let's leave alone the messy process of politics. But I'm not sanctimonious about this stuff. There are things that offend me. When I see Tom DeLay operating with complete impunity, or this White House manipulating the facts to advance its agenda, it can make me angry. But mostly this is a matter of how do you get stuff done."

And what if he failed to change politics? Would he inevitably disappoint his supporters? "That's too cynical," he said. "If the argument is that money is always going to have some influence in Washington, that politicians will always be more concerned with staying in office and maintaining their status, that men and women are flawed, evil, and sinful creatures, then yes, we haven't achieved heaven on earth. But the country was profoundly different as a consequence of John F. Kennedy. It's fair to say he helped to release the energy, that his presidency helped create the space for a whole generation to reimagine civil rights, to reimagine war, to think about America's relationship to the rest of the world, to start thinking about the role of women in society. I don't think there's any doubt that Ronald Reagan had a profound effect on our economy, on our politics, on our culture. That's what I thought was a pretty self-evident point that got the Clintons stirred up. I thought Bill Clinton brought about genuine change within the Democratic Party. It was a useful corrective to some of the excesses of identity politics and certain liberal dogmas in the way we approached the economy."

In the end, Obama preferred his legacy to be one of changing America rather than making politics pure. He just happened to believe that his best chance of changing the country was to change its politics along the way. If that didn't work, he could always win enough seats in Congress to get his way—as long as he did it in an agreeable manner. "If you've got a working majority, if the American people are behind you, then you can fear no man," he told one rally in Lebanon, New Hampshire, as he was still battling Hillary Clinton. "You can walk into a room with a sunny disposition. You can smile and say yes sir, no sir, yes ma'am and no ma'am. And if they don't agree with you, you've got the votes and you will beat them and you can do it with a smile on your face. That's how we're going to win an election. That's how we're going to bring change to this country. . . . We are happy warriors for change."

Did that make his bipartisanship phony? Or was he a liberal masquerading as a centrist? Both notions were indeed too cynical. His approach made him a pragmatic politician who could work with both sides, as long as there was some common ground. If there was no room for compromise, he would move ahead without them. He ultimately wanted to make the nation more progressive: with more support for those at the bottom of the economy, more health care coverage, better public schools, and a greener economy. "If you show him a moderate or conservative way to get something done and it was cheaper or more effective than the liberal way, he would do it—and would not hesitate to do it," said Robert Gibbs.

Obama's love of compromise led to some untenable positions. He signed strict ethics rules to prevent former officials from lobbying his administration and kept registered lobbyists out of his senior team. Yet he allowed a defense lobbyist to become his deputy defense secretary, and a banking lobbyist to become chief of staff at Treasury. He waved through Tim Geithner's tax problems at Treasury, yet failed to realize how he was weakening his own ethical image—and his future nominees. "There's a conflict and tension between changing the culture of Washington and building a government," said one senior Obama aide. "Experience in and of itself isn't bad. In fact, it's very useful in running a government." The tension was never fully resolved and the result was a poorly defined test for nominees, where relatively minor tax issues rose to the top of potential problems, ahead of influence peddling for big corporations.

The biggest casualty was his friend and mentor Tom Daschle. The former Senate leader was uniquely placed to work inside his administration and the halls of Congress to achieve universal health care, or something close to it. Daschle was not a lobbyist, but his earnings after losing his Senate seat suggested he worked in a gray area of political influence. He also suffered from tax problems like Geithner, and his problems emerged late in the process, in mid-December. There was no time to prepare the Senate for the revelations that he had enjoyed the use of a nominally free driver and limo. "It was either Daschle or Geithner who would go through," said one senior White House aide. "It was just a bad environment and a bad path going through the finance committee: the one part of the Senate that wasn't in love with him."

The White House was conflicted: many of Obama's longest-serving staff had links to Daschle, including Pete Rouse, who served as Senate chief of staff to both men. Others had no time for another Washington insider in the West Wing, never mind one with tax issues. When the president made a final call on Daschle's fate, there was little emotion involved. "He's prepared to make painful decisions when necessary," said one senior aide. In time, Daschle's crisis would look like a minor problem. "It's unfortunate for Daschle and I feel sorry for him," said Marty Nesbitt. "But six months out, it will look like a pimple on a gnat. I don't think the success of passing the health care plan is dependent on him."

Throughout the campaign, Obama's aides felt they needed to revive the renegade spirit whenever they grew too cautious or staid. Taking risks reminded them of the insurgent mood that created their organization and propelled them through two years of an election. "We were aware when we were playing it safe and we would catch ourselves and say, 'You know what? We're just being too cautious.' And you would go back to doing something differently," said Obama's leading pollster, Joel Benenson. "Maybe you would do the smaller town meetings, when you would take more questions from people. Maybe you're just doing different kinds of events. You roll the dice. You take a risk by the way you bail out of public financing and take the heat for that. It was a risky decision to play in some of the states we played in. The strategy was predicated on doing something differently, on defying conventional wisdom." The same dynamic played out in the early weeks of Obama's presidency: a veering between caution and risk. "The president's constant admonition is, 'Don't get too complacent. Don't get too conventional in your thinking,'" said David Axelrod.

In one area, Obama seemed to be ready to break with the conventional wisdom of the past immediately. He moved swiftly to demolish the foundations of President Bush's war on terror: ordering the closing of Guantánamo Bay and demanding plans for withdrawal from Iraq from his military leadership. But it was his tone with the Muslim world that was most striking for a candidate who shied away from most references to the religion during the general election. During the primaries he proposed a summit of Muslim leaders early in his presidency. "If I had a Muslim summit, I think that I can speak credibly to them about the fact that I respect their culture," he told me, "that I understand their religion, that I have lived in a Muslim country, and as a consequence I know it is possible to reconcile Islam with modernity and respect for human rights and a rejection of violence. And I think I can speak with added credibility."

He addressed the Muslim world in his inaugural address and continued the outreach in his very first television interview from the White House. He drew on his personal experience of living overseas—not to prove his qualifications for the job, but to prove his sincerity about diplomacy. "My job is to communicate the fact that the United States has a stake in the well-being of the Muslim world, that the language we use has to be a language of respect. I have Muslim members of my family. I have lived in Muslim countries," he told Al-Arabiya television. "My job is to communicate to the American people that the Muslim world is filled with extraordinary people who simply want to live their lives and see their children live better lives. My job to the Muslim world is to communicate that the Americans are not your enemy. We sometimes make mistakes. We have not been perfect." His tone represented a complete break from his predecessor's and from the politics of fear that had gripped the country in its wounded state after the attacks of 9/11.

Many of the ecstatic faces on the National Mall on January 20, 2009, wanted to witness the swearing-in of the first African American president. But the man himself was always leery of what that moment meant for the United States, even as he drew on the popular desire for such history to be written. The nation's deeply painful racial divide would never find a bridge in his election alone. "The impulse may be to write a piece that says Barack Obama represents a 'postracial politics.' That term I reject because it implies that somehow my campaign represents an easy shortcut to racial reconciliation," he told me just a few months after launching his bid for the presidency. "It's similar to the notion that if we're just all color-blind, somehow problems will be solved. I just want to be clear so there's no confusion . . . that solving our racial problems in this country will require concrete steps, significant investment. We have a lot of work to do to overcome the long legacy of slavery and Jim Crow. It can't be purchased on the cheap. I am fundamentally optimistic about our capacity to do that. And I do assert that there is a core decency in the American people and in white Americans that makes me hopeful about our ability to deal with these issues. But these issues aren't just solved by electing a black president."

So how would he start to deal with those issues? I wondered.

"I don't think that would be a particularly complicated task," he said. "As president I will go and visit some public schools right here in Anacostia and talk about the reading scores there. I think I can make that point very clear."

His first public school visit was not in Anacostia, but it did come early in his presidency. Less than two weeks after moving into the White House, he traveled with the First Lady along the eight-minute drive to Columbia Heights, one of the few truly diverse neighborhoods in the nation's capital. The Obamas were visiting Capital City Public Charter School, which is almost equally mixed between African American, Latino, and white children, and is more importantly mixed economically: more than half its students qualify for reduced-price lunch. The president read a book about Neil Armstrong's landing on the moon to a class of second graders, before asking what the students wanted to be when they grew up. One wanted to be an astronaut; others wanted to be a doctor or a sculptor. Another boy wanted to be president. "I think you might make it," the president said.

Maybe he couldn't deliver on the dream of racial harmony. But he could deliver on his personal dream to inspire children to work harder in school and aspire to greater goals for themselves. That was his vision when he decided to run for president. Even before he reached election day, his dream was becoming real. Over dinner with his close friends in the fall, Obama told how he had heard from a preschool teacher at an inner-city school that the children really responded to a few simple lines of encouragement: "Sit up like Barack Obama. Articulate your words like Barack Obama."

"That's a very powerful, fulfilling thing to hear," he told his friends. "The impact of this presidency could go far beyond whatever policy decisions I make. It could have a real positive social impact, even for very young kids." For a young man who had to find his own role models in the books he read; for a candidate who was the underdog for an entire year of campaigning; for a nominee by the name of Barack Hussein Obama, the notion that he was reaching schoolchildren whom he would never meet was like listening to the tale of the first man to land on the moon.

From their first days in office, Obama and his closest aides knew that their future—and quite possibly their place in history—would be defined by the economy. For all his grand ambitions about expanding health care and restoring America's place in the world, President Obama faced the simple, numerical judgment of the economic data. If the numbers bounced back, or seemed to be headed that way, he and his party could survive the midterm elections in 2010 and campaign for reelection from a strong base two years later. If not, the prospects were dismal. "Look, I'm at the start of my administration. One nice thing about the situation I find myself in is that I will be held accountable. I've got four years," he told NBC's Matt Lauer just before the Super Bowl game. "And, you know, a year from now I think people are going to see that we're starting to make some progress. But there's still going to be some pain out there. If I don't have this done in three years, then there's going to be a one-term proposition."

Well before he entered the White House, he knew how dire the economy was from extensive briefings that unemployment might rise into the double digits. Yet the scale of the challenge only seemed to lift his ambition even higher. "Did I want to throw the election at that point?" he quipped to me. "No, because, I mean, I said during the campaign and I've said subsequently, I actually think there is a convergence between what needs to be done in the short term and what needs to be done in the long term. I think we just showed that with the passage of the recovery act.

"The recovery act is not exactly how I would shape it. It was the product of navigating through 535 members of Congress who had very strong opinions themselves. But it reflects 85 to 90 percent of what I felt was needed, and embedded in it are a whole series of investments that lay the groundwork for progress on health care reform, energy independence, schools that work. And so I actually see this as a moment where we can move the trajectory of the country in a new direction."

Moving the trajectory of the country defined his ambition as president from his first days. It was just how he described Reagan's and Kennedy's legacies during the Nevada contest, in comments that annoyed former president Clinton so greatly. Even at the start of his presidential run, he used to cite Martin Luther King's comment that the arc of the moral universe was long, but it bent toward justice. He urged voters to put their hand on the arc and bend it themselves. And on his victory night in Grant Park, he praised his supporters and voters, who decided to "put their hands on the arc of history and bend it once more toward the hope of a better day."

Now, as president, he was putting his own hands on the arc of history. He enjoyed the scale of the challenges, which looked even more insurmountable than winning a presidential election as a freshman senator with a funny name and no money. "He was made for this job," said Valerie Jarrett. "I think this is the first time in his life that he has been challenged to this degree and thrived. This is a brain that needs to be exercised and he is finally getting a good workout. It's one explanation for why he's so happy now, and why he was always so restless before. He wants to have as great an understanding as everyone in the room, and really apply himself."

He shifted his reading list from nonfiction narratives to dry academic studies. "You know, I am actually spending an awful lot of time reading books on very specific subject matter," he told me. "Like the world financial system. I spend a lot of time reading about that. Or, you know, historical analyses of Afghanistan." He still drew on his old favorites for inspiration, but they sounded like distant reminders more than new sources of insight. "I do still use Lincoln's writings as a touchstone," he told me. "Emerson's writings. Niebuhr."

In the depths of crisis, he had the opportunity to do something more positive than rebel against the system: he could remake much of it entirely. He could rebuild some of the nation's biggest institutions—its financial sector, its health care system, its energy supply, and its schools and aim for more change than he ever thought possible. "Do I wish that a bunch of this money wasn't going into shoring up the banking system, with very little long-term payoff, beyond stopping the bleeding? Absolutely," he told me. "But I do think that it, in a larger sense, has been a wake up call to the country that we have to deal with some of these bigger issues, and it's not just the stock market or a housing bubble that led to our current problems.

"It's interesting. We had a meeting this morning . . . with our economic folks, who made an important point, which is that part of the problem here was not just a faulty financial regulatory system. Part of the problem had to do with huge trade imbalances, the capital that China and the Saudis and Japan were amassing as a consequence of us being dependent on foreign oil, an eroding manufacturing base, et cetera; then trying to find places to go, which leads them into a whole bunch of speculation and helps to create these bubbles. And so in that sense there are some underlying fundamentals that needed to be dealt with to prevent this cycle of bubble and bust, even if you had strong financial regulatory systems in place."

There was something radical about wanting to take the country back to the roots of its problems; something renegade about spending historic amounts of money in his first few months in office. Yet he could only have reached the seat inside the Oval Office with the self-discipline of some of his greatest heroes: King, or Gandhi, or even Malcolm X.

The balance between changing the world and running it was one that he had been searching for throughout the campaign and his political career. He discovered it late in the presidential campaign, as the financial system collapsed, and he loved it far more than the election itself.

"I enjoyed the fact that you had very clear substantive problems that took us out of the ordinary day-to-day political cycle," he told me. "And as president, I very much enjoy the intellectual challenge of figuring out how to get the country back on track."

His personal challenge was to be Renegade in more than just his Secret Service code name. He needed to change the nation before the nation's capital changed him; to lead in his own unconventional style, not to follow the familiar path of presidents past; to bend the arc of history before unseen hands wrested it from his grasp.

AFTERWORD

I never intended to write these words.

Covering the candidate was an extraordinary experience, and his campaign was clearly historic. I was one of a small handful of reporters to have a front-row seat from the very beginning: from his announcement in Springfield, to a summer and winter in Iowa, through the white-knuckle ride of the primaries and the heavyweight contest of the general. Early on, I thought he was likely to win his party's nomination and probably the presidency.

But a book? I wasn't convinced.

The candidate himself had a different plan in mind. It was two days after his speech on race in Philadelphia, and I had just finished interviewing him for a biographical story about Indonesia, his college years, and his youthful struggle with his own identity. I explained that his story was still largely unknown, even though he had written a bestselling memoir. "People want to know who you are," I said. "Who are you? That's the question people are going to ask six months from now and six years from now."

"You're absolutely right," he said, humoring me before engaging in what sounded like a little wishful thinking. "If I wasn't in this campaign, I would love to follow this election as an observer," he mused. "Why can't you write a book about it? Like Theodore White. Those are great books."

There's too much coverage, I said dismissively. People are consuming everything about the election. It's very hard to write something after the election. Besides, I said, publishers want partisan screeds nowadays. They don't want reporting.

The candidate looked crestfallen. "There *is* too much media," he said, recalibrating yet another dream about running for president. "I guess people are following too much of it."

Teddy White. How archaic. The poor man doesn't understand the media, I thought, as I walked back to my seat.

Still, I was intrigued by his wanting to observe the election at the same time as being its focus of attention. It sounded like one of his out-of-body maneuvers, a strategy for staying cool and detached while those around him were so overwrought. He was, of course, a wildly successful book author himself. And he understood the power of the writer and narrator to shape a story and perceptions. Maybe he wanted to write his own Teddy White story at some point. Or maybe he just wanted to read a Teddy White version of his own campaign. Either way, he was surely trying to nudge me into his own game plan.

In hindsight, the conversation sounded like a story his friend Marty Nesbitt had told me about a get-together at his home one night. Obama casually told Nesbitt and a few other friends that he wanted to run for the United States Senate, and they all laughed. It was only two years since he lost his congressional race against Bobby Rush, and their first reaction was to think he was ridiculous—until they heard him explain his strategy for winning. "He was prepared for this meeting. We weren't prepared for it," Marty told me. "He's always *way* ahead of you. Like he told you that you should write a book. He's way ahead of you on that. He's thought it all the way through. He's so *smooth* that he does it in a way that you think he hasn't thought it all the way through. But he has."

Just before he floated the idea about a book, the candidate asked me about my background. I told my family story in brief: how my mother was Moroccan and my father was British, a rare combination where I had grown up in England. For those who didn't know me, my Mediterranean complexion marked me out as different in a big city where brown meant Pakistani and black meant Caribbean.

"So they thought you were a Paki?" he asked, using the British term of abuse.

If they were being polite, I explained. If not, they added a few words of Anglo-Saxon for good measure. If they tried to be clever, they called me a half-caste, which I always found too Victorian to be truly offensive. Unlike the anti-Semitic insults, which hurt. Many of my friends found it alien and unsettling that I was Jewish. And even to my Jewish friends, I was an unusual mix of North African, or Sephardi, culture and the dominant Eastern European, or Ashkenazi, tradition.

In truth, what I faced was mild compared with the violence and hopelessness endured by the Asian and African Caribbean communities I grew up with. But I still felt the sting of insults hurled across a bus or in the street, on the soccer field or in a school hallway. I burned as friends or teachers or coaches spat out something racist in anger or jest, whether directed at me or another student.

Despite the vast gap in distance and culture, perhaps there were echoes in the experience of one of the few African American students in an elite Hawaiian high school.

"What you and I share is the ability to cross lines," he said.

We also shared a love of basketball. I never dreamed of being a professional player, as he had. But I had spent every spare hour in middle and high school shooting hoops at lunch and after school. And like him, my teenage game was good enough to let me scrape together a few minutes on court, or sit on the bench, while better players won the biggest trophies.

By this time, we had played a few times on primary days, and he had studied my limited game. When he walked back to talk to the rest of the press corps, they were curious to hear his assessment. "Richard has a good shot, but his drive leaves something to be desired," he said diplomatically. It's true, my drive sucked, but I salvaged my dignity by hitting my outside shots.

In our first game in Columbia, South Carolina, he was a little less tactful. "What's up with those layups?" he asked out loud.

I had noticed that his jump shot didn't have much lift to it, so it was time to hit back. "Hey, I can jump as high as you," I said.

"He's trash-talking me!" he said to his aides and Secret Service agents.

"I grew up on the mean streets, too, you know," I said. "They have them in England."

Two months after our Teddy White conversation, I finally figured out that he might be right. There wasn't just a book in this election; there was a vital story that could only be told by someone who was there to witness it firsthand.

"That idea of writing a book," I told him onboard the campaign plane as we flew out of Montana. "I think it's a good one."

"That's why I'm running for president," he replied with his broad grin. "Because I have good ideas."

I suggested that we should talk regularly to get some real-time insight into his experience of the campaign. "I will give you access. You'll get more access than anyone else," he explained. "The only problem is that I intend to win. So I have to be careful. I can't tell you what I really feel about some people. And then what happens if there isn't that much drama? What happens if we just had a plan and then went out and said, Let's execute it?"

A book was circulating onboard the plane about Bobby Kennedy's presidential run: Bill Eppridge's book of intimate photos, *A Time It Was.* Obama started flipping through the pictures, lingering at the scenes of a crowded stadium or the candidate in a diner. "That looks familiar," he said about one frame of some screaming fans. It was all too familiar, except for the fashion and the lack of security. The candidate's convertible Cadillac was only protected by a half-dozen people sitting on the back of it, in the open air, as they drove down a California freeway. Scout Tufankjian, a young freelance photographer who had also covered Obama from the start in Iowa, pointed out how close Eppridge was to the candidate, taking a photo of RFK curled up asleep on the floor of his plane. "Look at all that access!" she said.

"Yes, but it didn't end too well, did it?" Obama noted dryly.

Kennedy had no protection except for a single bodyguard whose job involved holding the candidate when the crowd tried to pull him away. I asked Obama about his Secret Service agents, and how he seemed to have bonded with them. He said he just tried to treat them like normal people. "I invited them into my home for Thanksgiving," he said. "It's Thanksgiving and they are away from their families. But they told me nobody had ever told them to come in and eat. Nobody treats them with respect."

Michelle had once told me that their daughter Sasha talked about the agents as "the secret people." Had they grown comfortable with the Service by now, after a year of their protection?

"They are very cool about it, very levelheaded," he said, softening his tone. He explained how they had adjusted effortlessly to the whole circus of the election. "You know, they have had maybe two tantrums in all their lives. They never play up or act up in any situation. They just take it in their stride. It's a testimony to how light a touch Michelle has. They do what she says. They are terrified of her without her ever saying or doing anything. Malia especially is very calm. She has a writer's sensibility. She has that sense of excitement that everything is new. She just wants to experience everything. I hope she never loses that."

Then he recounted what he had seen as he flew into Montana and traveled in his motorcade to Crow Agency, the home of the Apsaalooke tribe, sixty miles from the dull concrete blocks of Billings. It reminded him of the wonder he had felt when he traveled across the country with his mother and grandmother three decades earlier, visiting the continental United States for the first time, as a boy not much older than Malia. "Flying into Missoula or driving as we did today, you can go for an hour and see maybe one person," he said, sounding like someone who felt everything was new.

There are rare times when a whole country—and perhaps much of the world—wants to feel that same sense of excitement, to experience everything anew in politics or in their own community. This election was one of those moments, which return once in a generation. When strangers would walk up to share a personal story about their newfound activism, or their emotional response to the candidate, or their hopes for the election. It was a time when the candidate could correctly say the election was so much bigger than himself, even as his humility helped to motivate his fans and deflate the personal pressure.

I make no apologies for my close observations of the candidate, his inner circle, or the wider campaign. This election was too important to cover from a distance, and this candidate was too new and too complex to scrutinize from the comfort of an office. Given the decline of print media and the rise of the Web, there are many journalists who claim they can happily cover a campaign by phone and e-mail, beating the girls and the boys on the bus by several minutes to yet another blog post. That's true: they can indeed shave minutes off a Web item. I hope this book is a slow-food alternative to that fast and fried diet.

My job was neither to lift up the candidate nor to tear him down. It was to probe and challenge, to inquire and investigate, to observe and analyze, to explore and explain. Others will write comprehensive volumes about the rest of the field, or inside accounts of the Obama campaign, or anti-Obama rants. This is the story of what I covered as a magazine reporter and what I uncovered as an author.

As I write, I can hear the president's helicopters readying to take him to Camp David for the first time. They swoop overhead as decoys or the real thing. All you can see are the dark green underbellies and the sun glancing off their bright white tops. All you can hear is the throbbing beat of the blades, as they fade toward the Catoctin Mountain, leaving the sounds of a sunny Saturday afternoon: the squeaking of a seesaw that needs oiling, the spring of a hoop as a basketball drops from its arc and bounces away.

ACKNOWLEDGMENTS

Life on the road is an exhilarating, grinding, and depressing experience. I spent the best part of a year inside campaign planes, buses, and hotels, and could have survived none of it without the friendship and support of so many people on the road and back home. Without them, there would have been no *Renegade*, and no sanity.

For all that and more, I'm deeply grateful to Charles Ommanney, whose picture graces this book jacket, and who is quite simply the most talented photographer I have ever worked with; Shailagh Murray and Jeff Zeleny, two of the very best and hardest-working reporters in newspapers, whose writing is infused with intelligence and generosity; Michele Norris and Broderick Johnson, who are true friends and exceptional parents; Tichi Fernandez de la Cruz and José Andrés, my adopted sister and brother. Michele, Shailagh, and Jeff kindly read the manuscript of this book and made invaluable contributions to improve it.

This book is built on the thoughts and stories of many of its central characters and dozens of others associated with the candidate and his campaign. Above all, Barack Obama gave his time expansively, shared his thoughts freely, and planted the seeds of this book. Just as vital was his O-Team: Michelle Obama, David Axelrod, Robert Gibbs, Valerie Jarrett, Marty Nesbitt, David Plouffe, Pete Rouse, and Eric Whitaker. In many ways this book is the result of a rolling conversation with them, and I am greatly indebted to them all.

On the road, there were so many talented professionals who rarely receive thanks or acknowledgment, but whose work was critical to my writing and peace of mind. I cannot thank enough Linda Douglass, Ben Finkenbinder, Katie Hogan, Eric Lesser, Katie Lillie, Reggie Love, Marvin Nicholson, Jen Psaki, and Samantha Tubman.

I am grateful to all the policy wonks and consultants who politely ignored my stupid questions and chose instead to deepen my insight: Cornell Belcher, Joel Benenson, Greg Craig, John Del Cecato, Anita Dunn, Phil Gordon, Scott Gration, Larry Grisolano, Karen Kornbluh, Mark Lippert, Denis McDonough, Jim Margolis, Susan Rice, and Mike Strautmanis. And I am lucky to have known some of the people behind the fund-raising numbers: Leonore Blitz, Howard Gutman, Cathy Konrad and James Mangold, Susan Tolson and Charlie Rivkin, Wendy Wanderman and Mark Gorenberg.

My fellow traveling inmates made captivity seem almost fun. To all the TV embeds and TV crews, photogs, scribblers, and aircrews—you know who you are and how much we all leaned on one another. I would need neither Blue Moon nor cheese plate to step on another plane with Lee Cowan, Candy Crowley, Julianna Goldman, Mark Hudspeth, John McCormick, Nedra Pickler, Amy Rice, Mike Roselli, Alicia Sams, and our very own Dorothy Parker in red cowboy boots, Maureen Dowd.

My thanks to those who toiled at campaign headquarters, where it all came together: Bill Burton, Reid Cherlin, Stephanie Cutter, Josh Earnest, Jon Favreau, Katie Johnson, Ben LaBolt, Wendy Morigi, Dan Pfeiffer, Ben Rhodes, Nick Shapiro, Tommy Vietor, and Team MO—Kristen Jarvis, Katie McCormick Lelyveld, and Melissa Winter. And my thanks to those who built their field of dreams in Iowa, where it all began: Monica and Gordon Fischer, Steve Hildebrand, Tom Miller, Jackie Norris, Paul Tewes, and Peter Weeks.

A special thanks to those who shared their time and insight from the Clinton campaign: Jay Carson, Mandy Grunwald, Jamie Smith, and Howard Wolfson. And also to those inside and outside the Bush White House whose opinions and expertise I greatly respect: Dan Bartlett, Tony Fratto, Mark McKinnon, and Dana Perino.

To my surrogate family at MSNBC, it is a privilege to be part of your journalism. For your talent and courage, your good humor and support,

I thank you: Keith Olbermann, Izzy Povich, Gregg Cockrell, Katy Ramirez, Amy Shuster, Rich Stockman, Tory Wegerski, and the entire *Countdown* team; the deciders Phil Griffin and Mark Whitaker; the consummate professionals at *Meet the Press,* especially David Gregory, Betsy Fischer, and Shelby Poduch; Chris Matthews and the *Hardball* team; David Shuster and the *1600* team; Andrea Mitchell, Norah O'Donnell, Chuck Todd, Adam Verdugo, and the whole crew that keeps the dayside trucking at 30 Rock.

I would like to thank all my many friends at *Newsweek:* for all they taught me about reporting and writing over my six years at the magazine, and especially for allowing me to cover the campaign. I will always appreciate their support, good humor, and great skill.

Back home in Washington, I could never have embarked on the campaign or this book without the warmth and support of these friends: Randy Crowley, Julie Diaz-Asper and Tom Young, Nathalie Goldfarb and José Bassat, Jamie and Edward Hull, Gwen Ifill, Sarah Jessup and James Bennet, Cindy and Todd Klein, Karen Kornbluh and Jim Halpert, Anne Kornblut and Jon Cohen, Analia Porras and Charlie Bruetman, Susan Rice and Ian Cameron, Katharine Weymouth, Beth Wilkinson and David Gregory, Pary Williamson.

This book would never have appeared, never moved beyond an initial concept, without the enthusiasm and brilliance of Kris Dahl at ICM. I am truly grateful for her patience in listening to all my bad ideas, her belief in my abilities and my work, her honesty and her spirit. I am honored that she is my friend.

In Sean Desmond at Crown, I could not have dreamed of a better editor. His judgment is pitch-perfect, his direction is finely calibrated, and his vision is true. It has been a delight to work closely with him, as well as Stephanie Chan, Kelly Gildea, and Campbell Wharton. I am especially grateful to Tina Constable and Rachel Klayman for trusting me to deliver.

Acknowledgment does not come close to enough thanks for the Wolffes and Cuellos. To my parents, I am forever proud of all you have achieved, and forever the son you raised with love. To Martha and Claudio, I am incredibly fortunate to be part of your family and eternally grateful that you entrusted your daughter to me.

There is nothing I can write that could fill the gap of my absence, compensate for my distraction and self-absorption, or return the love of Paula, Ilana, Ben, and Max. These words were written with their laughter and strength, their ideas and dreams, their hunger for learning and hopes for the world, their kisses, tears, and tickles. To my wonderful monkeys: you teach me to open my eyes anew and open my arms for big hugs. To my wonderful Paula: you teach me what it is to love, to parent, to come home. For all your selflessness and sustenance—for all the manic mornings, long weekends, and empty evenings—I dedicate this book to you.

SOURCE NOTES

CHANGE

This chapter is based on my contemporaneous notes of the last forty-eight hours of the election, my contemporaneous notes of 2/15/07, and exclusive interviews with the following people: Barack Obama (11/4/08), David Axelrod (11/3/08, 11/4/08, 11/6/08), Reggie Love (11/4/08), Valerie Jarrett (11/6/08), Marty Nesbitt (11/6/08), Eric Whitaker (11/4/08), Wendy Wanderman (11/4/08).

I also drew on the following published sources: Lawrence K. Altman and Jeff Zeleny, "Obama's Doctor, Praising His Health, Sees No Obstacles to Service," *New York Times*, 5/30/08; transcript of the ABC Democratic primary debate, 4/16/08; David Katz's photographs for the Obama campaign, 11/4/08.

THE DECIDER

This chapter is based on exclusive interviews with the following people: Barack Obama (2/9/08, 3/4/08, 3/20/08, 6/20/08, 7/10/08), Michelle Obama (6/22/07, 2/12/08), Marty Nesbitt (7/11/08), David Plouffe (7/11/08), Maya Soetoro-Ng (6/29/07, 7/5/08), Eric Whitaker (7/11/08), Neil Abercrombie (8/14/08), Marian Robinson (2/12/08), Craig Robinson (6/27/08), Pete Rouse (8/1/08), Steve Hildebrand (7/11/08), David Axelrod (6/30/08, 7/15/08), Valerie Jarrett (7/11/08), Tom Daschle (8/15/08). It also relies on my contemporaneous notes of Michelle Obama on the campaign trail (6/22/07, 2/12/08) and a reader's letter to *Newsweek* (5/19/08).

I drew on Barack Obama's two books as follows: *The Audacity of Hope* (Crown, 2006: pp. 3, 5, 29–30, 66–67, 202–3, 205–6, 223, 225, 273, 275–76, 328, 329, 330, 331–32, 340, 354, 361); *Dreams from My Father* (Three Rivers Press, 2004: pp. xii, 5, 9, 11, 14–15, 16, 21, 22, 42–45, 47–48, 50–51, 54, 56, 75, 76, 85, 86, 121, 123, 126, 133, 211, 213–17, 397, 400–401, 407, 418, 420–22, 423). The chapter also refers to his speech to the Chicago Council on Global Affairs (11/22/05) and his statement on Hurricane Katrina relief efforts (9/6/05).

The following published sources were also invaluable: Janny Scott, "The Free-Spirited Wanderer Who Shaped Obama's Path," *New York Times*, 3/14/08; Mariana Cook, "A Couple in Chicago," *New Yorker*, 1/19/09; Richard Wolffe with Sarah Kliff, Karen Springen, and Roxana Popescu, "Barack's Rock," *Newsweek*, 2/25/08; Holly Yeager, "The Heart & Mind of Michelle Obama," *O, the Oprah Magazine*, 11/1/07; Scott Bauer, "Obama Leads Rally, Headlines Speech to Nebraska Democrats," Associated Press, 5/7/06; David Mendell, *Obama: From Promise to Power* (Amistad, 2007: pp. 307, 359, 373–74); Anne E. Kornblut, "For This Red Meat Crowd, Obama's '08 Choice Is Clear," *New York Times*, 9/18/06; and an NBC News transcript of *Meet the Press*, 10/22/06.

THREE
RULES FOR RADICALS

This chapter is based on exclusive interviews with the following people: Michelle and Barack Obama (1/2/08), Michelle Obama (6/22/07), Barack Obama (2/9/08, 9/18/08), Jerry Kellman (10/8/08), Jon Favreau (1/5/08, 10/8/08), a senior Obama aide who asked to remain anonymous, David Plouffe (9/30/07, 11/1/07, 5/6/08, 7/11/08, 10/10/08, 11/29/08), Steve Hildebrand (7/11/08), Paul Tewes (6/11/08, 12/1/08), Penny Pritzker (10/9/08), a Clinton friend who asked to remain anonymous, David Axelrod (6/30/08, 9/16/08), Tommy Vietor (10/8/08), a senior Clinton aide who asked to remain anonymous, Robert Gibbs (9/26/08), Marty Nesbitt (10/9/08), Valerie Jarrett (10/9/08).

The chapter relies on my contemporaneous notes of campaign events on 2/10/07, 7/2/07, 7/3/07, 7/4/07, 10/2/07, 10/4/07, 11/10/07, 12/8/07, 12/23/07, 12/27/07, 1/1/08, 2/21/08.

I also drew on these published sources: Saul Alinsky, *Rules for Radicals: A Pragmatic Primer for Realistic Radicals* (Vintage, 1989: pp. 12–13, 24); a photograph of Obama during his community-organizing days from his campaign website; a transcript of the *Rush Limbaugh Show*, "The Obama-Alinsky Connection," 8/26/08; Peter Slevin, "For Clinton and Obama, a Common Ideological Touchstone," *Washington Post*, 3/25/07; a transcript of Rudy Giuliani's speech at the Republican convention, 9/3/08; a transcript of Sarah Palin's speech at the Republican convention, 9/3/08; Barack Obama, *Dreams from My Father* (Three Rivers Press, 2004: pp. 133, 134, 139, 142, 146–50, 155, 162–63, 190, 223–26); "Where Is Barack Obama Coming From," Larissa MacFarquhar, *New Yorker*, 5/7/07; Nancy Benac, "Obama, McCain: By Their Offices Ye Shall Know Them," Associated Press, 8/11/08; Ashish Kumar Sen, "I Am Reluctant to Seek Changes to the N-Deal," *Outlook*, 7/21/08; Matthew Mosk, "The $75 Million Woman," *Washington Post*, 10/8/07; Jim Kuhnhenn, "Obama Raises at Least 32.5 Million, Leads Democrats in Fundraising," Associated Press, 7/1/07; Clinton campaign memo by Mike Henry, 5/21/07, published by the *New York Times*, 5/23/07; John McCormick and Mike Dorning, "Obama Gains $19 Million," *Chicago Tribune*, 10/2/07; ABC News/Washington Post poll, 10/3/07; Martin Luther King Jr., edited by James M. Washington, *I Have a Dream: Writings and Speeches That Changed the World* (Harper San Francisco, 1992: p. 151).

FOUR
FAILURE

This chapter is based on exclusive interviews with the following people: Barack Obama (1/2/08, 1/4/08, 9/18/08), David Plouffe (7/11/08, 10/10/08), Marty Nesbitt (7/11/08, 10/9/08), David Axelrod (1/6/08, 1/18/08, 5/8/08, 10/8/08, 12/11/08, 12/15/08), Tim Russert (1/7/08), Pete Rouse (10/9/08), Valerie Jarrett (6/30/08,

7/11/08, 10/9/08), Jon Favreau (10/8/08), Tommy Vietor (10/8/08), Bill Burton (12/15/08), Robert Gibbs (7/25/07, 10/30/08), Mark Gorenberg (11/5/08), Penny Pritzker (10/9/08).

The chapter relies on my contemporaneous notes of campaign events on 1/3/08, 1/4/08, 1/5/08, 1/6/08, 1/7/08, 1/8/08, 1/14/08, 1/19/08, 10/16/08, as well as my notes of the Dean campaign in the week of 1/20/04.

I drew on these published sources: transcript of *NBC Nightly News*, 1/7/08; transcript of ABC's *Good Morning America*, 1/7/08; Kate Snow, "Clinton Gets Emotional on Campaign Trail," ABC News Political Radar, 1/7/08; transcript of ABC News New Hampshire debate, 1/5/08; Barack Obama, *Dreams from My Father* (Three Rivers Press, 2004: p. 86); David Mendell, *Obama: From Promise to Power* (Amistad, 2007: pp. 128–33, 143–47); *The Autobiography of Malcolm X*, as told to Alex Haley (One World, 1999: p. 313); Barack Obama, *The Audacity of Hope* (Crown, 2006: pp. 106, 340); Daren Briscoe, "An Interview with Barack Obama," *Newsweek*, 1/12/09; transcript of MSNBC debate in Orangeburg, South Carolina, 4/27/07; Obama campaign press release, 6/7/07; Mike Glover, "Obama Calls Memo 'Dumb Mistake,'" Associated Press, 6/19/07; Adam Nagourney, "For Democrats, Primary Field Offers Reasons for Confidence," *New York Times*, 9/4/07; transcript of Joe Biden speech, Center for U.S. Global Engagement, 7/15/08.

I also gained valuable insight listening to Howard Wolfson speak at the Institute of Politics at the Kennedy School of Government, Harvard University, 12/12/08.

FIVE

BARACK X

This chapter is based on exclusive interviews with the following people: Barack Obama (6/27/07, 7/4/07, 3/4/08, 3/20/08, 5/6/08, 5/19/08, 7/10/08, 9/18/08), Michelle Obama (6/22/07), Cornel West (6/27/07), Maya Soetoro-Ng (6/27/07, 2/29/08, 7/3/08), Kathryn Takara (8/13/08), Bettylu Saltzman (6/20/07), Jerry Kellman (10/8/08), David Axelrod (2/27/08, 3/18/08, 12/5/08), Craig Robinson (6/27/07), Valerie Jarrett (6/30/08, 10/9/08), Bill Burton (3/7/08), Pete Rouse (11/26/08), Marty Nesbitt (10/9/08), David Plouffe (10/10/08), Eric Whitaker (5/4/08), Robert Gibbs (3/4/09).

The chapter relies on my contemporaneous notes of campaign events on 6/23/07, 7/3/07, 1/14/08, 1/21/08, 1/24/08, 1/26/08, 1/27/08, 2/12/08, 2/20/08, 3/18/08, 4/16/08, 5/5/08, 5/6/08.

I drew on Barack Obama's two books as follows: *Dreams from My Father* (Three Rivers Press, 2004: pp. 76, 77, 86, 89, 90–91, 123–24, 134–35, 274, 281–82, 284, 285, 294, 376, 429–30); *The Audacity of Hope* (Crown, 2006: p. 216). The chapter also refers to his speech to the Democratic National Convention, Boston, 7/27/04; his announcement speech in Springfield, Illinois, 2/10/07; his speech at Brown Chapel AME Church, 3/4/07. It also refers to Michelle Obama's speech in Orangeburg, South Carolina, 11/20/07.

I drew on these published sources: Alison and Frank Bruni, "McCain and Bush Revving Up Their Campaigns," *New York Times*, 2/3/00; Mark Penn's weekly strategic review, 3/19/07, published with Joshua Green, "The Front-Runner's Fall," *Atlantic*, 9/1/08; "State of Black America [sic]," C-SPAN, 2/10/07; "Black Support Helps Clinton Extend Lead," CNN.com, 10/17/07; Janny Scott, "The Story of Obama, Written by Obama," *New York Times*, 5/18/08; David Mendell, *Obama: From Promise to Power* (Amistad, 2007: pp. 125–26); Richard Wolffe and Daren Briscoe, "Across the Divide," *Newsweek*, 7/16/07; Ted Kleine, "Is Bobby Rush in Trouble?" *Chicago Reader*, 3/10/00; "Letter from a Birmingham Jail, 1963," in Martin Luther King Jr., edited by James M. Washington, *I Have a Dream: Writings and Speeches That Changed the World* (Harper San Francisco, 1992: pp. 87–88); Sarah Wheaton, "Clinton's Civil Rights Lesson," *New York*

Times, 1/7/08; Kate Phillips, '"The Clinton Camp Unbound," *New York Times,* 1/8/08; Katharine Q. Seelye, "BET Founder Slams Obama in South Carolina," *New York Times,* 1/13/08; Carl Hulse, "Civil Rights Tone Prompts Talk of an Endorsement," *New York Times,* 1/11/08; "Black Leader to Bill Clinton: 'Chill' on Obama," CNN.com, 1/21/08; transcript of the Democratic debate sponsored by CNN and the Congressional Black Caucus, Myrtle Beach, South Carolina, 1/21/08; Dick Morris, "How Clinton Will Win the Nomination by Losing South Carolina," Real Clear Politics, 1/23/08; Mason-Dixon poll, 1/22–23/08; Ron Fournier, "On Deadline," Associated Press, 1/25/08; Brian Ross and Rehab El-Buri, "Obama's Pastor: God Damn America, U.S. to Blame for 9/11," ABCNews.com, 3/13/08; *The Autobiography of Malcolm X,* as told to Alex Haley (One World, 1999: p. 442); "Obama's Minister of Hate," *New York Post,* 3/14/08; "Preacher with a Penchant for Controversy," *Washington Post,* 3/15/08; Katharine Q. Seelye and Julie Bosman, "Ferraro's Obama Remarks Become Talk of Campaign," *New York Times,* 3/12/08; "No Claims of Perfection," *Chicago Tribune,* 3/16/08; "On My Faith and My Church, by Barack Obama," Huffington Post, 3/14/08; Ben Wallace-Wells, "Destiny's Child," *Rolling Stone,* 2/22/08; Jodi Kantor, "Disinvitation by Obama Is Criticized," *New York Times,* 3/6/07; Daren Briscoe, "An Interview with Barack Obama," *Newsweek,* 1/12/09; James Cone, *Black Theology and Black Power* (Orbis, 1997: p. viii); William Shakespeare, *Hamlet,* act I, scene iii; Ron Fournier, "On Deadline: Why Obama Can't Close Deal," Associated Press, 4/22/08; Evan Thomas, "A Memo to Senator Obama," *Newsweek,* 6/2/08; CBS News Poll, 6/4/08; Washington Post/ABC News poll, 5/11/08; "Reverend Wright at the National Press Club," *New York Times,* 4/28/08; Jeff Zeleny and Adam Nagourney, "An Angry Obama Renounces Ties to His Ex-Pastor," 4/30/08.

I also gained valuable insight listening to David Plouffe and David Axelrod speak at the Institute of Politics, Kennedy School of Government, Harvard University, 12/11/08.

SIX
GAME CHANGER

This chapter is based on exclusive interviews with the following people: Barack Obama (6/27/07, 1/2/08, 1/4/08, 2/5/08, 2/9/08, 6/3/08, 6/20/08, 7/25/08, 8/28/08, 9/18/08), Michelle Obama (2/12/08, 8/29/08), Craig Robinson (6/27/07), Marty Nesbitt (7/11/08, 10/9/08), Jon Favreau (8/28/08, 10/8/08), David Plouffe (7/11/08, 10/10/08, 10/26/08), Pete Rouse (10/9/08, 11/26/08, 12/7/08), David Axelrod (1/20/08, 2/4/08, 2/26/08, 8/16/08, 8/28/08, 9/16/08, 10/8/08), Tom Daschle (1/24/08), Paul Tewes (12/1/08), Robert Gibbs (8/23/08, 8/28/08, 9/26/08), Valerie Jarrett (10/9/08), an Obama friend who asked to remain anonymous, five interviews with senior Obama aides who asked to remain anonymous, Susie Tompkins Buell (8/25/08), Ed Rendell (6/16/08), Jamie Smith (6/27/08), Linda Douglass (9/26/08, 11/1/08), Penny Pritzker (10/9/08), Tommy Vietor (10/8/08), Jim Margolis (8/28/08, 2/6/09), Joel Benenson (11/24/08).

The chapter relies on my contemporaneous notes of campaign events on 12/27/07, 1/2/08, 1/8/08, 1/14/08, 1/23/08, 1/26/08, 1/29/08, 2/5/08, 3/4/08, 4/28/08, 4/29/08, 6/3/08, 6/5/08, 6/27/08, 8/23/08, 8/28/08, 9/10/08.

I drew on these published sources: Barack Obama, *Dreams from My Father* (Three Rivers Press, 2004: pp. 78–79, 80); "Obama Favorites," *Chicago Tribune,* 11/14/08; transcript of *Hardball with Chris Matthews,* MSNBC, 9/26/07; Richard Wolffe, "Inside Obama's Dream Machine," *Newsweek,* 1/14/08; Maureen Dowd, "She's Not Buttering Him Up," *New York Times,* 4/25/08; Barack Obama, *The Audacity of Hope* (Crown, 2006: p. 211); transcript of ABC Democratic debate, 8/19/07; Adam Nagourney and Jeff Zeleny, "Obama Promises a Forceful Stand Against Clinton," *New York Times,* 10/28/07; transcript of MSNBC debate at Drexel University, Philadelphia, 10/30/07;

cartoon by Mike Luckovich in the *Atlanta Journal-Constitution*, 10/31/07; Alec MacGillis, "Clinton N.H. Official Resigns After Comments on Obama," *Washington Post*, 12/13/07; "Interview with Barack Obama," *Newsweek*, 11/3/08; Maureen Dowd, "There Will Be Blood," *New York Times*, 2/3/08; ABCNews.com video of Bill Clinton, Dartmouth College, 1/7/08; interview of Barack Obama by the *Reno Gazette-Journal* editorial board, 1/14/08; Mark Murray, "First Read: Bill Also Hits Obama on GOP Ideas," MSNBC.com, 1/18/08; Mark Murray, "First Read: Bill vs. Obama Continued in Buffalo," MSNBC.com, 1/21/08; Nedra Pickler, "Edwards, Clinton, Critical of Obama," Associated Press, 1/18/08; Sunlen Miller, "Political Radar: Is Bill Clinton Getting in Obama's Head," ABCNews.com, 1/22/08; transcript of John Kerry's speech, Myrtle Beach, South Carolina, 1/10/08; transcript of Ted Kennedy's speech, American University, Washington, D.C., 1/28/08; Eloise Harper and Sunlen Miller, "Political Radar: Clinton and 'The Fun Part,'" ABCNews.com, 12/7/07; "Obama's Mailings 'False'?" Factcheck.org, 2/24/08; "Clinton, Obama Exchange Attacks on Campaign Tactics," *Online NewsHour*, 2/25/08; Frank James, "At SOTU, Obama's Clinton Snub Was the News," *Chicago Tribune*, 1/28/08; transcript of Hillary Clinton's speech, *Online NewsHour*, 6/3/08; "Obama, Clinton Hold Talks in Feinstein's Living Room," CNN.com, 6/6/08; Patrick Healy, "Obama Donors Aren't Rushing to Aid Clinton," *New York Times*, 7/9/08; Federal Election Commission letter to Obama campaign lawyers Robert Bauer and Rebecca Gordon, 3/1/07; "Obama's Statements on Public Financing," Associated Press, 6/19/08; Libby Quaid, "McCain Admonishes Obama for Hedging on Accepting Public Funding," Associated Press, 2/15/08; Barack Obama video message to supporters, barackobama.com, 6/19/08; "The Politics of Spare Change," *Washington Post*, 6/20/08; "Campaign Financing Appears to Be Non-Issue for Voters," Gallup, 10/30/08; Jim Kuhnhenn, "Obama Opts Out of Public Campaign Finance System," Associated Press, 6/19/08; "McCain Attacks Obama for Opting Out of Public Financing," CNN.com, 6/20/08; Jacques Steinberg, "Russert's Son Sounds a Theme of Unity at Funeral," *New York Times*, 6/19/08; Mark Halperin and John F. Harris, *The Way to Win: Taking the White House in 2008* (Random House, 2006); Nedra Pickler, "Obama Says Bin Laden Must Not Be a Martyr," Associated Press, 6/18/08; transcript of "Celebrity" ad by McCain campaign, 7/30/08; transcript of "Embrace" ad by Obama campaign, 8/11/08; "Most Believe McCain's Attacks on Obama Unfair, Poll Finds," CNN.com, 10/20/08; Ryan Lizza, "Biden's Brief," *New Yorker*, 10/20/08; John McCormick, "One on One with Obama: His Plan of Attack," *Chicago Tribune*, 8/23/08; "21.7% of Households in Top Local TV Markets Watched Obama Infomercial," Nielsen Wire, 10/30/08; transcript of Obama ad "His Choice," 10/28/08; transcript of Barack Obama interview, *Today*, NBC News, 10/20/08.

I also gained valuable insight listening to David Plouffe and David Axelrod speak at the Institute of Politics, Kennedy School of Government, Harvard University, 12/11/08.

SEVEN

ALIEN

This chapter is based on exclusive interviews with the following people: Barack Obama (1/2/08, 3/4/08, 3/20/08, 4/10/08, 6/3/08, 6/20/08, 7/24/08, 7/25/08), David Axelrod (2/27/08, 6/5/08, 7/25/08, 9/11/08), Maya Soetoro-Ng (2/29/08, 7/7/08), Wahid Hamid (3/13/08, 1/25/09), Hasan Chandoo (1/23/09), a senior Bush official who declined to be named, Pete Rouse (6/23/08), Dan Pfeiffer (2/10/09), seven interviews with senior Obama officials who declined to be named, Scott Gration (1/10/08, 7/24/08), Susan Rice (1/10/08, 4/6/08, 7/15/08), Robert Gibbs (6/5/08, 7/24/08, 3/4/09), Marty Nesbitt (10/9/08), Joel Benenson (11/24/08), David Plouffe (10/26/08).

The chapter relies on my contemporaneous notes of campaign events on

12/28/07, 1/24/08, 1/29/08, 2/28/08, 2/29/08, 4/16/08, 4/22/08, 5/19/08, 5/22/08, 6/3/08, 6/4/08, 6/5/08, 6/16/08, 6/30/08, 7/3/08, 7/22/08, 7/23/08, 7/24/08, 7/25/08, 7/26/08.

I drew on these published sources: Andrew Malcolm, "'Top of the Ticket:' Breaking News: Obama Caves! Flag Pin Returns to His Coat Lapel," *Los Angeles Times*, 4/16/08; Sunlen Miller and David Wright, "Political Radar: Obama Says Flag Flap a Dirty Trick," ABC News, 11/7/07; CBS News/New York Times poll, 10/3–5/02; Pew Research Center poll, 10/10/02; Barack Obama's antiwar speech, 10/2/02, prepared text according to the Obama campaign (there is no recording of the speech beyond a few seconds of local TV footage); transcript of Hillary Clinton, *Meet the Press*, NBC News, 1/13/08; transcript of MSNBC debate, Orangeburg, South Carolina, 4/26/07; transcript of CNN debate, Charleston, South Carolina, 7/24/07; Mike Glover, "Obama Says He's Ready to Engage Rogue Nations," Associated Press, 7/29/07; "Interview with Barack Obama," *New York Times*, 11/1/07; Larry Rohter, "On McCain, Obama and a Hamas Link," *New York Times*, 5/10/08; Sunlen Miller, "Political Radar: Obama's Cup of Tea," ABC News, 12/28/07; Richard Wolffe, "Well, What Do You Know?" *Newsweek*, 8/6/07; Jeff Mason, "Hillary Clinton Calls Bosnia Sniper Story a Mistake," Reuters, 3/25/08; Mark Murray, "First Read: Hillary Questions Obama's Security Creds," NBC News, 3/6/08; Jeffrey Gettleman, "Fighting Intensifies After Election in Kenya," *New York Times*, 1/1/08; transcript of Barack Obama's speech to the Chicago Council on Global Affairs, 4/23/07; Jeffrey Gettleman, "Kenya Crisis Worsens As Opposition Cools to Talks," *New York Times*, 1/9/08; "Sliming Obama," Factcheck.org, 1/10/08; "CNN Debunks False Report About Obama," CNN.com, 1/23/07; an Obama campaign flyer in South Carolina, before the primary on 1/26/08; Michael Hirsh and Dan Ephron, "Good for the Jews?" *Newsweek*, 3/3/08; Michael Goldfarb, "McCain: 'Clear Who Hamas Wants to Be the Next President,'" The Blog, *Weekly Standard*, 4/25/08; "Obama Fact Check on Israel," RNC press release, 5/22/08; Howard Gutman, "Email to a Rabbi: Wrong or Wright?" Huffington Post, 4/9/08; Rupert Murdoch comments, All Things Digital Conference, 5/28/08; Andy Barr, "Roger Stone Claims Michelle Obama 'Whitey' Video Will Emerge Soon," *The Hill*, 6/2/08; Jeffrey Toobin, "The Dirty Trickster," *New Yorker*, 6/2/08; transcript of *Fox and Friends*, Fox News Channel, 1/19/07; Michael Wolff, "Tuesdays with Rupert," *Vanity Fair*, October 2008; Howard Kurtz, "Obama Met with Fox News Executives," *Washington Post*, 9/3/08; transcript of Joe Lieberman, CNN, 5/11/08; Azi Paybarah, "Lieberman on Confronting the Muslim Obama Rumor," *New York Observer*, 2/1/08; Paul Kane, "Lieberman Savoring Life on Both Sides of the Aisle," *Washington Post*, 6/6/08; Mark Hemingway, "Jewish Whispering Campaign," *National Review*, 6/10/08; transcript of Barack Obama interview, CNN, 6/5/08; Michael Cooper, "McCain Misspeaks on Iran, Al Qaeda," *New York Times*, 3/18/08; Richard Wolffe, "The Aide Who Went to War," *Newsweek*, 7/19/08; "Iraqi Leader Maliki Supports Obama's Withdrawal Plans," *Der Spiegel*, 7/19/08; Byron York, "Obama, Maliki and McCain," *National Review*, 7/21/08; Richard Oppel and Jeff Zeleny, "For Obama, a First Step Is Not a Misstep," *New York Times*, 7/22/08; Elana Schor, "Rabbi Criticizes Paper for Printing Stolen Obama Prayer," *Guardian*, 7/25/08; Sunlen Miller, "Political Radar: Obama the Dancing Bear?" ABC News, 3/1/08; Commission on Presidential Debates transcript, 9/26/08; Gallup poll, 9/28/08; Pew Research Center poll, 10/1/08; transcript of ABC News interview with Sarah Palin, 9/11/08; transcript of CBS News interview with Sarah Palin, 9/25/08; transcript of NBC's *Meet the Press*, 10/19/08.

EIGHT
THE RECKONING

This chapter is based on exclusive interviews with the following people: Barack Obama (9/18/08), three senior Obama aides and a participant in the White House meeting, all of whom declined to be named, Linda Douglass (9/18/08), Robert Gibbs (9/16/08), Pete Rouse (10/9/08), David Axelrod (4/24/08, 5/1/08), Dan Pfeiffer (2/10/09), Joel Benenson (11/18/08, 11/24/08), David Plouffe (4/24/08, 10/26/08), four senior Obama officials who declined to be named.

The chapter relies on my contemporaneous notes of campaign events on 1/14/08, 2/18/08, 4/14/08, 4/30/08, 6/17/08, 6/20/08, 7/10/08, 8/21/08, 8/26/08, 10/16/08, 10/29/08. It also draws on campaign pool reports from 3/28/08, 3/29/08, 3/30/08, and 4/2/08.

I drew on these published sources: "President Bush's Speech to the Nation on the Economic Crisis," *New York Times*, 9/24/08; Vikas Bajaj and Michael Grynbaum, "For Stocks, Worst Single-Day Drop in Two Decades," *New York Times*, 9/29/08; Ron Brownstein, "Obama and Blue Collars: Do They Fit?" *Los Angeles Times*, 3/25/07; Ron Brownstein, "Educated Women Climb Aboard," *National Journal*, 10/25/07; Ron Brownstein, "When Blue Collars Are a Tight Fit," *National Journal*, 5/3/08; Joe Klein, "Swampland: Obama Rides the Wine Track," *Time*, 11/30/07; "Kerry and Obama the Wine Men, Day to Day," National Public Radio, 1/10/08; Jeff Zeleny, "Obama's Down on the Farm," *New York Times*, 7/27/07; Evan Thomas, Holly Bailey, and Richard Wolffe, "Only in America," *Newsweek*, 5/5/08; John McCormick, "Obama Talks Arugula—Again—in Iowa," *Chicago Tribune*, 10/5/07; Mayhill Fowler, "Obama: No Surprise That Hard-Pressed Pennsylvanians Turn Bitter," Huffington Post, 4/11/08; transcript of Hillary Clinton at the Compassion Forum, CNN, 4/13/08; "Two Canadian Diplomats, One Evasion by Obama," *Washington Post*, 3/4/08; Leslie Wayne, "Obama's Tax Returns Show Donation Spike," *New York Times*, 3/26/08; Mike McIntire, "Clintons Made $109 Million in Last Eight Years," *New York Times*, 4/5/08; "Michelle Obama Rejects Elitist Characterization," Associated Press, 4/16/08; Brian Braiker, "Losing Ground," *Newsweek*, 4/26/08; exit polls in the Democratic primaries in Ohio 3/4/08 and Pennsylvania 4/22/08, CNN.com; Ruy Teixeira and Alan Abramowitz, *The Decline of the White Working Class and the Rise of a Mass Upper Middle Class*, Brookings Institution, April 2008; Ruy Teixeira, "Digging Into the 2008 Exit Polls," The Century Foundation: Taking Note blog, 11/11/08; "McCain Calls for Summer 'Gas-Tax Holiday,'" Associated Press, 4/15/08; Alec MacGillis and Steven Mufson, "Clinton Gas-Tax Proposal Criticized," *Washington Post*, 5/1/08; "How Many Jobs Could a Gas Tax Holiday Cost Your State," Obama campaign press release, 5/2/08; New York Times/CBS Poll, 5/1–3/08; Michael Shear and Juliet Eilperin, "McCain Seeks to End Offshore Drilling Ban," *Washington Post*, 6/17/08; Michael Falcone, "McCain Camp Calls Obama 'Dr. No' of Energy Security," *New York Times*, 6/24/08; Ben Rooney, "Americans Favor Offshore Drilling," CNNMoney.com, 7/30/08; Jonathan Weisman, "Obama Signals Support for Wider Offshore Drilling," *Washington Post*, 8/2/08; Jonathan Martin, "McCain Camp Amps Up Tire Gauge Gag," *Politico*, 8/4/08; Matthew Bigg, "McCain Takes Air Out of Tire Pressure Debate," Reuters, 8/5/08; Marc Ambinder, "A No Seal Zone Starting," *Atlantic*, 6/23/08; text of Barack Obama's speech to Resources for the Future, 9/15/05; transcript of Obama campaign TV ad "Quiet," 2/27/08; Andrew Malcolm, "Top of the Ticket: Obama's Sniper Tale?" *Los Angeles Times*, 5/15/08; transcript of interview of John McCain, Bloomberg TV, 4/17/08; Patrice Hill, "McCain Adviser Talks of 'Mental Recession,'" *Washington Times*, 7/9/08; Jonathan Weisman and Perry Bacon, "Gramm Stands by Recession Comments," *Washington Post*, 7/10/08; National Bureau of Economic Research, *Determination of the December 2007 Peak in Economic Activity*, 12/11/08; Jonathan Martin and Mike Allen, "McCain Unsure How Many Houses He Owns," *Politico*, 8/21/08; Jake Tapper and Sunlen Miller, "Political Punch: Obama Attacks McCain as an Economic Risk," ABC News, 9/15/08; transcript of Obama campaign ad "Seven," 8/21/08; Steve Holland, "McCain Suspends Campaign to Work on Wall St. Plan," Reuters, 9/25/08; Larry Rohter, "Real Deal on 'Joe the Plumber,'" *New York Times*, 10/16/08; Jake Tapper, "Political Punch: 'Spread the Wealth'?" ABC News, 10/14/08; Commission on Presidential Debates transcript, 10/15/08; Michael Finnegan and

Maeve Reston, "Candidates in Attack Mode Across Florida," *Los Angeles Times*, 10/30/08.

NINE

TRANSITION

This chapter is based on exclusive interviews with the following people: President Barack Obama (6/27/07, 2/7/08, 4/11/08, 2/25/09), a senior Bush official who declined to be named, David Axelrod (11/6/08, 2/11/09), Marty Nesbitt (10/9/08, 11/6/08, 2/11/09), Jon Favreau (2/10/09), a senior inauguration official who declined to be named, several senior transition officials who asked not to be named, Valerie Jarrett (10/31/08, 2/25/09), Robert Gibbs (3/4/09), Joel Benenson (11/24/08).

The chapter relies on my contemporaneous notes of campaign events on 1/7/08, 3/1/08, 10/31/08. I also drew on White House press pool reports of 2/3/09, 2/25/09; and Obama press pool reports of 12/23/08, 1/4/09.

I drew on these published sources: Barack Obama, *Dreams from My Father* (Three Rivers Press, 2004: pp. 230–31); Barack Obama, *The Audacity of Hope* (Crown, 2006: pp. 361–62); transcript of interview of President-elect Barack Obama by John King, CNN, 1/16/09; transcript of inaugural address of President Barack Obama, 1/20/09; White House transcript of the interview of President Barack Obama by Robin Roberts of ABC, 1/20/09; Pete Williams and Antoine Sanfuentes, "First Read: Biden Apologizes to Roberts," NBC News, 1/27/08; Margaret Talev, "Obama Retakes Oath of Office After Busy First Day," McClatchy Newspapers, 1/21/09; Greg Craig memo to President-elect Obama, "Transition Staff Contacts with the Governor's Office," 12/23/08; Martina Stewart and Dana Bash, "Clinton Foundation Reaches Written Agreement with Obama Camp," CNN, 12/18/08; Sharon Otterman, "Axelrod Puts Stimulus Plan at $675 Billion to $775 Billion," *New York Times*, 12/28/08; Congressional Research Service Report for Congress, *The Cost of Iraq, Afghanistan and Other Global War on Terror Operations Since 9/11*, 10/15/08; White House transcript of remarks of President Barack Obama, Elkhart, Indiana, 2/9/09; CBS News Poll, 2/5/09; Gallup poll, 2/9/09; CBS News Poll, 2/5/09; Ken Strickland, "First Read: Lindsey Graham vs. Obama," NBC News, 2/9/09; White House transcript of President Barack Obama's interview with Al-Arabiya television, 1/27/09; transcript of interview of President Barack Obama by NBC News, 2/1/09.

AFTERWORD

This chapter is based on exclusive interviews with Barack Obama (3/20/08, 5/19/08) and Marty Nesbitt (7/11/08) as well as my contemporaneous notes of events on 1/26/08, 3/20/08, and 5/19/08.

INDEX

   INDEX